"I am honored to have known Robyn for many years, watching her grow from a compassionate, empathetic teacher into a truly determined seeker of truth in the health field. This book is a compilation of Robyn's learning, over the past few decades.

As a Medical Intuitive, I am always on the lookout for good bodies of knowledge that I can refer people to. One that can help simplify the health journey into something that is practical, easy and manageable. Robyn Woods' book covers so many topics, from environmental health to your own feelings and how these impact your body and mind. Everything we experience affects us and Robyn has beautifully and gracefully covered this in her book, along with many strategies for coping and healing."

Carmel Bell – Medical Intuitive
http://www.carmelbell.com.au
Author of "When All Else Fails."

"In these crazy, hectic and turbulent times we cannot get too many reminders of what is really real... what really nourishes our soul and keeps us healthy and our hearts open. This book is one such reminder."

Deva Premal & Miten (devotional musicians)
http://devapremalmiten.com

"It takes one with great awareness and integrated life experience to capture and express, within the limits of language, such sound universal principles. Robyn Wood has managed to do exactly that in her book 101 Strategies for True Health and Empowerment. Whether you are new to the path of self discovery or a seasoned veteran, this book abounds with valuable information for personal health and empowerment, cleverly commingling 101 strategies within 12 categories and bridging individual experience with the oneness of an interconnected universe."

Christine Heart Savage
http://www.breatheforlife.com.au
Author of Living Beyond Stress, Anxiety & Overwhelm: 9 Steps to Freedom

"Through Robyn's guidance I have come to understand and believe that my autoimmune disease was in fact caused through unresolved emotional issues (blockages) some going all the way back to childhood. The sessions have empowered me to strive to resolve past issues and to create a mindful and truthful presence.

I also am now medication free from the crippling pain in my hips caused by the psoriatic arthritis. I would whole heartedly recommend Robyn's book as a way forward of being empowered to heal yourself from within and live an enriched life."

Josie Brennan

"As a general practitioner, I see a variety of health issues my patients come to ask me to assist with. And for no matter what the issue or concern is, its management can be facilitated by an optimal empowered response. In this book, Robyn offers us the benefit of decades of wisdom and distilled knowledge to help us all deal with whatever 'razorblades' life throws up at us. She shows us with clear simplicity where we can be powerful in response to illness and distress, but also more importantly to help us work and grow towards prevention of illness at the fundamental energetic level. Robyn's magnificent exercises and vignettes assist clearance of habits that keep us constrained and stuck, helping us dissolve these to allow a more complete, loving and expanded expression of our lives in each moment. Joy and love await, let us all be brave enough to follow the advice she offers."

Dr. Jenny Altermatt

"A groundbreaking transformative guide guaranteed to enhance vitality and personal growth. Robyn shares with genuine compassion and insight a detailed roadmap to deep lasting healing for mind, body and soul. The book is so extensive and detailed, covering topics such as depression, addiction, relationships, exercise, diet and so much more. It offers true and lasting solutions for change and healing, so comprehensive is its approach! A resource book that will stand the test of time and impact generations to come!"

Helen Paige,
http://www.helenpaige.com
Author of Guardian of the Light and Elephants and Angels.

101 STRATEGIES *for* TRUE HEALTH *and* EMPOWERMENT

Healing from Within

ROBYN WOOD

BALBOA. PRESS
A DIVISION OF HAY HOUSE

In this information age things are rapidly changing and whilst the references and hyperlinks in this book were correct at time of publishing, things can quickly become outdated. If you are aware of more current information, or would like to share some of your findings towards greater health, please feel free to contact the author Robyn Wood via the website. http://www.robynmwood.com or http://www.truehealthandempowerment.com

Many thanks for help with designs, graphics and Illustrations
Canstock http://www.CanStockPhoto.com
Justin Williams. http://www.ixplainit.com.au
Kath Gillies http://www.kathgilliesphotography.com
Robyn Wood http://www.robynmwood.com
Usagi Studios https://www.fiverr.com/iusagi

Balboa Press books may be ordered through booksellers or by contacting:

Balboa Press
A Division of Hay House
1663 Liberty Drive
Bloomington, IN 47403
www.balboapress.com.au
1 (877) 407-4847

Print information available on the last page.

ISBN: 978-1-4525-2812-0 (sc)
ISBN: 978-1-4525-2813-7 (e)

Balboa Press rev. date: 04/28/2015

BOOK DEDICATION

This book is dedicated to the future generations.

May we all awaken to the profound mind/body/spirit connection that deepens our awareness with all life and our magnificent Earth-mother.

As we build consciousness and address issues at the causal level we can free ourselves from past struggles of personal health challenges. We will then leave this world in a better place with greater wisdom, compassion, love and harmony that benefits all who walk this Earthly plane.

CONTENTS

PREFACE

I remember waking one morning some years back and getting a very clear sense of writing about healing that arises through releasing emotional pain and building awareness. At that time I didn't know who or what it was for. It didn't matter. The inspiration was really strong and I trusted it. I was already teaching many of these practices in my Expanding Consciousness classes and empowering my clients with some value added tools as a health care practitioner. I fantasized about the idea of business incorporating these consciousness-building strategies into the workplace and the profound benefits it would create for business owners, the profits of the companies and their employees – maybe one day.

I reflected, too, that it was more than two decades earlier when a mentor and health care practitioner I sometimes consulted advised me that cancer was in my energy field and I better do something about it. He had the ability to see energy and identify the emotional link with incredible accuracy. The truth of his words penetrated like icy spikes all over my body and I immediately knew I had to resolve the pain and resentment I was holding and get really serious about doing the essential inner work.

As the ideas continued to develop, it became obvious that I was writing about everything I had learned in my own healing journey from protracted sexual abuse as a child, depression, addiction, an earnest quest for truth, and understanding why things happen as they do.

Though my own search for meaning was long and included many years spent with a spiritual teacher, it was the world of spirituality and energy that made increasing sense to me. I discovered that the answers could really only be found through my own inner exploration into greater consciousness and reconnecting with my feeling body, where I had suppressed so much pain. I learned that under all that wounding was a growing truth and peace. The earlier dislike for myself continued to transform into increasing self-love, along with an expanding appreciation and love for Mother Earth and all her inhabitants. That we are all part of the whole became my knowing and not just a belief I adopted from others.

My humble thanks go to the Evolutionary Leaders of our time whose foresight and teachings recognize the spiritual essence of people and the connectedness of all life. Their awareness of energy and heart-focused work has inspired me along the way and opened the door to my own inner explorations, which are reflected throughout this work. In particular, I would like to acknowledge Tom Kenyon, Eugene Gendlin, Eldon Taylor, Lynne McTaggart, Esther & Jerry Hicks, Eckhart Tolle, Don Miguel Ruiz, Ken Wilber, Candace B. Pert, Debbie Ford, Bruce Lipton, Michael King, Cameron Day, Alicia Power, the Heart Math Institute, and many more who have shared their wisdom through their books and teachings. They awaken within us an eternal truth that we all own, not individually but in common.

With added thanks to those who have inspired many with their own recovery from terminal illness: people like Louise Hay, Brandon Bays, and so many others, whose own healing journey into greater awareness may not be publicized but has fed the collective global energies of consciousness to assist our own awakening into knowing the truth and power of our integral self.

To the Mavericks, whistle blowers and individuals of this world, who follow their heart and are willing to question all that influences our global family and insist upon truth and change, your courage inspires us all to arouse a greater level of individual responsibility.

I deeply thank Mother Earth, who many years ago became my anchor when meditating, helping to ground myself when I wanted to escape to the spiritual realms and avoid some of the harsher experiences of earthly life. I thank her for the many walks and sitting in nature that captured my heart and mind with her beauty and wonderful energy to bring me into presence and inspire me with answers to my inner questions and inspirations for the next bit of processing or writing. Perhaps strangely, it wasn't until the work was approaching completion that I realized this compilation of writing was going to become a book with 101 Strategies for True Health and Empowerment. Had I known that at the outset I seriously doubt I would ever have started.

I am eternally grateful to my precious family and partner Paul, including my beautiful extended family. Loving thanks also to all my dear friends. You know who you are. To Barb and Libby, thank you for always being there over this lifetime. I love all of you without reservation. To those who have gifted me with your trust to assist you on your healing journey, I am grateful that you have pushed my creativity to communicate these skills in a way that speaks to you. Your input has contributed to the succinct simplicity and alternatives offered throughout these processes.

To my editor, Venetia Somerset, thank you for your patience, precision, and tenacity in dealing with my submission of over a hundred different files instead of one.

I offer this book as a self-help program consisting of 12 Categories and 101 Strategies (plus bonus Consciousness Tips for Children) to those who are ill, distressed, or seek a better understanding of who they are and their place in this world. It is my sincere wish that you may find within yourself the power to heal and come to know the magnificence of your true self. I hope you can feel my love and compassion in the written word directed to you, the reader.

INTRODUCTION

We have reached a time in our evolution where we know that many of our health practices are not only ineffective but also can be damaging to our bodies. The side effects of many drugs actually create health problems; pharmaceutical companies appear to be more interested in making money than in people's health. A growing variety of foods we consume are foreign to our bodies, creating imbalance, and a large number of personal care products and cleaning aids commonly used in our homes are toxic for both our bodies and the Earth.

Even one of the most respected medical periodicals in the world, *Journal of the American Medical Association* (JAMA) published an article saying that doctors are the third leading cause of death in the U.S. The causes of these deaths included unnecessary surgery, errors in medication, and infections in hospitals. At the same time, cutting-edge science in quantum physics and epigenetics has made significant inroads into understanding our health and how the mind and our environment affect it. Interestingly, it was more than 80 years ago, in 1933, that Erwin Schrödinger, who won the Nobel Prize for Physics, said: "Quantum physics reveals a basic oneness of the universe" and yet relatively few have embraced this awareness.

Through his groundbreaking research, Dr Bruce Lipton discovered that genes and DNA could be manipulated by a person's belief. His work is bridging the gap between science and spirituality and affirming our eternalness as energy beings connected to everything in our environment – multidimensional beings with physical, emotional, mental, and spiritual bodies. He and many other evolutionary leaders are helping to return our conversations to the essential nature of our spirituality.

As we all deepen our understanding of our connectedness, we can make the critical changes that will benefit our personal health and wellbeing, which will at the same time help our ailing planet. It is very apparent that this Earth, which supports all life, is suffering as a result of our actions and inactions. We all know that continuing in the same way is unsustainable. Now is the time to think collectively and globally and find a way to live in harmony with our Earth Mother. After all, the Earth is everybody's home and will be home for our children and their children.

The Hard Facts

It is an unfortunate truth that serious health issues are on the increase, with obesity estimated to cause 123 thousand premature deaths over the next two decades; depression is the fastest-growing illness in the world today; 2.5 million people die from alcohol misuse each year and nearly three-quarters of adult Australians are affected by someone else's drinking (World Health Organization 2011). The misuse of drugs – both pharmaceutical and non-pharmaceutical – causes both short- and long-term health problems and can leave children of drug abusers vulnerable to neglect and sexual abuse.

This has quite devastating effects on individuals, their families, the companies who employ them, and society in general. A grim forecast is that our children today will have a shorter lifespan and die earlier than us. Of great concern also is that air pollution kills around 7 million people worldwide every year and has become the biggest environmental health risk.

As the World Health Organization has said, we all need to breathe.

Change is necessary to address these alarming trends, which affect not only our human selves but also our beautiful planet.

The doctor of the future will give no medicine,
but will interest his patient
in the care of the human frame, in diet and in the cause and
prevention of disease.
– Thomas Edison 1847–1931

It is time to wake up! Our bodies comprise a very complex system of interacting energies with a supreme intelligence that absolutely knows how to heal itself given the right nutrients and environment. Instead of feeling powerless and a victim to our reality, now is the time to embrace the immensity of our personal power, our connectedness with all life, and our spiritual essence as humans and caretakers of this Earth; now is the time to use it in a way that builds harmony, respect, and wellness.

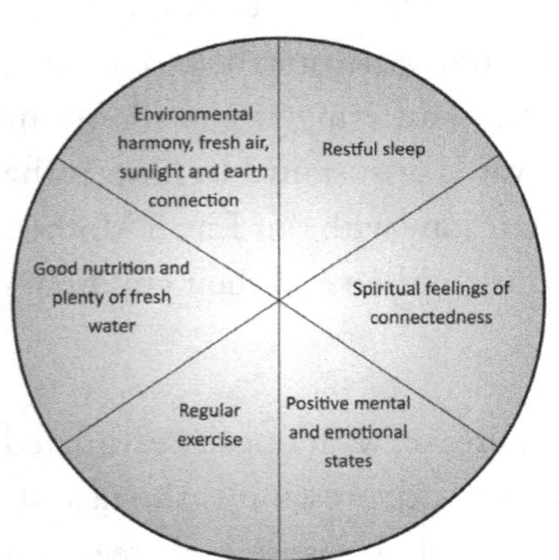

The Wellness Wheel

A healthy, happy person requires an environment that provides plenty of fresh air, sunlight, Earth connection, good nutrition, fresh water, restful sleep, regular exercise, positive mental and emotional states, and awareness of one's spirituality, which facilitates feelings of connectedness. All aspects make up the whole. No one aspect can be eliminated.

How To Use This Book

As you venture forth on this journey into the 101 Strategies for True Health and Empowerment, the one essential thing you need is to accept total responsibility for your whole self. This is fundamental to living an empowered, successful, and truly healthy, love-filled life – owning and claiming your authentic multidimensional self. Although I sometimes refer to your spiritual essence, all these Strategies are free of religious dogma and man-made rules.

This book is a holistic presentation of succinct and powerful life skills Strategies that build consciousness and assist your body to heal as you integrate them. Simply draw from these processes according to your own preference in any moment in time. You will discover that as you become more mindful, release resistance and attachments, your body's energy can return to flow and you will open up more to your own unique internal guidance system through your intelligent heart that helps you to navigate your way through life.

When you really connect with your body and the wealth of information it conveys, you realize that any health imbalance or pain is our body's way of saying "pay attention." Pain and illness is simply energy "stuck" within your vibrational field that you have attracted in your evolutionary journey.

The Strategies in this book attempt to provide an understanding of the energy play and how you can address your specific issue towards greater health and empowerment. Much encouragement is given throughout the book to attune to your heart and develop "heart coherence," a term science now uses to describe when the heart, mind, and emotions are all in energetic alignment and cooperation.

If you wish to understand the secrets of the Universe,
think of energy, frequency and vibration.
– Nikola Tesla, inventor, physicist and futurist

As you become more heart-coherent, you feel connected to your Higher Self. Other names are sometimes used to refer to the same thing: the I AM Presence, the God within, the Source connection. It is that beautiful, truthful, loving connection that is untainted by your life experience. It can be thought of as pure awareness that is not limited by conditioning or the illusions of the mind; that special part within that wants and knows how to move you forward towards truth and ever-increasing love, peace, and joy.

A core theme throughout these individual processes is building greater awareness to explore and deepen your understanding of self as an energy being: who you are, why you think and behave the way you do, and what you can do to bring about your desired change. Building consciousness deepens your understanding and gives you choice. Understanding and knowledge of self provides the power and impetus to change – it empowers you.

Mastering your own energy with the 101 Strategies for True Health and Empowerment will reap the results of transformation. These Strategies are embraced by 12 general Categories.

THE 12 CATEGORIES

The 12 Categories listed below describe general areas of self-healing. Their subjects reflect the growing health concerns of our Western world. Of these, Addictions, Depression, and Anxiety are massive and increasing problems that are having catastrophic impacts on individuals and their self-esteem, and ultimately affecting everyone in our world.

1. Addressing Addictions
2. Addressing Depression
3. Addressing Anxiety
4. Awareness and Mindfulness
5. Career and Goals
6. Communications and Relationships
7. Environmental Health
8. Everyday Essentials
9. Exercise for Life
10. Improving Self-Esteem
11. Nutrition for Life
12. Quick Stress Busters

A central element within the self-help resources of this book is the theme of awareness, as in Category 4, *Awareness and Mindfulness*.* The book also embraces some of the insights from psychoneuroimmunology and quantum physics that are currently illuminating both science and medicine. It is through awareness and understanding the role of the illusory mind and its interrelationship with body and spirit that we are able to make changes to bring about transformation and true healing.

Environmental Health provides information on what individuals can do to bring about personal behavioral change to support their own wellbeing, which has the added bonus of impacting on the wellbeing of the Earth. The microcosm affects the macrocosm.

Other Categories provide the essential tools to live an extraordinary life in an ordinary way. Vital information is included in *Improving Self-Esteem, Communications and Relationships, and Career and Goals* on how to deal with different emotional stressors; this will provide the core elements for individual growth and development and have a direct impact on your health and wellbeing.

Fundamental information is incorporated on *Exercise* and *Nutrition,* with some website links offered for your further exploration. *Everyday Essentials* are practices that over time need to be incorporated into your everyday living for optimal wellbeing and greater consciousness.

While there are some Strategies under the Category *Quick Stress Busters* that offer fairly immediate relief for stress or anxiety, the vast majority of these processes are proven life skills that you can apply and integrate at your own pace. You may even find that some are already part of your everyday behavior or perhaps are becoming so.

These processes provide the crucial tools for the transformation we need if we are to live a healthy, happy life. Many of them are consistent with teachings from world Evolutionary Leaders who have a deep understanding of the profound mind–body–spirit connection and live these principles. No one owns these teachings: they are just simple truths, some of which are intuitively known by many who are spiritually aware.

*In order to distinguish these from the names of the Strategies, Category names are presented in italics.

THE 101 STRATEGIES

Most of the Strategies require action in some way. To bring about the change you desire, there typically has to be an incentive, which is usually the result of a shift in understanding. Otherwise the egoic personality lacks the inspiration for change and prefers to stick to the old ways, even though there may be no positive outcome. Each of the processes aims to provide information to give that expanded view of things to inspire change in your attitude or behavior.

Applying these Strategies, you will learn a great deal about yourself as a multidimensional being and the patterns that have resulted as part of your conditioning.

At the top of each page of the individual Strategy are the Categories that apply to it.

Within some of the individual Strategies you will find more than one way of using the material. These variations, which do not affect the actual process of understanding and healing, are included to provide a different way of looking at things and may appeal to different personality types. Such are found in Thought Power and Control; Feeling Scattered: Unbalanced; Awareness: Building the Observer; and several others.

1. Accept Yourself
2. Affection
3. Affirmations
4. Allow Feelings
5. Asking for Help
6. Awareness: Building the Observer
7. Awareness: I Statements
8. Awareness of Awareness
9. Being: Mindfulness
10. Beliefs Challenge
11. Body Breath Awareness
12. Boundaries
13. Causes of Health Imbalance
14. Change Challenge
15. Change: Warmer Greeting
16. Clearing
17. Communications: Family Agreements
18. Communication Keys
19. Communication: When you…
20. Competition versus Cooperation
21. Conflict Resolution
22. Connect with Nature
23. Conscious Breathing
24. Control versus Preferences
25. Decisions: Heart Wisdom
26. Decisions: Motives and Impact
27. Deep Release Breathing
28. Do No Harm
29. Do Things You Enjoy
30. Environmental Health: Consumables

31. Environmental Health: Electromagnetic Fields
32. Environmental Health: General
33. Environmental Health: Personal Products
34. Environmental Health: Water
35. Exercise for Living
36. Feeling Agitated
37. Feeling Anger
38. Feeling Challenged
39. Feeling Disempowered
40. Feeling Fear
41. Feeling Grief
42. Feeling Guilt or Shame
43. Feeling Jealousy
44. Feeling Lonely or Alone
45. Feeling Rejected or Hurt
46. Feeling Scattered: Unbalanced
47. Feeling Stuck
48. Feeling Uncertain or Fearful of the Unknown
49. Feeling Unloved or Unlovable
50. Feeling Unsupported
51. Feeling Victimized
52. Feeling Worried
53. Forgiveness Process
54. Gag Gossip
55. Goal Setting
56. Going with the Flow
57. Gratitude
58. Grounding/Earthing
59. Help Another
60. Honor and Respect Differences
61. Ideas and Inspirations
62. If Seriously Ill: Understanding Integrated Healing
63. Intention/Counter-Intention
64. Jiggling
65. Judgment Effect
66. Kindness to Self
67. Laughter Medicine
68. Major Life Influencers
69. Manage Key Tension Areas
70. Mantras
71. Music to Uplift and Nurture
72. Nutrition: Best Food Options
73. Nutrition: Keys
74. Oral Health
75. Pain Dialog
76. Pain Focus
77. Personal Mission Statement
78. Projection
79. Protection
80. Quick Breath Affirmation
81. Relationships: Building Intimacy
82. Relationship: Key Question
83. Release Resistance
84. Release the Need to be Right
85. Reverse Count Breath
86. Review and Remake Your Day
87. Seek to Understand
88. Shadow Play
89. Should versus Could
90. Simplify Your Life
91. Sleep Tips
92. Solitude
93. Switching Process
94. Thought: Managing the Inner Critic
95. Thought Power and Control
96. Toning
97. Trust, Truth, and Honesty
98. Truth Lover

HOW TO USE THE STRATEGIES

The different Health and Empowerment Strategies fall within the 12 Categories and cover a broad range of issues, some of which may or may not be relevant to you at the time of reading.

There are several ways you can use the material in these Strategies. One way is to center yourself and hold the intention that you want to be drawn to the most helpful strategy for you at this time. Then just open the book in the Strategies section and see what you have attracted.

Alternatively, you can pick out from the list of Categories and Strategies what is most relevant for you; the Categories will be a general guide on where to look. The Categories *Addiction*, *Anxiety*, *Depression*, and *Self-Esteem* are so fundamental to ill health that you will find almost all the 101 Strategies illuminating for these conditions, and every one of them is reflected in the category *Awareness*. Much of the material is closely interwoven, so as you read you will see other correspondences at the end of the page to invite you to look up other Strategies.

As previously indicated, the same Strategy is sometimes relevant to different Categories. Clearing, for example, applies to 10 of the 12 Categories because of its universal impact in different areas of human life. The same is true for Thought Power and Control because of its association with the human mind. Boundaries certainly form a primary Strategy in *Communications and Relationships* but may also be relevant to other Categories such as *Improving Self-esteem* and *Career and Goals*.

It is the combination of these Strategies that provides the key to holistic wellness. Most of them are not one-minute wonders that you apply and then forget about. Rather, they are life skills with a core theme of heightening personal awareness and providing the tools to address the patterns that lie at the *causal* level of your physical or emotional imbalance.

Applying these practices allows you to undo the conditioning that all humans experience, enabling you to see the world through a much broader lens and to recognize your connectedness to all life. The practices help you to uncover the real you – your true essence as a multidimensional spiritual being having a human experience.

The following key points sum up the basics of all the instruction in this program of self-healing through personal empowerment and will be illustrated in various ways throughout the book:

- Emotion is a combination of thought and feeling.
- Our thoughts create a vibration that impacts on our whole energy system.
- Positive thoughts create positive feelings; negative thoughts create negative feelings.
- The emotional body is associated with the heart.
- The emotional/feeling body is your internal guidance system.
- The mental body is associated with the mind and ego.
- Mind is the cause of all pain and suffering.
- You are the thinker in charge of your mind's function.
- Your beliefs control your behavior.
- Most of what you believe is likely to be untrue – challenge all your beliefs.
- You can learn to manage the mind.
- All people experience conditioning.
- You are a multidimensional energy being with a physical, emotional, mental, and spiritual body that all interact together.
- Your physical body is your temple that requires good nutrition, exercise and a healthy environment to keep it in good working order.
- You are an energy being living amid a sea of other energies both seen and unseen.
- You are responsible for keeping your energy field clean in the same way that you are responsible for keeping your physical body clean.
- The child learns to suppress emotion as a coping mechanism to avoid pain.
- Suppressed emotion dictates all our behavior whether we are aware of it or not.
- Suppressed emotion blocks the flow of energy in our multidimensional self.
- Suppressed emotion/blocked energy will eventually manifest as dis-ease in the physical body.
- Your conditioning and your environment influence what you perceive and think.
- You can't heal what you can't feel.
- Your heart's innate intelligence knows how to move you forward.
- Your body has a supreme intelligence that knows how to heal itself.
- You are an incredibly powerful co-creative energy being.

As you integrate these transformative processes into your everyday living, you will experience greater personal awareness, improved self-esteem, more success in your career and chosen pursuits, and more harmonious relationships. Along the way you will realize that it makes no sense to continue doing what you've always done and expect a different result, though this is not an uncommon attitude.

There may be times when you need extra support. Don't hesitate to seek professional advice. If you have any serious health condition it is recommended that you work with these strategies in consultation with your health practitioner.

People tend to make change in one of two ways. One way tends to be reactive to a situation, such as when faced with a crisis, whether it be environmental or personal. Environmental disasters such as flood or fire tend to confront people with what is really important in their life and often unite a community; a personal crisis might be triggered by a serious car accident, or having a sudden heart attack, or being diagnosed with a debilitating illness. Experiences such as these can create massive upheaval in one's life and often promote deep personal reflection, which can then become the catalyst for change. Relationships may be elevated to a new high with a commitment to move on from past wounding; health can become a priority leading to regular exercise and healthy eating; long hours in work may be reduced to allow time for more recreation and life balance.

The other incentive for change comes when people are educated around the issues they are facing, providing a different or expanded perspective. Through education, understanding arises, facilitating willingness and a desire to make changes. Continuing improvement is enhanced with reinforcement and support.

This book has as its foundation the basics of psychoneuroimmunology and the recognition that everything and everyone is made of energy. The comprehensive Strategies it contains recognize the significance of the physical, emotional, mental, and spiritual aspect of all people and provide the keys for true health and empowerment.

Category 1
ADDRESSING ADDICTIONS

Addictions are on the increase and the cause of immense personal, family, and social problems, with huge financial impacts on families at a cost of billions each year to the business world. A common adjunct to addictions is depression, which is now considered the fastest-growing illness in the world today, affecting all age groups. (See *Addressing Depression*.)

What Is an Addiction?

An addiction is a long-standing compulsive behavior pattern or a psychological and bodily dependence on a substance or practice that is beyond voluntary control.

By contrast, a habit is a recurring pattern of behavior that is sometimes unconscious. Such examples might be putting your right foot in the leg of your pants before your left while dressing, or maybe folding your arms left over right, or clasping your hands always with the same thumb on top.

A habit is something that you can change with a little bit of effort without any great distress. It first requires consciousness that you have a particular habit and then, with that awareness, choosing to change the pattern. The difference with an addictive pattern is that it goes beyond the person's desire and will to change it. It is a behavior that is compulsive and cannot be voluntarily terminated without distress. It is an aspect of self that feels as if it is in charge of your life – a personality aspect that totally drives you.

There are all kinds of addictions. The types below appear to be the most common.

- coffee or caffeine in its different forms
- alcohol
- smoking

- drugs, illegal or prescription
- gambling
- food, much of which is caused by sugar addictions or artificial sweeteners or msg
- video games
- the internet can be the source of many addictions such as sex, porn, gambling, relationships
- sex – which can be the act of sex itself, or masturbation, pornography, or being obsessed about the opposite sex
- compulsive shopping
- television viewing
- social media
- work

Other addictions could be excessive exercise, people-pleasing, perfectionism, laziness, religion, crime or risky behaviors that provide an adrenaline rush, and so on.

One of the greatest addictions of humankind is "thinking," but very few even realize it. This refers to the constant flow of thoughts that just fills your head with the unconscious desire to avoid uncomfortable feelings.

Causes of Addiction

Everybody has to deal with emotional pain throughout his or her life. Yet most of us as children are not taught how to process it because our parents have not learned how to deal with their own pain. Without that training, it is impossible for them to teach us what they have never experienced.

The unaware but well-intentioned parent will often respond to the distraught child by trying to distract them from the focus of their hurt or pain rather than consciously acknowledging the distress and deepening their understanding of the situation. Common strategies could be offering some kind of oral pacifier, such as food or drink; or drawing attention to any number of things within their surroundings to divert the child. It may be telling some story about an event, or a person; or numerous other activities which all serve to distract from the upset that the child is feeling.

There are also many times when the developing child looks to the parent for reassurance; if this is warm and encouraging something like a minor fall will not have any lasting impact. If, however, the parent makes a big drama about it the child will respond accordingly, picking up on his or her energy. It can be challenging to find the optimal balance.

Some of the more obvious emotionally painful experiences could be if your parents or some significant other ignored you, or abused you in some way. There could be any number of different outcomes that do not help the child deal with the difficult emotions and so the child quickly learns to find ways to avoid and suppress them as a coping mechanism. Being ignored, not heard, not respected, or not valued conveys a message that you don't matter. The perception and interpretation of these events challenge the very core of our worthiness, leading to beliefs of "not good enough."

While these distracting tactics may temporarily elevate the child's mood, and can in their own way be beneficial, if it leaves the cause of the problem intact and unresolved, the child learns to suppress the painful emotions. These processes of distraction can become habitual and can lead to patterns of avoidance, denial, and sabotage.

Suppressing feelings leads to greater and greater levels of unconsciousness and increased risks of reaction to different triggers, so often accompanied by projection and blaming someone else. Unresolved emotion will impact, influence, interfere with, or sabotage any intimate relationship that you may pursue as an adult.

According to neuroscientists, around 5 per cent of our cognitive abilities are conscious and 95 per cent are driven by the subconscious programming that we all experience. That means that the way we process our current experiences is fundamentally running through the filters of the subconscious mind where all past hurts are stored. That is, until we begin the journey of awakening, which is the foundation of the work set out in this book.

All addictions are a means to quell anxiety. They can start in a seemingly benign way, such as taking some drugs to fit in with peers or developing a habit of having a regular alcoholic drink or two, or eating without any degree of consciousness or using some kind of media to dumb down any anxious feelings. It is an effort to manipulate the past unpleasant feeling to something more tolerable – to relieve some anxiety. This behavior appears to provide a temporary relief for the distress. It fulfills a role in some way. It gives you a false sense of empowerment, a feeling of being back in control.

The problem is that all it does is mask the pain, so that next time you feel that discomfort you are going to look for the same numbing effect. This becomes a coping strategy that does nothing to resolve the issue. Each time you feel the levels of discomfort and seek out the pacifier, you will have to exert *more effort* to keep the pain suppressed and so more of the distraction is required. This is how an addictive cycle is born and perpetuated.

The Inner Critic

A strong inner critic is always associated with addictive patterns. In fact, any obsessive, compulsive, or addictive behavior is strongly associated with an inner critic dynamic.

It is the "self-created" inner voice that is putting you down, telling you you're not good enough, and criticizing you. Everyone has an inner critic, and learning to manage it is an essential component in addressing addictions.

Along with your inner critic, you must become aware of your self-talk and the different inner voices that drive the addictive behavior and exercise control over you. Eckhart Tolle, in his book *A New Earth*, refers to the voice of addiction as a quasi-entity or energy field that periodically takes you over completely and may be saying, "You've had a rough day. You deserve a treat, why deny yourself one of the only pleasures left in life!"

You are likely to also have other personality aspects that want you to back off or that are criticizing you for actually doing the behavior. These different personality aspects could be ones that seek family harmony or business success. "Don't do that. You know it will end in misery. You know if you don't stop this behavior that your business will continue to slide downhill. You've got to pull yourself together and deal with this."

The Challenge

Overcoming addiction is challenging. We live in a world where addictions are encouraged through the media, such as promoting caffeine, high sugar and fat content foods. "Play these gambling games," it tells us. "Drink alcohol, take drugs, and buy these products that you really don't need." It creates a powerful environmental energy whose impact on us we must all learn to manage.

Moving beyond addiction is not about avoiding it, though this is helpful in the early stages. A behavior can hibernate if the emotions connected with it are not addressed. You can avoid something all you life, but it does not mean that you have transcended it or healed the wounds beneath it. This is a common pattern for people who give up one addiction and simply replace it with another, such as giving up alcohol only to take up smoking. Or trading food for cigarettes, or television for computers or other instant media.

Though you may desperately want to change and eliminate the addictive behavior, you will find your will is not strong enough to bring this about. Often people have to reach rock bottom before they will surrender to the necessary steps for transformation and healing.

You will know you have truly overcome your addiction or been "healed" when you can easily have access to the addiction and be totally uninterested. An example would be giving up caffeine or alcohol and still having it in the house.

In summary, any addiction is a means to avoid or suppress distressing feelings. It is an unconscious refusal to face and move through your own hurt or pain.

It's possible for a lifelong affliction to heal
rapidly with a mere shift of attitude;
but even though this shift may seem to occur in a split second,
it may in actuality take years of inner preparation.
– David Hawkins

No matter what the trigger for the onset of the addictive substance or behavior, every addiction starts with pain, and the desire to not feel it. It will also end once the pain is felt and transcended.

The reality is that you cannot heal what you cannot feel! So the healing process is one of allowing yourself to feel what you have suppressed, avoided, or denied.

The Healing Process

Where there are addictive tendencies there will typically be much guilt, shame, and possible depression because of it. The antidotes are compassion and building self-love. In the common event that there are feelings of deep hurt or betrayal, then forgiveness needs to be included as part of these essential steps to any healing.

It will be helpful if you can identify the role of your addiction. All addictive behaviors fill a role in your life; they provide an illusory comfort. Once you have identified that role then you have to release or transcend the need for it. The attachment is not so much to the substance or behavior but rather to the role that it plays.

An example may be in a co-dependent relationship where the other person plays the parent role while you fulfill the role of the child; or a gambling addiction that gives an adrenaline rush and provides a sense of power or excitement. Or some kind of food addiction that provides the nurturing and comfort you feel unable to get by other means. It may be a behavior that helps you to feel accepted by those you care about. These roles are not peculiar to the behaviors, just possible examples. Take particular note of what it is that triggers your desire for the addictive behavior. There will be a pattern in when it first started and what emotional challenge preceded it. And you may find that those patterns will be a reflection of the same coping mechanisms that your parents adopted and you learned through osmosis.

Remember, awareness gives you choice.

True healing requires an inner journey to address the issues that lie at the base of your emotional pain. This means a real commitment to working on self-love and self-awareness while finding new ways to deal with the pain.

It is common for all of us to attract people who reflect our own behavior, and so people with addictions will often attract other people with addictions. They may be our partners in life, or friends and associates who become part of our social network.

At a time when you need most support, be very discerning about being among those who exhibit the kind of addictive behavior you want to change.

This may also be a time for reevaluating relationships and setting new directions, though when you are in the midst of your healing journey, avoid making any major decisions.

You will need courage, so make sure you surround yourself with people who are supportive of your endeavors. Being in isolation during times of releasing addictive tendencies can make it more difficult to commit to the desired behavior.

Support yourself with the program of Strategies in this book that embrace the physical, mental, and emotional healing that is required. You can heal yourself and break free of addictions! It is a way to really honor and awaken to your authentic self.

Addictions seem to affect just about every area of your life and are often associated with depression. There will be anxiety and an impact on your self-esteem and it can have either a subtle or profound affect on your career and relationships. For this reason nearly every one of the 101 Strategies apply to this Category, though all may not be relevant to your current circumstances. In determining what might help you with your current dilemma, just scan the list and choose what feels most relevant.

David Hawkins, *Power vs Force*, Hay House, 2007, p223.

Category 2
ADDRESSING ANXIETY

LOVE

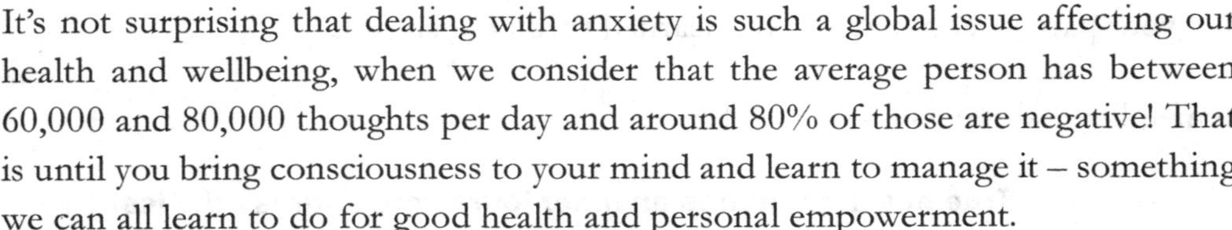

FEAR

It's not surprising that dealing with anxiety is such a global issue affecting our health and wellbeing, when we consider that the average person has between 60,000 and 80,000 thoughts per day and around 80% of those are negative! That is until you bring consciousness to your mind and learn to manage it – something we can all learn to do for good health and personal empowerment.

Anxiety and the various forms of fears that leave us feeling uncomfortable arise from our thinking mind or what is called the mental body, which is related to the personality or ego aspect of self.

Thoughts are real things, which have their own unique vibration or frequency that affects our whole body system. Just like colors, plants, or sounds, all words have their own energy signature. Thoughts with a more neutral quality to them have little impact on the feeling body. A thought that is energized (focused on) creates an associated feeling response in the body that we call emotion.

So we can say that thought is the parent and feelings are the child or the result of the thoughts. For example, thinking about a new job (the parent) could bring about feelings of excitement and anticipation, or they could be of anxiety and fear (the child); it depends on your perception and the quality of your thoughts: whether they were negative or positive. The combination of thought and feeling is emotion.

Emotion is sometimes referred to as "energy in motion." It is a strong feeling that *moves* us like anger, joy, or jealousy. All emotions have a resonance that can be measured on the emotional scale from fear to love, just as a thermometer uses a scale that reveals the rising degrees of temperature, or the keys on a piano ranging from low to high. This is reflected in the column of smiley faces.

Those emotions we would call positive leave us feeling good and have a high resonance that falls within the "love" bandwidth. This results in even heart rhythms that boost our immune system and facilitate optimal functioning of our body and our ability to process information. When we are feeling bad we are in the lower resonance and the reverse applies. These mixed emotions are part of the human experience. Scientists can observe how our emotions affect our bodies by measuring the patterns of our heart rate.

Used consciously, your heart, which is connected to your emotional body, is a most treasured asset to guide you through your life's journey. Building awareness of your feelings and learning to manage your mind and emotions is extremely empowering and can make a huge difference to your health, level of fulfillment, and the success you experience in your life.

Feelings without thought-forms are neither positive nor negative. They are simply neutral reports – our barometer to help us know what is happening within our own energy responsive world. Feelings are associated with the heart, and learning to attune to your feeling body will be a tremendous support for you through life because the body doesn't lie – it just feels.

You need a lot of discernment, however, when you work with the mental body. This is what some also call the ego or personality aspect of self that has experiences, thoughts, multiple beliefs and perceptions that all form part of our programming as humans. We can say that the overall function of the mind is to turn your beliefs into reality.

***FEAR* = *F* alse *E* nergy *A* ppearing *R* eal**

Conditioning

All humans experience conditioning as a child growing up, and this is the foundation that influences all our thinking. It is where our beliefs are developed and many of our anxieties are born. The experiences and relationships we have and their associated emotions basically dictate our behaviors, how we process life and our place in this world.

These everyday experiences, with the inevitable feelings of hurt and invalidation, give rise to our fears. It is our interpretation of events, or the story we tell ourselves, that is recorded by the brain, which then becomes a storehouse for all wounding that is not processed effectively in the moment.

And so we begin to understand that *mind that is the cause of all suffering.*

Brief Life Example

While every person is unique and their perceptions of their experiences are exclusive, creating a complex pattern of energy developed over many years, a very simplified example could play out like this:

> Imagine a four-year-old going to hospital to have his tonsils removed. It's just an overnight stay and parents are advised by hospital staff to go home and return in the morning. Despite the fact that they are deeply loving parents and doing what they feel is best to support their little one, the child may interpret the whole experience as "abandonment," and perhaps even that he is being punished in some way.
>
> The child has been taken to a hospital (unfamiliar environment) where he experiences a surgical procedure, which causes pain and difficulty swallowing. Due to a very heavy workload at the time, the nursing staff may not respond immediately to his cries. Increased fear may arise: Why is there blood is on my pillow? Where are mom and dad?
>
> Long after the physical body has healed the child could still hold fears about being left alone, or with strangers. He may become clingy or anxious about any kind of hospital environment. Perhaps he feels undervalued or even unloved, or maybe as though he did something wrong to bring this about. There are numerous possible perceptions, which will be influenced by the child's experiences up to that age and the filters through which he views life.
>
> In this example, if the fear of abandonment remains, the child will develop belief systems to support that fear. Possible beliefs like: people you love will hurt you, hospitals aren't safe places, loving care has a sting in the tail, I'm defective in some way. He may go through life and experience some important friendships that later desert him; or perhaps he is dumped by a girlfriend, or his business relationships falter. While the belief remains because of his unresolved painful experience/s as a child, the Universal Law of Attraction makes no judgment about what is good or bad, right or wrong and will simply support his pattern of thinking by attracting like and similar experiences back to him, basically validating many of the erroneous beliefs and perpetuating the negative emotions.

This is of course just one tiny fragment of a childhood experience among billions of others that will occur throughout those very early years influencing and moulding the child into the adult with all the associated illusory beliefs that form as part of conditioned existence.

Understanding your Behaviors

The adult egoic (personality) mind in its naivety will filter all your thinking through past experiences, most of which will be beyond your conscious awareness. It does this in an attempt to keep you safe by striving to avoid the repeat of any painful feelings; it does not understand or encourage the process of healing as your higher self does. The ego does not understand that you will keep attracting those same painful experiences because of the habitual nature of your thinking.

Consider this: The brain does not, of itself, select your thought forms. It makes no judgment and has no discernment. You, however, as the thinker in charge of your mind's function, have that ability. Imagine the brain is like a TV set with all the internal workings that make it work and you as the controlling thinker (mind) selects which channel or picture you want to see on the screen. You as the thinker have the ability to change the channel of the TV (brain) to something else. If you don't switch the channel it will continue to run the same programs, in the same way that water running down a hill will always take the path of least resistance. To alter the flow you will have to change some of the formation where the water flows.

Be alert to the egoic mind, which may attempt to justify why you don't need to change. It might be the desire to hold on to resentment and sabotaging behaviors as a subtle (but ineffective) way of fighting back. Fear may manifest from the inner work that is needed: guilt, shame or fear of change, and the possible loss of behaviors like addictions that provide comfort, despite the fact they are detrimental to health. You will understand the importance of challenging these thought-forms.

How Do I Address Anxiety?

An essential key to addressing all negative emotions and in fact, all healing is to accept total responsibility for your current situation. This *does not* mean you are to blame or that the other person's behaviour was not harmful to you. It means you have the power to heal your own body/mind and it is not dependent on another. Transmuting your own anxiety is really about changing your mind and letting go of some fixed perceptions that you are holding stuck.

Negative emotions can be healed or transmuted, by raising the vibration of the fixed energy and allowing it to go back into flow, in the space-time continuum. This is done by replacing any kind of resentment anger, or negative emotion with higher vibrational thought forms and feelings like, compassion, understanding forgiveness or acceptance. The cause of the emotional pain is your perception (judgment) that it is "wrong or should not have happened that way."

Of course it is totally human and natural to assess the situation and process it mentally until you realise the effect of judgment and that there is a better way.

Helpful attitudes are being open to a new perspective that invites a better understanding and acceptance of the situation thereby raising the frequency. Genuine forgiveness, which comes from the heart, allows this transformation to occur. Gratitude for the learning elevates the frequency, and even the desire for truth all assist to unlock the stuck energy.

Anxiety left unmanaged, will cause health imbalances. Treating just the physical body with chemicals and drugs without making changes in thinking and behaviour does not provide holistic healing. Unless the mental and emotional body - which lies at the cause of the health condition is addressed, the physical energetic body will manifest another imbalance.

You'll never medicate your way out of a disease
that you behaved yourself into.
Change your habits and change your life. KNOW THE CAUSE
– Dr. Roby Mitchell

Environmental Influences

Most anxieties arise from the conditioned mind, and you can certainly become masterful at addressing these. But there are environmental factors as well. Wherever you are or whatever situation you are in, your body and mind are in constant energy exchange with the physical environment around you, and this has a direct impact on your emotions and therefore your physical wellbeing. Anything that impacts on your physical health has a stress component to it and so will affect your level of anxiety as well.

- Strong winds can stimulate the liver and bring rise to anger.
- Environmental toxins that permeate our air can leave us feeling agitated and unwell.
- Living and working in highly built-up areas reduces our exposure to negative ions – those free radicals that our body needs.
- Without enough sunlight we can become quite depressed.
- While color is often subjective, it is common for black to create a resonance of negativity, depression, or power over you if you are surrounded by it for a protracted period.
- Different kinds of foods and other substances (mostly in excess) cannot only affect our physicality but also our moods.

- Loud noises, particularly if they are insistent, or the quiet sound of a mosquito sharing your bedroom.
- Planetary energies: when the planet Mercury goes retrograde, for example, it tends to interfere with our communication systems and our thinking mind.
- The monthly full moon reflects an increase in violent crimes, a rise in admissions to psychiatric hospitals, and suicide rates go up.
- Geopathic stress and geo engineering affects our Earth Mother and all her inhabitants.
- Electromagnetic radiation is permeating our world, conflicting with our own body's electrical system.
- Solar flares from the Sun affect the Earth's ionosphere and can interfere with our own natural circuitry.
- Unseen energies including negative thought forms from our self and others can leave you feeling anxious.

Being aware of these possible environmental influences can assist you in your understanding and create the potential to minimize the impact.

Which Strategies are Best for Me?

There are different kinds of energy healing processes with different impacts. When you are feeling any kind of anxiety or negative emotion and are looking for help from the Strategies, trust your intuition in the moment to see what mostly draws you. You cannot make a mistake. All the Strategies lead to greater consciousness, though some may be more supportive of your specific needs than others. Just one might be enough to bring about a positive change, and there may be times when you feel that several processes are needed to address the various aspects.

Remember these are life skills: behaviors to learn and integrate into your everyday life to build awareness, self-love, good health, and personal empowerment.

If you're really angry with someone you could draw from any of the following Strategies:

- Deep Release Breathing
- Feeling Anger
- Shadow Play

There are still others that may have more appeal to you at the time, such as:

- Challenge Your Beliefs

- Clearing
- Conflict Resolution
- Feeling Agitated
- Forgiveness Process
- Projection
- Thought Power and Control

Old hurts often have many layers, so it is a matter of chipping away at them. These layers occur because of the accompanying beliefs we develop that can become ingrained in our psyche and form the patterns that result from those beliefs.

Developing awareness of your multidimensional self and having an understanding how the body, mind, and spirit all work together can provide the incentive needed to take action by taking responsibility for all your feelings, emotions, and experiences.

When we choose to take full responsibility for our feelings we can then begin to become conscious of the false ideas we have adopted as part of our reality and commence the journey of healing and awakening. Critical to this healing process is learning to manage your mind, and nobody else can do that for you.

Loving patience and a commitment to greater truth will get you through. Developing an attunement to your feeling body and becoming an astute observer and manager of the mind facilitate awareness and open the doors to true healing, greater consciousness, and empowerment.

Nearly all of the 101 strategies are relevant to this Category *Addressing Anxiety*, though some may not seem applicable to you in your current circumstance. Just scan through and allow your eye to fall on what is most appropriate for your current situation.

Dr. Roby Mitchell http://www.drfitt.com/About-Us_ep_7.html

Category 3
ADDRESSING DEPRESSION

Depression is an all too common health imbalance, which is on the increase, and we need to take note and address the issues at the core, not just at the symptomatic level. While Western medicine has commonly treated this condition with drugs, there is now acknowledgment that they do little if anything to treat this most debilitating condition.

However, much help is available.

If you suffer from depression, you are not alone. Globally, there are more than 350 million people of all ages who suffer from depression. It is the third largest individual health problem in Australia after heart disease and stroke and could be the largest "untreated" illness in the Western world with more than eighty per cent of depressed people not seeking treatment. Research reveals that depression results in more absenteeism than almost any other physical disorder and costs businesses, billions per year in lost productivity, and absenteeism.

A source of statistics on depression: http://www.upliftprogram.com/depression_stats.html#2

What Is Depression?

Understanding depression and its causes empowers you to be able to turn it around. Depression is described as a mood disorder with a multitude of negative emotions. It is a label given to a health imbalance which at its core is hurt and pain and suppressed or denied emotional issues. This can be exasperated by environmental influences. If you are suffering from depression you may present with a depressed mood, a loss of interest or pleasure, feelings of guilt or low self-worth, disturbed sleep or appetite, low energy and poor concentration.

You may feel a loss of control or a sense of powerlessness over your life. Depression and sadness can be as a result of the emotion of anger turned inward. If you were depressed and attempted to describe your energy, you will find it is typically very heavy, as if you are carrying around excess weight. It is, in fact, a lack of "life force" energy or *prana*, which will contribute to feeling unmotivated.

Depression will impact on your physical, emotional, mental, and spiritual bodies. It can be chronic or recurrent and can seriously affect your ability to take care of yourself. Without treatment, at its very worst, depression can lead to self-harm and suicide.

Depression touches everyone throughout their life, either directly through their own experience or indirectly through contact with others. Recognizing this fact helps us realize that the only way we can really address this growing concern effectively is to participate actively by deepening our understanding of the energy behind depression, accept personal responsibility, and find ways to raise awareness and resolve any painful emotions and help others to do the same. This is, in fact, the essence of the spiritual pathway.

The Signs of Depression

- lack of interest in activities and life in general
- protracted feelings of being down
- protracted feelings of overwhelm
- protracted times of uncontrollable crying
- an inability to cry
- persistent strong negative emotions such as guilt, worry, anxiety, fear, doubt, sadness, and feeling helpless
- reduced self-esteem.

The Causes of Depression

The causes of depression vary, though there is consistently painful unresolved emotions as their basis. Each person on this Earth has their own unique gifts, talents, and abilities, and if you are not living your passion – doing the work you love – the core part of you lacks expression and you will feel depressed.

This can happen when you allow the mind with all its logic, practicalities and fear to be the driving force in your career path rather than attuning to the higher guidance associated with your heart.

Examples of some outward triggers can be grief over the loss of a loved one through death or rejection, trauma, change or loss of a job, moving house, child abuse, family disputes, and serious illness for self or loved ones, feelings of lost opportunities and addictions.

Increasing studies are indicating that a poor diet and an unhealthy gut can be a significant cause of depression and various other health conditions emphasising the importance of good nutrition.

Dr. R. Hawkins, in his book *Power versus Force*, states "In clinical practice, the most catastrophic depressions occur in people who have discovered that they've been spiritually deceived... Recovery is much more challenging in these circumstances."

Resistance to change is a significant contributor to depression and requires that you expend a lot of effort to maintain that resistance. This depletes the amount of energy available to you for your everyday functioning. Change is a constant in life because everyone and everything is made of energy and energy is always evolving. Depression and unmotivated behavior inhibits your spiritual essence, which wants to express itself through your heart's deepest desires.

Acknowledging that you suffer from depression is a very important first step. This will open the door to your healing and the multitude of resources available to help you return to wellness.

You cannot heal what you cannot acknowledge, and you cannot heal what you cannot feel!

Action is vital to bring about healing. True healing is an active internal process, whereby you willingly embrace that which you have previously denied or avoided and begin to attune to your own higher guidance, which is always leading you to greater love.

If you also suffer from any kind of drug addiction, please refer to Category 1, *Addressing Addictions*, for additional information and helpful tools and processes. There are many small everyday things you can do to help with depression. These are listed below. It is important to be gentle with yourself and ask for help if you need it. Sometimes just talking through a particular issue, and allowing the feelings to flow, can be instrumental in creating new perspectives and start the healing process.

Keys for Temporary Relief

- Acknowledge your feeling state and find a trusted person to share your emotions.
- Go outside into nature and consciously breathe in the fresh air. Our homes can be a very toxic environment and lack the purity and healing energy that nature provides.
- Connect to any of the Earth's natural surfaces with your bare feet to soak up the negatively charged free electrons that help our bodies to harmonize.
- If possible, go for a swim in the ocean, as the salt water is a natural cleanser to your energy field. Alternatively, regularly have a bath with rock salt, which has a similar cleansing effect.

- Avoid alcohol or sugar as these substances are depressive in nature and can become addictive.
- Avoid any kind of violent media or heavy metal music where the language used has a negative focus; instead watch comedies and play uplifting spiritual or joyful music.
- Activity is important to break the feelings of inertia. Break down your tasks into small chunks that only take a few minutes and take action with them. This will provide a small sense of achievement or satisfaction and leave you feeling better about yourself. Then do another small task and continue in this pattern.
- Find something to entertain or nurture yourself. Read a book or magazine, play a solo card game, potter in the garden, explore the Internet, connect with a friend, do a puzzle, clean out a cupboard, prepare a nice meal, gently massage your own body from top to bottom.
- Go for a walk, or do some other forms of exercise. This can create an increase in the endorphin levels in the brain, which elevate your mood.

Foods and Supplements that May Help Depression

Some research suggestions include improving your blood levels of Vitamin B12, which can be found in lean cuts of meat, fish, and poultry; and folate found in legumes, green vegetables, and orange juice.

Tryptophan is an essential amino acid found in some foods that our body then converts to serotonin, which can regulate mood. Foods that contain high levels of tryptophan include bananas, nuts, sesame seeds, milk, egg white, soy protein, chicken, and turkey.

St. John's Wort is a herbal supplement for sadness worry, nervousness and sleep difficulties. Omega Fatty Acids are found in fish and supplement form and assist normal brain function. Magnesium is a calming mineral that nourishes the nervous system and has many other health benefits. It is found in legumes, nuts, whole grains, and green vegetables, but these foods are not enough to meet your body's needs. Best to supplement.

Depression is considered a serious health condition and working with these Strategies in conjunction with support from your healthcare practitioner is recommended. Depression often goes in conjunction with addictions and each has a powerful impact on self-esteem. For this reason the vast majority of the Strategies are applicable. The level and cause of your depression will naturally influence which ones are relevant. Adopting any of the Strategies that begin to bring about upliftment is valuable, so just see what you feel you can manage.

Some primary ones to consider are the following:

16. Clearing
35. Exercise for Living
57. Gratitude
58. Grounding/Earthing
73. Nutrition Keys
86. Review and Remake your Day
94. Thought: Managing the Inner Critic

Category 4
AWARENESS AND MINDFULNESS

Awareness and mindfulness are terms often interchanged. Mindfulness is attentive awareness of the present moment. In their book *Breath by Breath*, Larry Rosenberg and David Guy draw upon a useful analogy that mindfulness is like a mirror simply reflecting what is there. It is a term that refers to your ability to perceive, sense, or feel that which may be an inner or an outer experience of your environment.

Mindfulness is not thinking, though you can be mindful of thought, but observing and accepting what is so in the here and now without reacting. It is as though you are just a witness of your experience without making any judgment about it. It is accepting all that is – allowing everything to be there: acknowledging and accepting your thoughts, feelings bodily sensations, and your environment.

Awareness, in its broad context, is the foundation of good health, personal growth, building happy relationships, and attaining a feeling of greater love. It is a state of observing what is, without any attachment – a state of perceiving all experiences, thoughts, and feelings equally. Nothing is clung to, explored, suppressed, repressed, avoided, or denied. It is just observed.

**At any moment of your day
you have the opportunity for greater awareness,
no matter where you are or what you are doing.**

Quantum physics tells us that our experience of reality is determined by our thoughts and beliefs, and that our bodies are made up of around 99% space. Yet we are not our thoughts, feelings, or behaviors, although these things may constitute our experience of life.

We are multidimensional energy beings living and interacting amid a sea of other energies. Developing awareness is a process of uncovering your true nature or authentic self.

Awareness is a state of being conscious of events, objects or sensations without reaction. On its own, your mind will perceive things as they are and comprehend the nature of what is. It is your *emotional response* to what you see, hear, or perceive about people, places, and things that creates different reactions. This is a form of judgment.

For example, if you were walking down the street and a stranger passing by says "I hate you," you could react in many different ways depending on your level of awareness and past conditioning. You may be shocked, or feel deeply hurt, you may laugh it off as some crazy joke or be disgusted at such a comment, or you may have no reaction, just noticing it. The likelihood is that the person is dealing with his or her own emotional pain.

In this situation let us allow for some sensitivity to such a surprise comment. If however you have a strong reaction, the passer-by has found a trigger, which is part of a program that *you* are running.

So being conscious in the moment becomes an opportunity for you to transform that reaction; to observe all the feeling sensations in your body without any attempt to alter them. Just remaining present with all that is will allow that energy to move and eventually dissipate.

Be clear and understand that any reaction is just that: a response to an earlier trigger that has been reactivated. If there is no reaction, consciousness is present. Within this context, presence is another term to describe conscious awareness.

The personality self or egoic mind has an investment in having its needs met and will attempt to keep you safe from facing any past hurts. These are the illusions that the mind creates which arise from the beliefs, experiences, and perceptions you have adopted as part of your conditioning. This is not a right or wrong, good or bad situation; it is just how it is. Every person experiences conditioning.

As you challenge all your beliefs, your perspective broadens and a greater truth is revealed to you. This activity of challenging your beliefs, being present, and developing awareness helps you to override the egoic mind, which will otherwise remain the driving force in your thinking and behavior.

Around 95 percent of the way you live your life will be driven by the subconscious mind rather than the conscious mind until you begin the journey into greater consciousness, which allows you to remove that programming and see it for the self-made mind story that it is – not to judge or react but rather notice from a neutral standpoint as the observer of your own mind. This creates a space between you as the personality aspect that reacts according to the programming in the subconscious mind, and consciousness, which is simply "presence."

Awareness is the function of paying attention to your intention. Learning to be totally present or mindful in everything you do. Without awareness you have no choice and you are at constant risk of repeatedly sabotaging yourself, reacting to an unconscious program.

It is only being in the present moment that you have the opportunity to dissolve the unconscious pain of the past within you. Raising awareness gives you choice and allows you to grow through a deeper understanding of yourself and others. This is the empowerment that allows you to change your habits, routines, and reactions – to change your entire life and allow you to create the life you want. It takes effort and focus to be mindful and raise awareness, but the rewards are well worth it.

When you choose awareness, acceptance and compassion for all your life events and experiences, you will continually develop greater love, peace, and wisdom.

All of the health and empowerment Strategies require a level of awareness to actually implement them. Hence they are all included in the *Awareness and Mindfulness* Category.

Larry Rosenberg with David Guy, *Breath by Breath: The Liberating Practice of Insight Meditation*, Shambhala Publications, 2004 p15

Category 5
CAREER AND GOALS

Career and Goals is incorporated in this Health and Wellbeing program because work consumes such a large portion of your life and because part of the human condition is "desire." Underneath all desire is the yearning to feel good. People are constantly wanting or wishing for things they do not have, or things they want more or less of.

Setting goals and working towards those goals has many benefits. Everyone likes to feel they have some control of their own life journey. Having a goal can be a tremendous help to those who suffer from any kind of illness, depression, addiction, or low self-esteem. It provides focus, a sense of purpose, and a sense of achievement when those goals are achieved. Often goals change before they have actualized. This is normal and natural as we, too, are in a constant state of change. Revisiting your goals regularly is important to maintain a sense of clarity and purpose, and it provides the opportunity to make any adjustments as you continue to move forward with your goals.

It is of the utmost importance is to follow your heart's passion. Your heart is the core of your feeling body. To do work that gives you pleasure or joy provides such a deep level of satisfaction that it radiates out in all directions and leads you to your greatest potential.

> **The work that you engage in is a way for you to manifest your love, your awareness, your consciousness, your mastery. It reflects back to you your personal expression and the places in yourself that are not clear, the places in yourself where you are muddled or chaotic. So if you find yourself unfulfilled by your work, unfulfilled by the way in which you are engaging the world through expressing your creativity and love, then we suggest that you look to those places in yourself where you are unclear about your intentions in that realm. The problem is not with work. The problem is how one engages or resists engaging the world through the energy usage called work or service.**
> – Tom Kenyon & Virginia Essene

Beware of feeling trapped in work that you don't like. It will be a constant drain on your energy and erode your sense of worthiness and wellbeing.

Hold the intention that you are willing to move on, and strive always towards your aspirations even if it's just starting with some small step. Let your mind ponder the possibilities that would fulfill your deepest desires.

As multidimensional beings we are in a constant state of creating our reality. What you are experiencing in your life now is largely a reflection of your prior thinking. What you wish to happen in the future is strongly influenced by what you think *now*. Whatever is the focus of your mind is what you manifest, in co-creation with what is happening in your environment.

The challenge most people face is that they focus on their current reality and/or what they don't want, which perpetuates their existing state. The spiritual teachings of Abraham through Esther Hicks suggest that worrying, for example, is like planning a future event of what you *don't* want to happen.

Such an example might be worrying about not having enough money to pay the bills, or being fearful of losing your job, or being discontented with your home or living circumstances. When you do focus on what you want, you are exercising your creative conscious mind, and your emotional body responds with good feelings. The energy waves created by your mind do not judge or discern the quality of your thoughts, they simply respond. You must bring consciousness to your thoughts to be able to select and manage them.

We live in a world of duality and contrast, and for everything that we desire there is also the opposite – what is *not* wanted. So as a co-creative energy being, your attention must be on what you desire, not the lack of it. A way to assist your focus on what you do want is to play the *"What if ..."* game and imagine what it would be like. *"What if ..."* is a popular recommendation by Abraham/Hicks to make you feel better.

Example of the "*What If ...*" game – (struggling to pay bills)

> What if I had loads of money to pay my bills? I would feel so free. I'd look at my bank balance and there would always be plenty of money to go around. What if I had plenty of cash in my purse – I wouldn't need to put so much on credit card, and even if I did I would always have plenty left over each month to pay it out in full and still be flush. What if I was always able to meet the bills on time? Oh it would be so liberating. What if ...

You can see in this example that the thoughts are focused around imagining what it would be like to have what you want. This engages the conscious creative mind and emotional body and you feel good. Any time you are feeling good, you are in the flow of positive energy. The mind does not know the difference between what is real or imagined. It simply responds to your thought, attracting like and similar energy.

Fundamental to success in career and goal manifestation is understanding yourself as an energy being and what the Law of Attraction actually means.

Your thoughts create a frequency or vibration, and the Law of Attraction then answers that vibration. Your emotions will always reveal to you if you are in the flow of positive loving energy or in resistance. You feel good, bad, or neutral. In these active (not neutral) states, you are attracting a like energy back to you.

Interestingly, it is very common for your strongest desires to also be the very thing you are deeply fearful of having. This fear of opening up to your heart's desires has many different causes, some of them to do with your programming or conditioning. Common among these sabotage thoughts that lie beneath conscious awareness can be the fear of success and the change that might bring to your life.

Gratitude or appreciation keep your vibration high and in alignment with your higher guidance. This also helps you to determine the next step. Gratitude can be for any number of things, which don't have to be related to your desire.

> Examples could be gratitude for a warm bed at night, for the abundance of food that you can choose from, for the beauty of our parks and gardens, for fresh water, for the birds that sing, even gratitude for public toilets when you need them. There could be gratitude for the friends you have, even for the person who pushed your buttons to reveal some unresolved pain within you that is now conscious.

When you focus on something for 17 seconds a matching vibration is activated through the Law of Attraction. The longer you hold the focus the stronger will be the manifesting energy. In the same way, when you throw a pebble into a pond, the resulting circles of energy are not the same as if you throw a large rock. It just creates more energy. This applies equally to what you want or don't want.

Working on self-love and self-worth is an integral part of manifesting. If you do not feel worthy you will undoubtedly sabotage yourself through unconscious belief patterns that play out. Ensure you are always working to build your self-esteem. This is a central part of human life and the spiritual journey.

Ensure your goals do not cause harm to another or are competitive with another. That kind of thinking comes from the subconscious mind and has its basis in past fears. Your conscious mind is naturally connected to your creativity and aspirations and positive thinking. There is abundance for all.

In order to achieve your own goals, help another to achieve their goals, which will also leave you feeling good about yourself. Any attempt to withhold information or retard the progress of another – perhaps because they may get greater recognition than you, or be more successful – has a direct impact on your own success because you have cut yourself off from the whole. As above, this is fear arising from the subconscious.

As energy beings, everything you do, say, or be has an impact on the total energy frequency of this Earth. Adding to the love vibration on the planet also adds to your own vibration. Choose goals that are respectful of the Earth, and this means the mineral, plant, animal kingdoms as well as the human kingdom.

Always attune to your heart and your higher guidance and do what feels good in each now moment, although it may not be what you initially thought or wanted, but now feel strongly compelled towards, even if it takes courage or is associated with some challenge. Honor those internal guidance feelings, as they will always serve you well.

All human beings have their own unique purpose for being here on Earth. Allow the connection with your conscious and creative mind to join with your heart to be your intuitive guide. Maintain a flexible attitude and honor the good feelings and inspirations that give greater clarity for your life purpose to evolve.

Your career and goals are central to living a happy, creative, and fulfilling life. Explore the many Health and Empowerment Strategies below that seem relevant to you for helping you to heighten awareness and achieve these outcomes.

1. Accept Yourself
3. Affirmations

4. Allow Feelings
5. Asking for Help
6. Awareness: Building the Observer
7. Awareness of Awareness
8. Awareness: I Statements
9. Being: Mindfulness
10. Beliefs Challenge
12. Boundaries
13. Causes of Health Imbalance
14. Change Challenge
16. Clearing
18. Communication Keys
19. Communication: When you…
20.Competition versus Cooperation
21.Conflict Resolution
22. Connect with Nature
23. Conscious Breathing
24. Control versus Preferences
25. Decisions: Heart Wisdom
26. Decisions: Motives and Impact
28. Do No Harm
29. Do Things You Enjoy
31. Environmental Health: Electromagnetic Fields
32. Environmental Health: General
34. Environmental Health: Water
35. Exercise for Living
36. Feeling Agitated
37. Feeling Anger
38. Feeling Challenged
39. Feeling Disempowered
40. Feeling Fear
41. Feeling Grief
42. Feeling Guilt or Shame
43. Feeling Jealousy
45. Feeling Rejected or Hurt
46. Feeling Scattered: Unbalanced
47. Feeling Stuck
48. Feeling Uncertain or Fearful of the Unknown
50. Feeling Unsupported
51. Feeling Victimized
52. Feeling Worried
54. Gag Gossip
55. Goal Setting

56. Going with the Flow
57. Gratitude
58. Grounding/Earthing
59. Help Another
60. Honor and Respect Differences
61. Ideas and Inspirations
62. If Seriously Ill: Understanding Integrated Healing
63. Intention/Counter-Intention
65. Judgment Effect
68. Major Life Influencers
69. Manage Key Tension Areas
73. Nutrition: Keys
77. Personal Mission Statement
78. Projection
79. Protection
80. Quick Breath Affirmation
82. Relationships: Key Question
83. Release Resistance
84. Release the Need to be Right
85. Reverse Count Breath
86. Review and Remake Your Day
87. Seek to Understand
89. Should versus Could
90. Simplify Your Life
91, Sleep Tips
92. Solitude
93. Switching Process
94. Thought: Managing the Inner Critic
95. Thought Power and Control
96. Toning
97. Trust Truth and Honesty
98. Truth Lover
99. Values
100. Who Am I?
101. Work Passion

Tom Kenyon & Virginia Essene, *The Hathor Material*, Orb Communications, 2006, p. 80.
Abraham/Hicks http://www.abraham-hicks.com

Category 6
COMMUNICATIONS AND RELATIONSHIPS

Communications and relationships are at the very core of our life as human beings. Despite the hierarchy that exists in business, politics, and numerous other aspects in our world, no one person is any better or worse than anyone else. From a spiritual perspective, no culture, religion, social standing, or individual opinion is anything more than a compilation of beliefs developed over time, despite the fact that different religions claim to know the eternal truth. Ultimately each one of us is left to choose what we will believe.

General Relationships

Communication is basically a process of transmitting and receiving. On every level of your multidimensional self, in all moments in time, you are choosing what to transmit and what to receive. To use the familiar parallel of yin and yang, yang is the more masculine energy related to transmitting and yin is the more feminine receiving energy. To have good communication happening we need a balance between the two energies.

Communication often suffers in relationships because presence is not there with one or more of the parties concerned. One person may be speaking and the other not listening – or one may be transmitting and the other is not receiving, but rather formulating in their own mind what they will convey when the speaker has finished.

We all recognize this communication play and it typically reflects that the receiver is more interested in his or her own story than truly wanting to hear and understand the other's. They may be physically present, but they are off wandering in their own mind and not really listening.

This kind of dynamic, common as it is, will lead to misunderstandings, conflict, and disharmony. Being a good listener requires you to focus on the other person and what they are saying – to be attentive and present with them.

Or there may be times when the reverse could apply: when one is open and wanting to engage, to receive and hear from the other, but there is nothing coming back from them and it seems like a one-way communication. In either situation, there is no balance, and there will not be good communication.

Presence

The term "presence" is often interchanged with consciousness. It is a felt experience of being aware of your own feelings, at the same time holding the space for another to be there with their feelings. It is a state of listening, accepting, sensing, and feeling without judgment. It is like the very opposite of what brings rise to our issues.

The more conscious you become, the more "present" you can be.

It is indeed very precious to be heard, to be listened to, to feel accepted and seen for the person you are. When someone is present with you it shows respect, that they care about you and that you matter; even if the other person does not agree with you they are still demonstrating by their presence and communication that you are worthy.

Being present with another is a life skill that takes time to develop, as the untrained monkey mind is so often busy thinking and processing the next sentence or beyond or delving back into the past.

The best gift you can ever give someone is your time – you are giving something that you will never get back. It's a way to truly honor and respect another for the person they are.

The greatest gift in any kind of communication is to be fully present with another.

Sources of Disharmony

If you reflect and identify the source of pain, hurt, and suffering that we all experience in our human journey, we will find that nearly all of it arises from some kind of *communication problem*. There may be times where you have not felt heard, acknowledged, respected, valued, or maybe even seen by another. This type of scenario plays out in our families, workplaces and communities.

All people like to feel heard and understood even if there is disagreement or conflict with beliefs and values. Listening shows respect for another. Effective listening is a skill and it takes practice.

Taking things for granted in relationships and making assumptions, adds to the risk of poor communications and will lead to conflict and disharmony.

Sometimes, for a variety of different reasons, the words we use may not be congruent with our feelings or with our body language. This also creates disharmony in our own body mind, which in turn, can seriously hinder clear and honest communications. We see and sense this play out with others as well.

Programming

All people experience programming and it's easy to become righteous about our own values and beliefs and totally ignore that the other person has experienced conditioning just the same as you have. Simply holding that awareness will already put you in a more open state of mind, facilitating an improved communication. They, like you, are acting out of their respective programming, and very often unconsciously. They have their own values and beliefs that could be a world apart from yours and this may be compounded by your different social, cultural, or religious beliefs. The key point here is not to judge the other because of your differences, and determine who is right or wrong, but rather seek to understand their perspective. This way you will both benefit.

The Gift of Conflict

While it seems natural for people to want to avoid pain and hurt in our communications, it is an inevitable part of life. Our pain and suffering is typically triggered by relationships. These people who may initially awaken feelings of anger, hurt, or frustration within us actually provide a true gift that can lead us to heal the wounds of our inner child.

They are our angels in disguise and they give us insight into our subconscious patterns by revealing our unresolved emotional issues, our beliefs and attachments, and our attempts to control. They often provide a mirror for our own disowned behavior, which happens when we project our feelings onto another, stopping us seeing the truth about ourselves.

A child's mind does not have the ability to discern and evaluate all the information it receives and the experiences it has, so children learn to suppress challenging emotions; their interest is more about basic survival. This leads us to processing around ninety five per cent of our thinking through the stored memories of the subconscious mind as we grow up.

As an adult, however, we have the capacity to see, reflect, analyze, be discerning, and question everything including the habitual thought forms that we run. We have the potential to undo the programming, to bring consciousness to our mind, feelings, and behavior patterns. We can learn and make choices that support our wellbeing and connections. We can change the destructive patterns and make the subconscious, conscious.

When you feel those emotional triggers, empower yourself by an *attitude of appreciation.* Your feeling body is giving you a message that something requires your attention and it is an opportunity to heal and gain greater consciousness. Your angel in disguise has come to help at this time, not to make you miserable. They are showing you what is there unresolved in your energy matrix. If nothing were there – there would be no reaction. That attitude alone will help to take some of the sting out of the emotional pain you are experiencing.

If you accept that relationships are here to make you conscious instead of happy, then the relationship will offer you salvation and you will be aligning yourself with the higher consciousness that wants to be born into this world.
– Eckhart Tolle

Conflict by its very nature implies an attachment to a belief, or situation and an unwillingness to let it go. Holding the intention of wanting to resolve conflict helps to shift that. Always strive to understand another person. A simple statement like "Help me to understand" can be the key to a turnaround. Of course you must support it with some genuine listening or receiving of information.

Be aware that it only takes one person to bring about change. When you change your attitudes, beliefs or behavior you also change your vibration – the unseen energy that you are radiating. The other person cannot use the same patterns to elicit the same kind of response. This means they have to find another way, and so when you change, so too does the other person.

Whenever you are confronted with an opponent – conquer him with love.
– Mahatma Gandhi

Health Impact

Quantum physics recognizes that our thinking has a direct impact on our biology. What we think and believe (mind energy) totally affects our health and wellbeing. So if we are thinking loving, positive thoughts about others we are sending out good vibrations. Science calls this "constructive interference." However, if we are thinking negative, fearful, angry thoughts we are sending out negative energy, which science refers to as "destructive interference."

Studies shows that people in loving, supported relationships generally feel happier and have fewer health problems. This includes those who may not have a human relationship but do have one with an animal.

> **Social relationships—both quantity and quality—affect mental health, health behavior, physical health, and mortality risk. Sociologists have played a central role in establishing the link between social relationships and health outcomes, identifying explanations for this link, and discovering social variation (e.g., by gender and race) at the population level. Studies show that social relationships have short and long-term effects on health, for better and for worse, and that these effects emerge in childhood and cascade throughout life to foster cumulative advantage or disadvantage in health.**
>
> - Debra Umberson and Jennifer Karas Montez

Relationship with an Intimate Partner

Everyone wants to be happy and many give their power away to another expecting that the other person will make them happy. This will always leave you wanting and brings with it an incredible burden for both you and your partner. As adults, we can only ever be responsible for self. Expecting another to make *you* happy creates co-dependent relationships, which will always result in pain.

Nevertheless, it is a common part of the human journey to initially attract these codependent relationships and learn from them, so that you can reach this understanding and become more conscious. The key is not to rely on another for validation that you are lovable and loved but rather to give that love to yourself by working on self-esteem, awakening to your spiritual essence and the fulfillment of your own desires.

Providing love, care, and support in relationships is a natural extension of good communication. Supporting another with their goals and aspirations is a way of also supporting your own self – it satisfies our natural instincts of connectedness and compassion. We all know how good and uplifting it feels when someone speaks kindly to us. Enjoy being in relationship sharing your love and support, at the same time honoring the independence of each other.

Relationship with Self

The most important relationship is the one you have with yourself. It is a way of honoring your spiritual nature as an eternal being. This is reflected by high self-esteem, which goes together with a commitment to looking after your physical body with a healthy diet, exercise, and positive attitude. Included also, is being truthful and assertive, expressing your own thoughts, feelings, and preferences while understanding and allowing another to have their own thoughts, feelings, and preferences and learning to say "no" without feeling guilty.

When your self-esteem is high you have a tremendous amount of love to give out to others and it is unconditional. So the more self-love you have, the less needy and the more harmonious will be your relationships with others.

The Law of Attraction Assembles Happy Relationships … Asking your relationship with any other to be the basis of buoying you up is never a good idea, because the Law of Attraction cannot bring to you something different from the way you feel. The Law of Attraction cannot bring you a well-balanced, happy person if you are not yourself already that. The Law of Attraction, no matter what you do or say, will bring to you those who predominantly match the person who you predominantly are. Everything that everyone desires is for one reason only: they believe they will feel better in the having of it. We just want you to understand that you must feel better before it can come to you. In simple terms if you are not happy with yourself, or with your life, the attraction of a partner will only exaggerate the discord, because any action taken from a place of lack is always counterproductive.

– Abraham/Hicks

Communicating effectively and honestly enhances relationships and helps you to get the things that are important to you. The keys to developing loving relationships and good communications basically comes down to undoing the programming that we all experience, building self-love, practicing good listening skills, developing awareness, being present, and supporting others. Opportunities for this exist in all moments in time in everything you do, think, or say.

As you work at building your communication skills and harmonious relationships, let your intuition guide you to the various communication Strategies in this book that may speak to you in the moment.

As you will see from the list below there are many that are relevant.

1. Accept Yourself
2. Affection
3. Affirmations
4. Allow Feelings
5. Asking for Help
6. Awareness: Building the Observer
7. Awareness of Awareness
8. Awareness: I Statements
9. Being-Mindfulness
10. Beliefs Challenge
12. Boundaries
14. Change Challenge
15. Change: Warmer Greeting
16. Clearing
17. Communications: Family Agreements
18. Communication Keys
19. Communication: When you …
20. Competition versus Cooperation
21. Conflict Resolution
22. Connect with Nature
24. Control v Preferences
25. Decisions: Heart Wisdom
26. Decisions: Motives and Impact
27. Deep Release Breathing
28. Do No Harm
29. Do Things You Enjoy
36. Feeling Agitated
37. Feeling Anger
38. Feeling Challenged
39. Feeling Disempowered
40. Feeling Fear
41. Feeling Grief
42. Feeling Guilt or Shame
43. Feeling Jealousy
44. Feeling Lonely or Alone
45. Feeling Rejected or Hurt

46. Feeling Scattered: Unbalanced
47. Feeling Stuck
48. Feeling Uncertain or Fearful of the Unknown
49. Feeling Unloved or Unlovable
50. Feeling Unsupported
51. Feeling Victimized
52. Feeling Worried
53. Forgiveness Process
54. Gag Gossip
55. Goal Setting
56. Going With the Flow
57. Gratitude
58. Grounding/Earthing
59. Help Another
60. Honor and Respect Differences
62. If Seriously Ill: Understanding Integrated Healing
63. Intention/Counter-Intention
65. Judgment Effect
66. Kindness to Self
67. Laughter Medicine
68. Major Life Influencers
70. Mantras
75. Pain Dialog
76. Pain Focus
77. Personal Mission Statement
78. Projection
79. Protection
80. Quick Breath Affirmation
81. Relationships: Building Intimacy
82. Relationships: Key Question
83. Release Resistance
84. Release the Need to be Right
85. Reverse Count Breath
86. Review and Remake Your Day
87. Seek to Understand
89. Should versus Could
91. Sleep Tips
92. Solitude
93. Switching Process
94. Thought: Managing the Inner Critic
95. Thought Power and Control
96. Toning
97. Trust, Truth, and Honesty

98. Truth Lover
99. Values
100.Who Am I?
101. Work Passion

J Health Soc Behav. 2010; 51(Suppl): S54–S66.doi: 10.1177/0022146510383501 http://www.ncbi.nlm.nih.gov/pmc/articles/PMC3150158/
Eckhart Tolle, *Practicing the Power of Now*, Hodder, 2002, p. 95.
Abraham/Hicks, *The Vortex: Where the Law of Attraction Assembles All Cooperative Relationships*, Hay House, 2009, p. 123.

Category 7
ENVIRONMENTAL HEALTH

In subtle and significant ways, environmental health hazards are increasing in our world and affecting human health as well as the health of the Earth. In the 19th and 20th centuries our evolution and advancement into new technologies led us away from the nature essence that supports our very existence. We lost balance and it is time to remember and respect all life and the interconnectedness we share on this planet. Nature provides immense learning if we merely observe her. We know that the practices that currently exist on our Earth are not sustainable and put our future and that of our children at great risk.

For our own health and wellbeing and that of our families, it is important that we educate ourselves about the energy connection and parallels between the wellbeing of humanity and the Earth.

Quantum physics recognizes that the environment has a direct impact on us. We are human energy beings interacting within a sea of other energies, both seen and unseen. There is increasing evidence that there is a direct correlation between solar activity and human achievement and that the Earth's ever-changing electromagnetic fields can have a profound affect on our body, mind, and emotions. (see Heart Math Institute http://www.heartmath.org).

The human body is an electrochemical organism and the more we destabilize it electrically or chemically, the more we stop that organism working to full capacity in all areas. The more we separate ourselves from the Earth through our everyday practices of wearing shoes and living in elevated homes, spending less time out of doors, the more we inhibit our ability to receive the multitude of health benefits that are freely available from nature and our flesh-to-Earth connection.

The diminishing vitality of the Earth caused by the decimation of our forests and the pollution of the land and oceans results in massive depletion of fundamental generators of oxygen, as well as depletion of the mineral reserves through agriculture. These are potent signs of humanity's disconnection from the very being that supports all life.

Our own behavior also reflects a lack of respect and understanding for the temple that is our own body. Lack of exercise and poor diet neglects the needs of our physical body. The suppression avoidance or denial of our emotional, mental, and spiritual bodies is evidence of our limited view of holistic health and wellbeing.

A wake-up call to all of humanity is the shocking reality that babies are born already polluted with hundreds of chemicals found in the blood of the umbilical cord! (research by the Environmental Working Group http://www.ewg.org).

According to the World Health Organization (http://www.who.int/en)

- Environmental hazards are responsible for about a quarter of the total burden of disease worldwide and as much as 30 percent in regions such as sub-Saharan Africa.
- In developed countries, healthier environments could significantly reduce the incidence of cancers, cardiovascular diseases, asthma, lower respiratory infections, musculoskeletal diseases, road traffic injuries, poisonings, and drownings.
- Environmental factors influence eighty five out of the 102 categories of diseases and injuries listed in The World Health Report.
- Worldwide, 13 million deaths could be prevented every year by making our environments healthier.

Geo-engineering, according to Wikipedia, is the deliberate large-scale manipulation of an environmental process that affects the Earth's climate, in an attempt to counteract the effects of global warming. Through the Internet there is growing publicity about alternative energy sources that are safe, sustainable, and inexpensive. As co-inhabitants that share this Earth, we each need to do our utmost to explore this subject in greater depth and take appropriate action.

The treatment of animals which form part of the food chain reveals some shocking truths about factory farming and live export, which raise questions about our level of responsibility to these creatures that share our environment.

We live in a sea of seen and unseen energy toxins, which have a mild to seriously detrimental effect on health. As well as affecting general health, these hazards occur in the areas of consumables, electromagnetic fields, personal products, and water (see Environmental Strategies 30–34).

Given the sometimes invisible nature of these hazards it is all too common for people to be unaware of these ubiquitous energies or complacent about them. An understanding of both ourselves and the Earth as energy beings, and the sheer number of environmental hazards, will allow you to make clearer choices, take more responsible action, and explore areas that may be influencing your health, including some conditions that may not otherwise be easily diagnosed.

Being open to new understandings and really questioning the source and motivation of many of the reported news articles is important to our education and establishing what really is true. Responsible action now benefits both current and future generations.

Some of the feeling Strategies have been included in this Category because there are so many unseen environmental energies that can be responsible for feelings of imbalance. Within this book, material on Environmental Health is found in the following Strategies:

3. Affirmations
5. Asking for Help
6. Awareness: Building the Observer
7. Awareness of Awareness
9. Being: Mindfulness
11. Boundaries
13. Causes of Health Imbalance
14. Change Challenge
16. Clearing
20. Competition versus Cooperation
22. Connect with Nature
28. Do No Harm
30–34. Environmental Health
36. Feeling Agitated
46. Feeling Scattered: Unbalanced
50. Feeling Unsupported
55. Goal Setting
57. Gratitude
58. Grounding/Earthing
62. If Seriously Ill: Understanding Integrated Healing
63. Intention/Counter-Intention
72. Nutrition: Best Food Options
73. Nutrition: Keys
79. Protection
87 Seek to Understand
91. Sleep Tips
101. Work Passion

On alternative transportation see_http://bluestarenterprise.com/
http://removingtheshackles.blogspot.com.au/2013/12/ring-on-consciousness-and-levitation.html
http://www.youtube.com/watch?v=piT7Vgc9sCw

On bridging science and spirituality see http://www.brucelipton.com

Category 8
EVERYDAY ESSENTIALS

Everyday Essentials is a compilation of 25 Health and Empowerment Strategies that are considered fundamental to everyday life. All have an element of raising awareness and clarity to enable you to transform old patterns of self-limitation and bring more love into your life. Love is the bottom line of what all humans innately strive for and is consistent with the personal and spiritual journey.

The list may seem a bit overwhelming at first if these are currently not part of your daily practice. However, some of the Strategies are very quick; they take just a few minutes and make a big difference such as Clearing, Thought Power and Control, Protection, and Gratitude. Sleep tips are only relevant if you don't get enough quality sleep. Exploring the Environmental Strategies may require minor or significant changes.

Focusing on differences rather than sameness will always lead to disharmony, so Honor and Respect Differences and Judgment Effect, are important for your understanding.

Many others are about self-observation, which can be done as you move through your day with all its experiences and activities. Chanting Affirmations will not intrude on your busy day but will help you to focus your mind and enhance your feeling state, as will the Strategies for managing the Inner Critic and focusing on Gratitude.

Still others will require a commitment of allocated time such as Exercise for Living, and Goal Setting. To adopt any new pattern of behavior, you will find it helpful to accompany it with another pattern or daily routine. An example would be doing a Gratitude list as soon as you get into bed, and the Grounding and Protection Strategies as soon as you get out of bed. Use daily triggers to practice the three Awareness Strategies, like each time you walk through a doorway, each time you have been to the bathroom, put down the phone, had a drink, either side of your daily shower or before meals, or any other regular daily practice.

Becoming familiar with the practices of Seek to Understand and Projection will likely require some deep inner reflection before they settle into your consciousness and habitual way of being.

It's not so much about starting these all at once, but rather building these practices into your way of being, so that they become second nature to you. Each time we learn something or adopt a new behaviour, new neuron connections are formed. The more we practice them the stronger the connection becomes. When we change our thinking, we change our behaviour and we change our life.

You may find it helpful to add these practices to your list of Goals. Use any kind of reminders to help you further. Write little notes that you paste around you – on the fridge, bedroom wall, car, etc. Use your phone to ding reminders at you. Create a daily checklist that includes any of these tools. Without reminders you are likely to fall back on old patterns and operate on auto pilot, continuing with behaviors that don't serve you. Adopting positive new behaviors that enhance your growth requires a level of consciousness and a commitment to your growth, along with patience and compassion for yourself.

The Strategies that are recommended as Everyday Essentials are:

1. Accept Yourself
3. Affirmations
4. Allow Feelings
6. Awareness: Building the Observer
12. Boundaries
16. Clearing
28. Do No Harm
30–34. Environmental Health
35. Exercise for Living
54. Gag Gossip
57. Gratitude
58. Grounding: Earthing
60. Honor and Respect Differences
65. Judgment Effect
73. Nutrition: Keys
78. Projection
79. Protection
83. Release Resistance
87. Seek to Understand
91. Sleep Tips
94. Thought: Managing the Inner Critic
95. Thought Power and Control

Category 9
EXERCISE FOR LIFE

No doubt you've heard it a hundred times before. Regular exercise is essential for good health and wellbeing. It helps to improve your health, and can prevent certain conditions or diseases from manifesting in the physical body. There may also be individual reasons. It may be to rehabilitate after an injury, to lose weight, to improve your fitness, to improve flexibility, to interact socially, to build your confidence, or just to feel good.

The human body is an incredibly complex energy mechanism and it needs regular maintenance to keep it in good working order, just as any machine needs regular care and maintenance. If you don't exercise regularly, your body will start to form blockages and all kinds of ill health conditions will result.

Dr. James L. Chestnut is arguably one of the leading international practitioners in the area of lifestyle wellness and prevention, embracing nutrition, exercise, and energy expenditure, belief systems, thoughts, emotions, and social interaction. He says that exercise is as important as vitamin C, or breathing, or love, or anything else and emphasizes that exercise must be seen as a required and essential nutrient for health and wellbeing.

Benefits Of Exercise:

- Helps you manage your weight; when you exercise you burn calories.
- Promotes better sleep; exercise can help you fall asleep faster and deepen your sleep.
- Can put the spark back in your sex life. When you exercise you feel more energized and look better. Exercise improves your circulation, which can lead to more satisfying sex.
- Helps your whole circulation system and so strengthens your heart and lungs, which facilitates more energy flow.
- Reduces the risk of developing and/or dying from heart disease.
- Reduces high blood pressure or the risk of developing it.
- Reduces high cholesterol or the risk of developing it.
- Improves muscle tone, strength, endurance, and motor skills.
- Improves coordination, agility, and flexibility.
- Improves glucose regulation and so reduces the risk of developing diabetes.
- Helps maintain bone strength.
- Reduces the risk of developing colon cancer and breast cancer.

- Improves general and psychological well-being: reduces feelings of depression and anxiety, and helps to manage anger.
- Improves self-confidence and self-esteem.
- Enhances work, recreation, and sport performance.
- Assists the removal of toxins from the body.
- Slows down your aging process.
- Increases your energy levels.
- Improves your brain power: promotes clearer thinking and boosts IQ.

The Australian Government's new guidelines for exercise (http://www.health.gov.au/internet/main/publishing.nsf/content/health-pubhlth-strateg-phys-act-guidelines) recommend:

Doing any physical activity is better than doing none. If you currently do no physical activity, start by doing some, and gradually build up to the recommended amount.

- Accumulate 150 to 300 minutes of moderate intensity physical activity or 75 to 150 minutes of vigorous intensity physical activity, or an equivalent combination of both moderate and vigorous activities, each week.
- Be active on most, preferably all, days every week.
- Do muscle-strengthening activities on at least two days each week.
- Minimize the amount of time spent in prolonged sitting. Break up long periods of sitting as often as possible.

The Strategies relevant to this Category are the following:

3. Affirmations
5. Asking for Help
6. Awareness: Building the Observer
7. Awareness of Awareness
13. Causes of Health Imbalance
14. Change Challenge
20. Competition versus Cooperation
25. Decisions: Heart Wisdom
26. Decisions: Motives and Impact
28. Do No Harm
34. Environmental Health: Water
35. Exercise for Living
36. Feeling Agitated
55. Goal Setting

58. Grounding/Earthing
63. Intention/Counter-Intention
64. Jiggling
73. Nutrition: Keys
89. Should versus Could

Dr. Chestnut: see his book *Innate Physical Fitness & Spinal Hygiene*, The Wellness Practice – Global Self Health Corp., 2005.

Category 10
IMPROVING SELF-ESTEEM

No matter what you think or how you feel about yourself today, there is always room for more self-love. Another term often used for self-love is self-esteem. Self-esteem is how you feel about yourself. It is made up of thoughts and feelings that you have about yourself. These carry a frequency or energy vibration, which impacts on your whole "beingness." The more positive the feelings, the higher your self-esteem; the more negative the feelings, the lower your self-esteem.

Self-esteem

- **Affects the way you live**
- **How you think, act and feel about yourself and others**
- **How successful you are in achieving your goals in life.**
- **In summary, it affects everything you "Do, Say, and Be."**

Many writers and teachers in the area of personal and spiritual development acknowledge that a growing child receives and perceives significant negative input despite having loving parents. All people have their off days including parents, and the child is exposed to many other environmental energies that also influence. Some argue that there is a 50:1 ratio of negative input to positive input. Using this scenario, it's easy to see how this impacts on your self-esteem. That is, for every time you are praised or reassured you receive 50 times the opposite kind of information, which results in limiting beliefs about your skills, talents, intelligence, abilities and self-worth, all of which affects your health and sense of personal empowerment.

Negative input cuts to our very core. Interestingly, numerous studies have concluded that negative emotions are experienced more intensely and have a longer duration than positive emotions. This has implications for all of us in attempting to understand our own emotional processes as well as the way we parent our children.

If you perceive that you were important, lovable, and valued by your parents, it would contribute positively to your self-esteem; and the opposite applies: if you perceived that you were a problem, a nuisance, or not as lovable or capable as one of your siblings, or maybe born at the wrong time or the wrong sex, then this would result in a negative perception of your self-worth.

These experiences will contribute to your thoughts, which when repeated develop into beliefs about yourself and the world you live in.

A developing child can easily go into overwhelm with negative emotions and as a survival mechanism will learn to suppress the more challenging feelings. There is really no choice for the child without a fully conscious loving adult who can guide her. Even if you grew up in a family where there is great love and affirmation of your worthiness, the environment, the world of duality and contrast that surrounds you will still challenge your self-esteem.

The innocent child lacks discernment and awareness of herself as a creative energy being. She learns by observing her environment. If her parents did not show affection to each other there will be a subconscious program about that kind of behavior when she becomes an adult and is in a relationship. Or if the father often yelled abuse then that will most often be the pattern that the child takes on into adulthood. If a parent was very nurturing this will be a natural behavior.

Some early life experiences often create a hub of multiple beliefs that become part of your programming and remain tucked away in the unconscious.

Such an example might be:

> As a 4-year-old you were put to sleep in your grandparent's house when visiting them on a farm. You woke to find no one coming to your cries and the house empty, although you may have had loving parents who at that time were just out of earshot in the garden.

Your perception as a vulnerable 4-year-old whose concerns are focused around survival and safety could thus initiate the following type of beliefs:

a. People you love will abandon you.
b. It's always risky to sleep and not safe to fully rest.
c. There's no point crying because nobody will care for you.
d. Farm life is no fun.
e. There must be something inherently wrong with me that people don't care about my feelings.

As the child grows these beliefs can form part of the wounding created by the personality aspect or the egoic (unaware) mind and could manifest as the associated following behaviors and patterns:

a. Having difficulty in fully trusting in relationships and so have a series of loved ones abandoning you.
b. Being a poor sleeper, never fully able to rest and let go.
c. Bottling up feelings, believing there is no point to their open expression as no one listens.
d. A general feeling that country living has no appeal.
e. Feeling unworthy of love and fundamentally defective in some way.

When a child is unable to process through painful feelings, she will suppress them to get by; they will remain in the subconscious and so the patterning becomes instilled with continued avoidance. The accompanying beliefs become the adult's uncomfortable truth reflected back to them by the Law of Attraction.

Fortunately you weren't born with beliefs and they can be changed. While a thought can be changed in an instant, the beliefs that develop and become part of your programming require a greater level of energy input to undo them.

In essence, what erodes your self-esteem is your perception of your life experiences and the relentless cascade of thought – all activities of the mind!

**Changing your beliefs is central to building self-esteem.
It may be the single most important thing you do –
the most empowering and the most difficult.**

You are born worthy … There is a part within all human beings that is untouched by their life experience and that is often referred to as the I AM presence, the higher self, the God within, or Source energy. This core essence is associated with your heart. It is your internal guidance system, the part of you that knows you are a creative spiritual being temporarily here on Earth in human form to express your gifts, talents, and abilities. It is the part that always strives to guide you through your feeling body.

You can learn to recognize this part because every time you do something that honors and respects *you*, you build your sense of worthiness. Every time you move towards your goals and aspirations you feel good about yourself and every time you ignore your internal guidance it will erode your self-esteem.

To ensure clarity, we are not referring to the narcissist self-love whose focus is on the separate self of the personality aspect, but rather that unconditional self-love that embraces your physical, emotional, mental, and spiritual energy bodies and recognizes the pure loving essence that resides within.

It is never too late to start working on your self-esteem, the key to which lies in unraveling the childhood programming, challenging all the beliefs and expanding your awareness as a sovereign multidimensional being. As you begin to awaken to new perspectives and change your life, there is a bit of lag time with the Law of Attraction in your processing. It will still reflect your old beliefs until the new begin to take firm hold. Persistence is vital at this time of transition when you are seeking confirmation for your efforts of change.

Of equal importance is to not judge yourself for any feelings of inadequacy as this will just erode your self-esteem and hold you in the pattern. So kindness and compassion to yourself is essential. Have the same compassionate attitude for yourself as you would for a small child learning to walk. After all, this life is a profound learning experience.

Be alert to avoid any comparisons with others. Such behavior will certainly drag you down. This is an activity of the egoic mind that does not recognize your uniqueness and connectedness with all life. Watch also for any tendency to walk in the shadow or the path of another. We each have our own path and our happiness is determined by how much we follow our own heart's guidance.

"Your task is not to seek for love, but merely to seek and find all the barriers within yourself that you have built against it."
– Rumi

Increasing your self-esteem and feelings of self-love brings with it many benefits including better health. Dr. Bernie Siegel says: "If I told patients to raise their blood levels of immune globins or killer T-cells, no one would know how. But if I teach them to love themselves and others fully, the same change happens automatically."

Other qualities include understanding, compassion, connectedness, harmony, joy, knowing, patience, worthiness, and trust. Increasing self-love requires a real commitment that benefits not only you but the whole planet, because everything you do, say and be has an impact. That is one reason why you will find that just about all of the 101 Strategies are useful for building your self-esteem.

There is no real right or wrong order of working with these processes. They are not something you do just a few times when you're having a bad day. They are strategies to bring about life change. They are tools of Mastery. Just see what you are drawn to and commit to integrating that and then embrace another and another until your daily experience is love and joy.

Definitions of "self":

Self: a sovereign energy being with a physical, emotional mental and spiritual body and a core essence of love.

Self-confidence: how we feel about our ability to perform a certain task. We all have varying levels of self-confidence in different areas. It could be as simple as making a meal, or cleaning the car.

Self-esteem: how we feel about our self, including our self-image. Our self-esteem is made up of thoughts and feelings we have about our self.

Self-love: is inextricably linked to self worth or self-esteem. It is being unconditionally loving and have positive regard for self, which precipitates love for other beings. To love and accept all parts of self without any judgment – including all learning experiences.

Self-mastery: to be conscious and aware in all moments, to choose love, truth, unity, compassion and harmony above all else, to have clearly defined boundaries, to posses the qualities of spiritual willingness and non-attachment. In summary, to live an extraordinary life in an ordinary way.

All 101 Strategies could apply to improving self-esteem.

Dr. Bernie Siegel, *Love Medicine and Miracles*, Rider & Co., 1999.

Category 11
NUTRITION FOR LIFE

The Health and Empowerment Strategies related to nutrition in this program are specific to the individual. However, to understand true wellness and nutrition, it is beneficial to consider the macro level in relationship to the Earth, which supports life. So many of our evolutionary leaders agree that human health is a direct reflection of the health of our Earth.

> *We are standing at a major crossroads in human history. We are being called to evolve to a higher level of consciousness, cooperation and co-creation of a world that works for everyone and all life forms. If we fail to answer that call, we risk the total destruction of all life on the planet.*
> *Jack Canfield http://www.evolutionaryleaders.net/inspire*

The very life force of Mother Earth, which provides all our food, is depleting because of human activities. While awareness is growing, the bulk of humanity has lacked comprehension of this fundamental truth, which recognizes the connectedness of all life.

The ancients understood this truth and always regarded the Earth with great respect and appreciation for her gifts. Unfortunately this deep insight has not carried through into our modern world and is having devastating effects all over the globe.

Deforestation results in tremendous decrease in oxygen levels, and we pollute our oceans so that the plankton or organisms which produce oxygen in the ocean are stunted. Aggressive mining and fracking generates billions of liters of toxic wastewater through hydraulic fracturing which drills deep into the earth. The savage pace of oil consumption is similar to draining the blood from a human body. Many harsh chemicals have been introduced into our environment through industrial or agricultural processes polluting the air we breathe, the food we eat and our water ways.

Continuing this pattern is clearly not sustainable for either the earth or humankind.

Some interesting food facts:

- The World Health Organization estimates that one-third of the world is well-fed, one-third is under-fed one-third is starving.
- One-third of all food produced lands in trash.

- Australians waste 4,000,000 tones of food each year.
- 1.3 billion tons of food is thrown away each year worldwide.
- When food rots in landfill, it gives off a greenhouse gas called methane, which is 25 times more potent than the carbon pollution that comes out of your car exhaust.
- The hidden impact? When you throw out food, you also waste the water, fuel, and resources it took to get the food from the paddock to your plate.

Factory farming of animals contributes to deforestation, pollution, and climate change. The treatment of animals in factory farms (around two-thirds) deprives them of their natural living circumstances and abilities to express their normal behavior. Research and Information compiled by Animals Australia http://www.animalsaustralia.org reveal:

- Caged egg-laying chickens are unable to nest, perch, forage, or dust themselves.
- Newborn chickens used for meat production are selectively bred to grow at 3 times their natural rate. This can result in heart and lung difficulties as well as leg problems, which in turn lead to an inability to support their weight, and so movement is inhibited and they may be unable to reach for water. They live in their own excrement for their whole short life, which can be around 5–6 weeks.
- A mother pig is legally confined to a cage, sometimes for months at a time so she can't turn around or reach out to her piglets. Piglets can have their tails removed, teeth cut, and be castrated without any pain relief.
- A dairy cow must produce a calf each year to provide milk for human consumption. When the calf is born it is taken from the mother within 12–24 hours after birth, causing much stress for both the mother and her calf. The cow is then sent for milking twice a day. Male or "bobby" calves are sent to slaughter from 5 days old and are legally not fed for up to 30 hours before slaughter.

The United Nations, climate change scientists, Oxfam and World Vision all agree that raising animals for food is one of the largest contributors to greenhouse gas emissions, and that eating less meat would benefit the world.

Some personal considerations might be:

1. If factory farms use more food than they produce is it a sustainable activity?
2. Are animals entitled to live their natural life on this planet in conjunction with humanity?

3. What is my attitude to animals on this planet?
4. If I care about animals and these issues what can I do to make a difference?

Nutrition is essential for the survival of the human species. We, like all life, are energy beings living on this Earth, and everything we do to the Earth and any of its kingdoms (mineral, plant, animal, human) will also impact on ourselves. It is wise to be mindful of this interrelationship when we make choices about nutrition and everything else that supports our very existence.

"Nothing will benefit human health and
increase chances for survival
of life on Earth as much as the evolution to a vegetarian diet."
– Albert Einstein

The 21 Strategies related to Nutrition do not aim to provide specific detailed information about this extensive topic. Rather, they strive to deliver key information to help the reader understand the essentials of nutrition and provide fundamental information to enable a healthy diet along with some easy to understand tips, with opportunities to perhaps explore further through various website links or other resources.

To address human health issues at its core level means we must also find new ways that sustain both ourselves and the Earth. This will come about by awakening to our connection with all life, expanding our awareness of food sources, and a change in values with respect and compassion at the forefront for our Earth Mother.

Finally, perhaps a useful question to ask yourself is: "Does the universal law of cause and effect apply to me?"

The following Strategies are relevant to this Category:

3. Affirmations
5. Asking for Help
6. Awareness: Building the Observer
7. Awareness of Awareness
13. Causes of Health Imbalance
14. Change Challenge
28. Do No Harm
30. Environmental Health: Consumable
32. Environmental Health: General
34. Environmental Health: Water

35. Exercise for Living
55. Goal Setting
57. Gratitude
62. If Seriously Ill: Understanding Integrated Healing
63. Intention/Counter-Intention
72. Nutrition: Best Food Options
73. Nutrition: Keys
74. Oral Health
83. Release Resistance
87. Seek to Understand
89. Should versus Could

On food facts, see http://www.thehills.nsw.gov.au/IgnitionSuite/uploads/docs/Food%20Waste%20NEW.pdf
Animals Australia. http://www.animalsaustralia.org
For information about Vaccines, GMO'S and Big Pharma www.boughtmovie.com

Category 12
QUICK STRESS BUSTERS

As we move through life with all its twists and turns, we will inevitably experience heightened emotional challenges of varying degrees. Of course this is always the body's way of saying "pay attention" and our opportunity for expanded awareness and healing, though circumstances may not always be conducive to exposing or addressing our wounds in that moment.

While it is never appropriate to continually ignore these signals, having some helpful resource you can apply at those times will get you through. Take care to watch for any behaviors that simply mask the problem, such as avoidance and distraction, or resorting to things like food, drugs or alcohol.

These quick stress busters may in some circumstances completely resolve the emotional trigger or will at least reduce your stress levels. At a later time you may like to explore some of the deeper practices to address the remaining issues.

If, for example, your children are driving you crazy, Jiggling or Laughter Medicine might be the perfect pacifier and you can even get them to join in. If you are worried about something, consider the Thought Strategies, or Gratitude. Playing some uplifting Music may draw your mind away from fearful thoughts and calm the senses.

If you find yourself amid some conflict, setting some Boundaries and using the Quick Breath Affirmation could be beneficial. Apply the Protection Strategy and make sure you do some Clearing as soon as possible to clean the negativity from your energy field that will undoubtedly result.

Feeling overwhelmed with anger? The action Strategies of Shadow Play, Deep Release Breathing, or Toning will release the intensity of that energy, or even just doing some vigorous Exercise will help. The Feeling Anger Strategy will provide a deeper understanding of the energy play.

Take time to familiarize yourself with these Quick Stress Buster Strategies so you can apply them in those challenging times when you need some immediate help.

The variation of these tools will appeal to your different moods, circumstances and type of stress trigger. The above examples are indicators only. Trust your intuition on what feels most appropriate to you at the time. They will give you instant relief if practiced properly and can contribute to a greater sense of wellbeing.

Some of the relevant Strategies to this Category are quite practical in nature and require action; others will help shift your understanding to enable a reduction in your stress levels:

3. Affirmations
4. Allow Feelings
12. Boundaries
16. Clearing
27. Deep Release Breathing
35. Exercise for Living
36. Feeling Agitated
37. Feeling Anger
46. Feeling Scattered: Unbalanced
57. Gratitude
58. Grounding/Earthing
64. Jiggling
67. Laughter Medicine
69. Manage Key Tension Areas
70. Mantras
71. Music to Uplift and Nurture
79. Protection
80. Quick Breath Affirmation
88. Shadow Play
93. Switching Process
94. Thought: Managing the Inner Critic
95. Thought Power and Control
96. Toning

Strategy 1
ACCEPT YOURSELF

CATEGORIES APPLIED

Addressing Addictions
Addressing Anxiety
Addressing Depression
Awareness and Mindfulness
Career and Goals
Communications and Relationships
Everyday Essentials
Improving Self-Esteem

Accept yourself where you are at, *no matter what*, including all those parts you prefer to disown or not acknowledge about yourself. Without acceptance you will always seek it outside of yourself from others and you will always be disappointed.

You might be feeling non-acceptance for your appearance, for your thoughts, beliefs, feelings, or behaviors.

What you resist will persist

The voice of non-acceptance in your head will undoubtedly arise from your childhood conditioning. And the repeated thought-forms of non-acceptance perpetuate the uncomfortable feelings.

Learn to recognize the self-created voice of the inner critic, which is always putting your down. Rather than doing battle with it, belittle it by singing "Happy Birthday" to it, or be grateful that it has popped in so that you can see a destructive pattern that you are working on changing. Adopting this tolerant attitude doesn't offer resistance, which can otherwise feed the problem. See also Strategy 94 Thought: Managing the Inner Critic.

Non-acceptance of self can also be related to a *shadow aspect*. Understand, however, that it is the actual resistance to these aspects of self that keeps it in place because you keep feeding energy through the denial of it. Even though everyone has a shadow side it only has power over you when you deny it or resist it.

Owning your shadow is not identifying with it but rather being aware of it and using your conscious mind to recognize it as the shadow. Accepting that it exists does not mean you need to act it out. It is about accepting and knowing that you are capable of whatever behavior the shadow reveals to you. It's a step away from resistance and a step towards wholeness.

Often your shadow self emerges through being critical or judging the behavior of another. It is so often easier to see in another what you cannot see in yourself. Some examples might be:

- Judging someone for being particularly miserly about something when it is part of your own behavior
- Being really critical about someone who gossips, which is something you also do
- Condemning a person who is verbally abusive, just like you.

Being aware of your mind and any attempt to project onto another will lead to greater awareness and freedom to choose another way.

"The person we choose to be, automatically creates a dark double – the person we choose not to be."
– Thomas Moore, *The Care of the Soul*

Acceptance is the first step, and an essential step, to embracing self-love and awakening to the truth of your core loving essence. From a place of acceptance of what is, change can really happen.

Retrain yourself by starting with the kind of acceptance you would have towards accepting things you are comfortable with, such as plants, the days of the week, the weather, the ocean. These are typically quite easy to embrace. Once you can really *feel* the effect of acceptance in your body, then move towards personal things about your appearance – your hair, eyes, hands – and keep moving towards the parts you least accept, which may be your weight, the shape of your nose, wrinkles, or behaviors. The objective of attuning your feeling body towards these benign things is to *give you the feeling of acceptance*; once you recognize this feeling you can use the mind to focus it on those challenging parts, so that you neutralize the negative feelings and retrain the mind by creating new brainwave patterns.

So bring in a feeling of acceptance, then think of what it is that you don't accept and hold that feeling at the same time of saying "I accept myself for…" (whatever it is).

Start with the aspects of yourself that are the least intense and work towards the stronger ones. Make it a daily habit to bring about acceptance and increased self-esteem.

Self-acceptance is learning to love the perceived unlovable.

On the journey towards self-acceptance and self-love you may find you need to do some *forgiveness work*. For any guilt or shame (see Strategy 42 Feeling Guilt or Shame) that you are holding stuck in your energy field. Guilt and shame serve no positive function and are very toxic to your body. This will always work best if you can have compassion for yourself, just as you would have for a child learning any new task. See Strategy 53 Forgiveness Process for guidelines.

The more self-acceptance, the more empowered you are to change things and awaken to your real self.

See also:

- Allow Feelings
- Awareness of Awareness
- Beliefs Challenge
- Change Challenge
- Clearing
- Forgiveness Process
- Gratitude
- Kindness to Self
- Projection
- Shadow Play
- Thought: Managing Inner Critic
- Thought Power and Control

Thomas More, *The Care of the Soul*, Harper, 1998, p 20.

Strategy 2
AFFECTION

CATEGORIES APPLIED

Addressing Addictions
Addressing Anxiety
Addressing Depression
Awareness and Mindfulness
Communications and Relationships
Improving Self-Esteem

Human beings all need affection and love. We know this at the core of our being because we all have this innate desire to love and be loved. There is something about skin-to-skin contact. We also know that touch is vital for survival in the very young and they will die without it. The babies who are showered with affection by their mothers are better at coping with stress as they grow up. Those who are touch-deprived have tendencies towards aggressive and violent behavior. Our need for touch does not diminish as we grow and develop.

"Being affectionate is good for you.
Affection can be a simple, non-pharmaceutical,
cheap way to reduce stress."
– Kory Floyd

Research validates what we feel and know to be true. Affection satisfies a basic human need and leads to more self-esteem, better mental health (less depression), better coping abilities, and less stress.

Affection is a key to happy relationships. It reflects that someone is there for you – caring and supporting you. It facilitates a deeper intimacy and a trusting bond.

Synonyms for the word "affection" are friendliness, care, regard, warmth, fondness, liking, and love. These are the qualities that we need to show to those we love. In order to receive affection we also need to give affection. Heartfelt expressions of affection are viewed positively, though in circumstances where one feels threatened in some way, they can be viewed negatively.

With the busy lives and many commitments so common in today's families, it can be all too easy to drop into a pattern of taking your loved one for granted and ultimately neglecting your primary support. It's like saying everything else is more important than you. If these deep emotional needs for affection are not met, your relationship will undoubtedly suffer.

We can live without religion or meditation,
But we cannot survive without human affection.
– The Dalai Lama

Ways to show affection:

- Giving genuine compliments – "I love your smile", "You look so beautiful."
- Holding hands when out walking of just sitting beside each other
- Hugs: Experiment with different kinds of hugs, a good morning or hello hug, a good night cuddle, comforting hugs, playful hugs, a thank-you hug
- Give a small gift
- A little love note
- Kind or supportive words
- A phone call for no particular reason other than just wanting to connect
- A foot rub
- A back rub or massage
- Some gentle stroking
- Fingers through your loved one's hair
- A loving glance or wink
- Kissing: A study by a group of German physicians and psychologists in cooperation with insurance companies made a surprising discovery when researching long life and success. They found that those who kiss their spouse each morning:
    - ✓ miss less work because of illness than those who do not
    - ✓ have fewer auto accidents on the way to work
    - ✓ earn 20–30% more per month
    - ✓ live about 5 years longer.

In explaining their findings, according to Dr. Arthur Szabo, "A husband who kisses his wife every morning begins the day with a positive attitude. A positive attitude heals."

So basically giving your loved one a morning kiss enhances your relationships, boosts your self-esteem, makes you healthier, wealthier, and longer living.

See also:

Change: Warmer Greeting
Communication Keys
Communication: When you…

For a very humorous 5-minute presentation on affection with men and women, check out Amanda Gore's website http://www.Amandagore.Com *Why Women Are Different From Men And Vice Versa* https://www.youtube.com/watch?v=vQFl4a0xiBE

Kory Floyd, *Communication Quarterly*, Spring 2002.
Arthur Szabo, *Bits & Pieces*, July 25, 1992, pp. 4–5.

Strategy 3
AFFIRMATIONS

CATEGORIES APPLIED

Addressing Addictions
Addressing Anxiety
Addressing Depression
Awareness and Mindfulness
Career and Goals
Communications and Relationships
Environmental Health
Everyday Essentials
Exercise For Life
Improving Self-Esteem
Nutrition For Life
Quick Stress Busters

Affirmations are simply short powerful statements where you consciously control your thoughts. They are positive statements, comments, or compliments. All words and thoughts carry a particular resonance or vibration. Repeating affirmations not only creates a positive vibration and assist in your desired manifestation, but will significantly contribute to reprogramming your mind and overcome the brain's tendency to memorize the negative. Note, however, that everyone has an inner voice that seeks to sabotage; awareness of these negative voices is important if you are to steer your way around them.

There are an infinite number of affirmations related to all kinds of different subjects. Include them in your everyday language to assist you in all aspects of your life.

Some guidelines are:

Make them succinct. Phrase them in present tense, not in the future. Placing the word "now" in the phrase ensures the present tense, e.g. "I am now enjoying a loving intimate relationship."

State what you *do want*, not what you don't want. Ensure that your affirmation feels totally right for you; adapt it to suit your language style. Repeat them often and with real feeling; 500 a day would be good. (It is estimated the average person has 68,000 thoughts each day, so having 500 positive thoughts reflecting what you want in your life is not an onerous task.) Chanting affirmations for a period of 21–30 days is highly beneficial. This timeframe has a very positive impact on reprogramming the subconscious mind, particularly if they are said either side of sleep or in meditation when the brain enters the alpha level of the subconscious mind.

If you find that your affirmation creates some resistance within you because it is too far away from your current beliefs or reality, then adding the words "I am willing..." or "I choose..." before the affirmation can create the desired energy shift. For example, your affirmation may be "My new business is flourishing and prosperous." If you are really struggling to build a new business, and you feel frustrated or disbelieving, then the following amendment would read: "I am willing to have a new flourishing and prosperous business" or "I choose to have a new flourishing and prosperous business." You will notice these words shift the feeling of contrast while remaining quite affirming and create a more allowing state.

While it is highly beneficial to stick with the same affirmations for a period of time because of the cumulative desired energy created by repetition, it is also beneficial to adjust them according to your immediate need or from what you are experiencing or want to experience. For example, when you notice that you are running fearful thoughts, replace them with affirmations, and when wanting to build your own sense of self-love chant affirmations to reflect this.

You may feel challenged by a situation where you need an immediate lift. Such a situation might be doubting your own willpower about abstaining from some favorite foods while doing a detox over a few days. A suitable affirmation might be "I am strong, focused and determined," or, "I lovingly nurture my body with nutritious healthy food."

Or it may be a situation where you feel suddenly challenged where conflict has arisen. Affirm to yourself: "I choose to feel calm, and communicate clearly, honestly and respectfully," or "I love the creative way I find easy solutions to conflict."

Remember that what you express is what you will attract. It is the energy behind the thought or the affirmation that gives it the desirable manifesting power. So really try to connect with the feeling of the affirmation and your desire.

Listed below are some areas of affirmation that may offer inspiration for you. Or you might prefer to create your own. The important thing is that they feel good for you.

Self-Worth And Self-Esteem

- I am enough, no matter what.
- I love and approve of myself exactly as I am.
- I am worthy of love and all good things.
- Being love in all moments is my natural state of being.
- Love flows to me easily and effortlessly and in surprising ways.
- The more love I give, the more love I receive and the happier I feel.
- My heart and mind are filled with gratitude love and light.

- I am loved beyond measure, I am cherished and I am worthy.
- I deeply love and accept myself, for I am sacred, you are sacred, all is sacred.
- I am 100% powerful, loving, and balanced at all times.
- I am loving, whole, and complete within myself.
- I am loving and lovable no matter what.
- I am the master of my life, and my subconscious mind is my friend and servant.
- I am filled with an unlimited, inexhaustible supply of divine love.
- I am comfortable knowing that I am loved for who I am because I am a unique expression of creation. I am in love with my true self.
- I have an attitude of gratitude.
- I am powerful, centered, and loving at all times.
- I am loving in all moments.
- I am lovingly powerful and powerfully loving.
- I choose love in all moments.
- I choose to be 100% decisive in everything I do.
- My conscious mind, my subconscious and my source are a mighty manifesting force.

Growth And Expansion

- I am the power, the master, and the cause of my attitudes, emotions, and behavior.
- I have perfect self-control and self-mastery in everything I do.
- I have everything within me to move forward in life.
- I move forward to my greatest potential with ease and grace.
- I always experience "button pushers" as angels in disguise and as opportunities for my growth.
- I am a center of pure self-consciousness and will, with the ability to direct my energies wherever I choose.
- I embrace change with confidence, courage, trust, and anticipation.
- I love challenges and embrace them with excitement and anticipation.
- Every day in every way I am expanding my awareness.
- I am willing to change and grow.
- I choose to know the truth no matter what.
- I enjoy change and stretching my boundaries.
- Everything always works out for me. *

Health And Wellbeing

- My body is in perfect health.

- I love my body and nurture it with good food, exercise, sleep, and a positive attitude.
- All of my energy bodies are perfectly aligned and perfectly healthy.
- Every day, in every way, I eat, drink, and exercise to nurture my body.
- All of my body systems and all of my body's organs function in perfect harmony.
- I choose to be my perfect weight of __ kilos.
- I find positive creative ways to address all disharmony.

Pain

- I choose to release all resistance and allow all feelings.
- I release all resistance and avoidance and simply surrender.
- I now choose to surrender equally to pleasure as to pain.
- I surrender to allowing my higher self to work through me in love.
- I release this energy that is not of me and return it to its original source (because of our relationship with others we can often unknowingly carry their pain, hence the importance of clearing your energy field regularly).

Relationships

- I am always attracting positive loving relationships into my life.
- I choose to see the beauty in all people.
- I choose to know the truth and am willing to challenge all my beliefs.
- Positive loving people are naturally attracted to me.
- I recognize all people as reflections of me and appreciate them. We are one.
- I communicate clearly and effectively no matter what.
- I love the way I always find something positive to share with others.
- I speak with compassion and truthfulness.

Success And Abundance

- I choose abundance and success as my natural state of being.
- I am the power, the master, and the cause of my attitudes, emotions, and behavior.
- I am constantly creating the energy to expand my income each week.
- I choose positive new habits that support my goals.
- I choose to do everything necessary to make the changes to attract abundance and success.
- I love what I do and I do what I love, and I am successful.
- I claim my power. I prosper wherever I turn.
- Money flows to me easily and effortlessly and in surprising ways.

- The more I earn, the more I give, the more I receive and the happier I feel.
- I trust that I can have what I want and I am unattached.
- I express my desires around success and abundance, and trust and let go.
- Everything I need comes to me in perfect timing and sequence.
- Money keeps expanding and expanding in my life.
- Financial abundance is my natural state of being.
- I enjoy great success. I love my work and I am richly rewarded creatively and financially.
- I am clear on my goals, and they manifest easily and effortlessly.
- My life is blossoming in total perfection.
- I have everything within me to live my life successfully.
- I am conscious of all my thoughts and choose only positive supportive thoughts that nurture me and lead me to my potential.
- I choose to constantly move forward in the direction of success and abundance.
- Success and abundance is my birthright and everyone else's.
- I am the master of my life.
- I think, see, feel, and express financial abundance and success. It is my birthright.
- My potential is manifesting now.
- I choose love, trust, success, and abundance in all moments.
- I am successful in all areas of my life.
- Money success and abundance is a natural state for me.
- If it is to be, it's up to me.
- I naturally seek the positive in all situations.

Spiritual Desires

- There isn't anything that I cannot be or do or have – I am a creative spiritual being.
- Everything always works out for me.*
- I am not my thoughts, emotions, sense perceptions, and experiences. I am not the content of my life. I am Life. I am the space in which all things happen. I am consciousness. I am the Now. I Am.
- I awaken to the Divine Light which is at my core.
- I awaken to my pure essence of love.
- I am a powerfully loving spiritual being.
- I am one with the environment and the environment is one with me.
- All of my energy bodies and energy connections are perfectly aligned to and from source.
- I seek universal truth in every aspect of my life.

- I am a sovereign being.
- I am sovereign, I am free, I choose love through eternity.
- I am a multidimensional all-powerful loving being.
- I am one with all life.
- I can reclaim my power and energy from any concept or belief that I have adopted.
- I am filled with the power of my divine core.
- I can create or un-create anything that exists within my reality.

Using the words "I AM" within the affirmation is powerful because it is said to be the creative word: the initial word that produced creation and from which all creation springs. Below is what is known as the I AM mantra.** Each statement is powerful on its own or can be joined together as one.

I AM
I AM all that I AM
I AM one with the universal mind
I AM one with the source of all life
I AM one with all life forms and they are one with me
I AM love
I AM light
I AM peace
I AM truth
I AM
I AM sovereign
I AM free
I AM love through eternity

See also:

- Quick Breath Affirmation
- Thought Power and Control

* This is a commonly used affirmation by Abraham/Hicks.
** Inspired by Michael King, Insight Foundation.

Strategy 4
ALLOW FEELINGS

CATEGORIES APPLIED

Addressing Addictions
Addressing Anxiety
Addressing Depression
Awareness and Mindfulness
Career and Goals
Communications and Relationships
Everyday Essentials
Improving Self-Esteem
Quick Stress Busters

Feelings are the gift we have as humans to guide us in our evolution; they are sometimes referred to as the eyes to the soul. Feelings are experienced through our emotional body, which interpenetrates with the physical, mental, and spiritual bodies that make up a complex life-maintaining system within this vast universe. It is through our feelings that we are able to connect with our intuition or higher guidance.

Your feeling body never lies to you – it just feels. Yet the mind, by contrast, can and will deceive you because of its association with the ego/personality and subconscious programming, which will be full of many erroneous beliefs. Your feeling body feels and senses and your mind interprets these feelings. Feelings and emotions are often used interchangeably, though to be more specific it is thought and feeling that create emotion.

Feelings include all the physical sensations associated with the human senses, as well as feelings and sensations of the subtle worlds in our environment. Human beings are electrochemical organisms and we can pick up all kinds of different feelings and sensations that do not arise from within but rather from outside of our bodies, like other people's feeling state, environmental and planetary energies, which are all interconnected.

This process is focused on the inner feelings arising from the subconscious and unconscious mind; its focus is on understanding and learning to work with your emotional body, where thought and feeling are combined.

Your physically felt body is in fact part of a gigantic system of here and other places, now and other times, you and other people in fact, the whole universe. This sense of being bodily alive in a vast system is the body as it is felt from inside.
– Gene Gendlin, originator of Focusing. http://www.focusing.org

All feelings are valid irrespective of what they are.

While we tend to label feelings as either positive or negative, they are simply an indicator to reveal what is happening in our human energy system and the world that surrounds us. Feelings show us the contrast of what we like and don't like and so also offer us inspiration to move towards greater love, which we all want at the deepest level.

When we are feeling "bad" it is an indication that we have the potential to move toward a more harmonious state. When we are feeling "good" there is contentment and a kind of *rightness* in that state and all is well. The body *en-joys* that experience because it is its natural aligned state.

Emotional triggers are a reminder of something from our childhood that we were unable to process out into a harmonious state at that time, and so we suppress the emotion. The energy of the negative feeling stays in the body and is reawakened when something similar happens.

The trigger might be feeling ignored by a work colleague. The origin could be as simple as being ignored or chastised as a small child for trying to get your parents' attention over something that was important to you. Any kind of repetition of similar situations can perpetuate a thinking pattern of not feeling valued or worthy that continues into adulthood, very often without any consciousness of the origin.

SUPPRESSING EMOTIONS

Suppressing any kind of hurt or painful emotion becomes an unconscious coping mechanism, at the same time planting seeds of unworthiness. This pattern continues into adulthood and so we can become increasingly disconnected from our ability to trust our feeling body as an innate intelligence that knows how to move us forward to greater love, expansion, success, and connection with all life. Instead we give power to the mind, and the more we do this, the more we feel disconnected from our higher guidance and everyone around us.

The better you feel, emotionally, the more you are allowing your alignment with Source. The worse you feel, the more you are resisting Source. When you are offering no resistance, your natural state of alignment resumes—and so does the alignment between your cells and their Source.

– Abraham Hicks

Suppressing emotions is like continually adding to a storehouse of negative energy within our bodies – energy that drives every aspect of our life in an unconscious way. It is like severing our natural healing processes that help us to comprehend our feelings and behaviors.

We just don't want to feel bad, so without understanding how to process these challenging emotions we will use all kinds of strategies as a means to avoid or deny the disharmony that our emotional body is communicating to us. We pursue everyday distractions like watching television or engaging with any kind of media, eating, drinking, shopping, working, being busy, or any kind of activity that helps to avoid the uncomfortable feeling state.

The problem is that, as the saying goes, "what you resist will persist." And so the source of disharmony, unaddressed, is likely to lead to more suppression, and the distracting behaviors then develop into addictions.

Suppressing emotions leads to addictive behaviors.

Generally speaking, we are not actually taught to allow feelings, but rather to distract ourselves from them or learn to control them.

Having an uncontrolled angry outburst projected at another person may release some of the tension within you, but is unlikely to result in a harmonious outcome or resolve the initial pain that has been awakened. So learning to manage your emotions is appropriate. Nevertheless, it is important to be able to transmute the challenging feelings in order to return to wholeness.

Projection

Another way we avoid our own painful feelings is to project our discomfort onto another. It is very common to be able to see in another what you cannot see in yourself. Accusing another of being critical, for instance, might reflect a behavior of your own that you deny. Projection always keeps you stuck because there is no acknowledgment or acceptance of your own behavior. You are basically giving responsibility to the other person for how *you* feel, leaving you powerless and stuck with the energy of the disharmony. By contrast, taking ownership for your feelings is very empowering and enables you to address them. See Strategy 78 Projection for more information.

Discussing Emotions

During times of distress, talking about painful issues can give rise to emotion and can help to bring about a new understanding. New understandings lead to new perceptions, and so to a shift in your energy (emotional) body. However, being fixated on a particular issue and unwilling to embrace another perspective, explore it further or seek a greater truth will ensure you keep the disharmony in your body. The same is true when you choose to block something you perceive as too painful and so pretend that nothing happened, or have an attitude of "it's all in the past so it's resolved" – *it's not.* Your body remembers and records all your life experiences and it will be responding to the resonance or vibration whether you are aware of it or not.

You will know when it's resolved by the way you feel.

We all enjoy the feelings of love and joy that lie at the core of our being. This is our natural state. When we are *not* experiencing love, joy, or periods of neutrality, we innately know that something is out of balance.

A Feeling Exercise

To deepen your understanding of the different resonance related to feeling and to help you transmute the energy, do this exercise.

Just close your eyes, take a couple of deep, slow breaths and then *feel into* the quality or vibration of the word "judgment." Not a mental definition with the mind, rather a feeling description with your emotional body. Do it now …

You will notice how restricted and limiting it is. It carries the energy of confinement, inflexibility, and self-righteousness – a cold and final energy where there is nowhere to go from there. It is judgment that holds energy stuck within our subtle bodies.

By contrast, feel into the quality or resonance of gratitude. Do it now before you read on …

Gratitude has a buoyancy and light feeling about it, a kind of fluidity.

We always have choice to think what we want.

As energy beings we are in a constant state of change, and allowing our energy to be in a constant state of flow keeps us healthy and well.

Understanding How To Transform Feelings

There are different ways to address difficult emotions. For integrated healing, all of them require that you allow the feeling to come into consciousness, though you don't have to understand what it relates to with the mind. Remember, "you can't heal what you can't feel."

One of the keys to dealing with the energetics of painful issues is to allow the free flow of feelings through you, not holding it stuck. It is a state of surrender to what is, a transition from resistance to acceptance. Without consciousness, it can be challenging to totally be with how you feel without distracting yourself. This extreme discomfort happens when you lose presence and become absorbed in an emotion.

So what is presence? Presence is conscious awareness. It is accepting a whole state of being. It is being conscious of and allowing whatever is there without resistance – a state of being all-accepting. It is being aware of the aliveness in your body while also retaining awareness of whatever else is there in your environment. Everything that you experience is happening in the present moment.

Emotions are a form of energy and energy can never be eliminated; it can only ever be transformed. To address painful feelings, we need to raise the frequency of the feelings from the lower fear bandwidth into the higher love bandwidth, just like the rising temperature on a thermometer. We do this by allowing whatever has been suppressed to arise.

This occurs by *releasing any judgment* about these previously held emotions, which enables the energy to get back into flow. Depending on your particular emotion, it may or may not require forgiveness; if it does, it needs to be true forgiveness from the heart, not just forgiveness with the mind. The emotional body must be engaged.

When you stop avoidance or denial and just feel, simply allowing the feelings (without any mind story), you are invoking the higher vibrational qualities, which include allowance, acceptance, and tolerance. It is a state of surrender in the moment, and it is as though the state of allowing carries those feelings to their home within the space-time continuum, without you needing to know any detail or where they originated.

Each time you allow uncomfortable feelings without resistance, it is like calling back parts of your energy into flow. The result is that you are more whole and complete and the release of the negativity obviously leaves you feeling better and raises your frequency and brings more light into your body. It's as if you are emptying out the negativity of your multidimensional body and discovering that there is this beautiful loving being within. The more you can feel and allow *without judgment*, the more a greater truth will unfold for you.

A Process To Allow Feelings

Come into a state of presence. When presence is there, you do not become consumed by the emotion; you do not allow the mind to get lost in a story, which perpetuates the emotion. When you are absorbed in thinking you have lost presence. In presence you allow your body to feel what it wants to feel while retaining awareness of everything else around you. This allows the energy to flow, and whatever has been suppressed and seeks your attention can rise to the surface.

An example of being present might be:

> Being aware of the chair you are sitting on, other furniture in the room, the walls of the room that surround you, the floor and earth beneath you, any sounds you may hear, the lighting in the room and how it splashes on different areas, the space that surrounds you, the temperature of your body and the room you are in, the tightness in your belly, the constriction in your throat, the flow of your breath, the air around your face, the thoughts that come and go.

Strive to have a curious, compassionate, and non-judgmental attitude as you retain your presence and allow your feelings to arise. Realize that the feeling is simply a part of you that wants expression; it is a part that you have previously suppressed. *Your body naturally wants to heal, it knows how to heal* – you just have to allow it to assume its natural higher vibrational state. Gratitude for your body's supreme intelligence, or for the one who has bought your wound to the surface, will ease the intensity of the uncomfortable feelings. No resistance, no mind story, just breathing, allowing feeling, and staying present. Complete allowing for less than a minute and it will begin to dissipate. So an extension of being present when an emotion starts to arise could play out like this:

> ... Noticing the flow of your breath, the air around your face, the thoughts that come and go... Chest starting to constrict, breathing becoming more rapid, throat feeling dry, a sense like a hard blob in your belly, feeling turbulent, now like a knife stabbing. Still aware of the support of the chair and the Earth beneath your feet, air seems warmer somehow, blob in the belly seems to be breaking up, a thought that someone is very cross, tears welling up, more saliva in your mouth, choosing to feel and allow without judgment or wanting it to go away. Appreciating that your body is trying to express and release what has been stored, a sense that Father is angry, breathing becoming easier, belly turbulence subsiding, muscles relaxing, belly feeling softer, breathing easier, a magpie's song, a deep sigh, peace.

Notice there is no mind story here, just presence with what your body is expressing and noticing any thoughts that arise. Allowing feelings is not dwelling in depression, self-pity, or repeatedly running negative mind stories. Allowing feelings is the simple act of allowing the flow of energy through you without resistance so that the uncomfortable feelings that you are holding in your body can be released.

When you focus, allow feelings, and maintain presence, the shifts can be minor or significant depending on the layers that may exist and your ability to be present and manage your mind in an emotional feeling state. With regular practice you will become increasingly skilled and comfortable working with this process. You will often find there are more feelings beneath the surface ones. Celebrate every opportunity to heal. Allow any tears to flow because they also offer release.

"Tears are like little bits of fear melting into love!"
– Linda King

There may be times when you sense that the uncomfortable feeling is actually a projection coming from another person. As your sensitivity builds with this process you will become more attuned to those outside energies affecting you. Then you simply need to clear that energy. See Strategy 16 Clearing for more information.

There are many Strategies to process painful emotions. Make Strategy 4 Allowing Feelings part of your daily routine to bring about transformation. Learn to work with your body's innate feeling intelligence and the immense wisdom and freedom it offers.

Personal or spiritual growth is the process of transmuting negative emotions (which all come under the heading of "fear") into love. It is perhaps obvious that the more unconditional love you feel, the happier you are and the higher your vibration, which radiates out to all life around you. These are the spiritual initiations of life that remove the sense of separateness, awaken the love that is within you, and help you feel the connectedness you have with all of life.

Do not hesitate to seek professional help to address painful emotions.

See also:

- Accept Yourself
- Awareness of Awareness

- Being: Mindfulness
- Clearing
- Deep Release Breathing
- Feeling Agitated
- Feeling Anger
- Feeling Challenged
- Feeling Disempowered
- Feeling Fear
- Feeling Grief
- Feeling Guilt or Shame
- Feeling Jealousy
- Feeling Lonely
- Feeling Rejected
- Feeling Scattered: Unbalanced
- Feeling Stuck
- Feeling Uncertain or Fearful of the Unknown
- Feeling Unloved or Unlovable
- Feeling Unsupported
- Feeling Victimized
- Feeling Worried
- Forgiveness Process
- Going with the Flow
- Projection
- Shadow Play
- Thought Power and Control

Abraham Hicks, *Getting into the Vortex*. Guided Meditation CD #409.
Gene Gendlin, originator of Focusing. http://www.focusing.org

Strategy 5
ASKING FOR HELP

CATEGORIES APPLIED

Addressing Addictions
Addressing Anxiety
Addressing Depression
Awareness and Mindfulness
Career and Goals
Communications and Relationships
Environmental Health
Everyday Essentials
Exercise for Life
Improving Self-Esteem
Nutrition for Life

People give different names to the essence of Spirit within all human beings. Some people call it the Universe, God, Universal Consciousness, the I Am presence, Source energy, Real self, or even gut instinct. It is a trust and faith within self – not the "little self" driven by the subconscious mind with all its conditioning, but a kind of omnipresent self that is connected with your heart and knows how to move you forward.

If, instead, we give our power to the mind it is as though we turn off a switch to this wise, knowing spiritual essence within. It's not that it has gone anywhere, but a busy mind or a lot of external distractions disconnects us from the feeling, knowing state that is part of our spiritual essence. It remains for us to attune to that connection within, somewhat like trying to find a clear channel on a radio station.

This amazing resource is always available for support and higher guidance. Take the time and care to connect to this higher vibration for help often, and especially in times of immense challenge or distress.

Tips To Reconnect

- Start by placing yourself in a column of pristine light.
- Spend several minutes focusing on some deep, long, slow breathing. This helps to slow down the mind and connect you more with your intuition and feeling body.
- Hold the intention that you want to attune yourself to this higher vibrational spirit essence within.
- Using your imagination, and even pretending, can be really helpful to build the connection. Pretending is a way of opening you up to the possibilities of linking together and releasing self-doubt.

- Then it is a matter of holding your quiet Attention on your Intention, and not allowing yourself to be distracted by the multitude of energies surrounding you.
- Put forward your questions, ask for inspiration, courage, whatever help you need. Be specific.
- Become really focused on your feeling body. Notice the subtle sense of energy shifts like when someone comes close to you; notice the impressions that arise, the impulses, the instant dialog or instant knowing. This is much faster than the logical mind, which typically has to work through the filters of the egoic or personality mind. If you are distressed you may notice that you immediately take a deeper breath and an increased sense of calm comes over you, perhaps a greater sense of clarity.
- It is important to learn to trust those instant feelings and instincts that come to you. Ensure you park the doubting mind in those moments of insight.
- If you lose focus, start again.

When you are connected to your higher guidance it will have a good feeling. Hence, you will understand the value of becoming really aware of your feeling body.

While this spiritual guidance within is always there, we are generally not taught as children to nurture this special connection, and so it can take some training to reconnect. It's somewhat like building a muscle that is already in place. Anyone can do this; it just needs practice or repetition to strengthen it.

Typical of the practices that enhance this type of learning are being aware in the present moment, meditating, and feeling your way into the energy center of your heart. These are practices that teach you to focus the mind and be more attuned to your feelings or gut instincts.

Other ways to help you build this connection is to spend time in nature and be totally present with all different aspects. Most natural settings have a more pristine energy free of contamination by lower resonant energies, and they provide a variety of different frequencies. Take time to just sense the vibration or frequency of different flowers, plants, rocks, or the Earth itself. Be totally present and sense the vibration of a bird or a snail or butterfly going about its instinctual life.

Looking after your physical body with nutritious diet and plenty of fresh water and exercise also helps maintain a purer vehicle for sensing, and of course you can also ask for help to support this discipline.

Ask for help in understanding your expanded sense of self, to help clear any blockages in your life, to have courage and overcome fear and doubt, to know the next steps in your journey and to take the next steps towards your heart's longing.

Your spiritual essence is always there ready to help.

See also:

- Allow Feelings
- Awareness of Awareness
- Clearing
- Deep Release Breathing
- Gratitude
- Grounding/Earthing
- Intention/Counter-Intention
- Mantras
- Protection

Strategy 6
AWARENESS: BUILDING THE OBSERVER

CATEGORIES APPLIED

Addressing Addictions
Addressing Anxiety
Addressing Depression
Awareness and Mindfulness
Career and Goals
Communications and Relationships
Environmental Health
Everyday Essentials
Exercise for Life
Improving Self-Esteem
Nutrition for Life

At any moment in time you have the opportunity for greater awareness, no matter where you are or what you are doing. It is a state of observing everything in your world. "Awareness is the state or ability to perceive, to feel, or to be conscious of events, objects or sensory patterns" (Wikipedia). Awareness, consciousness, observation are all terms with the same meaning in this context.

Awareness is EVERYTHING!

Awareness is the first step to creating lasting change. Without awareness we will be driven by the egoic mind, which is where all our subconscious programming resides. Ego is all about I, me, and mine, and separates us from our true multidimensional self, our connection with our spiritual essence and that of all others. The mind stores every experience we ever had along with our illusory perceptions. Developing psychological clarity about our life experiences is part of the process of increasing consciousness.

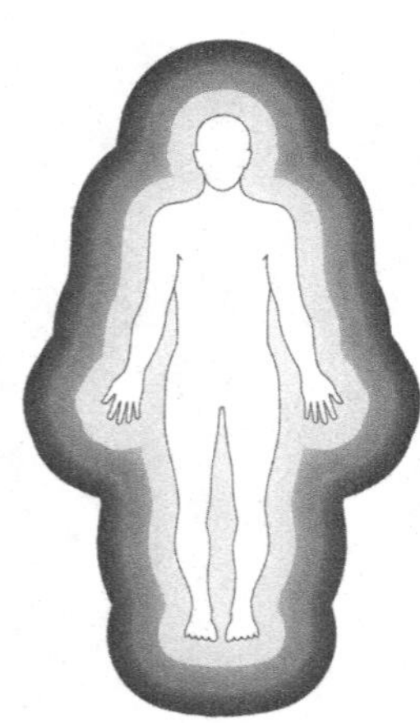

The more aware you become, the more you can direct your life towards what is important to you, rather than reacting or being a pawn of your subconscious or unconscious mind and the painful triggers that evolve as part of your childhood programming or conditioning.

The human being has 4 primary bodies, each with different functions, which make up our multidimensional self.

1. The physical body – to act and experience
2. The emotional body – to feel
3. The mental body – to think and visualize
4. The spiritual body – to reflect our unlimited potential.

As we grow in our awareness we become increasingly conscious of each of our bodies and their functions. Our psychological clarity increases with a deepening understanding about our life experiences. As we continue our efforts to clear the subconscious mind of its programming, the effect is that this raises our frequency and connects us to the unlimited potential of all that is. We are then able to bring that through our bodily form so that we can express our individual unlimited potential.

Increasing awareness doesn't come from books, though they can guide you along the path. Awareness comes from the practical experience of observing what is so – of being mindful of the "now" moment.

At any moment in time there are myriad things going on in your body and all around you, so there is always an opportunity to observe "what is." Building awareness of your feeling body gives you the precious gift of linking up with your higher self or your internal guidance system because of its association with the heart. This, in conjunction with becoming an astute observer of the mind, brings freedom from all suffering.

He who knows others is wise.
He who knows himself is enlightened.
– Lao Tzu

Building The Observer

Practice each of the 4 exercises below to heighten awareness.

1. Five–10-minute self-observation exercise

You can complete the different aspects of this exercise one at a time or in one sequential sitting for a more complete self-observation.

- **Breath.** Sit upright in a chair and give your full attention to your breath. It will help if you close your eyes to avoid any outer distraction. Simply focus all your attention on your breath. Notice how it feels as it travels throughout your chest; notice where you first feel the breath as it enters the body, notice any movement of your body as you breathe the breath. As your awareness goes to your mind and your thoughts – and it will – just bring it back to your breath.
- **Body.** Now feel into your body. Take your awareness fully there. Notice how your body feels. Notice the contact points of your body on the chair. Notice the temperature of your body, any tension, discomfort, pain, ease, or relaxation in your body. Notice any sensations that you feel. Notice any emotions that may be there: any

vulnerability, frustration, agitation, or perhaps anticipation, excitement, love. Just feel and notice without any resistance, any judgment, or any attempt to change anything. As your mind wanders – and it will – just bring your attention back to your body. Just notice/observe.

- **Thoughts.** Then take your awareness to your thoughts and simply notice your thoughts. Do not try to change anything. Notice the quality of your thoughts, the quantity of your thoughts. Notice any space between your thoughts. You are just observing yourself quite intimately without judgment and without trying to change anything. It's somewhat like being on the platform of a station, observing your train of thoughts as they go by.
- **Environment.** Then turn your attention to any sounds or other things going on in your environment. You may notice a particular scent or smell; you may get a sense of warmth or movement around you. Whatever it is, give it your full concentration and again when you mind wanders off; simply bring your attention back to your point of environmental focus.

You will have noticed in this exercise that you focused your awareness on different aspects of self. You controlled your awareness by bringing it back to the focus after your mind wandered off, which it will always do. As you focused in on different aspects of yourself you not only controlled your awareness but you also noticed more about those parts. This is the role of the observer.

The conscious observer is simply "Feeling Awareness."

2. One-minute self-inquiry observation

Ask yourself:

Q "Where is my awareness…what am I thinking, and how am I feeling?"
A "I'm thinking about completing that project and I am feeling anxious."

Building awareness of your thinking process is extremely important and ultimately very empowering, because Thought + Feeling = Emotion. You begin to realize that when you monitor or change your thinking you can change how you feel.

After you've practiced identifying the thought and feeling for a while, expand the awareness exercise by asking yourself:

Q *"What else am I aware of?"*

A *"I'm thinking I have so much information to wade through and it's unfair I don't have help".* These are further thoughts. *"I am aware that my teeth are tightly clenched, my shoulders are tight, and my breathing is fairly shallow."* These are bodily sensations.

You can expand that further by extending your awareness out to the *environment* around you using all your senses and noticing what you see, the temperature, any movement or sensations of different energies around you, any smells or sounds. *I'm aware of a slight perfume like the smell of jasmine, I'm aware the window is open and a squeak in my chair as I move and the floor beneath me feels really solid and I hear the soft buzz of the air-conditioner and voices in the background."*

Awareness gives you *choice* and the ability to refocus your thoughts and think positively, perhaps *"I'm actually learning quite a lot that could be helpful in the future"* and attune to what else might be influencing you. It also provides the option to unclench your teeth, drop your shoulders, deepen your breathing, embrace more of the pleasant perfume of jasmine, and connect with the support that surrounds you, all of which would facilitate more harmonious feelings.

3. Watching the mind

This exercise builds awareness of your mind. Building awareness of the mind is like watching your train of thoughts as they pass by while you stand on the station platform observing your thoughts.

When you are absorbed in your thoughts you are on the train, unaware that you are thinking. Then when you become aware that you are thinking consciousness is present. It is as though you have hopped off the train and are now on the platform observing the train of thoughts and any gap between the thoughts. There is a space between you as the thinker and you as the observer on the platform.

You can expand this exercise to include observation of your feelings and body sensations as well.

Developing awareness of the body-mind can be done separately or as one. Extremely important is to adopt a curious friendly attitude about yourself, free of any self-judgment or any projected judgment onto another. This is particularly important if you experience an emotional trigger. Without awareness, you will likely project emotional triggers onto others. Any pattern of projection will ensure that you remain unconscious and you get to keep the problem.

4. Observing Emotional Triggers

Emotional triggers are part of human existence. They are always felt in the feeling body and are triggered by our perception or thought-form from the mental body. They are a good indication that there is some emotional clearing to do, and an opportunity for healing and greater awareness.

The more you build the observer within you, the more peace and harmony you experience and the more control you have over your life. A key is learning to recognize that you are feeling triggered, rather than lamenting some undesirable behavior after the event – like an uncontrolled angry outburst. It is about creating a space between you as the observer and your feeling response. Note these three steps to building your observer and the examples:

1. Reflect on your own behavior: the thoughts, feelings, and actions *after* the experience. Ensure that you do not judge your behavior, just observe.

    Your partner makes some comment and you react angrily. You have *re*acted to a trigger that your partner found by their remark. This is an example of being unconscious. You observe and notice what has happened without judgment – just noticing. You are aware or mindful *after the event.*

2. Observe your thoughts, feelings, and behavior *during* the experience, noticing in the moment what you are doing.

You could respond with a level of awareness. Feel the anger at the remark, while observing your own bodily reactions and still respond angrily. Here you are again reacting, but aware you are reacting. You are aware *during the event.*

3. Observe your feelings, thoughts, emotions, and behavior *in all moments* of your experience. That is being so aware and present with all the body-mind responses that you can immediately stop any unwanted behavior in an instant. This is being in the "now moment."

   Now you would feel the anger rise as your partner pushed that button, but rather than react angrily you notice the feeling response, which may be felt in your belly, neck, shoulders, chest, throat, or jaw. You may also notice that your breathing becomes shallow. You take one or two breaths and choose how to respond. That could be any number of different ways, but with presence it will be a controlled response. The key thing is you are conscious in the moment and *choosing* your response rather than *reacting.* You are in a state of mindfulness, present with what is. You are aware *in all moments* of this experience.

It takes time to build the observer. It is just a matter of practice. It is a process of creating a space between your observer and your feeling response. Building the observer allows you to see and feel every thought, motive, impulse, or pattern before it takes you over. Building the observer brings unconscious patterns into your awareness and gives you choice.

A conscious person does not react but rather responds.

Take time every day to turn your awareness inward, to tune into your body and notice what you experience in your body, your mind, and your surroundings. Observe your thoughts, motives, behaviors, feelings, desires, and all that is around you. This is a great way to develop not only your awareness but also your intuition as you become more astute at interpreting and responding to the omnipresent energy within and around you.

See also:

- Awareness of Awareness
- Awareness: I Statements
- Being: Mindfulness
- Body Breath Awareness

- Conscious Breathing
- Deep Release Breathing
- Grounding/Earthing
- Reverse Count Breath
- Thought Power and Control

Strategy 7
AWARENESS: "I" STATEMENTS

CATEGORIES APPLIED

Addressing Addictions
Addressing Anxiety
Addressing Depression
Awareness and Mindfulness
Career and Goals
Communications and Relationships
Improving Self-Esteem

"I" statements are a simple form of self-expression about your feelings, beliefs, and values that not only facilitates greater personal awareness but can make a huge difference to effective communications with others and even how you *feel* about yourself. "I" statements build trust, and create healthier, happier relationships. *

"You" messages create a distance from your own feelings, which can be obscure even to you, leaving you lost in a sea of general opinions rather than identifying what is really part of your personality. Expressing your opinion as a subjective fact can alienate others and result in conflict. It makes the assumption that everyone feels the same as you do. Naturally people are going to have different opinions about different things for a multitude of different reasons.

For example, if you were to say, "If you live in the country, it is so isolating and really inhibits social interaction," this assumes that others share your opinion and it could be offensive to those who find living in the country a rewarding experience, perhaps even facilitating a more meaningful social life. This can certainly lead to disharmony and disconnection. Notice the difference and feeling behind the contrast if you said: "I reckon living in the country would be really isolating and I imagine it would be a real inhibitor to establishing any kind of social network."

This is a softer statement that takes responsibility for your feelings, discloses something about you and your opinion, and also leaves the conversation open for others to share their opinion. "I" statements include a level of self-disclosure and this tends to build trust and diffuse potential conflict.

Beware of "I" statements that include "you." These sentences can be disguised and include expressions like "I feel like you ..." or "I feel that you ..." Here there is an implied judgment that is a step away from you owning your own feelings and it also puts the other person into a lesser position.

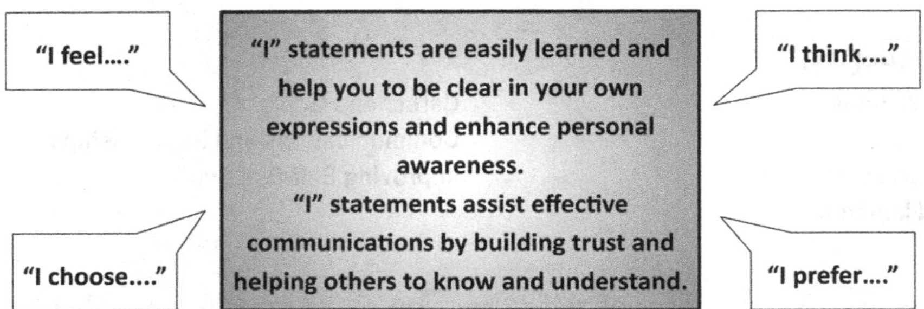

"I feel...."
"I" statements are easily learned and help you to be clear in your own expressions and enhance personal awareness.
"I" statements assist effective communications by building trust and helping others to know and understand.
"I think...."
"I choose...."
"I prefer...."

Good communications are the key to harmonious relationships.

See also:

- Awareness of Awareness
- Awareness: Building the Observer
- Communication Keys
- Communication: When you…

Strategy 8
AWARENESS OF AWARENESS

CATEGORIES APPLIED

Addressing Addictions
Addressing Anxiety
Addressing Depression
Awareness and Mindfulness
Career and Goals
Communications and Relationships
Environmental Health
Everyday Essentials
Exercise for Living
Improving Self-Esteem
Nutrition for Life

Awareness is a state of observing everything in your world about what is – so no judgment, no emotion, just awareness. It is a state of consciousness that is continuous.

Deepening awareness is the key to change and greater happiness. Awareness, consciousness, and observation are all interchangeable in this exercise. Practice these awareness processes often to deepen your consciousness of real self.

Exercise 1

Find a comfortable position where you will not be disturbed. Observe what is so – your thoughts, feelings, sensations and what you perceive in your environment. Then observe what you think about what is so.

Then ask yourself, "Why am I thinking that?" "What would happen if I was to listen to that voice?" "What would happen if I thought something else?"

Then as you change your thoughts, notice what happens in your feeling body.

The key to growth is the introduction of higher dimensions of consciousness into our awareness.
- Lao Tzu

Exercise 2

Find a comfortable position where you will not be disturbed. Close your eyes. Observe your thoughts.

Then move your attention away from your thoughts and observe yourself as the thinker of your thoughts. It is as though you are standing back watching your thoughts. To use the analogy we've had before in Strategy 6, imagine yourself on the platform of a train station; here you are the observer. Then imagine a train going through that represents your train of thoughts; here you are the thinker. Periodically you will be on the train, thinking and unaware that you are thinking. Then consciousness will arise and you will become aware that you are the observer standing on the platform of the train station observing your thoughts. You will move in and out of this pattern of being the observer or the thinker.

Start with Exercise 1 and do it often. It encourages mind and body awareness. When you feel you are accomplished with this exercise – which will be different every time you do it – then go on to Exercise 2.

Exercise 2 may or may not seem a little more challenging. Don't have expectations of what will unfold. Rather, learn from the process of what you are doing, increasing your awareness of consciousness.

Do these consciousness-building exercises as often as you like.

See also:

- Awareness: Building the Observer
- Being: Mindfulness
- Switching Process
- Who Am I?

Strategy 9
BEING: MINDFULNESS

CATEGORIES APPLIED

Addressing Addictions
Addressing Anxiety
Addressing Depression
Awareness and Mindfulness
Career and Goals
Communications and Relationships
Environmental Health
Improving Self-Esteem

Being is recognition of your existence – being here now. While many great philosophers have their interpretation, in this context, "being" refers to a receptive, passive state: the experience of being in the "now moment," present to what is so without any judgment. Life is made up of a series of present moments, but the unmanaged mind is rarely present, instead focusing on past and future.

Being offers no resistance and embraces many qualities such as allowing, flow, surrender, receptivity, patience, unity, trust, knowing, connectedness, and awareness.

In a state of "being" you may find yourself enjoying the song of a bird or soaking up the gentle warmth of the sun on your face, or feeling a soft breeze caressing your hair. You may be enchanted by the way the sun casts some shadows around you or the uprightness of the grass at your feet.

You may observe others going about their day, or find that some unpleasant feeling that you have been suppressing bubbles to the surface for transformation, or some kind of inspiration arises providing the solution to a problem you've wanted to solve.

In a state of being you may find yourself deeply connected with your surroundings, feeling a deep sense of tranquillity and yet aliveness. Whether you are in a state of being or not – something is always happening. *Being allows your awareness to embrace more of what exists.*

The common obstructions to these "being" states are typically caused by a busy mind: thinking about the past or the future, or engagement in some activity. Hindering a state of being can be a belief that "I am only worthy if I am doing."

Interestingly, however, if you don't create these passive times that allow you to connect to your own beingness, which embraces your heart's guidance, you are unlikely to live your passion or fulfill your primary purpose.

Creating times for just "being" reduces your stress levels, has an analgesic effect on pain, and facilitates greater awareness and connection to your higher self. It is similar to a meditative state, inasmuch as you are aware of yourself and your surroundings. But there is no endeavor in focusing the mind as there is with meditations that might count the breaths or chant mantras. It is not better or worse, just different.

Being

Find a place to just sit and be. There is nothing to do. Being can happen anywhere, but nature is typically a far clearer environment than your own home. Nature facilitates a cleansing, rejuvenating effect on your energy field as well as providing more appealing surroundings, arguably enhanced without the common distractions of everyday existence.

Close or open your eyes, as you prefer. In a state of being you are not directing the mind, though you may observe the mind and any thoughts that arise There is no self-judgment, no activity, just being, feeling, noticing, and observing. Consciousness is present.

Mindfulness

A variation of being can be the practice of mindfulness or awareness. The primary difference here is that you retain that awareness of yourself and your surroundings, but it is not necessarily passive. It can be while brushing your teeth, eating, working, driving, washing the dishes, walking – whatever activity you do. It is a moment-by-moment experience without any judgment. Mindfulness is awareness of your body, mind, feelings, sensations, and everything in your surroundings.

Mindfulness can be applied to any and every passive state and doing state.

See also:

- Awareness: I Statements
- Awareness of Awareness
- Awareness: Building the Observer
- Body Breath Awareness
- Connect with Nature
- Going with the Flow
- Grounding/Earthing
- Who Am I?

Strategy 10
BELIEFS CHALLENGE

CATEGORIES APPLIED

Addressing Addictions
Addressing Anxiety
Addressing Depression
Awareness and Mindfulness
Career and Goals
Communications and Relationships
Improving Self-Esteem

Beliefs are simply repeated thought-forms, habitual ways of thinking that become energized, then, by their simple repetition, activate the Law of Attraction, thus reflecting what you believe. Beliefs dramatically affect everything in our life: our health, relationships, vocation, the world we live in, who we are, how we perceive our place in the world, and our understanding of God or spirituality.

Some beliefs are deeply imbedded like those associated with religious doctrines. These and others can be very challenging to identify because you don't even notice them. It is as though they become ingrained into who we are. An enormous amount of our behavior (which reflects beliefs) is automatic: the subconscious mind is the driving force unless there is awareness. Beliefs influence every action that we take, and every inaction.

The more we think a particular thought the more it becomes a belief, which then becomes entrenched into the collective consciousness.

Numerous evolutionary leaders agree that most beliefs (over 80%) are simply not true and yet we live our life according to them!

Many of the beliefs we adopt as our own come from our parents, carers, schools, the media, society, religion, and culture. They are typically someone else's first, and most are formed without any level of consciousness. Particularly in our formative years, we normally didn't ponder and decide that I agree to a particular belief ... It's more as if we pick up by osmosis from those around us, taking on board the beliefs and values of others.

There are an enormous amount of beliefs associated with worldly affairs affecting our lives that are totally fear-based, providing misinformation intentionally touted by some people in power and misleading news reports that require considerable discernment. Because of the unconscious manner in which we adopt so many of our beliefs from people in our environment, we often feel disconnected from our true essence, which can leave us feeling depressed, a bit lost, or stuck. Our behavior might reflect the beliefs and values of others rather than what is really important to us, yet we may not even associate that awareness with our feeling state. This can leave us feeling out of integrity with our real self.

Much of this occurs through the programming of the innocent child, whose mind absorbs information in those formative years and takes on board all kinds of thought-forms and beliefs without an understanding of either his capacity to choose or the effect of those beliefs.

This seriously impacts on our perceptions, attitudes, and behaviors, until we start questioning and deprogramming, or practice the raising of awareness of our thought-forms and beliefs that is essential for personal and spiritual growth.

Your current life is a reflection of the beliefs you hold. Your expectation always reveals your beliefs. Do you expect to fail or succeed? Do you expect good things to happen to you or not? Any self-limiting beliefs will be validated by the subconscious or unconscious mind and the actions you choose to take or not take. If, for example, you felt betrayed by another in a relationship, then holding the belief that "lovers will betray you" or "you can't trust men or women/men" will be continually reflected back to you with recurring betrayals. The repeated thought-forms set up a strong energy that mirrors back to you so you can see what you are creating. When you do see it you can change it. The universal Law of Attraction makes no judgment; it is just energy attracting like energy.

Our new science now recognizes that it is our responses to our environment that are controlled by our perception, and that, as Dr. Bruce Lipton says in *The Biology of Belief*, our perception controls our biology. If a child was frightened by the sudden appearance of a barking dog approaching her, her perception could be that dogs are really scary – particularly if the parent response was a panicked look and verbal outcry that the child witnessed. Another child whose environmental experience was a parent smiling and encouraging the approaching dog with a pat may perceive dogs to be fun and playful. Fear sets off a negative response and fun a positive energy response.

Thoughts and beliefs all have a vibration attached to them. The quality of your beliefs directly reflects the quality of your life, your health, who you are, and how you live your life. Change your beliefs and you change your biology.

Some beliefs may feel so strong that there is absolutely no doubt. Be aware, however, that this doesn't mean that those beliefs are "true." If we were to use a scale from 1 to 10 we could say that absolute convictions are at a 10 and others that seem somewhat uncertain are at the other end of the scale around 1–2. Then there will be a significant portion of your beliefs that sit somewhere in the middle.

Many hold opposing beliefs that can create confusion and sabotage behaviors. For example, a businesswoman believes women are equal to men and on a deeper, maybe unconscious level, believes men are superior. Or a man believes it's really important to be ethical and honest, and yet plays out a conflicting belief that says what people don't know won't hurt them and cheats on his insurance.

The one you believe the most is the behavior that you will do. Depending on your own level of consciousness, you may or may not be aware of these opposing beliefs you hold. If you are aware, then doubt exists and this provides a stepping-stone towards change.

We need to celebrate our awareness when we identify these opposing beliefs. Once they are conscious we have the first bit of information needed to initiate change. It is impossible to bring about change without awareness of the behavior you want to change.

A useful benchmark to determine the quality of your beliefs is to decide if they are moving you forwards in life in terms of building loving connections with others, doing work you enjoy, feeling good about yourself, feeling that your life has purpose.

Beliefs can cause great suffering and steer us away from what we innately know is true. According to leading neuroscientist Mark Waldham, it is a natural neurological process that when we believe in something, it also creates a contrasting non-belief, which explains why human beings can be so prejudiced.

The brain will reject any information, or any person, that interferes with that belief. At its most extreme, wars are fought and lives are lost as a result of attachment to beliefs. Hence the importance to constantly remind ourselves that we are so much more than just the body/mind. And just because we believe something, it doesn't mean that it's real.

"Knowledge of others people's beliefs and ways of thinking must be used to build bridges, not to create conflicts."
– Kjell Magne Bondevik

When we are feeling loving, loved, and connected, there is a kind of rightness to it. Nothing needs to be fixed or changed – all is well in our world. Our beliefs will be congruent with true self. When this is not our experience, our beliefs will be the cause of our suffering. The empowering part is:

You created them … and you can change them.
In fact, you are the only one who can!

Tips to identifying your beliefs

Take a notebook, answer the following questions and take note of the different observations. Reflect on your life and particularly the areas you would like to change. Then explore your beliefs associated with those different areas.

1. Ask yourself "Who taught me what I know about men, women, family, money, sex, love, the environment, food, drugs, animals, work, ethics, values, self-love, friendship, politics, community, different cultures, values, personal power, or other key things in my life."

2. Ponder and note, who or what do I listen to? Family, friends, significant others, work colleagues, television, newspapers, the Internet?

3. Notice what is happening in your life now. It is a reflection of the beliefs you hold. Take particular note of the areas you feel unfulfilled. If for example you would like a loving partnership but your current life is not reflecting that, delve into the possible beliefs you have around it.

4. What are your expectations? They will always reflect what you believe.

5. Be aware that you will always behave according to your beliefs even if they are unconscious, so take note of your behavior, particularly in the areas where you feel unfulfilled.

6. If there is disharmony with another in your life, be assured that their beliefs and behaviors make sense to them, just as yours do. Seek to understand the other person as well as challenging your own beliefs related to the specific issue.

7. Observe your self-talk and spoken language, particularly anything that follows "I Am…" This can reveal either your resistance or your alignment with your true core self:
   - I am always struggling to pay the bills.

- I am hopeless at saving money.
- I am stuck in this job and can't afford to leave.

Clearly this reflects some issues around money. So explore what are your beliefs around money. Perhaps, growing up in a poor family, you may have inherited beliefs that money is for greedy people, or money corrupts, or you can't be spiritual and have money too.

8. Notice any beliefs that reflect "I am this way because XYZ has happened to me." It is as though you have made a form of agreement through the self-talk you have created around your life experiences. The stories that you run become part of your beliefs and become entrenched into your perception of who you are and leave you in a powerless situation, a victim to your life experience. Remember that your higher self is untouched by your life experience. These erroneous beliefs are part of the egoic or personality self that has a very limited view of yourself and the world.

9. Watch out for the all too common negative beliefs around worthiness like:
    - I'm not worthy.
    - I'm not smart enough, intelligent enough.
    - I'm not strong enough.
    - I'm powerless.
    - I'm not lovable.
    - I don't deserve.
    - I am defective.

These are erroneous beliefs that hold you back from reaching your true potential and realizing your true core essence. *Recognize that you were born worthy.* So really question where on Earth have these deprecating beliefs come from. Then decide whether you want to keep them or not.

"There is nothing that can help you understand your beliefs more than trying to explain them to an inquisitive child."
– Frank A. Clark

Changing Beliefs

You cannot change your beliefs unless you are conscious of them. It doesn't require strength, just awareness, though in some instances it may require courage. Being aware of your beliefs provides the choice to either maintain or change them.

A shift in understanding assists an easy transition to a new belief. For example, if you believe someone betrayed you and you later find out that it was their way of trying to protect you from being hurt, you are likely to find it easy to adjust your belief. Without a shift in understanding change is unlikely. That is why it's important to question the source and validity of your beliefs and to expand your perception and understanding, including the omnipresent world of energy that is constantly interacting with you. It will be easier to do this with some beliefs than with others; identifying and changing some of the more engrained core beliefs will require a more concentrated effort.

Be alert to any need to justify your belief/s; this can be the egoic self, feeling threatened. An example might be justifying that you have no choice but to stay in a job you don't like because you can't afford not to. If you dig deeply into this belief you might find that you just don't want to face some of your fears about retraining, or exploring possible new job opportunities. You may believe that opportunities are limited, or you don't feel worthy, or you're too old to retrain.

You may hold a belief that men are users and you have a history to vindicate that. Remember that the universal Law of Attraction will continue to support your beliefs no matter what they are. There is no discernment here, just energy attracting like energy.

The potential to change is there wherever there is doubt about your belief. Moving from conviction to having a suspicion shows openness; your attachment to the belief has relaxed a little. Understand that you can retrain your mind. Just as water running down a hill will always take the path of least resistance, so too will your thinking continue to follow in the same patterns until you redirect the flow, which consciousness allows you to do.

Being open to a greater truth or a new understanding is a great asset in changing beliefs. When the mind is fixed or closed there is no opportunity for expansion. This general attitude of being open to a greater truth will serve you well as you journey through life.

Once you have identified your beliefs, ask the all-important question. "Is that *really* true?" "Does what I believe about … support me moving forward?" "Would my higher self or core essence agree with that belief?"

Connecting to your heart energy is the real key to assessing the value or authenticity of your beliefs. This is because all thinking from the mind must filter through the subconscious where all the programming is stored, so it can be challenging to determine what is true and what we just think is true because of a strong and usually unconscious pattern.

When we are connected to our heart's energy we are more connected to our spiritual essence. We know through research that when the heart is in a coherent state the signals the heart sends to the brain to inform the frontal cortex are stronger and more accurate. Basically we have greater access to information and intuition. The heart will always lead you to greater love, ease, wisdom, peace, and connectedness.

Our conditioning is such that any time you challenge the subconscious programming fear may arise. This is where all your beliefs are stored. Once something like this becomes conscious there is likely to be an inner battle between the part that has held the belief, believing it to be right and true, and the other part of you that doubts it and is open to changing it.

Remind yourself that it is an old pattern that you created or adopted as your own without awareness, and that you can also change it. Connect to your heart energy as above and allow it to guide you.

When choosing to eliminate beliefs that no longer serve you and integrate new ones, it can be helpful to go through some kind of symbolic clearing process such as writing down the old beliefs, thanking them for their service, and then burning them; then recording the beliefs you choose to embrace and creating affirmations that reflect them and chanting them hundreds of times until they become integrated. Your task is to create new neural pathways so that the mind will generate a new pattern that supports you. Use different reminders, such as messages on your phone or notes pasted around you, then begin to do the behavior that supports your new way of being. It will likely feel uncomfortable at first but that is simply because it is new and unfamiliar. Be persistent and you will soon reap the rewards and embrace a new way of being. See Strategies 3 and 14, Affirmations and Change Challenge, for more information.

Be aware that like all people, you have been programmed to believe certain things, so if you don't bring consciousness to your beliefs others will continue to impose their beliefs upon you for their own purposes, and this may not support your preferences. Be willing to challenge all your beliefs, no matter what they are. Open your mind up to new possibilities – awaken to your authentic self and let your heart be the driving force in your life. Pretend you have a blank canvas and you are creating your life anew. What kind of beliefs will you choose to support you through life?

You have to change your beliefs to change your life.

As you do this, your map of the world or your truth will also evolve, leading you on your journey to an ever greater truth and love in your life.

With practice in attuning to your heart you will be able to assess the value of your beliefs and create beliefs that will support your core essence and expansion. This process will help you remove the self-created illusions of limitation, doubt, and fear and will expand your awareness into recognizing the amazing multidimensional energy being that you truly are.

To create the life you want, deliberately program your core beliefs.

See also:

5. Affirmations
6. Awareness of Awareness
7. Awareness: Building the Observer
8. Change Challenge
9. Major Life Influencers
10. Thought Power and Control
11. Values
12. Who Am I?

Bruce Lipton, *The Biology of Belief: Unleashing the Power of Consciousness, Matter and Miracles*, Mountain of Love/Elite Books, p. 135.
http://www.BruceLipton.com

Kjell Magne Bondevik is a Norwegian statesman, born 1947.

Mark Waldham, 10 Mind Blowing Discoveries about the Human Brain: Neurowisdom and the secrets to happiness and success, no. 7.
http://www.NeuroWisdom.com

"There is nothing that can help you understand your beliefs more than trying to explain them to an inquisitive child." Frank A. Clark, American politician (1860–1936).

Strategy 11
BODY BREATH AWARENESS

CATEGORIES APPLIED

Addressing Addictions
Addressing Anxiety
Addressing Depression
Awareness and Mindfulness
Improving Self-Esteem

This simple process is great for those who struggle to identify their feelings. It builds awareness of body, mind, and feelings, which is critical to developing intuition and following your higher guidance. It is also through the feeling body that true healing takes place. It is learning to trust those instincts that will manifest through the emotional body and then transfer into thought-forms through the mind.

As a child growing up and experiencing wounding (as we all do), the natural coping mechanism is to disconnect from painful feelings. Typically this kind of behavior is repeated time and again, creating a pattern, until as adults we often don't even register some of our feelings and at times don't even know how we feel, and so the illusory mind becomes the often misguiding force.

Step 1. In this first step your objective is to feel the extremes of the breath. Take a deep breath in until your lungs feel expanded and hold it there. You will feel a tightness or tension in your chest; you may even feel your heart pumping. Just stay with it, observing that sensation for as long as you can, holding the breath while the tension builds to the point that you have to exhale.

Then, when you feel you must, exhale and notice the feeling of relief, fully experiencing that sensation in both your physical and emotional body.

Repeat this extreme breath process several times until you are more acutely aware of the bodily sensations working with the breath.

Step 2. To deepen your awareness further, move on to observing just your normal breathing and its qualities and sensations over several breaths, while still noticing how this impacts on your physical and emotional body. This will be a more subtle kind of feeling, so a deeper inner attunement will be necessary.

It is best to close your eyes to minimize any external stimulus, then breathe in and notice the quality of the breath. It may be smooth, stilted, expansive, limited, even, or various other sensations. You may be aware of a kind of energizing feeling as the breath enters your body. Often a sensation of rising, expansion, or upwardness, as you feel the subtle sensation of the rise of your chest.

Then, as you exhale, notice the quality of the breath and any other sensations. You may experience a feeling of letting go, release, downwardness, and relaxation. It is as though the whole breathing process provides a yin and yang experience of in and out, expansion and contraction, tension and relaxation. The breath provides balance when we breathe with conscious awareness of the breath.

Repeat this process regularly to heighten awareness of the subtleties of your feeling body and your breath.

Your feeling body and your breath are your constant companions and provide an immense amount of information if you choose to take notice.

See also:

- Awareness: I Statements
- Awareness: Building the Observer
- Being: Mindfulness
- Conscious Breathing
- Deep Release Breathing

Strategy 12
BOUNDARIES

CATEGORIES APPLIED

Addressing Addictions
Addressing Anxiety
Addressing Depression
Awareness and Mindfulness
Career and Goals
Communications and Relationships
Environmental Health
Everyday Essentials
Improving Self-Esteem
Quick Stress Busters

Boundaries are an important means of respecting yourself and keeping you feeling at your best. They reflect self-care, self-love, and provide a degree of protection. Boundaries promote wellbeing, integrity, and a feeling of being in control of your life.

Other people and environmental energies affect us all, whether we realize it or not. We have all had the experience of feeling good and then going to places or being with some people and coming away feeling depleted or agitated. We have also felt uplifted after some positive experience or exchange with others.

Boundaries are applicable in every aspect of your life: your family, home, money, possessions, relationships, sexuality, work, and spiritual practice.

Clear boundaries also respect others, as they make clear statements facilitating a greater understanding of who you are and what is acceptable to you. Boundaries vary for different people, and when you are clear it enables others to know you better. Having clear boundaries facilitates mutual respect, supports communications, and can enhance relationships. People know where they stand, which may avoid the likelihood of resentment that can happen when someone steps beyond your boundaries.

Without strong boundaries you are likely to experience people invading your space or possessions; feeling depleted, agitated, or unwell; feeling that your values have been compromised; not feeling respected; feeling resentment; and having stronger swings in your emotional state.

It is your responsibility to keep your boundaries strong and not make assumptions that others should know what they are. Setting yourself boundaries enables you to choose what kind of energies you wish to transmit or receive within your own energy field.

If someone has a stronger will than you, and you leave yourself open, you may find yourself in situations that are not of your choosing and sometimes even wondering how you got yourself into that predicament. This is common where there is low self-esteem, which results in wanting to please another, and insufficient will and awareness on your part to counter the other person's will. You will need to be alert to this situation so that you can hold your boundaries strong, speak your truth and meet any challenge from other people.

Some boundaries need to flexible. A fixed boundary may be that no one smokes in your home. A flexible boundary may be when a close friend with whom you normally share your deepest stories starts to speak about an issue that has arisen for her at a time when you have another commitment; then you will need to adjust according to your priority at that time.

Discern in each moment in time how the other person is, so that you adjust your boundaries appropriately. If you are feeling very open-hearted and you connect with some someone who is highly stressed you will be vulnerable to picking up their energy, so you must determine what feels the best thing for you to do at that time. You can still be compassionate and understanding while holding your boundaries firm.

If you notice, after the event, that your boundaries were compromised in some way, take time to reflect and identify how it happened. Understand that if someone crosses your boundaries, it is your responsibility because it indicates that you have not been clear. Ask yourself why this happened. When you have awareness you can create the appropriate boundaries that will avoid a recurrence.

Clear boundaries require a level of awareness, will, and self-respect.

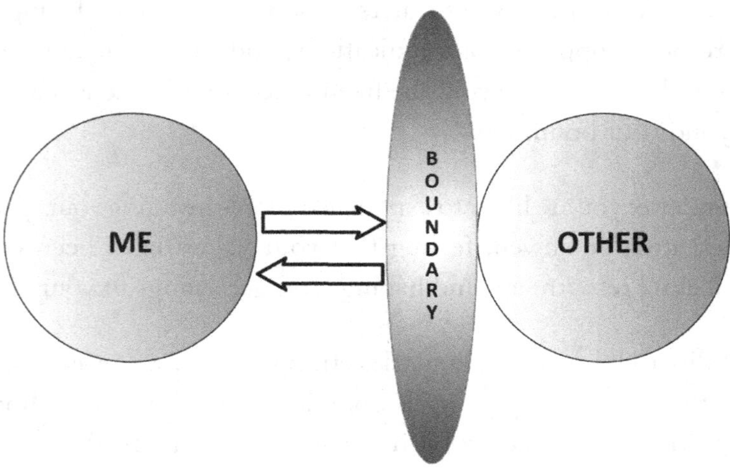

Boundaries that serve you positively are:

1. Speaking your truth of what is acceptable/important to you in order to respect your space, relationships, possessions, or anything else.

2. Ensuring that you don't allow yourself to get sucked in to any circumstances where another has a strong or stronger will than you.

3. Not buying into a negative story that is being told.

4. Avoiding associating with people who are exhibiting negative attitudes and behaviors.

5. Avoiding heavy metal music or any other recreational activity that has a negative connotation.

6. Being aware of those people who actually draw from your energy leaving you feeling depleted.

7. Learning to say "No".

8. Being discerning about what you will watch on television or your exposure to any other media. This may mean avoiding programs like the news or movies that have a strongly negative theme.

9. Avoiding any involvement in gossip. Sharing information with more than 3 people is considered gossip if those people don't need to know.

10. Avoiding any groups, which project negativity. Beware of any "support" groups that reinforce any kind of victim mentality. This will inhibit your growth.

11. Consciously choosing food or drink to enhance your physical health and wellbeing.

12. Meeting your exercise needs for a fit and healthy body.

13. Being aware and careful to minimize environmental toxins.

14. Setting time constraints that facilitate harmony in your life: balancing time for family, work, social, exercise, sleep, creativity, spiritual practice.

See also:

- Awareness of Awareness
- Major Life Influencers
- Projection
- Protection
- Solitude

Strategy 13
CAUSES OF HEALTH IMBALANCES

CATEGORIES APPLIED

Addressing Addictions
Addressing Anxiety
Addressing Depression
Awareness and Mindfulness
Career and Goals
Communications and Relationships
Environmental Health
Exercise for Living
Improving Self-Esteem
Nutrition for Life

Your natural state of being is wellness. Health imbalances come in many different forms and are basically any state that is not considered harmonious for any aspect of the human multidimensional body. To address health imbalances effectively and holistically you need to embrace your whole self. This includes your physical, emotional, mental, and spiritual bodies. They are constantly interacting with each other and are affected by everything in your environment. In a multidimensional being there is a profound link between the mind, body, and spirit that is often overlooked when attempting to understand health imbalances.

The cure of the part should not be attempted
without treatment of the whole,
and also no attempt should be made to
cure the body without the soul,
and therefore if the head or body are to be
well, you must begin by curing the
mind: that is the first thing ... for this is the
error of our day in the treatment
of the human body, that the physicians
separate the soul from the body.
– Plato, *Chronicles*

While many innately know how to be healthy, there is very often a conscious, subconscious, or unconscious avoidance of the healing processes. This typically occurs because it means some kind of perceived discomfort or deprivation – a change that must be made in order to restore health.

Without understanding the cause of any imbalance, you will likely keep trying to address symptoms and be frustrated why your health issue is not resolving or why, when something appears to heal, you soon develop some other condition.

There are seven primary causes of health imbalances:

1. Genetic disorders
2. Inadequate exercise
3. Karma
4. Harmful oral consumption (includes lack of nutrition)
5. Insufficient sleep
6. Environment
7. Unresolved emotional issues.

1. **Genetic disorders**

   A gene is a segment of DNA that contains the instructions to make a specific protein (or part of a protein). Genes are contained on chromosomes. Chromosomes, and the genes on those chromosomes, are passed on from parent to child. Errors in the DNA that make up a gene are called mutations and can lead to diseases. Thus a genetic disorder or disease is one that is passed down from parent to child, for example Huntington's disease or Cystic Fibrosis.

2. **Inadequate exercise**

   The human body needs exercise to help it function at its optimal level. Exercise is required for flexibility, cardiovascular health, and strength.

3. **Karma**

   Karma is the out-play of cause and effect. It is the unconscious conditioning that you are born with, an expression of choices made in this and previous lifetimes, which impact on you, others, and the larger universe. Karma is the effects of a person's action, which determine his or her destiny in the next incarnation. We are all responsible for cleaning up our own karma. Karma diminishes with increasing presence or spiritual awakening.

4. **Harmful oral consumption and lack of nutrition**

   Poor eating habits can contribute to many chronic lifestyle and health imbalances that not only cause ill health, but can lead to death, for example an excess of certain food types such as sugar, fats and salt. A lack of fresh water causes dehydration and many other health problems. Know the source of your food. A growing body of evidence reflects health problems related to foods that are genetically modified and contain other chemicals and additives. Irreparable damage can be caused by:

   - unhealthy diet or lack of nutrition

- alcohol
- cigarettes
- recreational drugs
- some medications
- lack of fresh water

Your body needs the right fuel and maintenance to keep it in good working order. In conjunction with exercise, this can be met by plenty of fresh water, fruit, vegetables, nuts, and legumes.

5. **Insufficient sleep**

   Insufficient sleep is the leading cause for stress-related diseases such as diabetes, obesity, depression, and cardiovascular disease.

   Sleep helps to eliminate stress, fights off disease, restores energy levels, and repairs damage to bones, muscles, cuts, sores, and bruises. Sleep deficit is associated with a higher incidence of behavioral problems and irritability, anxiety, depression, reduced coping skills, motor vehicle and machinery-related accidents, risk-taking behaviors, and a weak immune system.

6. **Environment**

   Injury through personal or work accident can be minor or result in years of ongoing treatment. Trauma or injury with intent can be life changing in its impact. Then there are environmental hazards which are becoming increasingly insidious, with many of them creating massive pollution, reducing our oxygen levels, and leaving us bombarded by unseen energies that pollute our bodies and upset our natural circuitry. The effects can reduce the body's immune system and be the cause of feeling not quite right, and mild to serious ill health. Among these are electromagnetic fields, which power our homes, appliances, and workplace equipment. Insecticides, pesticides, synthetics plastics, chemicals, solvents, and heavy metals are all part of the toxic mix. A reduction in mineral levels results in less nutrition from food sources: artificial hormones, antibiotics, genetically modified foods, and geopathic stress can result in mild to severe health problems and even death.

   Allergies can reflect a kind of fear response in your body. Do what you can to identify the source of any allergic reactions and really tune into identify what may be bothering you. More insidious allergies can come through food supplies that have been contaminated with chemicals, antibiotics or GMO's.

As human beings we are electrical in nature and our modern lifestyles have disconnected us from the Earth and all her natural healing properties that support life. This lack of flesh-to-Earth connection due to shoes, raised beds, and elevated buildings all contribute to reduced health by inhibiting our ability to equalize our energy to the living source of negatively charged electrons arising from the Earth's surface. This can result in inflammation, reduced immune system, reduced blood flow, disrupted body rhythms, pain, poor sleep patterns, reduced energy, etc. (See Strategy 58 Grounding/Earthing for more information.)

While too much sunlight can be an environmental hazard and result in burned skin and even lead to skin cancer, sunlight is fundamental to good health because it provides the essential Vitamin D we all need that is not available from food sources. Just ten minutes a day helps to strengthen bones, aids in weight loss, improves digestion, helps control sleep patterns, enhances liver function, body temperature, and sex drive, and elevates your mood.

7. Unresolved Emotional Issues

Painful emotions are part of human existence and as a small child we learn to suppress them as a coping mechanism. This leads to unconscious patterns of avoidance and denial and over time the unresolved emotions will eventually manifest in the physical body of the adult. Numerous health issues can be the result, from a mild headache to more intense muscle aches and pains, depression, addictions, or diseases like arthritis, diabetes, or cancer. While the ancients have long known about the mind-body-spirit connection, our science now identifies psychoneuroimmunology as the study of interaction between psychological processes and the nervous and immune systems.

Stress levels are compounded by any health issue, and the individual's search for help to address these concerns often results in medication or drugs to alleviate symptoms. Just medicating or treating the physical body does little if anything to permanently resolve these maladies.

"Drugs can never treat conditions you 'behaved' yourself into."
– Dr. Carolyn Dean

Self-help tools, counseling, adopting meditation and mindfulness practices, and working on self-esteem are strategies to address the imbalances in the emotional, mental, and spiritual bodies. You are never too old to start.

Understanding Physical Pain

Pain is the body's way of saying, "take notice." It lets us know when something needs our attention and when we are out of balance. It is a gift of insight that encourages us to really explore what is happening in our multidimensional body. Pain can be physiological or emotional; in terms of your whole self they are not separate. Pain is a signal that something needs to change. Denying these messages from the body's intelligence or just popping a painkiller will ensure that the underlying cause remains. Integrated healing requires that you work at other levels and practice presence so that you can attune to your body's message and surrender to what is.

While it is extremely common to want to fight pain, it can actually worsen the intensity of it. It is the egoic mind's way of saying "I don't want this," which adds to the tension and decreases the flow of natural healing energies. Surrender, by contrast, is when you stop allowing the egoic mind to be the driving force and open yourself up to the higher intelligence within your heart that is always available in the present moment. In a state of surrender you are open and allowing the body to do what it can to restore balance. Energy can then shift, resistance can dissolve, insights can arise, new behaviors can be instigated, and the transformation can begin. Strategies 75 Pain Dialogue and 76 Pain Focus offer further insights.

"Pain is inevitable. Suffering is optional."
– The Dalai Lama

To be healthy, it is not so much about doing behaviors that make you healthy as it is about stopping the behaviors that make you unhealthy. This includes addressing both your physical and emotional activities and the environmental energies that are within your power to change. Everyone vibrates his or her own unique energy signature, which is reflected by one's conditioning. The essential components to good health and wellbeing comprise an environment which provides plenty of fresh air, sunlight, Earth connection, good nutrition, fresh water, restful sleep, regular exercise, positive mental and emotional states, and an awareness of one's spirituality, which facilitates feelings of connectedness.

Note: It is important to understand that a doctor's treatment is different to what is called whole or integrated healing. A doctor's cure may resolve the health condition at the physical level, but the other components of your multidimensional self must also be addressed to embrace integrated healing. The quotation from Plato above tells us that the ancients knew this and we have forgotten. This can happen, however, if you change the behavior that may have been underlying the cause.

Health imbalances in the human body reflect health imbalances on the Earth. The neglect and denial of our own health is a mirror of our behavior towards the very Earth that supports us. Our Earth's vitality is diminishing, with decreasing oxygen levels. Human beings are decimating the forests, contaminating food supplies with artificial chemicals, extracting the oil, depleting the mining reserves, polluting the air and the oceans. This disconnection between our Earth Mother and our own humanness must be remedied in order for true healing to take place.

See also:

- Awareness: Building the Observer
- Clearing
- Environmental Health: Personal Products
- Environmental Health: Consumables
- Environmental Health: General
- Environmental Health: Electromagnetic Fields
- Exercise for Living
- Grounding/Earthing
- If Seriously Ill: Understanding Integrated Healing.
- Major Life Influencers
- Nutrition Keys
- Oral Health
- Thought Power and Control

Carolyn Dean, MD, ND. "Drugs can never treat conditions you 'behaved' yourself into." http://drcarolyndean.com

Strategy 14
CHANGE CHALLENGE

CATEGORIES APPLIED

Addressing Addictions
Addressing Anxiety
Addressing Depression
Awareness and Mindfulness
Career and Goals
Communications and Relationships
Environmental Health
Exercise for Life
Improving Self-Esteem
Nutrition for Life

Change is about the only constant in all of life. Our Earth, the galaxies, and even our bodies are in a constant state of change, with cells dying and being replaced all the time. Change is an integral part of growth.

Growth and the fulfillment of goals require change. The natural human condition is desire. It could be for more harmony in relationships, greater self-love, a move to a new place, greater consciousness, better health, and so on. Fulfillment of that desire requires that we constantly make changes.

Change requires that you move out of your comfort zone.

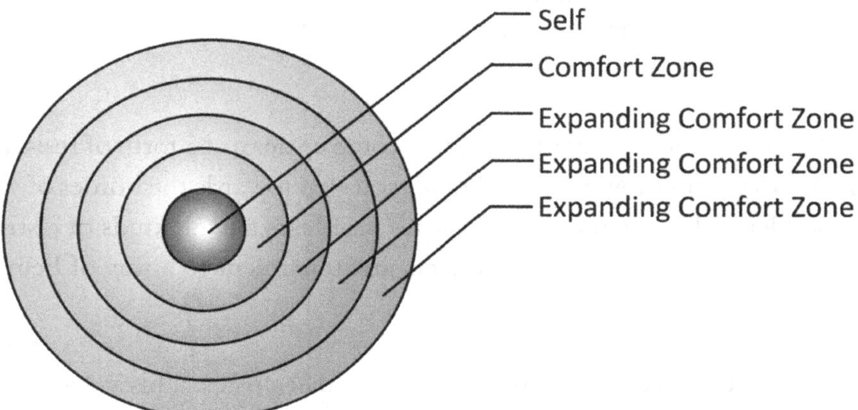

Expanding your comfort zone means moving into new territory: going beyond your previous experience, moving away from the familiar boundaries that are known, into an area that is unfamiliar or new.

To do this typically requires a new understanding. Unless there is some kind of incentive to change, you will not move of your own initiative.

Change can certainly be forced upon us – such as being retrenched from your job or dealing with some kind of unexpected crisis or more everyday things like missing your train to work, cancellation of an event you may have committed to, or a family member being unwell and plans having to be altered.

The more risks you take, the more changes that come your way, the more choices are available to you. Your world keeps expanding. You become comfortable with uncertainty, and it literally means that fear is no longer the driving force in your life. Once you are in that new territory, it becomes your new comfort zone. Your comfort zone has enlarged: you are embracing more of the world that is available to you. This results in feelings of contentment and personal power and you feel good about yourself for having had the courage to do this. You begin to feel comfortable with being uncomfortable. Your attitude can shift from fear and hesitation to one of excitement and anticipation about the new.

Change can be about doing something differently, stopping some behaviors, starting some new behaviors.

"Your life does not get better by chance,
it gets better by change."
– Jim Rohn, American speaker and author

Fears

In most cases as you contemplate change, you will come up against a form of resistance because you are stepping into the unknown. It's as though you step towards the border of your comfort zone and then suddenly the subconscious activates past fears and all kinds of justifications say why it's best to stay with the old ways. It reflects an attachment to a way of being and a lack of trust.

You really want to take notice of the quality of your inner voices. This voice associated with the egoic mind is often full of fear. Part of the reason for that is the brains propensity to store negative memories. Its objective is to keep you safe based on past hurts, and thinking will always be filtering through past pain or experiences irrespective of whether it has any relevance.

You may be contemplating going for a job promotion and the inner voice may run messages like: "Remember what happened last time you went for an interview! What if they reject you? There's bound to be something you don't know or like about it. Management won't really consider your expertise, just stay where you are" – and so it goes on. Where there is a similar unresolved feeling, the egoic mind will always be promoting the negative, even if it is relatively minor to the potential gains.

There are occasions when, consciously, you might really want to change something about your own behavior but seem to lack the willpower to do so. We see this play out regularly when people make New Year's resolutions and start out okay but soon revert back to old ways of being. The subconscious with its old familiar patterns has resumed the driver's seat in your life. However, *all these response patterns of the mind can be changed.*

Then there is the inner critic that all human beings have. This is a self-created inner voice and it will be constantly putting you down, telling you you're not good enough or can't do, or don't deserve. Neither of these inner voices is likely to be supportive or encouraging.

There is, however, an aspect of self that is always striving to move you forward. It is associated with your heart and provides the inspiration you receive through your feeling body that connects to your higher mind. It is commonly referred to as your higher self, the I Am presence, the God within, Real self, or your Spiritual aspect. This is the part which recognizes that growth requires action or behavior change, not just thought or desire. It wants you to grow, to awaken to your authentic self and fulfill your potential. It is the voice of support, love, inspiration, and courage.

Discerning the quality of your inner voices helps you identify the mind games and bring consciousness to the inner conflict that so often exists when contemplating change. It can also help your understanding, which is a prerequisite for change.

Be aware, however, that just as water will always take the path of least resistance, so too will the subconscious mind always revert to old patterns of thinking and behavior. To overcome this we have to *bring consciousness* to these patterns. We can do this first by recognizing them and then holding both an *intention* of what it is we want to change as well as holding our *attention* on this desire. Together, intention and attention bring consciousness. So we can understand that change requires real focus.

If the desire for change is strong but is accompanied by fear – such as a self-defeating addictive behavior like obsessive eating, or smoking – then a more powerful inner conflict will exist. This is because there is an attachment to the addictive behavior and a longing to be free of the power it has over you. All addictions are a means to reduce anxiety, irrespective of what they are.

When you allow fears to inhibit your growth, it will result in a lack of self-esteem and dramatic limitations to the fruition of your desires and goals. This can also manifest as stuck feelings and lead to depression. Sadness is a reflection of opportunities lost. Every time you feel inspired to move forward in some way and ignore it, you will feel unhappy with yourself.

"We cannot change what we are not aware of, and once we are aware, we cannot help but change."
– Sheryl Sandberg

Wanting Others To Change

There are times too, when people don't move out of their comfort zone because they are waiting and wanting the other person to change so they can feel better. This is futile behavior and will seriously inhibit any resolution of your problems and potential for growth.

Understanding Facilitates Change

In order to make this transition you will need to alter your understanding to help you release your attachment to the behavior you want to change. The behavior (obsessive eating, for example) offers a brief release of anxiety. But it does nothing to address the root cause of the anxiety and so the addictive patterns continue, driving you and eroding self-esteem because of the inner conflict of wanting to be free of the addiction and at the same time not wanting to be without it.

The primary reason or energetics behind this is suppression of unresolved pain or wounding and an attachment to food as a way of pacifying the anxiety. The conscious mind might be very keen to give up obsessive eating, but without a shift in understanding, the subconscious mind will remain the driving force.

This deeper understanding of the energy play brings about an expanded awareness. Analysis on its own is insufficient. You need information, knowledge, and some analysis to create the shift. This is a big leap to a greater awareness.

Not all change threatens to expose pain and wounding, which is common with addictive behaviors, though overcoming some of the suppressed fears can be a massive morale booster. Change in all its forms expands you into something more.

Risks Of Change

Each time you resist your desire to go for what you want and step into the unknown, it is a drain on your energy, because fear drains energy and lowers your feelings of worthiness. It can also be the trigger for jealousy. Jealousy is when you are observing someone who has had the courage to go for what they want and it reminds you that you haven't.

Gifts Of Change

Each time you move beyond your resistance, you develop into more of your potential. This not only has the effect of overcoming your fears so you feel better, but also moves you closer to your goals; and every time you do that you build your self-esteem and step closer to your potential. As you willingly embrace change you are allowing your heart or your higher guidance to lead you. You are expanding into more of your authentic self and it feels so good.

Keys To Change

1. Start by making some small non-threatening changes regularly; this builds your confidence and expands your comfort zone. A change a day will help you get comfortable with being out of your comfort zone. These non-threatening suggestions help to open you up to new energies and new ways of being.

- Dry yourself in a different way after bathing.
- Travel to work a different way.
- If you always have take away food on Friday nights change it to Thursday.
- Explore a different restaurant or café.
- Turn off the T.V. and talk with your family or play games.
- Do many different things with your non-dominant hand.

Then venture outwards from there. Practice talking to new people, visiting new places and exploring new ideas and possibilities – always with a sense of optimism of what might be the positive outcomes.

Then begin to take action steps towards your goals. Push through the resistance; watch the play of the mind and its old stories to overcome any of your own sabotage behavior.

It maybe enrolling in a new course, finding a new way of relating to someone, looking for a new job, initiating contact with someone you find interesting, or following through on that business idea you've had. These will typically be ideas that have flashed into your mind and you have discounted because of the potential discomfort of having to do things you've not done before or done before with negative outcomes. If the latter occurred use the experience to learn how to do it differently.

2. Explore your understanding of the situation where you want to bring about change. Gather information, bring it together with the knowledge you have both about yourself and your desired change, and then analyze it all. Along with some really honest self-reflection this will lead to greater awareness. Why is the current situation so? What do *you* want the change to bring about? Is *your* heart or intuition guiding you towards this change? What is the likely outcome if *you* don't change?

3. Be willing to let go of your attachment to a behavior, a thing, a belief, or a way of being. Change is impossible with attachment. Be open to change your understanding in order to release attachment.

4. Anchor yourself in a column of light. While holding yourself in a column of light is always beneficial, it is even more important as you address some of your fears or resistance to provide support and a protective field of energy.

5. Focus your attention and intention on your desired change, not on what is. You might like to support yourself with reminders of little Post-it notes pasted around the house, or set up your phone for reminder messages. Choose an affirmation to support your intended growth and chant it often to retrain the mind away from the old patterns.

6. Bring in feelings of gratitude often. Gratitude elevates your feeling body to higher states of wellbeing. Find gratitude in the stepping-stones of change and for all kinds of different things.

7. Call upon the qualities of courage, surrender, willingness, gratitude, optimism, and trust. Just by feeling into the meaning of these words, you will activate them in your mental and emotional body. Initiating change puts you in a position of power.

8. Ask for help from the higher intelligence within: the aspect of self that is striving to move you forward. Invite the spirit of change to move through you.

9. Adopt an attitude of optimism, excitement, and anticipation about change and all the magic of potential, success, growth, expansion, and awareness that it offers. This keeps the energy levels high and flowing and redirects the mind away from patterns of negativity and fear.

10. Learn to love change because more of the world is available to you, and the more you are willing to change and grow the more awareness and potential there is to awaken to your Authentic Self.

See also:

- Asking for Help
- Beliefs Challenge
- Change: Warmer Greeting
- Decisions: Heart Wisdom
- Intention/Counter-Intention
- Release Resistance
- Seek to Understand
- Values

Sheryl Sandberg, *Lean In: Women, Work, and the Will to Lead* Deckle Edge, 2013.

Lean In: Women, Work, and the Will to Lead is a 2013 book written by Sheryl Sandberg, the chief operating officer of Facebook, and Nell Scovell, TV and magazine writer.

Strategy 15
CHANGE: WARMER GREETING

CATEGORIES APPLIED

Awareness and Mindfulness
Communications and Relationships
Improving Self-Esteem

This is a lovely exercise to build your self-confidence, enhance relationships, and add a little more love into this world at the same time. It requires that you move out of your comfort zone in terms of your normal way of greeting people, which will vary for different relationships.

Our way of meeting or acknowledging another tends to be habitual, enabling us to stay in our safe zone. There is often little thought given to an introduction to new people. Some may avoid any kind of exchange due to their own lack of confidence and fear of rejection. If there is low self-esteem it will be more of a challenge, but your courage could also attract wonderful rewards.

To expand yourself, simply make a habit of greeting another person more warmly than you usually do. Of course you must use your discretion here to avoid stepping over anyone's boundaries or compromising your own.

A smile is always a lovely gift, particularly if someone doesn't have one.

Some examples:

- If passing another whom you would not normally greet at all, give them a smile.
- If you normally shake hands when you greet a particular person, add a smile and if appropriate, use your other hand to clasp over theirs or give them a brief hug. If you normally smile and give a brief hug, hold that person a little longer or add a kiss to their cheek.
- If your greeting is via the phone, add more warmth to the conversation, perhaps by asking something personal about their weekend, their family, or their health. Use your discernment here. Make sure you smile at the same time to relax the facial muscles. This is often detectable in the tone of your voice.

Generally speaking, being warm and interested in others will create positive impressions. While this more outgoing behavior may initially feel uncomfortable, these genuine efforts to connect more warmly will bring the benefits of expansion and those kindly gestures will soon return to you. Don't wait for others to take the initiative.

See also:

- Affection
- Communication Keys

Strategy 16
CLEARING

CATEGORIES APPLIED

Addressing Addictions
Addressing Anxiety
Addressing Depression
Awareness and Mindfulness
Career and Goals
Communications and Relationships
Environmental Health
Everyday Essentials
Improving Self-Esteem
Quick Stress Busters

We are all exposed to all kinds of different energies and experiences that impact on our physical, emotional, mental, and spiritual bodies. Everything is made of energy and has its own unique frequency or vibration.

Every thought we ever had still exists and forms part of the sea of energies surrounding us and what we see in our reality. These vibrations of energy are often transmitted from one to another and can be problematic without awareness, because there is transference of the emotional and mental state from one to the other person and vice versa.

"If you wish to understand the secrets of the Universe,
think of energy, frequency, and vibration."
– Nikola Tesla

There are many reasons to make clearing a regular daily practice. All energy workers understand the importance of keeping the body's energy in flow and removing anything stagnant to maximize mobility and health. Sometimes we can feel as though something heavy has stuck to us and some movement or a good shake or jiggle can leave us feeling clearer.

There may be times when you suddenly feel angry for no reason and then someone you know pops into your mind. This can be an indication that you have connected with the other person. So whatever they are feeling can easily be transferred to you: when they feel happy you feel happy, when they feel sad you feel sad. This may or may not be intentional; it is just a sign that energy connections need to be cleansed.

Judging another person is also an indication that you are connecting to them. Judgment is rife in this world and creates much disharmony. It is one of the most important challenges to address as you increase consciousness and develop self-mastery. Strive as much as possible to use discernment instead, which has a much higher frequency and no negativity – it is neutral.

There is absolutely no point being critical or resentful of another person for these energy transfers. The mostly likely thing is that they are unaware of their influence upon you or any one else. No doubt you have also done the same thing throughout your life. Knowledge gives you power and choice. We are all responsible for our own energy field, which includes all our thoughts and beliefs and actions and the boundaries we create.

Most people will have experienced the impact of walking into a room that did not feel good without knowing why. You are also likely to have been in a space that felt peaceful or happy with or without anyone being in there. In these circumstances, you are picking up on the energy of what is or what remains in the room.

Particularly in close relationships such as family or business associates, you may feel that you are strongly influenced by their thinking and find yourself getting sucked into a situation that you don't want and maybe later you wonder how that happened.

If you do not keep your energy field clear, you are vulnerable to the thoughts and emotions of others. You might have a goal to move house to a particular area, and find that someone close to you would prefer you stayed in your existing house. Their thinking is consistently around about you staying put, while yours is about moving. You may find yourself overpowered by their thought-forms (with or without awareness) and wonder why it's such a struggle to make the move happen. It is a form of counter-intention. See Strategy 63 Intention/Counter-Intention.

Another reason to adopt regular clearing is to offset the common experience of disharmony in close relationships. One may be growing and developing and the other is not, or gossip may prevail. Gossip forms an energy matrix that links people on a collective consciousness level in a dysfunctional way. (See also Strategy 54 Gag Gossip.)

Extremely widespread is the experience of going into a shopping center with the intention of buying certain items, but finding that you purchase more than you had on your list. This occurs when you step into the field of many who have a similar objective of shopping for particular items. The combined sales hype of all the different stores vying for your dollar and the shoppers who are out to purchase various items can be like trying to swim against the stream to retain your focus. These unseen energies, which include the myriad thought-forms of other people in our environment, can have a dramatic impact on your thinking and how you feel, influencing your purchases and leaving you feeling depleted.

We are all exposed to these kinds of resonances, most often unknowingly, and we need to be discerning in these situations. You only ever want to allow positive, loving energy transference from one to another. Be aware also that when you have a strong heart connection to another (common in families), your open heart can leave you vulnerable to their "stuff."

Once a child grows to maturity it serves both adult and child to be discerning and develop strong boundaries. Love and compassion are so very important in relationships, but it does not benefit either of you to allow one to feed off the energy of the other. Perceiving the other person as a victim or dependent and projecting your pity onto them creates a lower vibrational thought-form. The only appropriate response to that person in these circumstances is compassion, which has a much higher resonance. This applies in all relationships including adult children, partners, siblings, or close friends.

To be of ultimate support you need to be in your highest vibrational state, strong and positive. If you lower your energy to sympathy or pity, not only do you deplete your own energy and allow them to draw from you, but it is also disempowering to them and their connection to their higher self. The best way to help is to see them happy, well, vibrant, whole, and complete. They can then access that higher vibrational energy.

When you understand the omnipresence of the various unseen energies and the different qualities and vibrations, you will recognize the value in doing some personal energy clearing and establishing strong personal boundaries (see Strategy 12 Boundaries). This is extremely important if you suffer from depression or addictions, or if you struggle to make things happen or maintain your power in relationships.

Just as you clean your physical body each day, and take precautions to keep it protected, so too you need to clean and protect your unseen subtle bodies regularly. A clean and strong energy field enhances your health and wellbeing. Every time you do this, you also make a small impact on the collective consciousness. Many traditions and cultures have age-old forms of clearing, but the Western world has been slow to understand and adopt these practices, though wafting incense through a church or temple has a similar aim.

Other indicators of the need to do some clearing are in the following situations:

- When you are feeling down, depressed, or emotionally challenged
- When you have a sudden downturn in energy without knowing why
- If you have been around others, or in a place where people have been arguing
- Any kind of media that has a negative impact on you
- In large groups, particularly where there is intense emotion
- Around people who are unwell or needy
- When you have undesirable feelings and someone pops into your mind
- When you are feeling manipulated or overpowered by another
- When you are struggling to sleep
- When you wake feeling depleted or depressed
- When you are struggling to maintain focus and your thoughts are negative
- When you are exposed to a lot of electromagnetic radiation and feel a loss of vitality.

This is a key strategy for people who suffer from depression or who feel unwell or anxious.

Clearing can make a dramatic difference to how you feel and is one of the most beneficial things you can do to optimize your health and wellbeing and keep your subtle energy bodies free of interference. It is effectively bringing more light into your energy matrix. Make it a regular daily practice and you will strengthen your field, optimize clarity, build intuition and wellness.

PERSONAL AND ENVIRONMENTAL CLEANSING PROCESSES

The light-flush and deep cleanse processes which follow the heart breathing preparation are done in a meditative state. Include one or both of them as part of your morning routine and/or before sleep to maximize your sense of wellbeing and clarity.

1. Preparation: heart breathing

Sit quietly and breathe into your own heart. You may find it helpful to close your eyes and place your hand over your heart to assist your focus. Then bring to mind something that inspires gratitude within you. The feeling of gratitude will raise your frequency to a higher state. As you breathe some long, slow breaths imagine that your heart is filling with light and expanding out to embrace your whole body and beyond; this will also embrace your higher self. Do this for about 10 breaths, or until you feel a heart connection.

1a. Light-flush

Now focus your attention on the Earth and send your energy down from your own heart through your body deep into the heart of Mother Earth. You can imagine this as streamers of light connecting you. Then bring in feelings of appreciation for all her gifts that allow you to sustain life, and imagine her beautiful energy as light beams coming up through the soles of your feet and through your whole body, penetrating into every cell in your body. This process helps you stay grounded and connected as you proceed.

Then imagine you are connecting to the highest vibrational light-form in this galaxy. Some may call this God or Source energy or you may prefer to draw upon the energy of the Sun. Visualize or sense it to be the most brilliant, pristine light and bring it down through the top of your head and send it all the way down and through every cell in your body and into the Earth and beyond. Particularly focus the light on any area where you may feel pain, discomfort, or an imbalance. Hold your focus in this way for anything from 2 to 20 minutes depending on your need at the time.

Next, hold the intention to call back any energy that you have displaced through your own thought projections or any unconscious agreements you may have made in any space-time reality. This is important to ensure you take responsibility for your own energy and can fully reclaim your sovereign self.

To further enhance this light-cleanse and your own intuitive processes, include the following deep cleanse.

1b. Deep cleanse

With your body filled with light, and still feeling your connections to your heart, the Earth, and Source hold the intention that you want to see or sense any dark patches (i.e. negative energies) so that you can clean them away. You might find it easier if you imagine that you are looking at a smaller image of yourself against this brilliant light, rather than just feeling into your own multidimensional body.

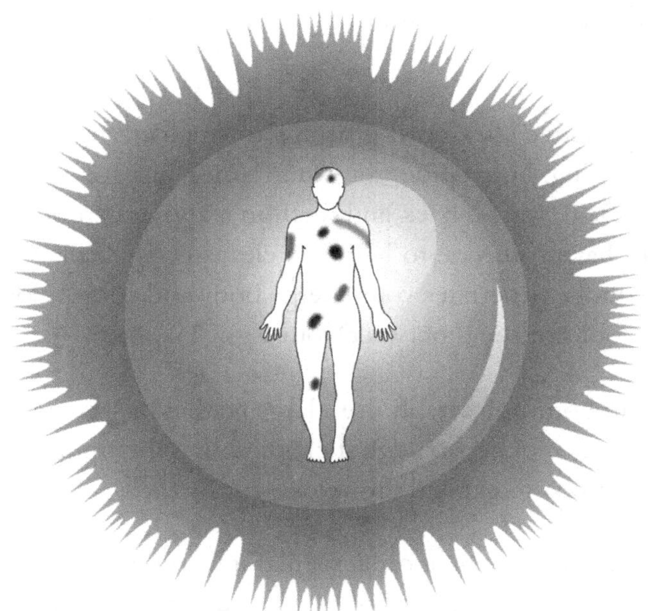

Then imagine a galactic vacuum cleaner facing your body and direct any stuck or dark energy into it. Direct it to suck out all the negativity or dark spots and transmute the energy. Home in on any areas of imbalance. Be aware that where there is physical or emotional pain or discomfort there will be lower vibrational energy present.

If you are not a visual person and have difficulty identifying these energy imbalances, pretend you can – it opens up your creative intuitive aspect. Trust the process; you will soon feel the benefits. Clean the front of your body then attend to your back and sides. *Holding the intention for cleansing is a key factor.* Remember that energy goes where your attention flows.

2. Smudge clearing

Smudge clearing comes from the Native American tradition. A smudge stick is usually made from dried white sage bundled tightly together and lit at one end to get it smoking. It is the energy signature of the plant that facilitates the clearing or purification.

While these are readily available in stores, you can make your own from any sage you may have in the garden, perhaps adding some lavender and/or rosemary, which also have astringent qualities. This more dynamic kind of clearing is extremely effective, though exercise caution if you have any respiratory problems.

The process: Hold the intention to clear all undesirable energies and call upon your higher self to assist.

Light one end of your smudge stick until it begins to smolder/smoke. You can blow on the end to stimulate the burning, but you do not want flames, just smoke. If your intention is to clean your own energy field, waft it back and forth in a zigzag manner all over your body. It is preferable if you can have someone to help you cleanse your back. Otherwise do the best you can to ensure the smoke penetrates your energy body and comes close in to your physical body including under your arms and between your legs.

If you are smudging your home, preferably use a large feather or several swatched together and waft the feather/s over the smoking smudge stick, directing the smoke through the area to be cleansed. The feather is a way to expand the smoke out further.

Smudging is great to do in your home or car at regular intervals as well. The frequency depends on how you and your home feel. Any kind of prolonged agitation, difficulty focusing, feeling unusually tired, are all common indications that a cleanse is needed – and most particularly if there has been conflict, or sickness. When you smudge your home make sure you waft the smoke into all the corners of each room and any accessible tucked-away places like under chairs or tables When complete, place the ignited end in a small container of sand or earth to cease smoking till the next time you wish to use it.

3. Grounding/earthing

While the science is relatively new, there is ample evidence about the improved state of wellbeing following flesh-to-Earth contact. This is because the Earth has a constant flow of negatively charged ions at its surface and when we stand barefoot she immediately starts to equalize our electrical body with hers. This is extremely helpful to reduce the effects of electromagnetic fields that deplete our health. There are many additional healing benefits such as reduced pain and swelling, increase in energy levels, and reduced anxiety, improved sleep, and blood flow. See also Strategy 58 Grounding/Earthing for more information.

4. Ocean swim

Take a swim in the ocean to provide a wonderful cleanse to your whole four-body system. It will also leave you feeling more invigorated because of the wild water and added nature energies. It has long been known of the many health benefits and natural curative powers of the ocean, though from a scientific perspective this is not fully understood.

On a physical level, ocean water has been known to help heal cuts, minimize swelling, lessen the pain of osteoarthritis, and leave you feeling uplifted. Even just breathing in ocean air will leave you feeling better with all the negative ions or anions. These invisible molecules increase oxygen flow to the brain, improving our mood and leaving us feeling more energetic and alert.

5. Salt bath

Salt is a natural cleanser. The human body is composed of around 75% water and the fluid is a salty water solution. Dentists often recommend gargling with salt water to help any kind of infection. Having a bath with a cup of rock salt for about 20–30 minutes will assist to cleanse your energy field. It is a wonderful backstop when you just don't have the energy or convenience for any other kind of personal cleansing.

6. Fresh air clearing

Spend time outdoors in nature to soak up the plethora of cleansing and healing energies she provides. The more pristine the environment the better: outdoors in a city environment with lots of traffic will have much less of an impact than being down by the beach or in some beautiful forest or parkland. To cleanse your home or car regularly open all the doors and windows to allow the free flow of fresh air from nature to cleanse away any stagnant energy. This is most beneficial on a windy day to facilitate the free flow of air.

7. Sound clearing

Playing beautiful music (classical or spiritual) can also assist to cleanse your own energy field and the environment because of its high sound resonance. Spiritual chants like *OM* have a lovely clearing, peaceful effect.

Once you have completed any of these 7 cleansing processes, create a protective field of energy for your body, car, or living environment. A simple form of protection is to imagine yourself in a ball of light with a mirror facing outwards. That means that any energies coming towards you are deflected back to the source. See Strategy 79 Protection for details.

We live in a world of duality where there are a lot of dark forces which impact upon us. Some are a result of an unintegrated shadow aspect of self, and many are a reflection of the collective unresolved fears of humanity. Over thousands of years these have gathered in our psychic atmosphere and can enter our field of energy. These and other unseen negative forces can trigger fear as we feel the vibration in our energy field that awakens our nervous system to something that does not feel good. While the topic of dark energies is rarely desirable, being aware of their influence and having the tools to address them empowers us and disempowers them. The more we build our consciousness, clear our energy field, and awaken to the outside influences, the more we contribute to love and harmony in this world. What we clean up today not only benefits us personally but all beings around us and all future inhabitants of this Earth.

Claiming your sovereignty sends a powerful message to these unseen forces that you are aware of their influence and demand that this ongoing abuse cease. Repetition of the clearing processes and in particular the deep cleanse will help to eradicate them including chanting affirmations that declare your awareness and sovereignty. These are empowering reminders to your authentic self as well.

> I am sovereign
> I am free
> I choose love through eternity
>
> I am sovereign, I am free, only I can govern me
>
> I am sovereign and no one is allowed to take my energy. I am sovereign and no being or non-being is allowed to infringe on my sovereign space. *

See also:

- Allow Feeling
- Boundaries
- Connect with Nature
- Deep Release Breathing
- Environmental Health: Electromagnetic Fields
- Environmental Health: General
- Feeling Agitated
- Feeling Anger
- Feeling Challenged
- Feeling Disempowered
- Feeling Fear
- Feeling Grief
- Feeling Guilt or Shame
- Feeling Jealousy
- Feeling Lonely
- Feeling Rejected or Hurt
- Feeling Scattered: Unbalanced

- Feeling Stuck
- Feeling Uncertain or Fearful of the Unknown
- Feeling Unloved or Unlovable
- Feeling Unsupported
- Feeling Victimized
- Feeling Worried
- Forgiveness Process
- Grounding/Earthing
- Jiggling
- Protection
- Shadow Play
- Toning

* Cameron Day http://www.ascensionhelp.com

Strategy 17
COMMUNICATION: FAMILY AGREEMENTS

CATEGORIES APPLIED

Addressing Addictions
Addressing Anxiety
Addressing Depression
Awareness and Mindfulness
Communications and Relationships
Improving Self-Esteem

All people are unique and as such have different likes and dislikes, different values, goals, and preferences. When people live together in families these differences will inevitably arise and can create much emotional pain and disharmony if not resolved. This can lead to stored wounding and patterns that become unconscious through life's journey.

Irrespective of age, the basic human need is to feel loved, heard, and acknowledged. When these fundamentals are not met they lead to problems with self-worth and relationships that carry through into adult life. As a parent, attempting to deal with the needs of your spouse and children, and maybe extended family, can present many communication challenges, particularly if you lacked some of these basics in your own childhood.

Making prior agreements about dealing with conflict or major family decisions facilitates the potential for all to feel safe in the knowledge that they will be heard. It provides a soft formula to address any conflict and can accelerate the potential to find a harmonious solution and build closeness. If children are old enough, involve them in establishing the agreement process and record it so that all can refer to it. Adding everyone's signature can strengthen the commitment.

Once you have determined your process you might all agree to trial it for a month to see how it goes with the intention to review it.

Establishing family agreements for addressing conflict generally requires fairly emotionally mature people. Being acknowledged and heard is so important to feeling valued, creating good self-esteem, and healthy connections.

While there is no one formula that works for all families, the guidelines below embrace some of the fundamental human needs in communication that you might like to table.

Guidelines for family agreements

1. All family members will be listened to or heard without interruption. This shows respect and allows the person to feel validated, and this feeling then opens them up to other perspectives.
2. The listener/s will acknowledge and ask questions to ensure they fully understand the situation. It is important to really understand what the issue is and listen carefully; you are in receiving mode and this is not the time to share your own perspective.
3. All agree to be open to a new understanding. Being fixated on your view inhibits good communication.
4. All agree to express their feelings honestly and respond honestly without attacking another.
5. All people will use "I" statements to ensure clarity and ownership of feelings. "You" statements tend to generalize and inhibit clear understanding.
6. The upset person agrees to look at their role in the situation and accept responsibility.
7. The focus will remain on the resolving the problem rather than on making personal attacks.
8. All agree to avoid blame but rather seek to understand. Try putting yourself in the other person's shoes.
9. At the conclusion, all agree to express genuine gratitude for taking time to listen to each other.

See also:

- Affection
- Boundaries
- Communication: Keys
- Communication: When you…
- Conflict Resolution
- Honor and Respect Differences
- Relationships: Building Intimacy
- Projection
- Release the Need to be Right
- Seek to Understand

Strategy 18
COMMUNICATION KEYS

CATEGORIES APPLIED

Awareness and Mindfulness
Addressing Anxiety
Addressing Depression
Career and Goals
Communications and Relationships
Everyday Essentials
Improving Self-Esteem

Having good communication skills increases your potential for being understood and getting your needs met, while also really understanding others and developing strong relationships. It takes time to develop expertise in this area, and it is greatly enhanced with a commitment to expanding your own self-awareness. Effective communication builds harmony, trust, and respect and improves your opportunities in almost every area of your life. Communications always work better if you show genuine interest in the other person's feelings and point of view. Really listen with your whole self while the other person is speaking and avoid the common pattern of thinking about your response at that time. Give them the gift of your "presence" and your relationships will be enhanced.

1. Apply the acronym **SOLER** for good communication tips:

S Face the person **Squarely:** This reflects your bodily involvement and attention.

O Have an **Open** body posture: No crossed arms or legs.

L Lean towards the speaker: This reflects a more attentive manner.

E Maintain **Eye** contact.

R Reflect back what the speaker has said to ensure you understood.

2. Withhold judgment. Be aware that all humans are a result of their programming and are conditioned to certain thoughts, beliefs, and behaviors – just like you. Judging another for their different values, beliefs, or behaviors seriously inhibits your understanding of them and will detract from your own self-esteem. Judging another is also an indirect form of judging yourself.

This behavior creates a story or a conceptual identity about who they are; such perceptions impair communications because of your attachments to beliefs around them.

A simple comment like "Help me understand" can show not only that you are listening, but also that you really want to understand their point of view.

3. Listen with both ears and an open heart that does not judge and is patient. Be interested and ask questions to really tune into what is being expressed, with the intention of really wanting to understand.

Listening can occasionally mean that you want time to pause or ponder what they have said. A comment like "I appreciate what you have said, but would like a minute to reflect" shows that you are listening, and allows you time to digest without reacting. Interrupt only to seek to really understand the other person, not to put your own story forward. Try putting yourself in their shoes and be open and flexible to a new understanding.

4. Give up trying to control another, which causes a great deal of pain and disharmony. Any attempt to control reflects an attachment to a belief or an outcome. Really seek to understand the other person. Remember also that it's okay to have preferences, just as it is for the other person, and it's okay to agree to disagree. Be an example with your own behavior, so that the other person can witness and learn.

5. Build your emotional awareness. Emotions can play a big part in any kind of communication. Feelings come from our emotional body and thoughts from our mental body. These develop through our life experiences and conditioning as a child growing up. Building emotional awareness not only benefits your own self-understanding but also helps you empathize with others and certainly facilitates harmonious communication.

If you are emotionally triggered, understand that you are having a reaction. Your internal wound has been activated and in that moment in time you have an opportunity to heal.

Pause, breathe deeply, seek clarification if needed and respond mindfully. You may find it helpful to move away from the situation and return to it after you have processed your own feelings.

It takes time to build emotional awareness. Always hold the intention to be open to a greater truth and to accept responsibility for your own feelings and not blame someone else. This will allow you to move forward. Blame will keep you stuck.

6. Warmly acknowledge your relationships. All people like to be heard, understood, and feel valued and respected. Remember not to take relationships for granted. Regularly acknowledge your relationships with genuine warmth, which may be a smile, a hug, an expression of appreciation or whatever feels appropriate for the particular person and situation. Be willing to step outside of your comfort zone, while totally respecting people's boundaries.

7. Show affection to your loved ones. For your family and more intimate relationships, ensure you take time to express affection, which shows them your love and gratitude for who they are and for being in your life. Kind words, hugs, small gifts, genuine compliments, and regular kisses not only enhance relationships, but build self-esteem, reduce stress, and improve wellbeing.

Spread the love … it helps EVERYONE!

See also:

- Affection
- Awareness: Building the Observer
- Comfort Zone Expansion
- Communication: When you…
- Competition versus Cooperation
- Conflict Resolution
- Honor and Respect Differences
- Projection
- Relationship: Key Question
- Release the Need to be Right
- Seek to Understand

Strategy 19
COMMUNICATION: WHEN YOU...

CATEGORIES APPLIED

Addressing Addictions
Addressing Anxiety
Addressing Depression
Awareness and Mindfulness
Career and Goals
Communications and Relationships
Improving Self-Esteem

This is a simple assertive communication tool that will facilitate your self-awareness and assist others to really know you. It uses the skill of self-disclosure in an appropriate manner; it doesn't reveal too much of yourself, which can leave you feeling vulnerable without appropriate boundaries, or, sometimes, put people off.

It helps you to identify and express how you feel and reveal your beliefs and values. Your feelings are your feelings – unlike facts, they are not debatable. It is important to recognize that you are responsible for your own feelings no matter what they are. It is also important that you remain open to a new understanding, which means not being attached to your story. There may be valid reasons why things happened as they did that could change your perspective. Any fixation will hinder the process. All people deserve respect and this is an essential tool in communications.

Central to the effectiveness of this strategy is the use of "I" statements*, which may of course include "me" and "my," in your conversation. Ensure you maintain responsibility for your own feelings and avoid blaming others, which will almost certainly add to the disharmony. "I" statements assist clarity of expression by avoiding general statements where no ownership is really taken of your feelings and assumes that other people feel just like you.

An example would be "You know how you feel really annoyed when someone doesn't put the top on the toothpaste properly" versus "I feel really annoyed when someone doesn't put the top on the toothpaste properly."

The great value in this tool is that it retains mutual respect, and as such allows communication to be open without invoking a defensive response. As you improve your communication skills you will add to your self-esteem and enhance your relationships.

There are four aspects that identify behavior, feelings, effect, and desire. It's really a matter of filling in the gaps to: "When you … I feel … because … Would you please …"

1. *When you …* reveals to the other person what triggered your feeling and identifies their behavior. You are giving them information, so they at least have the chance to do something about it. It may be possible that they are otherwise unaware of the circumstances. Generally people cannot read minds and so may not even realize they are intruding in your space or overstepping your boundaries, which inhibits any incentive for change.

TIPS:

- Report accurately and objectively.
- Describe what actually happened without embellishment.
- Avoid including your guess at the other person's motive or feelings.
- Avoid any character assassinations and swearing.
- Avoid absolutes such as "never," and "always"; instead use "frequently" or "sometimes" *as* appropriate.
- Concentrate on one behavior at a time; do not wait till breaking point and bundle a whole lot of issues in together.
- Make sure you assert about the actual issue rather than selecting trivial matters.

2. *I feel …* "I" messages allow you to express your feelings without attacking another person. When you are honest and express your feelings it assists your own awareness and clarity. It may reveal something about your own conditioning and unresolved emotions that need to be addressed. It also helps the other person to understand you better. Sharing your feelings can really build bridges in your communications and relationships. As a result it can increase the likelihood of the other person changing their behavior.

BEHAVIOR	**When you…** (gives information)
FEELINGS	**I feel…** (helps take responsibility)
EFFECT	**because…** (discloses and enables negotiation)
DESIRE	**Would you please…** (allows clarity of your desires)

TIPS:

- Accurately report your feeling, e.g. amused, annoyed, baffled, concerned, confused, contented, curious, depleted, disappointed, delighted, enthusiastic, frustrated, furious, grateful, happy, horrified, hurt, mad, optimistic, sad, surprised, scared, terrified.

- Use the words *"I feel..."* rather than *"You make me feel..."* Avoid *"I feel that..."* as this is an opinion, not a feeling.

  This acknowledges that you are accepting responsibility for your feelings. Remember, you produced the feeling. For example, say

  "When you don't put my car in the garage after you have used it, I feel annoyed" rather than *"You make me annoyed when you don't put my car in the garage after you have used it."*

3. *Because* ... Here you are describing how the other person's behavior has actually affected you. Expressing the clear effects of the other person's behavior can help them to understand, perhaps in a way they did not previously:

- Costs you money
- Causes damage or harm to your possessions
- Consumes your time
- Interferes with your work effectiveness
- Causes extra work for you.

TIPS:
Take care not to blame the other person. For example:

> *When you don't put my car in the garage after you have used it, I feel annoyed because I got totally drenched in the rain when I ran out to where you had parked it.*

versus

> *When you don't put my car in the garage after you have used it, I feel annoyed because it's less convenient for me to cart things back and forth, and it's protected from the weather so I don't get wet if it's raining; plus it helps to keep the car clean.*

4. *Desire....* This may not always need to be stated because it could become clear in the above 3 aspects of your communication. Use your discernment. For example:

> *When you don't put the rubbish out, I feel frustrated and let down because you had agreed to accept responsibility for that task and then I am left to do it or it doesn't happen.*

In these last two examples it is obvious that you want the other person to maintain their commitment, and asking to "please put the rubbish out" or "please put my car in the garage" may seem superfluous to your communications.

> *When you are late getting that report to me, I feel anxious because I have less time to prepare my submission before the meeting, then I get the flak from above. Would you please ensure you get them to me on time.*
>
> *When you cancel out at the last minute, I feel disappointed and angry because it doesn't give me time to make other plans that I might otherwise prefer without you joining me. Would you please give me more notice in the future.*

In these two examples, while your desire is implicit, you are stating the consequences of their action or inaction to you and clearly stating your request.

TIPS:

- Remember, it's totally okay for you to set boundaries and protect your money, time, possessions, and work, no matter how trivial the other person may consider them to be.
- Be specific and brief.

When you are communicating with anyone, be respectful both of your own feelings and those of the other person. Relationships help you to identify your own conditioning and wounding. Using this Communication Strategy can assist you to resolve some issues.

See also:

- Awareness: "I" Statements
- Communication: Keys
- Conflict Resolution
- Feeling Unsupported
- Feeling Rejected
- Honor and Respect Differences
- Relationships: Building Intimacy
- Relationship: Key Question
- Seek to Understand

* Clinical Psychologist, Thomas Gordon and colleague of Carl Rogers first coined the term "I" messages in the 60's. He is widely recognized as a pioneer in teaching communication skills.

Strategy 20
COMPETITION VERSUS COOPERATION

CATEGORIES APPLIED
Addressing Addictions
Addressing Anxiety
Addressing Depression
Awareness and Mindfulness
Career and Goals
Communications and Relationships
Environmental Health
Exercise for Living
Improving Self-Esteem

While considered a "healthy norm" by many, competition does not always produce a healthy outcome. The people who can attest to that are those who have felt stress from the competitive involvement, or emotional pain and reduced self-esteem from being the loser in a competitive situation.

Given the prevalence of competition in our world it can be useful to look at some research. It appears that cooperation produces more favourable outcomes than competition.

> Researchers have found that competitive structures reduce generosity, empathy, sensitivity to others' needs, accuracy of communication, and trust. These results follow naturally and logically from competition itself; the problem does not rest with the individuals involved and the way they approach a contest. Moreover, contests between teams teach that the only reason to work with others is to defeat another group of people who are working together. Cooperation becomes the means; victory is the end. (Kohn Alfie)
>
> There are considerable data indicating that higher achievement, more positive relationships and better psychological adjustment results from cooperative rather than from competitive or individualistic learning. (Johnson & Johnson)

As human beings, we thrive on love, fun, and connectedness. Competition, which relies on one person succeeding at the expense of one who does not, is unlikely to be considered a fun experience by all or assist any kind of relationship bonding.

If our objective is to create harmony and wellbeing, both individually and globally, then it is best to look at our own motive for any competitive involvement. This is not to make a judgment about being right or wrong, but simply to understand oneself so that more conscious choices can be made which facilitate these fundamental life skills that support wellbeing.

What is your motive? Dig deep … What is behind any desire for competitiveness?

- Is it jealousy: are you observing someone else achieving something you actually want?
- Is it about "feeling less than" and striving to find a way to be acknowledged or noticed?
- Do you need to have power over another, or to feel superior in some way?

These reasons are unlikely to result in harmonious outcomes. However, if it is to prove something to yourself, then there is a quite different energy behind it. You are in fact competing against yourself in some way, striving to better yourself and meet a personal challenge that will lead to growth.

It is positive to want to go first, provided
the intention is to pave the way
for others, make their path more easy,
help them, or show the way.
Competition is negative when we wish to defeat others,
to bring them down in order to like ourselves.
– The Dalai Lama

The more you question your motives the more conscious awareness you bring into your life, which opens up your inner world to greater choice.

The more you follow your own heart's passion the more you will discover that it's not about competing against anyone else, but rather living your own empowered creativity that is uniquely you. We can learn much from the laws of nature, which is about cooperation, not competition.

See also:

- Accept Yourself
- Communication Keys
- Control versus Preferences
- Do No Harm
- Help Another
- Seek to Understand

Kohn Alfie, *The Case Against Competition*, revised edn, Houghton Mifflin,1992. http://www.alfiekohn.org/teaching/compinCL.htm

Johnson & Johnson 1989, *Cooperation and Competition: Theory and Research.* Interaction Book Co. http://www.cdtl.nus.edu.sg/success/sl17.htm

Strategy 21
CONFLICT RESOLUTION

CATEGORIES APPLIED
Addressing Addictions
Addressing Anxiety
Addressing Depression
Awareness and Mindfulness
Career and Goals
Communications and Relationships
Improving Self-Esteem

Conflict is a very destructive energy to be around, whether it is in the home, workplace, social situations, or within your community. It leaves a negative unseen energy, whether it is verbalized or not. Conflict occurs when people disagree about something they consider important, which is usually values, desires, or perspectives.

If it is handled in a respectful and positive way, however, it can be a genuine growth experience, sometimes providing a deeper understanding and enhancing the bond between people.

Very commonly, conflict occurs when two people are attached to their beliefs or their story, which are in opposition to each other, and there is resistance or an unwillingness to let it go. These beliefs or stories may be true for either person.

Behind conflict is often a lack of understanding, and so it is important to listen and strive to comprehend the whole situation. It might be that one feels disrespected, unsafe, insecure, or just in need of acknowledgment or greater closeness.

Conflict also manifests when someone uses his or her power to manipulate or control another. This "power over" mentality is driven by the egoic mind and lacks empathy for the other.

Complaining is also a form of conflict. Put another way, you don't have complaints, complaints have you. That is because you are the one losing energy over it.

Tips To Address Conflict

1. **Bring awareness to your own feelings and behavior.** With awareness you have choice and are able to control your own emotions and clearly communicate your desires and preferences. This could be the most important thing to do because understanding yourself could bring about a total shift and resolution.

a. Notice if you are being *triggered* by an unresolved past event. It might be that someone has criticized you for something, which has reminded you of the way your father so often criticizes you. Recognize that deep wounding can help you take more ownership for your own feelings. It helps to share feelings as well as the facts in any discussion. It can really help another to understand you better. Facts are debatable, feelings are not.

b. Notice if you are *projecting* and seeing in another person an aspect of your own behavior that you deny. Maybe you feel some information is being withheld and you have not been kept in the loop. Check within to see if this is part of your own behavioral pattern. Projecting is a way of keeping those shadow aspects of self suppressed.

2. **Be willing to really hear the other person.** Listen attentively without processing your response while they are venting.

3. **Acknowledge the limitations of your knowledge**. The other person may be more informed than you, and owning these limitations helps to build trust.

4. **A simple statement** like "Help me to understand" or "I want to know what you are really hoping for" can be the key to a turnaround. Put yourself in the other person's shoes and really try to understand what it is like from their perspective. Of course you must support it with some genuine listening and at least being open to a new perspective. See also Strategy 87, Seek to Understand

5. **It takes two to have conflict.** But it only takes one person to bring about a transformation, and despite common wishes and a lot of effort you cannot change another person – you can only change yourself. When *you* adjust your attitudes, beliefs, or behavior you also alter your vibration and the energy that you are radiating. The other person therefore discovers that they cannot use the same patterns to elicit the same kind of response. This means they have to find another way, and so when you change it allows the other person to change.

6. **Intend harmony.** Maintaining your attention on that intention assists the direction and focus and also connects you with your heart. Conflict can quickly resolve if the intention is to come from your own loving heart. Understand that it is fear, not love, that evokes the attachment to your area of conflict: a fear of being out of control, not getting what you want.

7. **Look for common ground** before focusing on the differences. Acknowledging these commonalities can build a bridge.

8. Beware of any **need you might have to be "right."** This reflects a low self-esteem and a "power over" attitude. Needing to be right sets up a "pushing against" kind of energy that attracts the same kind of energy back and inhibits the potential for resolution.

9. With conflict, emotions are often heightened. Pause and see **the other person in a column of light**. It is a way of acknowledging them as a spiritual person just like you. Holding them in light also attracts a higher vibrational energy. Put yourself in the light also.

10. **Avoid any name calling or yelling.** If the other person is being verbally abusive, state that there is little point discussing with this tone and you are happy to return later when things have settled down.

11. **Heart-based decisions** lead naturally to harmonious outcomes. Focus on your heart, and hold the other person with compassion. Breathe deeply and ask your heart "What would love do now?" The consequence of then acting out the behavior based on love is the most powerful act and one that can have a positive domino effect.

12. **Be willing to forgive.** Holding on to resentment leaves you losing energy over the conflict.

13. **Postpone any discussion** to resolve conflict if either person is under the influence of drugs.

14. Be willing to **agree to disagree** and walk away if the discussion is not moving towards harmony in some way.

"The opponent strikes you on your cheek,
and you strike him on the heart
by your amazing spiritual audacity in turning the other cheek.
You wrest the offensive from him by
refusing to take his weapons,
by keeping your own, and by striking him in
his conscience from a higher level.
He hits you physically, and you hit him spiritually."
– Mahatma Gandhi*

See also:

- Awareness: Building the Observer
- Boundaries

- Communication Keys
- Communication: When you …
- Competition versus Cooperation
- Control versus Preferences
- Feeling Challenged
- Forgiveness Process
- Honor and Respect Differences
- Projection
- Relationship: Key Question
- Release the Need to be Right
- Seek to Understand

* Quoted in Stanley Jones, *Portrayal of a Friend*, Abingdon, PR 1993.

Strategy 22
CONNECT WITH NATURE

CATEGORIES APPLIED

Addressing Addictions
Addressing Anxiety
Addressing Depression
Awareness and Mindfulness
Career and Goals
Communications and Relationships
Environmental Health
Exercise for Life
Improving Self-Esteem
Quick Stress Busters

Our ancestors had immense respect for nature and the Earth. They spent much more time outdoors, working with the land, observing the skies and the creatures, and intuiting the myriad messages that seemed to speak to their souls. We have lost that feeling of connectedness to the very essence of our life support. Being among nature is "natur-ally" very healing. Our homes and workplaces have become very toxic and many of these unseen contributors of toxicity build up, having a negative impact on our health and wellbeing, hindering our natural instincts, and causing a reduced immune system which can result in illnesses like allergies, asthma, headaches, poor concentration, depression, and cancer.

There is a strong argument that our children's health today (a quarter of Australian children are considered overweight or obese) is dramatically affected by the lack of outdoor exposure because they spend so much time in front of some kind of media screen, and overprotective parents drive their children everywhere, minimizing physical activity. This is an important message for both the adult and the parent.

The air around us has both positive and negative ions. These are electrically charged particles. Humankind has created an imbalance in the environment we live in today, with far more positive ions than in the past, creating an electrical imbalance in the air and in our bodies. Positive ions are known as free radicals. These free radicals, which have a detrimental impact on our health and contribute to the aging process, are caused by many everyday things in our environment, for example:

- radiation from telephone towers, meter boxes, microwave ovens
- televisions, computers, radar systems, mobile phones, heating and cooling systems
- exhausts and cigarette fumes, smog

- harmful chemicals and toxins found in personal care products, household cleaning products, and home ware products.

When feeling stressed, depressed, or out of balance, go out into nature, preferably a garden or well-treed area where there are more healing energies and fewer pollutants. Down by the beach or moving water is also great because of the release of the healthy negative ions.

The potential health benefits of negative ions include:

- Enhances the immune system.
- Increases alertness and concentration.
- Increases lung capacity.
- Reduces the severity of asthma attacks.
- Relieves sinus pain, allergies, and hay fever.
- Relieves headaches.
- Has a stabilizing effect on brainwave activity.

While in this nurturing place, focus your full attention on some aspect of nature. Watch every movement of a bird feeding on the grass and listen carefully to every note you hear it sing; examine a flower as though it is the first thing of beauty you have ever seen; gaze at the expansiveness of the sky and its constant changes; dig your toes into the soil and attune your hearing to all the sounds that pierce the air. Feel the rays of the Sun penetrate your body. Talk to the trees and take time to marvel at the beauty and balance that nature provides. Breathe the air as though you've been locked indoors for weeks.

These simple activities will bring you into present time, alleviating anxiety, stress, and worry.

These are easy processes that allow you to focus your mind fully, rebuild your connection with Mother Earth, assist your intuition, and at the same time experience the beautiful healing energies of nature.

Repeat them often.

See also:

- Awareness of Awareness
- Being: Mindfulness

- Clearing
- Grounding/Earthing
- Environmental Health: Electromagnetic Fields
- Environmental Health: General
- Environmental Health: Personal Products
- Environmental Health: Consumables
- Environmental Health: Water

Strategy 23
CONSCIOUS BREATHING

CATEGORIES APPLIED

Addressing Addictions
Addressing Anxiety
Addressing Depression
Awareness and Mindfulness
Career and Goals
Improving Self-Esteem
Quick Stress Busters

Breath is life and most people do not breathe properly to fulfill the needs of the body and brain. It is the brain that tells the body to breathe based on oxygen and carbon dioxide levels in the blood, and other influencing factors such as exercise, fear, dehydration, drugs and alcohol, or various health conditions like asthma or heart or lung conditions.

Breathing is the only bodily function that we do both consciously and unconsciously. It is both voluntary and involuntary. When we learn to regulate the breath the body-mind will follow.

The normal rate of breathing for an adult is around 15 breaths per minute when at rest. It is measured by counting the number of times the person's chest rises and falls within one minute. Quick shallow breathing is common with stress and is detrimental to health on both a physical and emotional level, and longevity is decreased.

When we bring consciousness to our breath we can affect our body, mind, and the involuntary sympathetic nervous system responsible for the fight or flight response. Correct breathing brings oxygen into the body and affects almost every bodily function in the following ways:

- Increases the flow of oxygen into your body, nourishing both body and brain.
- Improves blood circulation.
- Creates more energy.
- Strengthens the immune system.
- Helps to reduce anxiety and clear the mind.
- Helps to release tension from the body.
- Helps to balance the left and right brain.
- Improves sleep.
- Improves quality of life.

The breath is the chi, *prana*, or life force energy that sustains us. When you fully focus on the breath it is also a way of stopping thought. It brings your focus into present time and is used extensively in the art of meditation.

Despite the dramatic changes and health benefits that effective breathing can bring, it is rarely taught outside of prenatal, yoga, or meditation classes.

Focusing on your breath brings you into presence and facilitates an expanded awareness of your feeling body. It puts you in a space of allowing and gives you the ability to notice, observe, and feel whatever may have been resisted that can be at the base of health issues. It assists your alignment and connection to your higher self and facilitates clearer thinking.

Why is this important?

Many things happen in the body without awareness. Your feeling body is associated with your heart and your internal guidance system. Your heart has an intelligence that is sometimes referred to as the heart brain. The heart brain communicates with the head brain and can influence your emotional experience, how you perceive things, and your higher mental processes. It holds the secrets to your expanded awareness and means for transformation. Commonly people disconnect from their feeling body in order to alleviate pain and suffering and so allow the mind to dominate. Ultimately this will only lead to increased disharmony and suffering.

Conscious Breathing Processes

Ensure an upright posture. Conscious breathing is preferably done with your eyes closed to assist your focus and eliminate the distraction of external stimuli. Breathing is always best done through the nose unless otherwise instructed. (If your nose is blocked due to a cold, hay fever or some kinds of health imbalance then breathe through the mouth.)

1. **Conscious breathing**

The more you do this, the quicker you will be able to attune to some of the more subtle messages through your body as well as providing the nourishment for your body and mind.

- Close your eyes and focus fully on your breath and simply observe your breath.
- Notice where it comes in through the nose, and where you feel it when it is expelled from the body. This may be at the nostrils or the upper lip.
- Notice the temperature of the breath.
- Notice the texture of the breath.

- Notice any sound of your breathing.
- Notice the length of the in-breath and the length of the out-breath.
- Notice the turning point of the breath and where it changes from an in-breath to an out-breath.
- Notice any other subtleties about your breath.

This is not about changing your breath, it's just about observing and being totally present with your breath. Being aware and present with your breath. Start with once a day for just 5 minutes and build to a minimum of 3 times a day.

"In and out. Just breathing, breathing, breathing, breathing, breathing. If you would just do that, your chaotic world would smooth right out. It would. Just by focusing on breathing for fifteen minutes every day. Fifteen minutes of breathing, really breathing..."
– Abraham/Hicks

2. **Deep conscious breathing**

Preferably ensure an upright posture. In this deep conscious breathing process the whole focus is on making each breath long, deep, and slow. A powerful strategy to reduce anxiety, build life force energy, and bring you into the present moment.

Take 5 deep, long, slow breaths in and out while expanding your lungs to capacity. Develop a slow rhythmical pattern of deep breathing. Repeat 5 deep breaths × 10 times a day or 10 deep breaths × 5 times a day. This not only has an immediate calming effect but also has a cumulative effect over time.

Extending deep conscious breathing for 10–20 minutes or more significantly compounds the health benefits and can be used as a form of breath-based meditation.

3. **Alternate nostril breathing**

Generally we don't breathe evenly through our nostrils most of the time; one will be favored, though typically unconsciously. The left nostril will access the right, feeling hemisphere of your brain and the right will access the left, thinking hemisphere of your brain. Yogic practice refers to alternate nostril breathing as the purifying breath because it provides access to and activates your whole brain.

Ensure an upright posture, comfortable with spine erect. You can use either hand for this exercise, but the following instructions will be for the right hand. Simply adapt if you prefer to use your left hand.

Using your right hand, place your index and middle fingers on the point between your eyebrows.

Both the thumb and the ring finger will be used to open and close either nostril. You may find it more comfortable to support your elbow of the hand you are holding to your face with the opposite hand.

a. Use your right thumb to close off the right nostril, leaving the left nostril open and slowly breathe up through the left nostril.
b. Hold the breath for a few seconds.
c. Close the left nostril with your ring finger and release the right thumb off the right nostril and slowly exhale through the right nostril.
d. Hold the breath for a few seconds.
e. Keeping the left nostril closed, now inhale up the right nostril.
f. Hold the breath for a few seconds.
g. Close the right nostril, with your thumb and slowly exhale through the left nostril.
h. Hold the breath for a few seconds.
i. Keeping the right nostril closed, now inhale up the left nostril.

Repeat steps b.– i. for around 10 minutes.

Correct breathing practice is arguably one of the easiest and most effective ways to address both short- and long-term physical and emotional health.

See also:

- Awareness of Awareness
- Awareness: Building the Observer
- Body Breath Awareness
- Deep Release Breathing
- Quick Breath Affirmation
- Reverse Count Breath

Strategy 24
CONTROL VERSUS PREFERENCES

CATEGORIES APPLIED

Addressing Addictions
Addressing Anxiety
Addressing Depression
Awareness and Mindfulness
Career and Goals
Communications and Relationships
Environmental Health
Improving Self-Esteem

Control in this context refers to the behavior that is exhibited in order to control another person's conduct.

It is a behavior that is so often exhibited because it provides some comfort and predictability. It is an attempt to make yourself feel better, and underneath is a level of fear and a lack of trust in the flow of life. Control is a form of attachment and attachments will always cause you pain. It can even be an attachment to being right. When you attempt to control another person it can create a lot of disharmony, dependency, and conflict.

Some self-reflection will help you understand what is behind your motivation to control.

A controlling attitude typically develops from childhood. There are parents who often unknowingly control their children to a point where they actually inhibit their learning and emotional development. While the intention might be to lead towards a particular desired outcome, the result can be a lack of understanding of the expected behavior and so the child's learning is limited. The child may reject the request or may do the behavior because she is being told to do it without any comprehension of why. Ultimately this pattern could lead to the child becoming dependent, and even the parent becoming resentful. If awareness is not bought to this kind of pattern the reliance will continue into adult life and the person will likely move into a co-dependent relationship.

All people are unique and will naturally respond to different cues. It is unrealistic to expect everyone to agree with you. However, when people understand *why* a particular behavior is requested of them, they are more likely to comply. In fact research shows that by the inclusion of the simple word "because" when making a request, the compliance rate soars. This explanation shows respect for the other person and appeals to their intelligence.

Giving genuine praise or compliments is a powerful way to acknowledge another that can result in cooperation. When people feel good they are more likely to want to help. You really can't acknowledge someone too much! Human behavior is such that a few kind words of appreciation help us feel good about ourselves.

Rather than attempting to control another, have *preferences* instead. State your preference so that the other person has an awareness that allows them to choose from an informed state. This is a much softer way to bring about compliance and maintain harmony without having an attachment.

Also relevant (in some circumstances), is the importance of trusting that the other person has the ability to change in their time. Attempting to force or control another to make changes is assured of conflict. Rather, be an example to show them the way.

Hold the awareness that you can lead and give direction without making someone else wrong and often avoid conflict in so doing.

Remember,

- Fear is at the root of a need to control.
- Look within to identify what is your need to control.
- Acknowledge that the other person may have different ideas, values, or ways of doing things and respect it.
- Acknowledge the other person's preferences.
- Explain the reason why you want something.
- Release your attachment and have preferences instead.
- Trust in the other person's ability to change over time.
- Lead by example.

See also:

- Communication Keys
- Competition versus Cooperation
- Going with the Flow
- Honor and Respect Differences
- Release the Need to Be Right
- Seek to Understand

Strategy 25
DECISIONS: HEART WISDOM

CATEGORIES APPLIED

Addressing Addictions
Addressing Anxiety
Addressing Depression
Awareness and Mindfulness
Career and Goals
Communications and Relationships
Improving Self-Esteem

It is common behavior to make decisions with the mind, which may embrace logic, practicalities, reason, anticipated outcomes, etc. These are all useful mental processes and they can serve you well. But because the mind experiences conditioning it can and will deceive you, depending on your level of personal awareness. The objective is to connect to the higher mind, which takes its guidance from the heart.

The subconscious part of the mind is the internal program that drives our thinking and behaviors until we raise awareness and make the subconscious, conscious. It is the storehouse for all our history and fears.

Without awareness, it is the subconscious mind that strongly influences our decision-making, and this can perpetuate the same limiting patterns. Often behind it there is a naive belief that we will be safe from challenging circumstances. In its negative aspect, the mind is so powerful that it can seriously inhibit the magic and miracles of so many possibilities that the heart inspires.

Your heart is an amazing energy center and its magnetic field can be measured several feet away from the body. Research shows that when we move into a state of coherence, the heart and brain operate synergistically, like two systems that mesh into one. Your heart has its own brain with extensive sensory capacities and can act independently of the cranial brain. It actually sends more signals to the brain than the brain does to the heart. The heart signals to the brain can influence perception, emotional experience, and higher mental processes.*

We have all experienced gut instincts or intuition. It is the signals from the heart that guide us to go a certain way, to do something, to call someone, or any number of other things that will serve us positively. A feeling can alert you to things before they take place; such instant feelings occur without the manipulation of the egoic mind. They are also the gut feelings that often arise when we are not thinking about anything in particular.

Attuning to your heart actually gives you more access to information and increases intuition. It increases your creativity and innovative problem-solving. It is as though we have access to universal energies through our heart. When you are in a balanced feeling state the signals from the heart have a stronger effect on brain activity, informing the frontal cortex more accurately and strongly.

"Anyone who wants to know the human psyche will learn next to nothing from experimental psychology. He would be better advised to abandon exact science, put away his scholar's gown, bid farewell to his study, and wander with human heart throughout the world."
– Carl Jung

Energy goes where attention flows; focusing on this energy center is a way to connect you to your higher self or the higher wisdom that we all have. When we focus on positive heart feelings such as gratitude or kindness our brain actually functions better. If we focus on frustration or negative feelings the brain's function is inhibited.

When the heart is in a coherent state, the actual feelings or sensations may be experienced as a subtle flutter, tingling, or tightness, or just a shift in the way you feel or an inner knowing. It is an internal guidance system that all humans are born with and yet we often begin to disregard it as we grow into adulthood.

Throughout history, different cultures and spiritual traditions have a universal regard for the human heart as a source of great wisdom, intuition, and love, and so it makes sense that learning to trust our heart when we make decisions will support our journey throughout life. You will also find that you attract more loving people and experiences into your life, and your energy radiates out, creating a positive impact on others.

Remember, your higher self is always guiding you towards more love in your life, even when it takes you out of your comfort zone – as it must for your growth. Growth and expansion is about embracing new things and new challenges. If it is new it will not have a familiar feeling, and yet interestingly, people often seek the familiar feeling as a form of guidance. Be aware of this play.

Avoid asking others' opinions related to any decisions you want to make. Their response will have to work through the filters of their life experience; even though they may be well intentioned their response could take you off your path. The reverse also applies.

Be alert to any counter-intention that may be coming from outside of you. Be discerning about what you choose to share with others, realizing they may have a different agenda to you. Keep your energy field clear of any contamination that could hinder your decision. See Strategy 16 Clearing for more information.

Practice with the 4 processes below to build your heart wisdom. They can be used separately or together. Your heart, because of its association with your feeling body, provides the most truthful lenses with which to view your reality.

Note: Avoid making any decisions when you are feeling negative emotions as this impairs clarity.

Adopt these 3 preparation steps before any of the processes below:

1. Hold the intention that you want to tap into your heart's wisdom to make a decision about … (whatever it is)

2. Breathe some deep, long, slow breaths to help you slow down the mind. When you feel your mind has slowed down, imagine you are breathing in and out through your heart.

3. Find something to be grateful for, and focus on gratitude for a minute or so. This helps to build your heart connection.

   This could be just 4–5 breaths or it may take several minutes depending on your current state of mind … and then proceed with the following processes.

Process 1. Feeling Your Heart
Focus all your attention on your heart and the energy center around it. You may find it helpful to actually place your hand on your heart. Then just feel into your dilemma – no mind story, just feeling. Notice what your instincts tell you and act on it.

Process 2. Step Into Your Heart
Imagine yourself as a very small being, who actually steps into your heart. Have a deeply loving and compassionate attitude towards this tiny aspect of yourself. When you feel you have a

trusting connection, then inquire in a curious and compassionate way what it actually needs at this time. Relate this to your dilemma.

Process 3. Heart Question

Asking the question "What would love do now?" is effectively accessing your heart's inspiration. While it engages the mind, you are inviting the response through love, which comes from the heart. This is always associated with the higher self.

Process 4. Test The Option

A way to use both your mind and your feeling body to guide you is to take a few steps relative to your decision. It's like having a sample experience. Your feeling body and your mind can work together in a coherent way to help you decide. If, for example, you are contemplating moving to a new area, go there, spend time and explore, take a walk around the streets and shopping centers and chat to others who live there. Being present in the area provides the opportunity for your body to get a feel for the situation and for using the intelligent mind.

WISDOM is power, will, and love in perfect balance.

Learning to trust your intuition to make decisions. You may find:

a. You head off to your favorite café to buy some lunch, but you feel the desire to go across the road to another café. Following through on this could result in meeting someone in the café who becomes an important connection in your personal or professional life.

b. You get in your car to drive home from work and get a strong feeling to go a different way. You later discover that there was an accident on the road and traffic was held up for hours; another possible outcome could be that you might have been the one in the accident.

c. You go to the doctor's because you were having some digestive problems and he reports he can't find anything and suggests some kind of antacid. Because of the strong feelings you decide to pursue the matter and later find there is some kind of growth in the large intestine, which was missed in the first diagnosis.

d. You just somehow know. It can be similar to the kind of knowing you have if someone is staring at you and you look around and catch someone's glance. It is a feeling and a belief in something. It will often give rise to excitement, courage, and an inspiration to act. You don't need anyone else's approval, You just know that this is what you must do.

e. You are in conversation with someone or listening to a song on the radio and something that you hear strikes a chord in you (a feel-good vibe) that may then go on to inspire you towards a new business venture.

Whatever choice you make, understand there are no wrong decisions. Whatever you do will provide greater clarity. It will either lead you towards what you are wanting or it won't. If it doesn't, you will know you need to change direction, and so you have learned from your actions and can choose again. If you're feeling really good about your decision then you are in alignment with your higher self and totally on track.

See also:

- Awareness of Awareness
- Clearing
- Decisions: Motives and Impact
- Going with the Flow
- Ideas and Inspirations
- Intention/Counter-Intention
- Personal Mission Statement
- Values
- Work Passion

*Paraphrased from HeartMath Institute. http://www.heartmath.org/about-us/about-us-home/hearts-intuitive-intelligence.html

Strategy 26
DECISIONS: MOTIVES AND IMPACT

CATEGORIES APPLIED

Addressing Addictions
Addressing Anxiety
Addressing Depression
Awareness and Mindfulness
Career and Goals
Communications and Relationships
Improving Self-Esteem

Making decisions about anything and everything can be challenging when you don't really recognize or understand your deepest motives or what internal programming you are responding to. Our thinking runs through the filters of the subconscious mind where all the belief systems and life experiences are stored. Any negative or fear-based experiences, particularly those that are unresolved, will be influencing your motives and decisions through the egoic mind. This can seriously impair your ability to expand into more of your potential and realize your true self.

We have the gift of free will and everything you *do, say*, and *be* has consequences. Everything we see and experience in our world is a result of our actions and inactions. It includes all our interactions with others and everything in your environment. We all leave our mark on this world, and those with any degree of consciousness would prefer to have a positive impact. The basic universal law of cause and effect applies: all actions and inactions have consequences and produce results. So it becomes clear that our decisions, thoughts, and actions either add to or detract from our sense of wellbeing and the quality of our vibration, including the quality of all our experiences and the broader world.

While the response of others is on one level none of your business, if we don't strive to be conscious of the impact of our decisions and the reactions we evoke in another, we seriously run the risk of increasing disharmony and unsustainable practices, which will ultimately destroy the very foundations of the Earth that supports us.

Such behaviors are in total contrast to our true nature of love and compassion; when we do not behave in a way that reflects this, it erodes our sense of self-worth and our potential for happiness.

A simple gauge to assess motives and decisions is whether they add to the overall love or fear balance on this planet. Understanding your intention is all-important.

For example, intending to cause harm of some kind in another would obviously have a negative impact and add to the fear quotient. This could be something like saying unkind things to another person, or trying to get someone drunk so that you can manipulate them in some way.

By contrast, being supportive or loving towards another has a positive impact and adds to the love quotient. It may be as simple as giving a compliment or helping someone with a task. Even a kindly look with a big smile can evoke a positive effect and provide a lift for the other person and satisfy something within you.

While we may never know the outcome of the ripple effect of our actions, we all know it happens because we are constantly experiencing this in our own life. A kind word can enhance another's day, prompting them to share a little more love than they may have otherwise. Of course, the opposite can contribute to a negative spiral.

Being aware of your motives as well as the impact of your energy gives you the possibility of contributing in a positive way by always choosing to add to the higher vibrations of love.

Below are some reflective questions that will facilitate greater consciousness and may help you with decisions:

- Have I set clear boundaries to honor and respect myself?
- Would my intended actions add to the love balance on the Earth?
- Would sharing the truth as I perceive it, wound another? If yes, it may be best not to act. Strive to speak your truth with compassion and sensitivity.
- What would love do now?
- Am I in integrity? Am I being honest?
- Am I adding more harmony as a result of my existence here?
- Am I respecting the wholeness within the other person and recognizing they are conditioned just like me and learning just like me?
- Am I accepting responsibility for all of my feelings and not projecting onto another?
- Are my actions done with a loving intent? (Resentment will add to the fear balance)
- Are my motives clear?
- Is this what my heart is guiding me towards?

To dig a bit deeper, ask yourself, "What is the motive beneath my motive?"

Sometimes this may reveal a hidden agenda. An example might be declining a dinner invitation because you can't afford to dine out. While funds might be a bit tight, if you dig a bit deeper you may find the real reason: you don't want to go because someone you have issues with will also be there and you would feel uncomfortable.

This is not about a right or wrong dynamic. Depending on the situation, it may even be a way of honoring your boundaries. *The point is to be honest with yourself and know your true reasons,* which helps to increase your consciousness.

Where appropriate, share your truth with another. Such a situation might occur if there was another family member who wanted to go to the dinner with you and would otherwise be misled by your initial decision. Truthfulness obviously creates an honest communication, which is the very foundation of all good relationships.

To avoid hurting another person choose your words carefully with consciousness. Honest self-reflection assists your own mental clarity, builds your awareness and sense of self-worth and can ultimately be the impetus for you to find a way to address the disharmony between yourself and the other person.

Ultimately, all your decisions that add to the love balance will not only benefit you, but everyone and everything. That is no small impact!

See also:

- Awareness of Awareness
- Decisions: Heart Wisdom
- Ideas and Inspirations
- Values
- Work Passion

Strategy 27
DEEP RELEASE BREATHING

CATEGORIES APPLIED

Addressing Addictions
Addressing Anxiety
Addressing Depression
Awareness and Mindfulness
Improving Self-Esteem
Quick Stress Busters

There are different kinds of focused breathing practices, all of which ultimately facilitate a greater level of awareness, health, and wellbeing. Deep Release breathing is sometimes referred to as abdominal breathing because of the engagement of the diaphragm muscles, which help the expansion and contraction of the lungs. It is a great resource when feeling really agitated, anxious, or stressed. At such times, your breathing can often become very shallow and stilted as your body goes into the fight-or-flight response. Other physiological changes may include perspiration, an increase in heart rate, or increased muscular tension, all of which have the effect of blocking the flow of energy within your body and creating tension.

Unlike most other breathing processes where the breath is inhaled and exhaled through the nose, in this one you are encouraged to breathe in through the nose, hold it, and then out through the mouth with an audible sigh.

Process 1

A. Hold the intention that you are going to release any distress from your body with every out-breath, and come back into present time, Do not allow your mind to take you off somewhere. Start by observing your breath and how it causes the rise and fall of your chest and abdomen.

B. Place one hand on your chest and the other on your abdomen. (A clue to the correct breathing is to notice that the hand on your abdomen will rise higher than the one on your chest as you inhale, ensuring that the diaphragm is taking the air right down to the depth of the lungs.)

C. Then begin to breathe very deeply and slowly in through the nose to the count of 5. At the same time, imagine you are inhaling the qualities of peace and calm … and allowing your lungs to fill to capacity; then hold the breath for the count of 5 before you exhale.

D. Then exhale with full audible breath (sigh) to the count of 5 or more and let go of any tension and stress. Ensure full expiration from the lungs as this determines the depth of your next in-breath. Repeat this for a few minutes or several cycles, or until you feel the calming and balancing effects.

Once you have mastered this Deep Release Breathing with the guidance of your hands on chest and abdomen, you will be able to do it without your hands. Closed eyes will facilitate a deeper more focused experience.

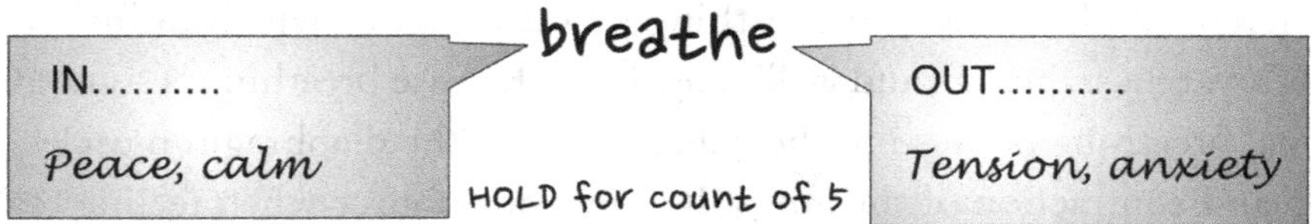

Process 2

Deep Release Breathing can be accomplished while participating in numerous other activities like traveling, washing the dishes, out walking, shopping, or having a shower (just delete B). This will have a reduced benefit because of the diminished focus, but it will have value.

Process 3

Adjust the deep release breathing by eliminating the counting or any effort to maintain evenness. Just breathing in deeply through the nose and out fully with an audible sigh through the mouth. Continue for several minutes until your anxiety reduces.

See also:

- Awareness: Building the Observer
- Being: Mindfulness
- Body Breath Awareness
- Clearing
- Conscious Breathing
- Feeling Agitated
- Feeling Anger
- Feeling Challenged
- Feeling Disempowered
- Feeling Fear
- Feeling Grief
- Feeling Guilt or Shame

- Feeling Jealousy
- Feeling Lonely
- Feeling Rejected or Hurt
- Feeling Scattered: Unbalanced
- Feeling Stuck
- Feeling Uncertain or Fearful of the Unknown
- Feeling Unloved or Unlovable
- Feeling Unsupported
- Feeling Victimized
- Feeling Worried
- Forgiveness Process
- Quick Breath Affirmation
- Reverse Count Breath

Strategy 28
DO NO HARM

CATEGORIES APPLIED

Addressing Addictions
Addressing Anxiety
Addressing Depression
Awareness and Mindfulness
Career and Goals
Communications and Relationships
Environmental Health
Everyday Essentials
Exercise for Living
Improving Self-Esteem
Nutrition for Life

It is a common misconception that "First Do No Harm" was part of the Hippocratic oath taken by physicians when they entered medical practice. The origin of this Latin phrase (*Primum non nocere*) is uncertain (see Wikipedia). Some consider it to be a universal spiritual law that recognizes the connectedness and sacredness of life.

In a model that leads to ongoing destruction, we see a lot of damage and harm done to our fellow human beings, the creatures, and our planet. What we witness in the world at large also reflects the inner turmoil of our human self, since the microcosm affects the macrocosm. When we see an outer conflict, it resonates with something that is already within. To fix the problems in our world we must fix the inner conflicts within ourselves.

Love and compassion are necessities, not luxuries.
Without them humanity cannot survive.
– The Dalai Lama

So many of the challenges in life provide the lessons that grow us spiritually. We learn sooner or later that if we hurt another, with words or actions, then through the law of attraction and the law of cause and effect we also hurt ourselves.

We have the opportunity every day to trust our intuition, which comes from our higher guidance. When we are feeling good and loving there is a *rightness* to it – nothing needs to be fixed or changed. All is well in our world.

When we are connected to our higher self or spiritual essence there is a good feeling and it feels totally natural to be loving and kind. We feel empowered and secure in our existence, and when these feelings preside there is no desire to cause any harm to another. Doing so would go against our authentic self. We would be acting out of fear.

This is more than just having a conscience, which can be totally influenced by your conditioning and beliefs. It is something deeper: something innate within us that is connected to our core essence ... a kind of inner knowing.

There may be times when you feel hurt or betrayed, and the desire to hurt back can be very strong. You may feel justified or vindicated to exercise some kind of payback. If revenge is exercised, there may even be an initial feeling of satisfaction that payback has taken place. Yet if you dig a bit deeper you will likely find that there is a negative feeling under that and it may even give rise to guilt, grief, or shame immediately following or sometime later. Then of course there are the karmic implications. We are all responsible for cleaning up our own mess.

There will be times when your perception will be completely off, as though you are looking through blinkers, unable to see all that surrounds and influences your experience. Deep regret can follow when you react and process through the limited lens of your subconscious mind and are unwilling or unable to see from a higher perspective.

It is important to recognize that it is your "lower" mind that is dominant in this kind of situation. Your inner child is hurting and needs your love to heal, though it might also want to be loved and approved of by another. Effectively you have chosen fear over love, and like any kind of negativity it will lead you down a destructive spiral, ultimately compromising your true loving nature, which then precipitates low self-esteem.

Hanging on to resentments and pain or seeking revenge is effectively giving some of your energy to the other person. Neither person can benefit. Forgiveness puts you back in the power position along with strong boundaries. See Strategy 53 Forgiveness Process.

Perhaps a useful subject for your own deep contemplation is the question: Could Do No Harm remedy the destructive pattern so prevalent in our world? Could it diminish the need for the myriad other rules that humanity has created? Would it automatically show respect? Would our considerations to all other beings be paramount with the focused intent of Do No Harm? And if so, would that cultivate kindness, compassion, respect, support, unity, peace, connectedness, harmony, appreciation, discernment, and trust. And if so, is it likely that we would feel really good about ourselves and because of that nurture the connection to our higher self?

Only your own heart can really make that decision.

See also:

- Awareness of Awareness
- Awareness: Building the Observer
- Communication Keys
- Competition versus Cooperation
- Gag Gossip
- Honor and Respect Differences
- Intention/Counter-Intention
- Judgment Effect
- Seek to Understand

Strategy 29
DO THINGS YOU ENJOY

CATEGORIES APPLIED

Addressing Addictions
Addressing Anxiety
Addressing Depression
Awareness and Mindfulness
Career and Goals
Communications and Relationships
Improving Self-Esteem

People will often put off or just not do the things they really enjoy. They justify this by saying they don't have time, they don't have enough money, they're giving priority to another thing or person, or feeling that they don't deserve it.

When you are doing things that give you pleasure and warm your heart, you are connected to your higher self or the I AM presence within. It is a key means to nurture yourself, build your self-esteem and maintain your alignment. You function better as a person, and because of the effect on your energy system, you are also better to be around.

Doing things you enjoy has a feel-good physiological response. Choose from the following list of easy ways to increase your vibration and add anything else that gives you pleasure.

- Dance
- Sing
- Play with children
- Play with anyone or anything
- Potter in the garden
- Paint
- Draw
- Create things
- Walk on the beach or in the park
- Gaze and talk to the moon and stars
- Pet your dog or cat
- Pamper yourself with a facial or massage
- Look at art
- Do work you love
- Take yourself on an outing that gives you pleasure

See also:

- Connect with Nature
- Going with the Flow
- Grounding/Earthing
- Kindness to Self
- Laughter Medicine
- Music to Uplift and Nurture

Strategy 30
ENVIRONMENTAL HEALTH: CONSUMABLES

CATEGORIES APPLIED

Addressing Addictions
Addressing Anxiety
Addressing Depression
Awareness and Mindfulness
Environmental Health
Everyday Essentials
Improving Self-Esteem
Nutrition for Life

Determining healthy foods can be immensely challenging when you are up against big companies with huge marketing budgets whose interest is more about profits than your health or the environment. The preservatives and additives in many foods, for example, can be extremely toxic.

While there are some foods that can be more likely to cause an allergic reaction than others, the reality is that anyone can have an allergic reaction to anything. The everyday food products listed below appear to be the most common and perhaps the most insidious.

This information only serves to awaken you to possible areas that may be impacting on your health without your knowledge. Investigate to your own level of satisfaction. Sources of information are provided below.

Additives. Food additives are chemicals that keep food fresh or enhance its color, flavor, or texture. These include colors, preservatives, food acids, antioxidants, mineral salts, vegetable gum and thickeners, humectants, emulsifiers, flavor enhancers, and artificial sweeteners. These all require your body to detoxify at some later stage. They can be the cause of respiratory and digestive difficulties and skin problems, also nervous disorders, commonly seen as hyperactive behavior in children. Ensure that you read the labels on your foods and determine what chemicals are safe. (http://www.fedupwithfoodadditives.info/information/additivesall.htm)

Coffee. Coffee is probably the most consumed beverage on the planet, with millions of dollars spent on its promotion. There are conflicting studies about its effects on health. According to Wikipedia, "excessive amounts of coffee can cause life-threatening adverse effects."

Coffee is an addictive substance and causes withdrawal effects. It's a stimulant, which can make you feel agitated and cause heart palpitations. It increases your risk of insomnia, stroke, and heart disease. It is also a laxative, and is known to disrupt absorption of vitamins and minerals that are essential to the body. It can be the source of stress and toxicity to your body.

With so much conflicting evidence about coffee you will ultimately need to explore to your own level of satisfaction. If you are a coffee drinker, perhaps the best guideline is really noticing how you feel with a protracted period of being without coffee. Many people drink it moderately with no ill effects.

Energy drinks. Hundreds of different brands are now marketed, with caffeine content ranging from a modest 50mg to an alarming 505mg per can or bottle. Some contain the equivalent of fourteen cans of Coke and few include warnings of the potential health risks of caffeine intoxication. In addition, they are very high in sugar. Both can lead to addiction. Caffeine intoxication is marked by nervousness, anxiety, restlessness, insomnia, gastrointestinal upset, tremors, rapid heartbeats (tachycardia), psychomotor agitation (restlessness and pacing), and in rare cases, death. (Eurekalert http://www.eurekalert.org).

Genetically modified foods. The benefits, risks, and ethical concerns regarding GM foods are still being researched and debated. Little research has been conducted into the long-term health risks of switching to GM food, though increasing claims of negative effects are arising. There is an urgent need for long-term, independent investigations into the performance of GM crops in the field including the longer-term effects on the mineral, plant, animal, and human kingdoms of this Earth (www.geneethics.org).

Common GM foods include soybeans, corn, squash, potatoes, pineapples, strawberries, canola, sugar papayas, zucchini, cotton wheat, rice. Beware also of dairy cows injected with the GE hormone rBGH/rBST; these animals are possibly fed GM grains and hay.

Be cautious of "experts" in their field such as Monsanto – one of the largest providers of GM foods, whose studies claim to prove their GM foods are safe. These same experts also advised that PCBs, Agent Orange, and DDT were safe, and we now know those claims were far from accurate.

The safest thing is to eat 100% organic food and purchase products specifically labeled as non-GM or GM-free.

Monosodium glutamate (MSG) is commonly added to foods to enhance flavor. It can produce headaches, heart palpitations, flushes, sweating, tingling sensations, shortness of breath, fatigue, obesity, and depression. While it is commonly associated with Chinese food, it is found in many pre-packed meals, soups, snacks, and fast foods.

For research on MSG go to: http://articles.mercola.com/sites/articles/archive/2009/04/21/msg-is-this-silent-killer-lurking-in-your-kitchen-cabinets.aspx

Soy products. There is increasing evidence of serious health risks associated with unfermented soy products, including digestive problems, hormonal problems, and serious problems for babies on soy formula. Added to this is the volume of GM soy being produced without knowing the longer-term effects. For more information see http://search.mercola.com/results.aspx?q=soy%20products.

http://www.westonaprice.org/soy/soy_studies.html

Sugar substitutes. Saccharin is a sweetener which belongs to a class of compounds known as sulfonamides. It can cause allergic reactions such as headaches, skin problems, diarrhoea and possible breathing difficulties.

A good sugar substitute is either Xylitol (extracted from various fruits and vegetables) or Stevia (a herbal leaf sweetener).

Water, bottled. Ten major brands of bottled water tested by the Environmental Working Group found an alarming array of contaminants, including cancer-causing by-products of chlorination, fertilizer residue, industrial solvents, and even caffeine. http://www.ewg.org

In addition, these plastic bottles create massive pollution all over the world.

- Drink filtered tap water instead of bottled or unfiltered tap water.
- Mix infant formula with filtered, non-fluoridated water.
- Carry water in safe, reusable containers.

Wheat. In our Western world wheat is the dominant grain and many people develop intolerance to it while remaining unaware of the imbalance it can cause. Wheat is used in an enormous amount of processed foods including cereals, sauces, dressings, soups, baked and packet foods, pastas, and some alcoholic beverages.

Common symptoms that often go undetected include tiredness, skin disorders, irritability, and bloating. A wheat allergy can result in more severe and additional symptoms. There are many alternatives such as spelt, amaranth, rice, rye, buckwheat, and quinoa.

When making food and beverage choices, consider both the impact on your health and the health of this planet and decide if you really want to support companies that disregard these essentials for life.

Care with Food that Naturally Contain Poison

Apple Pips contain cyanide, which can lead to vomiting if enough are eaten.

Almonds. Raw bitter almonds when eaten turn into hydrogen cyanide, which is poisonous. The heating involved in processed bitter almonds make them safe.

Brazil Nuts are great source of selenium, which is known to fight cancer, heart disease, and even aging. However, they are also one of the most radioactive foods in the world, have high amounts of aflatoxins which are carcinogenic. A few nuts several times are week are safe.

Cherries. The pips contain the chemical hydrogen cyanide, which are much more dangerous if chewed and can cause vomiting, breathing difficulties, and even kidney failure.

Rhubarb. The green leaves of rhubarb contain oxalic acid which can cause breathing difficulty, burning in the mouth and throat, diarrhoea, and eye pain.

Mushrooms. Around 5% of mushroom varieties are toxic if eaten, with 15–20 species potentially lethal. They are often mistaken when foraging for non-toxic ones.

Kidney Beans in their raw state contain high levels of haemagglutinin that make them unsuitable for consumption and can cause severe vomiting and diarrhea. Haemagglutinin is destroyed by traditional cooking methods of soaking then boiling.

Nutmeg contains a substance called myristicin, a narcotic with a very unpleasant toxic effect if taken in large quantities (1–3 whole nutmegs at one time). Ingestion of small amounts is harmless.

Potatoes. Green potatoes have extremely high levels of the glycoalkaloid poison, which is highly toxic.

Puffer Fish. A Japanese delicacy that can lead to paralysis and death if not properly cooked. Chefs train for 2–3 years to ensure they cook it properly.

Other Useful Sources

- ProActive Health (https://proactivehealth.net.au/index.php?mp_id=53)
- Environmental Working Group (http://www.ewg.org)
- My Green Australia (http://www.mygreenaustralia.com)
- Gene Ethics Network (http://www.geneethics.org)
- Proven Dietary Help & Research(http://www.feingold.org)
- AUST. Conservation Foundation (http://www.acfonline.org.au)
- Dr. Mercola - (http://www.mercola.com)
- Dr. Carolyn Dean MD ND (http://drcarolyndean.com)

See also:

- Environmental Health: Electromagnetic Fields
- Environmental Health: General
- Environmental Health: Personal Products
- Environmental Health: Water
- Nutrition Keys
- Oral Health

Strategy 31
ENVIRONMENTAL HEALTH: ELECTROMAGNETIC FIELDS

CATEGORIES APPLIED

Addressing Addictions
Addressing Anxiety
Addressing Depression
Awareness and Mindfulness
Career and Goals

Electricity is a form of energy that involves the flow of electrons. Electromagnetic field (EMFs) is the term used to describe that part of the electromagnetic spectrum known as carrying extra low frequencies, most of which power our homes and appliances and workplace equipment.

Quite apart from the massive pollution generated by the production of electrical power that sickens our Earth, EMFs also diminish human health.

Twenty-four hours a day we are exposed to electromagnetic emissions from dozens of household and workplace products that produce large magnetic fields. These include fridges, dishwashers, microwave ovens, toasters, hair driers, televisions, dishwashers, electric toothbrushes, sound gear, computers, office equipment, and other sources outside of our homes: satellite dishes, military installations, industrial machines, high-tension power lines and transformers, meter boxes, smart meters, and frequencies broadcast from radios, televisions, and mobile phones.

The human body has natural electromagnetic circuitry working the brain, nervous system, muscle contraction, and cell function. Our constant exposure to these external energies pollutes our bodies and upsets this natural circuitry. The effects can impact on the body's immune system and be the cause of that feeling of not being quite right, and mild to serious ill health.

Wireless radiation and electromagnetic pollution are everywhere and cause inflammation of the cells in your body; this can lead to diseases like brain cancer, heart disease, chronic fatigue, fibromyalgia, and more. See research by Dr. Stephen Sinatra https://www.youtube.com/watch?v=XumPQLTzPWI

Symptoms of Radio Wave Sickness

(excerpted from *No Place to Hide* April 2001)

- *Neurological:* headaches, dizziness, nausea, difficulty concentrating, memory loss, irritability, depression, anxiety, insomnia, fatigue, weakness, tremors, muscle spasms, numbness, tingling, altered reflexes, muscle and joint paint, leg/foot pain, flu-like symptoms, fever. More severe reactions can include seizures, paralysis, psychosis, and stroke.

- *Cardiac:* palpitations, arrhythmias, pain or pressure in the chest, low or high blood pressure, slow or fast heart rate, shortness of breath.
- *Respiratory:* sinusitis, bronchitis, pneumonia, asthma.
- *Dermatological:* skin rash, itching, burning, facial flushing.
- *Ophthalmologic:* pain or burning in the eyes, pressure in/behind the eyes, deteriorating vision, floaters, cataracts.
- *Others:* digestive problems; abdominal pain; enlarged thyroid, testicular/ovarian pain; dryness of lips, tongue, mouth, eyes; great thirst; dehydration; nosebleeds; internal bleeding; altered sugar metabolism; immune abnormalities; redistribution of metals within the body; hair loss; pain in the teeth; deteriorating fillings; impaired sense of smell; ringing in the ears.

Be aware! The only known cure for radio wave sickness is to stop being exposed to it.

Some Tips To Minimize Effect

Turn off all electrical equipment that is not in use at the wall switch and save money too.

Be aware that electromagnetic energy passes effortlessly through walls, so don't delude yourself that if you can't see it you are safe from these rays.

As the bed is the place where most of us stay in one place for an average of eight hours, it is very important to minimize our exposure to electromagnetic energy. Ensure your bed is not on the opposite, internal wall of a meter box. Avoid placement of any EMR product close to you, particularly your head – e.g. clock radios, phones, lap tops, television, stereo, touch lamps. Turn off all electricity not required while sleeping.

Cordless telephones are similar in effect to mobile phones. Ensure your head is not in between the aerial on the handset and the desk set. Better still, replace them with corded phones.

Clock radios emit a radiation that is typically close to a sleeper's head. Any appliance that is able to run on battery or mains power has a transformer within it. This steps the power down from 240V to 12V and electromagnetic radiation is given off. Use only battery-operated or wind-up clocks.

Dimmer switches and halogen lighting emit a particularly strong electromagnetic field. These are best to avoid.

Electric blankets interfere with the body's own energy circuit. The obvious is to do without them. But the impact would be reduced if you used the electric blanket to heat your bed and then removed the plug from the outlet when you got in it. However, even when the electrical plug is withdrawn from the socket the copper in the blanket can still attract electric fields and carry the negative vibration. Hot water bottles are definitely a better option for your health and better still, a non-spring mattress without the wire coils.

Metal-based beds can be conductors of an electrical current if an electric blanket is used. This also applies to mattresses with metal inner springs. See above.

Meter box. Avoid near an entrance that you have to walk by. Avoid any regular seating or bedding on the internal opposite side of the wall.

Smart meters use very high frequency radiation from telecommunications and microwave digital towers. This is continuous radiation, and the information suggests they use an extra 4GHZ, which is considered way beyond safe limits and the cause of many health problems. Explore to your own level of satisfaction and choose accordingly. (Doctors report on www.youtube.com/watch?v=n7L21XOC2wA&feature=player_embedded)

Microwave ovens. The debate continues on the detrimental effect on microwave ovens and their effect on food, and the environment. Microwave ovens create unsafe hot spots in your food and alter its chemistry. The radiation from microwaves is linked to leukemia; affects your heart and high exposure is know to cause cataracts. It is best to not be in the same room as them when in use. Consider doing without them. (For a comprehensive review visit http://articles.mercola.com/sites/articles/archive/2010/05/18/microwavehazards.aspx)

Mobile telephones emit a radiation that leaves the head and brain most vulnerable because of its obvious close proximity when in use. Limit use and/or use an extended earpiece, or have the phone on speaker. Avoid carrying in your pocket, which radiates waves to the corresponding part of your body. Avoid use of your phone when it has fewer signal bars. It means that it emits more radiation to get the signal to the tower. Texting uses less power/radiation than voice and avoids the phone near your ear to hear. Turn off when at home and use a landline.

Office. Rearrange your office so you have minimal exposure to electrical equipment.

Phone chargers, CD players, and cassette players contain a transformer (see clock radios above). Ensure they are located away from your body and turned off at the power point when not in use.

Television and computers. Limit exposure to these appliances, turn off at power point when not in use, and create as large a distance as possible from them with a minimum of 3 meters. Best to use laptops on battery only and recharge when you're not around.

Water beds. The electrical current charges the water and holds it while you sleep. It is best to change beds.

Wireless router. Replace with Ethernet cables.

Be Aware

A new review of recent studies supports the classification of RF radiation as a probable rather than a possible carcinogen. http://www.sciencedirect.com/science/article/pii/S0928468013000035

Dr. Olle Johansson of the Karolinska Institute in Sweden warns about the potential irreversible damage being done to DNA of our children by exposure to RF radiation from cell phones and transmitters, Wi-Fi internet, smart meters etc. http://emfsafetynetwork.org/?p=9990

Even if you can't see them, energy, frequencies, sounds, and vibrations are all around us and impacting on our health. Because these waves of energy are unseen, they are often not considered as a possible cause of ill health. Our homes are increasingly becoming polluted with all kinds of health hazards.

Apart from minimizing your exposure, explore the Internet for possible aids for protection from electromagnetic fields.

Learn more about the Emerging EMF public health issue from Scientists, Physicians and Other Experts at:

http://www.sciencedirect.com/science/article/pii/S0928468013000035

Dr. Martin Blank: http://www.youtube.com/watch?v=jr8RQQUqEV8

Dr. David Carpenter, Dean of School – Public Health and Director of Institute for Health and Environment

www.youtube.com/watch?v=n7L21XOC2wA&feature=player_embedded

www.ElectromagneticHealth.org

http://emfsafetystore.com/

http://www.electricalpollution.com/solutions.html

http://sagereports.com/smart-meter-rf/)

http://smartmeterwarnings.wordpress.com

See also:

- Environmental Health: General
- Environmental Health: Personal Products
- Environmental Health: Consumables
- Environmental Health: Water

Strategy 32
ENVIRONMENTAL HEALTH: GENERAL

CATEGORIES APPLIED

Addressing Addictions
Addressing Anxiety
Addressing Depression
Awareness and Mindfulness
Career and Goals
Environmental Health
Everyday Essentials
Exercise for Life

The Earth is everybody's home, and yet many manufactured items are causing not only serious health issues for humankind but also creating toxicity in the planet generally. These practices are not sustainable. Decide: *Do you really want to support companies that have disregard for the Earth and future generations?* Be aware of your purchases and investments.

The human body is an electrochemical organism and the more we destabilize it electrically or chemically the more you stop that organism working to full capacity in all areas.

There is a plethora of toxins that now permeate our Earth and the air we breathe, reducing the oxygen levels. Make sure you get plenty of fresh air and spend time in nature breathing deeply. Seaside and heavily treed areas offer the cleanest air. Ensure that you always sleep with fresh air coming into your bedroom, even if it is just a small amount. Ceiling fans help move air and dissuade pests from that room. They also attract fine airborne particles away from you, which means you will need to clean your fan blades regularly.

Toxic air is even affecting our unborn. The Environmental Working Group's (EWG) groundbreaking research has found hundreds of chemicals in the umbilical cord blood of newborn babies. It proves that some newborns have already been exposed to toxic chemicals.

The environmental toxins that cause the most problems are pesticides, solvents, and heavy metals. The primary damage caused by the solvents and major pesticide classes is to disrupt neurological function. In addition to being neurotoxic, these compounds are profoundly immunotoxic and are often toxic to the endocrine system as well. The adverse health effects are not limited to those systems only, as these compounds can also cause a variety of dermatological, gastrointestinal, genitourinary, respiratory, musculoskeletal, and cardiological problems.

The nation's worst pollution is found inside our homes and workplaces. There are thousands of toxic killers found in the air we breathe, the food we eat, bathroom products, household paints, carpets, cleaning products, cosmetics, cooking aids, water, and foods. Some reports state there are over 75,000 synthetic chemicals being used in everyday products. Just a few examples are:

- Some *floor cleaners* contain solvents nitrobenzene, formaldehyde, and ethylene glycol ethers, which provide a protective coating against general wear and tear and may cause headaches and respiratory irritations during application.
- *Dishwashing detergents* containing chlorine let off an invisible gas called chloroform when it mixes with organic molecules in the water and is often inhaled via steam when you open the dishwasher door.
- *General antibacterial cleaners.* Triclosan is a chemical used in antibacterial soaps, sprays, and cleansers, which is linked to heart attacks and damage to heart and muscle tissue.
- *Surface cleaners* commonly have formaldehyde, which kills most bacteria and fungal spores but is also a known carcinogen.
- *Toilet cleaners* often contain harsh acids, which cause irritation to the skin and eyes.

The good news is that numerous studies have proven the effectiveness of houseplants as a way to purify the air within our homes and workplaces. These include: Aloe Vera, Azalea Bamboo palm (also known as Reed Palm), Chinese evergreen, Chrysanthemum, Dracaena, English Ivy, Gerbera, Golden Pothos, Peace Lily, Philodendron (Heart Leaf), Snake Plant (also known as Mother-in-law's tongue), Spider plant, and Weeping Fig (Ficus).

Air pollutants come from the discharges of gases and particles, mainly from industry, motor vehicles, and domestic wood burning. There are also natural resources such as windblown dust and smoke from bushfires. Avoid the use of home air fresheners, which can be very toxic when inhaled.

Insecticides and pesticides. Over the last 50 years many human illnesses and deaths have occurred as a result of exposure to pesticides, with up to 20,000 deaths reported annually. Much of these toxins are carried through the air and end up in our water systems and soil, which obviously affects vegetation, bird, marine, animal, and human life.

Geo-engineering. The reader is encouraged to explore **geo-engineering**, which is the deliberate large-scale manipulation of an environmental process that affects the Earth's climate. (http://www.geoengineeringwatch.org)

Chemtrails are just one aspect of geo-engineering. Chemtrails are chemicals or biological agents deliberately sprayed at high altitudes for a purpose undisclosed to the general public.

Smoking contributes a considerable amount of cadmium into the body as well. Cadmium is a chemical element similar to the metals of zinc and mercury. It is used in the manufacture of batteries. Cadmium can affect the kidneys, lungs, and bones.

Oils, heavy metals and other chemicals enter waterways from a variety of potential sources, including urban and agricultural runoff, industrial and mining operations, landfill leaching, and transportation or industrial spills.

These chemicals can have drastic impacts on freshwater and marine ecosystems. This may vary in severity from reducing growth and reproduction to directly killing plants and animals. The effects of many toxic chemicals are increased by their ability to remain and build up in the environment over a long period. The results can be particularly destructive in wetlands and bays where flushing is limited.

Copper water pipes may play a role in the eventual onset of Alzheimer's, as can too much iron in your system. Contributors to excess iron can be cooking with iron pots or pans and particularly when cooking acidic foods. Also drinking well water that is high in iron.

It is critically important to dispose of household paints, batteries, asbestos, and other chemical cleaning products according to recommended guidelines. This is especially important in the dumping of car tires. There are millions upon millions of car tires that traverse our roads at any one time and leave wear particles that contaminate our water and air. They contain heavy metals like zinc cadmium, hydrocarbons, latex, and sulfur-containing compounds.

Heavy metals poison a diverse range of enzyme functions, affecting virtually every system of the body. The greatest exposure to heavy metals is from dental amalgam fillings and other metal dental appliances (See Strategy 74 Oral Health). Heavy metals contribute up to 80% to the causes of all diseases (www.nissenmedica.com).

Common problems include hormonal imbalances, cancer, thyroid problems, neurological disturbances, learning problems, depression, food allergies, and parasites.

Dry cleaning. Perchlorethylene is a cleaning solvent commonly used in dry cleaning and a suspected carcinogen that has been linked to cervical, lung, and bladder cancers. Ensure you air your clothes after you bring them home; better still, find a dry-cleaner that doesn't use it.

Synthetics and plastics. Plastic requires petroleum in its manufacture and is not generally degradable, creating massive landfill. Marine litter is now 60-80% plastic reaching as high as 95% in some areas. Many chemical additives that give plastic products desirable performance properties such as flexibility and soft texture also have negative environmental and human health effects, which include direct toxicity, as in the case of lead, cadmium, and mercury; carcinogens, diethylhexyl phthalate (DEHP); and endocrine disruption, which can lead to cancers, birth defects, immune system suppression, and developmental problems in children.

Adopt a policy of reduce, re-use and recycle. Find alternatives to plastic products whenever possible.

Some specific suggestions to reduce plastics and improve personal health and Earth sustainability:

- Buy food in glass or metal containers.
- Avoid food items individually wrapped with plastic.
- Drink filtered tap water.
- Avoid heating food in plastic containers, or storing fatty foods in plastic containers or plastic wrap.
- Refill toner cartridges, pens, and other office supplies and avoid purchasing equipment that disregards sustainability.
- Do not give young children plastic teethers or toys.
- Choose long-lasting wooden or metal toys for children.
- Avoid disposable products (razors, pens, lighters, bags).
- Shop using your own (non-plastic) shopping bags.
- Use natural fiber clothing, bedding, and furniture.
- Look for packaging labelled BPA-free. Bisphenol A (BPA) is found in plastic bottles and the inside coating of cans.
- Avoid all PVC and styrene products.
- Contact and ask the manufacturer of products to use recyclable packaging if they don't.

Sound frequencies. There are certain kinds of sound frequencies that can be extremely abrasive, adding to stress levels, affecting human health and performance. Sound from every source emanates frequencies that are beneficial or detrimental to your psyche and body. Discord is created with many environmental sounds and modern music, affecting not only humans but also plants and animals. By contrast, much classical music has proven to have nurturing and calming effects on sick patients, and has also been shown to assist plants to flourish and help animals become more gentle and receptive.

Geopathic stress includes fault lines, ley lines, certain mineral concentrations, underground cavities, and subterranean running water. Exposure to these Earth stressors can result in all kinds of health symptoms including:

> *Neurological.* Headaches, dizziness, nausea, difficulty concentrating, memory loss, irritability, depression, anxiety, insomnia, fatigue, weakness, tremors, muscle spasms, numbness, tingling, altered reflexes, muscle and joint paint, leg/foot pain, flu-like symptoms, fever. More severe reactions can include seizures, paralysis, psychosis, stroke (possibly MS as well).
> *Cardiac.* Palpitations, arrhythmias, pain or pressure in the chest, low or high blood pressure, slow or fast heart rate, shortness of breath.
> *Respiratory.* Sinusitis, bronchitis, pneumonia, asthma.
> *Dermatological.* Skin rash, itching, burning, facial flushing.

Such an impact is more prevalent if your bed is over one of these kinds of Earth stressors. Not surprisingly, the causes of these health conditions are often overlooked. A useful tip is to notice if you feel better when you are away from home. A trained geomancer using dowsing rods would be able to identify any kind of geopathic stress.

These are just some of the unseen energies that affect how we feel.

Mineral reduction in soil and waterways results in less nutrition from food sources and increases the need for food supplements such as antioxidants, vitamins, and minerals. This is a great incentive to grow your own food.

According to Wikipedia - causes of resource depletion are:

- Over-consumption, excessive or unnecessary use of resources
- Non-equitable distribution of resources

- Overpopulation
- Slash-and-burn agricultural practices, currently occurring in many developing countries
- Technological and industrial development
- Erosion
- Irrigation
- Mining for oil and minerals
- Aquifer depletion
- Forestry
- Pollution or contamination of resources.

Water covers 71% of the Earth's surface and is fundamental for all life-forms. Water plays an important role in the world economy as it functions as a solvent and facilitates industrial cooling and transportation. Approximately 70% of the fresh water used by humans goes to agriculture. Better management is needed to preserve this precious commodity. Rubbish dumping from ships, chemicals, and oil spills pollute our oceans and create havoc in marine life. Air pollution contaminates our water, and there are issues with floods, droughts, and irrigation causing high levels of salinity, which affect agriculture and biodiversity. The human body is around 70–80% water, and we need clean fresh water to refresh ourselves and keep our body and brain hydrated. See also Strategy 34 Environmental Health: Water.

Sunlight is essential to good health and wellbeing. It can cure depression, boost our immune system, and even lower blood pressure. We innately know it is good for us because we like the feel of it on our skin and it can help heal numerous skin disorders as well as improve sleep quality. While too much sunlight can result in skin cancers, we need sunlight on our bodies to provide the essential Vitamin D that doesn't come through the food chain to keep us healthy.

Health issues associated with lack of sunlight or Vitamin D are: weak bones, prostate cancer, seizures, depression, diabetes, and fibromyalgia. More recent research suggests that Vitamin D is also necessary to provide protection against more chronic diseases such as cancer, heart disease, infections, multiple sclerosis, and periodontal disease. Vitamin D receptors are present in virtually every tissue and cell in your body, so exposure to the sun is the best way to optimize your vitamin D level. Aim to have some sunlight on your bare skin every day.

A people–planet connection. The Institute of Heart Math has been looking into the energetic connection between people and the Earth's magnetic field environment. So far research has found scientific evidence of a relationship between human beings and the Earth's magnetic forces – why certain magnetic rhythms heighten our awareness and make us feel better, while other rhythms seem to trigger confusion, anxiety, and uncertainty. http://www.heartmath.org

Other Useful Sources Of Information

- Pollution Issues www.pollutionissues.com/Na-Ph/Pesticides.html
- Environment Protection Authority http://www.epa.vic.gov.au
- Synthetic polymers in marine environment http://www.ncbi.nlm.nih.gov/pubmed/18949831
- David Steinman and Samuel Epstein, *Safe Shoppers Bible*, Wiley John & Sons Inc., 1995
- Eve Hillary, *Children of a Toxic Harvest* https://proactivehealth.net.au
- Environmental Working Group www.ewg.org/
- Gene Ethics Network www.geneethics.org
- Geo-engineering http://www.geoengineeringwatch.org
- Proven Dietary Help & Research www.feingold.org/
- Skin Deep www.cosmeticsdatabase.com
- AUST. Conservation Foundation www.acfonline.org.au
- Dr. Mercola - www.mercola.com
- Dr. Carolyn Dean MD ND www.drcarolyndean.com/
- Wiser Earth - www.wiserearth.org
- Story of Stuff - www.storyofstuff.org/
- Heart Math Institute - https://www.heartmath.org
- www.mercuryfreenow.com/layperson/symptoms.html
- www.ecologycenter.org/factsheets/

See also:

- Environmental Health: Electromagnetic Fields
- Environmental Health: Personal Products
- Environmental Health: Toxic Consumables
- Environmental Health: Water
- Oral Health

Strategy 33
ENVIRONMENTAL HEALTH: PERSONAL PRODUCTS

CATEGORIES APPLIED

Addressing Anxiety
Addressing Depression
Awareness and Mindfulness
Environmental Health
Everyday Essentials
Improving Self-Esteem

Thousands of toxic killers have invaded our lives, through the air we breathe, the food we eat, and even what we use on our bodies. There are over 75,000 synthetic chemicals being used in everyday products. The nation's worst pollution is found inside our homes. Hazardous and toxic chemical concentrations 2–5 times higher than outdoors are found in the typical home.

Personal Bathroom Products

There are toxic chemicals used in products that are not only toxic to our own bodies but also feed back into Earth systems. In addition, a great deal of cruel and unnecessary animal testing is carried out by some makers of cosmetics and toiletries. A product that kills 50% of lab animals through ingestion or inhalation can still receive the federal regulatory designation "non-toxic" – even though it can have a negative impact on children's health. (http://www.your-health-and-wellness-guide.com/Childrens-Health-or-Toxic-Chemicals.html)

Products that include carcinogens, neurotoxins, and reproductive toxins are freely used in human products and often include labels like herbal, natural, and organic! Take care to choose sustainable products from companies that cause no harm to the animal kingdom and are guaranteed safe for you and your family. Understand that cosmetics are unregulated and commonly made from poorly tested chemicals. There are no safety tests or recall of harmful products. Environmental Working Group is a good resource for establishing safe products. See www.ewg.org

Of the 17,000 chemicals that appear in common household products, only 30% (5100) have been adequately tested for their negative effects on our health – *leaving 11,900 that nothing is known about.* Fewer than 10% have been tested for the effect on the nervous system, and nothing is known about the combined effects of these chemicals when mixed within our bodies. (World Resources Institute, *The 1994 Information Please Environmental Almanac*).

Our skin is the largest organ in the human body. A general guideline is that if you wouldn't eat it then don't put it on your body.

Antiperspirants block perspiration, and so prevent the natural release of toxins in the armpits and deposits in the lymph nodes. Choose a deodorant instead; though check to ensure it does not have toxic ingredients. An alternative is crystal deodorant sticks.

Aluminium, found in some deodorants, is used to block sweat ducts and can break through the skin. It is linked to a number of diseases and can increase risk of Alzheimer's disease.

Bar soap. Many are made from animal fat or lye (from sheep). This leaves dirt and grime in the bath, also clogs the pores of the skin. Avoid any bar soap or liquid soap with Triclocarban or Triclosan, which is an antibacterial component and can compromise your immune system. See also SLS below.

Baby wipes. Avoid chemicals of 2-bromo,-2- nitropropane- 1,3-diol or bronopol, found in baby wipes, conditioner, liquid soap/body wash. It is a known toxicant to human skin, the lungs, and the immune system, and an irritant to skin, eyes, and lungs.

Coal tar used in skin care products and anti-dandruff shampoo can cause potentially severe allergic reactions including rash, itchiness, breathing difficulties, swelling, dizziness, and sores.

Fluoride. There is huge debate about the use of fluoride in drinking water and its impact on health. While it is reported that the use of fluoride in water increases resistance to tooth decay, there are other reports that reveal how fluoride destroys your health by damaging your brain, immune and gastrointestinal systems, and bone and skeletal structures through fluorosis and other diseases. Poison warning signs must now be printed on toothpaste labels. Ensure that no children under 2 years old use fluoride toothpaste when it might be swallowed. It is recommended that you investigate to your own level of satisfaction. See Fluoride Action Network www.fluoridealert.org

Fragrances and perfumes are found in cleansers, cosmetics, laundry detergents, and air fresheners. Products with "Fragrance" on the label can contain hundreds of chemicals and trigger headaches, coughing, vomiting, skin discoloration, asthma, and allergic reactions. Avoid these products and choose fragrance-free products.

Glycerine, found in many products including skin care, is a drying agent; it drains moisture. Ensure that your skin care products have no glycerine.

Hair conditioners. Many contain tallow, an animal fat that is known to attract bacteria and pollutants to the hair. It is commonly used in candles and soaps.

Hair shampoo. Many have ingredients linked to cancer, developmental/reproductive toxicity, allergies and other concerns linked to neurotoxicity, organ system toxicity, irritation to skin, eyes, and lungs, enhanced skin absorption, and contamination concerns. Many contain ingredients such as propylene glycol, triethanolamine (TEA) and sodium lauryl sulphate (SLS).

Hair straighteners can cause cancer, allergy, skin and scalp irritation, hair damage, and hair loss.

Hair dyes. The dark permanent dyes are linked to cancer.

Insect repellent. Harsh chemicals can cause skin and eye irritation and could be linked to carcinogens. If used, ensure you wash any clothing before wearing it again.

Makeup. Only five major vats make all makeup products in the world. It is argued more expensive brands are no better than cheaper ones. Approximately 25 cents is the material cost in makeup. The remaining cost is in advertising and promotion. Beware also of "Play Make Up" for children, including lipsticks, nail polish, fragrances, and cosmetics; 884 of the chemicals available for use in cosmetics have been reported to the government as "toxic substances" (National Institute of Occupational Safety and Health U.S.A). A safety guide to cosmetics and personal care products is available from researchers at the Environmental Working Group http://www.cosmeticsdatabase.com/

Mercury is found in some fish, thermometers, and fluorescent light tubes and amalgam dental fillings. Mercury can cause brain and nervous system damage. It is linked with Alzheimer's, heart disease, Parkinson's disease, congenital abnormalities in pregnant women, autism, and multiple sclerosis. Mercury vapors in teeth are released with any kind of stimulation such as brushing teeth, chewing, teeth grinding, or hot fluids.

The remedy is to change to porcelain or composite fillings only with an astute holistic dentist who takes all necessary precautions. Take care to educate yourself prior to any dental work about this highly toxic substance. Also www.IAOMT.org

Mineral oil is a petroleum by-product. It clogs and dehydrates skin, can cause skin break-outs, and may often be a carrier of carcinogenic impurities. It is common in baby wipes.

Propylene glycol is used in soaps, cosmetics, and many household cleaning items, flavorings, drugs, and cosmetics, as well as in a compound used to make antifreeze and de-icing solutions for cars, airplanes, and boats. It is also a major ingredient in automatic brake fluid, antifreeze, floor wax, paint varnish, and liquid laundry detergent. Over exposure to PG can cause liver abnormalities and kidney damage. It is also linked to cancer, developmental/reproductive toxicity, allergies/immunotoxicity, and irritation to skin, eyes, or lungs.

SLS (sodium lauryl sulphate) is an artificial detergent chemical derived from coconut oil. It is common in most cleansers and moisturizers such as shampoos, conditioners, skin care products, toothpaste, etc. It creates bubbles/foam, and is used as an industrial degreaser. It is employed in labs and medical facilities as a standard skin irritant that scientists use to test healing agents. It is a known mutagen, which means it damages the genetic information in cells of the body. The membranes of the cells in a poisoned organ begin to degenerate, and cause the mutation of newly generated cells. SLS is absorbed through the skin and is retained in the brain, heart, and liver and damages the eyes.

Sunscreen. There are some ingredients that may be potentially carcinogenic or have other health risks. With such a common product do your research well.

Studies have shown that Vitamin D, gained from exposure to sunlight, has preventative benefits for many diseases, including heart disease, diabetes, and breast cancer.

Skin lighteners can cause skin irritation and damage.

Talcum powder has an inhalation risk. The use of talcum powder around the genitals is linked to ovarian cancer for women (*The West Australian*, September 29, 2008). *Cancer Epidemiology Biomarkers & Prevention*, September 1, 2008, 17, 2436–44.)

Toothpaste. Read labels on boxes (not on tubes), which tell us that most contain SLS (see above). Also avoid toothpaste with Triclosan. Under the tongue is the most absorptive area of body, hence use of therapeutic homeopathics and essences used in this manner. See also Fluoride above.

Become aware of the products you use on your body and the likely impact on your health and in turn the likely impact of the health of this planet that supports you.

Yes, our world is a minefield of toxicity. The Environmental Working Group provides the resources to look up a product or ingredient using a rating system and find safer alternatives: www.ewg.org

USEFUL SOURCES

www.goodguide.com
www.eh.org.au
www.ewg.org
www.drrapp.com *Dr. Doris Rapp Environmental medical specialist "Is This Your Child's World.*
www.mercola.com/Downloads/bonus/truth-about-water-fluoridation/default.aspx?gclid=CPGN-9vC858CFSAkagodH1c6YA
www.cosmeticsdatabase.com
www.IAOMT.org

See also:

- Environmental Health: Electromagnetic Fields
- Environmental Health: General
- Environmental Health: Consumables
- Environmental Health: Water
- Oral Health

Strategy 34
ENVIRONMENTAL HEALTH: WATER

CATEGORIES APPLIED

Addressing Addictions
Addressing Anxiety
Addressing Depression
Awareness and Mindfulness
Career and Goals
Environmental Health
Everyday Essentials
Exercise for Living
Improving Self-Esteem
Nutrition for Life

Water is life. Every system in your body depends on water. The average adult human body is 60–80% water, but the number of molecules in your body actually consists of over 99% water molecules. Drinking plenty of fresh water each day is fundamental for good health. Be aware that the body has no stored water to draw upon if you become dehydrated.

If you do become dehydrated, water will clear any toxic deposits that form in the kidneys, liver, joints, brain, and skin. Insufficient water or dehydration can result in chronic pains in joints and muscles, lower back pain, headaches, constipation, and fatigue. So it is important to drink regularly throughout each day.

Drinking water is needed to help the cells in the body to hydrate. It is needed for the production of all hormones made by the brain, including melatonin, which assists sleep, and for the efficient manufacture of all neurotransmitters, including serotonin. Sodium helps to regulate the amount of fluid in the body. Maximum recommended is one teaspoon a day of natural sea salt.

Drinking water

- Can cure headaches due to dehydration and helps to reduce stress, anxiety, and depression.
- Helps your skin by clearing impurities and giving your skin a healthy glow. It can help you to look younger.
- Helps to flush toxins and waste products from the body.
- Leads to better cell repair and regeneration.
- Can greatly assist weight loss by replacing calorie-loaded drinks and act as a suppressant to appetite.
- Greatly increases the efficiency of the immune system and reduces health risks.

- Provides the electrical energy and power for all brain functions and thinking so you also work better.
- Assists to integrate mind and body functions.
- Helps reduce and reverse addictive urges, including alcohol, caffeine and some drugs.

How Much Water Should I Drink?

Exercise requires you have additional water, preferably both before and after exercise to keep you hydrated. Exercise without water can hamper your athletic activities.

The average urine output for adults is 1.5 liters a day. You also lose water through sweating, exhaling, and bowel movements, with other factors as indicated below contributing to the overall picture. Your food contributes to around 20% of your total water intake.

Generally speaking, there are two guidelines to determine the amount of water your body needs each day. This refers to the common sources of tap water or tank water (not the higher-vibrational water referred to at the bottom of this page).

1. The replacement method, which effectively suggests around 2 liters
2. The guideline, which recommends drinking half your body weight in ounces of water each day or 1–2 liters.

Influencing factors on your water intake include:

- The more exercise you do the more water is required.
- Hot or humid weather can make you sweat and requires additional intake of fluid.
- Indoor heating can cause our skin to lose moisture, resulting in conditions like dry mouth.
- High altitudes can result in loss of fluid reserves due to increased urination and more rapid breathing.
- Health conditions such as vomiting, diarrhoea, or fever, all drain fluids, so more water is needed.
- Pregnant or lactating women require additional fluids to stay hydrated.

Thirst can be influenced by hot weather, health conditions like diabetes, high salt foods, or even a heavy meal.

TIPS

Drink water regularly throughout your day – don't wait till you are thirsty.

1-2 cups of warm water and lemon juice first thing in the morning and half an hour before breakfast is a great start to your day. Drunk on an empty stomach, it is great for the digestive system and assists elimination of waste products.

Research by Dr. Masaru Emoto on water has found that words and music have a dramatic impact on the water due to the vibration it creates. He found that the words "love and gratitude" transformed water into the most beautiful crystalline form. See the contrast created by the effect of the words "You make me sick" images shown in Strategy 57 Gratitude.

**Before drinking, place your glass, jug,
or bottle of water on a coaster
with the words "love and gratitude."
This will significantly increase
the vibration of the water.**

There is an increasing amount of research and experimentation, which reflect that thought, words, sound, events, and energy can be imprinted into water and as a result dramatically change the quality or vibration of water due to water's ability to retain memory. This is proving to have a huge impact on health and wellbeing to all who consume it, including the Earth.

Water carries an electrical current. To charge your water before drinking, pour water from an elevated vessel to another through the air to electrify it. Stagnant water has no electricity. It lacks life force.

There are all kinds of water available today including structured water, hexagonal water, crystal water, living water, miracle water, oxygenated water, regal water, and more. You are encouraged to explore to your own level of satisfaction.

See also:

- Environmental Health: Consumables
- Exercise for Living
- Nutrition Keys

Strategy 35
EXERCISE FOR LIVING

CATEGORIES APPLIED

Addressing Addictions
Addressing Anxiety
Addressing Depression
Awareness and Mindfulness
Career and Goals
Exercise for Living
Improving Self-Esteem
Nutrition for Life
Quick Stress Busters

There is much research around these days proving the unquestionable benefits of exercise for good health, emotional wellbeing, longevity, and the prevention of disease. Regular exercise can elevate your mood; it can improve your energy levels, your sex life, and your general quality of life. It can have an immediate and long-term benefit.

Although exercise is considered beneficial and essential for your everyday health care, there can also be personal reasons for exercising. It may be to rehabilitate after an injury, to lose weight, to improve your fitness, to improve flexibility, for social reasons, to build your confidence, or just to feel good.

If you don't take time to exercise,
sooner or later you better make time to be sick!

Seize daily opportunities to exercise:

- Before you get out of bed do a few stretches or spinal twists
- Use the stairs in place of an elevator
- Walk or cycle instead of taking the car on short trips
- Regularly stand and stretch
- Walk the kids to school

There are an enormous amount of exercise options and they have different outcomes. Basically your body needs aerobic activity, stretching, and strengthening exercise for overall health benefits.

1. 30–60 minutes of **aerobic activity** every day. This type of exercise increases your breath rate by increasing the body's need for oxygen. It will make you feel a little out of breath. Possible examples are:
    - jogging

- brisk walking
- cycling
- aerobics classes
- swimming
- dancing
- team sports.

If you are stressed it's best to avoid the competitive kind of sports (squash, tennis etc.), which can elevate your stress levels instead of having the opposite relaxing effect.

2. Your body needs some type of **stretching** activity.
   Stretching helps your body to be flexible – you will feel a bit of tension in the muscles being stretched. Examples of this are Tai Chi, Pilates or Yoga.

3. **Strength training** improves your muscular strength and tone and can totally alter the appearance of your body. It also helps to offset the muscle mass reduction that occurs with the aging process and lack of exercise. (Recommended twice a week.)

   Weight training, resistance training, and isometric training are all different forms of strength training that can improve muscle strength, help to lose weight, protect against injury, and improve bone density.

Try to make exercise fun so that you really look forward to it.

- Listen to your favorite music or talk while exercising.
- Join a class with a friend, work colleague, or neighbor
- Play ball with children, family, or friends
- Take the dog for a brisk walk.
- Try jumping on a rebounder, gym ball, or trampoline.
- Play skip rope on your own or with others.

If you are new to regular exercise it is best to start gradually and slowly build up. As a general guide, you should be able to hold a conversation while exercising. If you have any pain or medical conditions it is best to consult your doctor.

TIP Have 2–3 glasses of water first thing in the morning before breakfast and then go for a 20-minute walk. This will result in a need to use your bowels, which is detoxifying to your body.

See also

- Environmental Health: Water
- Nutrition Keys

Strategy 36
FEELING AGITATED

CATEGORIES APPLIED

Addressing Addictions
Addressing Anxiety
Addressing Depression
Awareness and Mindfulness
Career and Goals
Communications and Relationships
Environmental Health
Everyday Essentials
Exercise for Life
Improving Self-Esteem
Quick Stress Busters

When you are feeling agitated it is your body trying to communicate to you that something needs your attention. Identifying the source can be extremely helpful so that you can address it in the most effective manner by treating the cause rather than symptoms.

Sources Of Agitation

- Something you have consumed, such as coffee or a food source that disagrees with you or a digestive problem which has built up over time
- Nutritional deficiency, such as magnesium, iron, or Vitamin B6
- Medication
- Drug withdrawal
- Onset of a health issue
- Hormonal imbalance
- Inadequate sleep/rest
- A product you have put on or in your body
- Trying to sort out a problem
- Your own negative self-talk
- A peak stressor such as family sickness, breakup, moving house, job change.
- An emotional trigger that is bringing an old wound to the surface
- Negative thought-forms directed to you from another person or persons
- Fearful thought-forms from the collective consciousness that become more prevalent with any widespread distressing news like floods, fire, shootings, political unrest.
- A multitude of unseen environmental energies such as electromagnetic radiation, air pollutants, some kind of geopathic stress, negative unseen energies or chaotic weather.

Really endeavor to tune in to identify what is the source of this inner unrest or irritability. Taking some time for consideration or a mini-meditation; a quiet mind can provide valuable insight and therefore an effective resolution. While this reflection may not always reveal the desired clarity, it is an excellent process to build your skills of greater awareness. Muscle testing and dowsing can also be a helpful resource.

If you are able to recognize the source of your agitation, then it is easy to select an appropriate process. Simply doing Strategy 11, Body Breath Awareness may bring greater awareness and shift the agitation.

If, for example, you can see that you have been feeding yourself a lot of negative self-talk, then consider the Strategies Thought: Managing the Inner Critic (94) or Thought Power and Control (95). Gratitude (57), Affirmations (3), or Kindness to Self (66) might also be an appropriate option or addition to the thought strategies.

If your body is feeling agitated and you sense it's not related to any "mind story," then perhaps explore external sources such as any oral substance you have taken that may be causing an imbalance or something you are deficient in. A 30-minute footbath with half a packet of Epsom salts may reveal, by the calming effect, that you are lacking in magnesium, and so you can explore appropriate avenues for taking this supplement regularly to build up any deficiency. Clearing (16) may be the perfect Strategy to clean away negativity that is contaminating your energy field.

In a situation where someone has pushed an emotional trigger for you, exploring Projection (78), Deep Release Breathing (27), Forgiveness Process (53), Boundaries (12), or one of the Communication strategies may resolve the issue. Alternately, it might be Seek to Understand (87), Shadow Play (88), Release the Need to Be Right (84), or Release Resistance (83).

As you explore the range of health and empowerment options, just trust your intuition as to what feels most appropriate. One of the processes might be all that is required to restore a sense of harmony, or there may be two or more depending on your situation. It may be helpful to review Category 2, *Addressing Anxiety*, for a broader perspective.

Be alert to the tricks of the unaware mind that may prompt you to towards *distracting behaviors* as a coping means: watching television, comfort eating, turning to drugs or alcohol, working to be busy, or any number of other activities that only serve to suppress anxiety. The repetition of distracting behaviors leads to addictions.

Fundamental to emotional wellbeing is always looking after your physical health with appropriate nutrition, exercise, and restful sleep. Some mindfulness exercises or meditation are lifelong skills that will also enhance wellbeing. It may also be wise for you to take some kind of supplement like tissue salts, essences, herbs, minerals, or vitamins to support you through a period of Feeling Agitated (36).

Because of the plethora of seen and unseen energies impacting on us all the time, Strategies 30–33 on Environmental Health are worth exploring, and Clearing (16) is arguably one of the most important daily practices. It can make a profound difference to how you feel, particularly as you build your confidence with the process. Connect with Nature (22) and Grounding/Earthing (58) are most likely to bring about positive effects within 20–30 minutes. It is the nurturing and healing properties that emanate from the Earth that are able to restore a sense of balance and rhythm in our bodies, allowing us to absorb the negative electrons up through the soles of our feet.

Remember this Strategy if your child is hyperactive or agitated. Remove their shoes and take them outside to run around on the Earth for around 30 minutes to bring about a calming balancing effect.

See also:

- Allow Feelings
- Awareness of Awareness
- Clearing
- Connect with Nature
- Deep Release Breathing
- Feeling Fear
- Grounding/Earthing
- Thought Power and Control
- Thought Management: The Inner Critic

Strategy 37
FEELING ANGER

CATEGORIES APPLIED

Addressing Addictions
Addressing Anxiety
Addressing Depression
Awareness and Mindfulness
Career and Goals
Communications and Relationships
Improving Self-Esteem
Quick Stress Busters

There are numerous health conditions that have anger and irritability as a side effect, and even medication may be a contributing factor. This information is primarily to address the toxic effects of stored anger that is held in your heart and, in fact, in the cells of your body.

There is a lot of power behind anger and it is very toxic to the human body. Anger can turn into bitterness, resentment, and depression. It can lead to revenge and can be very dangerous and volatile. Stored or suppressed anger becomes uncontrolled anger, and acted out without consciousness it is very destructive. It can destroy relationships, cost you your job, cause you physical pain, ill health, and even your life. Holding on to anger also blocks growth.

Anger can arise from all sorts of circumstances depending on how you perceive the situation. It may be triggered by feelings of betrayal or loss, such as a lost business transaction or a job you missed out on, by the death of someone close, or physical or emotional abuse, or just not getting what you want. There is frustration and that can lead to rage and hatred.

Being in a challenging relationship, financial or job stress can all play a role. Anger can also be accompanied with a strong desire to be "right" – making the other "wrong." Sometimes there can be an emotional investment in wanting to hang on to this state of being, perhaps because you perceive it as validating you in some way, or maybe it serves some other function that you find satisfying.

A very important factor in addressing anger is to accept responsibility for it, and not see yourself as a victim and blame others for the cause of your anger. Accepting responsibility does not suggest that you are to blame for the situation. It simply means that the emotion is yours and you are the only one who can resolve your own feelings. Your feelings are your responsibility.

Although it is most often considered negative, anger is nevertheless a real and valid emotion. It is as real as any other emotion like jealousy, grief, compassion, or love. If anger is what you feel – so be it. Owning your feelings is essential for being able to address them in a constructive way that enables you to transmute it.

In its positive aspect, when used with consciousness, anger can be useful as a source of empowerment and to bring about change. It has been behind many great social or environmental changes within our world where there has been inequality, victimization, injustice, or cruelty to creatures or destruction of the environment.

Drawing upon the inner resource of power and anger may be important if you are about to be attacked while walking down the street. It might be precisely what you need to get you motivated to make some positive change if someone crosses boundaries that were weak or nonexistent beforehand.

Anger is a step up for a depressed person who feels powerless. It requires a lot of energy and effort to keep anger bottled up and doing so can lead to depression and a sense of powerlessness. Harboring anger will eventually manifest in illness and disease, literally festering or eating away at the physical body. Of course it is often not appropriate to express anger openly, like yelling at your boss, or venting your angry emotions recklessly at anyone in your surroundings, but it is important to release it from the body.

The widespread denominator in any of the causes of anger is
feeling you cannot control the situation.

Another common element is unconscious feelings of anger towards self. It is often easier to project it out onto someone else rather than accept that you feel anger towards yourself, perhaps for allowing the situation to occur. Such an example might be feeling anger that you have allowed someone to have control over you in some way. While the anger might be outwardly directed to that person, underneath there can be anger towards yourself for allowing this to happen and not standing up for yourself. Be aware also that if you are critical of your own feelings of anger, you may limit the positive power that it offers to create change.

Ways To Address Anger

1. Accept full responsibility for your feelings. Avoid blaming others, which will render you powerless and unable to move beyond the angry state.

2. Consider forgiveness as a solution. Hurt and resentment holds energy stuck within your body. When you forgive you free up that energy and regain your personal power. See Strategy 53 Forgiveness.

3. Identify your own beliefs about anger. If you hold a lot of judgment about anger being negative and inappropriate you will suppress it. Maybe beliefs like "Spiritual people aren't angry; loving caring people don't express anger; anger is too scary to feel." Beliefs like this suppress anger and inhibit its transmutation. Just accept that you feel anger and that it is okay and then do what you can to change it. Acceptance must come before you can resolve it.

4. Sometimes, having someone hear your story and validate your experience may be all you need to enable you to move on. Ensure your listener is someone who can really hear your pain and empathize without reinforcing a sense of victimhood. Consider a professional counsellor.

5. Be aware of your self-talk since this will reveal a lot about how you perceive the situation and whether you are willing to move on. When listening to those inner voices, ask yourself often, "If I were to listen to you, where would that lead me?"

6. Observe any attachment you may have to being right, or maybe wanting to hang on to the story. Ask yourself "How is it serving me?" Awareness of your motives will lead to understanding and the ability to move on.

7. Ensure you set clear boundaries. Get clear in your own mind what is acceptable and unacceptable to you. Where appropriate, state those boundaries to inform others. This shows mutual respect. See Strategy 12 Boundaries.

8. Where there is conflict, do your best to resolve it and be open and *willing to embrace a new understanding*. Accept that this is your perspective and there are probably others who feel equally strong about the situation. Remember, it is not so much the event that is the trigger for your anger as it is your perception of the event. See Strategy 21 Conflict Resolution.

9. Be really conscious of your words and actions to ensure no harm is done to another or regret that may come later.

10. Release the stored anger by thrashing your body about in a safe environment like in the ocean, a pool, or on your own bed. See Strategy 88 Shadow Play.

11. Clear your energy field to ensure you are not being contaminated by undesirable energies, which can be the projection of others. See Strategy 16 Clearing.

Do not hesitate to seek professional help if you have any concerns.

See also:

- Awareness of Awareness
- Boundaries
- Clearing
- Conflict Resolution
- Do No Harm
- Forgiveness Process
- Judgment Effect
- Projection
- Release the Need to be Right
- Seek to Understand
- Shadow Play
- Thought Power and Control
- Toning

Strategy 38
FEELING CHALLENGED

CATEGORIES APPLIED

Addressing Addictions
Addressing Anxiety
Addressing Depression
Awareness and Mindfulness
Career and Goals
Communications and Relationships
Improving Self-Esteem

Feeling challenged in this context refers to those times when there is an expectation about doing something new or doing something differently. It might be part of your job responsibilities – a direction that comes from outside of your chosen preferences. Perhaps you've been asked to learn some new technology or give a presentation for the first time.

Maybe it's more a self-imposed challenge where you want to lose weight and are making some changes to your diet and exercise regime and struggling to get away from the TV and go for a walk. It really matters little what the circumstances are – *it's how you perceive it that matters.*

Striving to achieve your goals is likely to create feelings of discomfort because the very nature of going for your goals will take you out of your comfort zone.

Interestingly, many people give up when they come up against obstacles or realize they have to do something that is totally new to them and not previously experienced. They react to the subconscious inner voices, some of which may be telling you, "you're not good enough," or "it's too hard," or "it will be stressful," or "it's not worth it because your relationships will change," or "you will have less time for other things," and so on.

Tips To Address The Challenge

Being aware of your inner voices is critical to you moving through the challenge. Ask yourself "If I were to listen to you where would that lead me?"

Being adaptable and unattached to what is familiar_will help to free you up. This is simply an attitude shift, but it's easier to move when you understand the irrational thought structures so often behind the feelings of challenge.

Everything is in a constant state of change. You just need to look at Nature and the natural laws of evolution to understand this law that affects all beings.

Find something to be grateful for about the situation to keep you in the higher vibrations and connected to your inner guidance. It is an opportunity to learn something new and grow, and maybe express your creativity.

It's interesting how common it is to look for something familiar as a kind of reassurance. This is a ploy of an unaware mind. Keep affirming to yourself that "anything new will naturally be unfamiliar and it's okay."

Every time you feel inspired to do something and then give up on it, your self-esteem will be eroded. Every time you feel challenged and move beyond, it adds to your self-esteem. Such is the experience of personal growth and high achievers.

See also:

- Accept Yourself
- Ask for Help
- Awareness of Awareness
- Beliefs Challenge
- Clearing
- Change Challenge
- Feeling Agitated
- Feeling Anger
- Feeling Disempowered
- Feeling Fear
- Feeling Grief
- Feeling Guilt or Shame
- Feeling Jealousy
- Feeling Lonely or Alone
- Feeling Rejected or Hurt
- Feeling Scattered: Unbalanced
- Feeling Stuck
- Feeling Uncertain or Fearful of the Unknown
- Feeling Unloved or Unlovable
- Feeling Victimized
- Feeling Worried
- Grounding/Earthing
- Thought: Managing the Inner Critic
- Thought Power and Control

Strategy 39
FEELING DISEMPOWERED

CATEGORIES APPLIED

Addressing Addictions
Addressing Anxiety
Addressing Depression
Awareness and Mindfulness
Career and Goals
Communications and Relationships
Improving Self-Esteem

As babies and children we learn to communicate our needs through our bodies, voices, and facial expression. It can be challenging as a child to get our needs met, and to some degree all children experience disempowerment. These feelings can be carried through into our adult years, and be triggered by our parents or our own children, or numerous other relationships or situations. It is not uncommon for women to feel disempowered in this world. Disempowerment often reflects a feeling of being out of control or overpowered by another and can result in anger and depression.

Disempowerment can arise anywhere: in families, sporting and community groups, education, social groups, health care, and the workplace. This is often associated with feelings of being excluded, not listened to or consulted, overlooked, deprived, devalued, worthless, or discriminated against.

To overcome these feelings will require some action on your part.

1. First, accept responsibility for your life and realize that you are in charge of your own happiness. Do not be reliant on the words or actions of another.

2. Recognize there really is a choice available to you, even if you don't like the options. Understanding this immediately softens the feelings of disempowerment.

3. Then, get clear on what it is you are wanting. Make sure you frame it in the positive as what you *do* want and not what you *don't* want. When you identify, vocalize, and embody what you want, it empowers you and elevates your feeling state. Focusing on what you don't want feeds the undesired negative aspect through the Law of Attraction and leaves you feeling down.

4. Be prepared for change. Remember that you can't change anyone else, only yourself. Hold the intention that you are willing to make changes and regularly do some deep breathing while feeling your way into courage. Taking these forward steps will also elevate your self-esteem.

5. Manage your mind and take care not to run a negative story around the disempowerment, as this too will feed the undesired negative aspect. See Strategy 95 Thought Power and Control for more information.

6. It's important to honor your truth, which will build your self-esteem, and this will likely take courage. It may at times mean that you need to have discussions with others or address some kind of obstacle that is before you. Rehearse it in your mind beforehand so that you are planting the seeds for change.

7. Find something to be grateful for to elevate your mood and keep you connected to your heart. In this way you can follow the lead of your higher guidance, which will always be striving to move your forwards.

8. Assess if you need to establish some strong boundaries such as saying "no" and being willing to stand firm on this.

Whatever the source of your feelings of disempowerment, strive to remedy this situation with a sense of balance, cooperation, and harmony.

See also:

- Asking for Help
- Awareness of Awareness
- Boundaries
- Clearing
- Competition versus Cooperation
- Control versus Preferences
- Major Life Influencers
- Seek to Understand

Strategy 40
FEELING FEAR

CATEGORIES APPLIED

Addressing Addictions
Addressing Anxiety
Addressing Depression
Awareness and Mindfulness
Career and Goals
Communications and Relationships
Everyday Essentials
Improving Self-Esteem
Quick Stress Busters

Fear is what we feel when we sense that we are threatened in some way. It can be real or imagined. It is an unconscious response of the brain and causes a flight-or-fight response which activates the body's sympathetic and parasympathetic nervous systems. This is an inbuilt primitive reaction, which all animals possess as well. It is our survival instinct, which prepares the body by sending a surge of energy that makes us primed to be able to fight and protect ourselves or flee from any danger.

This surge of energy is meant for short periods of release only and cannot be sustained without ill effects. Fear affects our health, diminishing our sense of wellness and even safety, and creates pressure on our heart and other bodily functions. Fear inhibits our ability to think clearly, communicate effectively, access our intuition, or make optimal decisions. It is the most universal and most paralyzing of all our emotions.

Types Of Fear

There are myriad everyday fears, also commonly referred to as anxieties. For some it may be as a result of an emotional trigger where someone has activated an old wound that has now surfaced. It can be worrying about someone, health issues, financial concerns, doing something for the first time, any kind of change, perpetual negative thoughts about self that seem to create a surrounding cocoon of fear and doubt and an endless array of different scenarios.

Eckhart Tolle says of fear:

> **The psychological condition of fear is divorced from any concrete and true immediate danger. It comes in many forms: unease, worry, anxiety, nervousness, tension, dread, trepidation, phobia and so on. This kind of psychological fear is always of something that might happen, not of something that is happening**

now. You are in the here and now whilst your mind is in the future. This creates an anxiety gap.

Some really common fears are of public speaking, heights or deep water, flying, sickness, loneliness, and financial problems. More persistent and intense fears of an object or a situation are called phobias. Phobias may not be based on any kind of rationality, and people will go to great lengths to avoid the object of a phobia, which can be very disruptive to their lifestyle.

Then there are fears tucked beneath our greatest desires, like longing to be successful but fearful of actually being successful. The same could apply to financial abundance or losing weight. Without awareness of these fears you will constantly sabotage your goals.

Fear has an extremely debilitating impact on you and your health and wellbeing. It is often said that FEAR is an acronym for False Energy Appearing Real. This is because the illusory mind and our conditioning play such a big role in determining how we feel in each moment.

The mind does not know the difference between what is real and what is imagined.

The mind (mental body) thinks and the feeling body (emotional body) responds accordingly.

Thought +Feeling = Emotion

It is the feeling of emotional pain or fear that is a very clear sign that something needs to be addressed. Whenever that imbalance is there, grabbing our attention, we can recognize it as stuck energy in our multidimensional body.

Your childhood conditioning will influence any stuck energy. It affects who you are today and how you process everything that happens in your life. Conditioning is something all humans experience as they grow up, and it will affect every relationship we ever have, how we feel about ourselves, the world in which we live in, and every decision we make.

Any unresolved wounding will remain in our energy field and can be triggered spontaneously through some similarity of the emotional pain. It awakens what is stored in the subconscious mind.

It is the typical iceberg effect. The conscious mind represents the tip of the iceberg and what is seen above the water line or in awareness, and the subconscious represents what lies beneath the water, often unseen and unknown but the huge foundation of all that is above it – that is, until we begin the spiritual journey into greater awareness.

Any trauma that you were unable to process effectively will remain stored in the body's energy field and can slip into the subconscious or unconscious mind with an acute stress response activated by some similar circumstance. A familiar smell, like the original one linked to the fear, can immediately activate the same response. Smell is the only sense that bypasses the thinking mind; it is triggered by the amygdala in the brain, which means that as soon as you experience the same smell, your body makes an immediate energy response without involving the thinking mind.

Becoming aware of the feeling body and managing the mind is the powerful combination we have to guide us through our human life. When we are feeling good and happy there is kind of inner knowing, a "rightness" to it: nothing needs to be fixed, all is well in our world, and our thoughts will be positive.

Clarifying Your Fear

The more specific you can be about the cause of your fear the more appropriate can be your strategy to address it. Some self-reflection will assist this process. Being an astute observer of the mind in all situations is always beneficial and will lead to greater consciousness. Deepening your understanding enables energy to shift. It is the precursor to change.

Sometimes fear can seem all-consuming, as though it is who you are. Just moving your perspective to realizing that it is *something in you* that is feeling fearful creates a shift in intensity. You see that it is not the whole of you but a part within that wants your attention. This attitude assists you to build self-compassion and helps to free up any resistance that will otherwise hold the emotional pain or fear stuck.

The list below sets out what are arguably the most common reasons for fear. All stem from our conditioning, all are interlinked, yet separating them out into these headings can make them more manageable; it can provide greater empowerment and insight on where to apply your focus for greater consciousness and self-healing.

Some remedies are offered beneath each of the following topics, and the relevant Strategies are listed at the end of the document.

1. Feeling emotionally triggered
2. Lack of self-love

3. Inner critic
4. Negative thinking
5. Worry
6. Identifying with another's pain
7. Soul fragments
8. Environmental energies
9. Other people's energies
10. Collective fears
11. Trauma.

1. Feeling emotionally triggered. This feeling state will generally arise from someone you know pushing your buttons, and it will very often be associated with projection. Projection is when you can see in another what you cannot see or own about yourself. This is a conditioned response associated with your subconscious or unconscious programming and is present as a reaction to the trigger.

A younger part of you (typically a child part) is reacting to something you have experienced previously which was, from your perspective, never resolved or healed. It has been tucked away in your unconscious or subconscious, and now your cellular memory through your body-mind has been awakened by this current experience and has exposed your wound. It will reflect a parallel or similar feeling that the child part of you was unable to process effectively at the time. There may or may not be conscious memory about the particular event.

Your response could be any number of different emotions: feeling agitated, angry, fearful, criticized, threatened, or feelings of loss or grief, or just feeling bad. Your emotional body is clearly stating that this does not feel good.

The interaction with the other person has found that button and exposed your wound. The painful feeling has arisen and without any degree of consciousness you will project your criticism onto the other person, which means that *you can't heal.*

An emotional trigger can also arise from a strong judgment about that person's behavior, which is totally opposed to yours. It shows an attachment to a belief about what is right and what is wrong. All attachments will cause pain.

> *Remedy:* Your attitude is crucial here. First and foremost, accept responsibility for your own feelings and recognize this as an opportunity for your own healing which will

require both honesty and courage. Be aware that that person's behavior makes sense to them. Ask yourself "Is this part of my own behavior?" And/or "Am I judging them for something that is opposed to my beliefs?" Understand that right or wrong is merely a personal opinion. See Strategy 78 Projection for more information.

2. Lack of self-love arises from our personal perception about self: how worthy or valuable we think we are as a human being. The very core of all beings is deeply loving, yet our *perceptions*, based on our experiences, are often filled with judgment, insecurity, fear, doubt, feeling unloved, devalued, rejected, and separate. When these negative thought-forms are repeated enough they become beliefs, which then play out as fears and erode our self-esteem and self-worth.

Remedy: Become very conscious of your thinking, eliminating any negative thought-patterns. Challenge all your beliefs. Replace the negative thoughts with positive, loving ones. Affirmations can be a great help, as is the practice of always reaching for a better feeling or thought. Do things for yourself that show love and respect for you – and make sure you don't leave that responsibility to others. Love the perceived unlovable within you. View your life as a series of learning experiences, not as mistakes.

As we process our wounding, it is the same as releasing darkness and bringing light and love into our energy field. So our resonance, how our multidimensional being vibrates, becomes finer or higher. Our heart chakra becomes expanded and we develop a deepening sense of love and compassion for self and all others. Our sensitivity increases and we can feel the connectedness and oneness with all life.

3. The inner critic is a self-created inner voice that you come to believe. Everybody has one. When you observe the voice of the inner critic you will find that it is more critical of you than any other person is of you.

Remedy: Self-observation and monitoring of your mind is crucial to controlling the inner critic. Acknowledge it by singing "Happy Birthday" to it as a way to belittle the inner critic. Avoiding or criticizing it is unhelpful. See Strategy 94 Thought: Managing the Inner Critic.

4. Negative thinking is just a habit that can be changed. It develops through lack of awareness about the way you think and can be contaminated by other negative influences in your energy field. If you do not monitor your mind and allow yourself to dwell on negative thoughts and stories it will take you down a negative spiral within minutes, leaving you feeling anxious and fearful. Fortunately we all have free will, and the more positive thoughts you have, the more positive will be your feelings. It is a matter of training your brain, aiming for a 5 to 1 positivity ratio.

> *Remedy:* Monitor your mind and ensure you choose positive, loving thoughts. Ensure you clean your energy field regularly to avoid contamination by others. Four of the Strategies will help: 10 Beliefs Challenge, 16 Clearing, 94 Thought: Managing the Inner Critic and 95 Thought Power and Control.

5. Worry. Worry is a negative emotion that can seriously activate fear. It is effectively putting your creative energy into something *you don't want to happen*! It might be worry about health issues, finances, a loved one's safety, your job, or any number of things – even the state of the world.

> *Remedy:* Use your creative mind instead to put your thinking into the desired outcome. Think, sense, and see things happening just the way you want. Imagine your loved ones safe, surrounded in light, in vibrant good health, and the world working in perfect harmony. Fantasize about the contrast of your concern and how wonderful it would be for everything to be working beautifully. See Strategy 52 Feeling Worried.

6. Identifying with another's pain. Most often it is our own painful experiences that help us to empathize with another who is in distress; it is as though we really understand what that person is going through. If we have managed to heal our own trauma, we will have genuine empathy and compassion, and this may be a great support to the other person. However, if we have not managed to heal our own wounds, our emotions are more likely to be raw and unbalanced. Any efforts to help another may not actually prove beneficial.

> *Remedy:* When the pain of another triggers you, see it as a reminder and an opportunity to heal your own wounds and draw upon any of the self-help processes. General ones like Strategy 27, Deep Release Breathing, or the more specific range of Feeling Strategies from 36 to 52. If your own pain is healed you will be more able to be supportive and act with compassion and consciousness.

7. Soul fragments. "Soul" means different things to different people. In this context, it refers to those parts of consciousness that carry through from previous lives. It can be that irrational kind of fear that you cannot link to any prior experience. As an example, if you are fearful of being in a large boat out at sea in deep water, it may be that there was trauma or death associated with the ocean in a previous incarnation.

> *Remedy:* While these feelings are obviously older and deep within, all can be healed in the "now moment." Various healing processes can be utilized, some of which are shown throughout this program. If there is great trauma, an energy healer may be helpful.

8. Environmental energies. There are also a multitude of environmental energies that could affect our level of anxiety. Some we can manage and others we cannot. Things like astrological energies, geopathic stress, solar flares, and stormy weather with lightning and strong winds may be beyond our control, but we still have the potential to manage our mind's response.

> *Remedy:* Attempt to isolate the source and address it accordingly. Clean your energy field (Strategy 16 Clearing). Keep your mind in presence, focus on Gratitude Strategy 57 to assist your feeling state, and manage your mind. See Strategy 95 Thought Power and Control.

9. Other people's energies. There are times when you may feel anxious, without having any idea about what might be the cause. All we know is that our body is experiencing a stress response. It is not uncommon for loved ones or other relationships to pick up on each other and wear their negativity. This arises when we have not maintained good boundaries and kept our energy field clear, which then results in being vulnerable to whatever they are feeling: if they are feeling good, we feel good and if they are feeling bad, we feel bad.

We can be affected by anyone who might project some kind of verbal attack upon us, either directly or indirectly. The energetic impact can be felt irrespective of geographical distance. Of course the same applies for any negative thoughts you have about others and highlights the importance of taking responsibility for your own thought processes.

> *Remedy:* Ensure that you clear your energy field daily, more often if you are in a really vulnerable situation. Also use energetic protection. Redirect your mind away from judgment and any thoughts that precipitate pity, dependence, or sympathy. Replace them with compassion. See Strategies 16 Clearing and 79 Protection.

10. Collective fears such as those expressed in news broadcasts can affect us as individuals or have a mass impact on the collective consciousness. Wars, or natural disasters like bushfires or floods that have destroyed homes, taken lives, and had devastating affects on communities, can effect our energy as well, even though you might not be directly affected or even living in the same country. It can awaken our own feelings of vulnerability and connectedness. The single tragic loss of life like murder or rape has the ability to arouse a whole community, creating grief and fear.

> *Remedy:* Ensure your alignment with source, clear your energy field, be discerning about engaging with the media, manage your mind. See Strategies 16 Clearing, 46 Feeling Scattered, 95 Thought Power and Control.

11. Trauma. While all these health strategies lead to greater consciousness and healing, if terror or trauma remain in your energy system there may be times that some support or assistance from an energy healer or other professional is appropriate.

> *Remedy:* There are some trauma release exercises that safely activate the body's natural reflex mechanism by shaking or vibrating in a pleasant way without needing to go into any story about the circumstances. Practitioners trained in trauma release can be found on the web. Trust your intuition and seek help if you need it.

See also:

- Affirmations
- Accept Yourself
- Allow Feelings
- Asking for Help
- Being: Mindfulness
- Beliefs Challenge
- Boundaries
- Clearing
- Connect with Nature
- Conscious Breathing
- Deep Release Breathing
- Feeling Agitated
- Feeling Anger
- Feeling Challenged
- Feeling Disempowered

- Feeling Guilt or Shame
- Feeling Jealousy
- Feeling Lonely or Alone
- Feeling Rejected or Hurt
- Feeling Scattered: Unbalanced
- Feeling Stuck
- Feeling Uncertain or Fearful of the Unknown
- Feeling Unloved or Unlovable
- Feeling Unsupported
- Feeling Victimized
- Feeling Worried
- Forgiveness Process
- Gratitude
- Grounding/Earthing
- Pain Dialog
- Pain Focus
- Projection
- Protection
- Quick Breath Affirmation
- Release Resistance
- Seek to Understand
- Shadow Play
- Toning
- Thought: Managing the Inner Critic
- Thought Power and Control

Eckhart Tolle, *Practicing the Power of Now*, Hodder Headline Group, 2001, p. 27.

Strategy 41
FEELING GRIEF

CATEGORIES APPLIED

Addressing Addictions
Addressing Depression
Addressing Anxiety
Awareness and Mindfulness
Career and Goals
Communications and Relationships
Improving Self-Esteem

Grief affects everyone at some period of his or her life. It is a reflection of what has been lost. It can be grief over a relationship that has come to an end, the death of someone close, the loss of a job, a home, a beloved pet, financial security, perhaps a situation you can't control or diminishing health.

This sorrow and emotional pain is a very normal and natural state and simply takes time to make the adjustment to your loss. Common stages of grief identified by Dr. Elisabeth Kübler Ross are denial, anger, bargaining, depression, and acceptance. There is no "normal" timeframe for the grieving person. It is a highly individual process and may take weeks, months, or even years. There may be protracted periods of getting on with life until latent triggers like anniversaries and family celebrations occur, which may plummet you back into deep mourning.

People behave differently as they work through such pain. Some weep openly, some retreat inwardly, yet the depth of grief can be comparable. The most universal feeling is one of deep sadness.

The death of a family member may set up conflict as the remaining bereaved attempt to organize things in a way that they feel expresses their connection with their lost loved one. For some it's a last opportunity to make some kind of statement or contribution. Disputes can arise in funeral arrangements, seeking some kind of memoir, or perceived entitlement.

Some Tips To Help You Through

1. Allow yourself to fully feel your grief – cry, scream, belt your pillow, or go for a run. Suppression will not make it go away and can lead to more complex emotions and health issues. Avoid any self-medication with drugs, alcohol, or other substances.

2. Your body is under great stress at such times, so taking care of yourself is important. Try to get as much rest as possible, eat nutritious food, get some exercise, and spend time in the healing energies of nature.

3. Grief is often compounded when elements of guilt, regret, and lost opportunities arise. Write about these feelings in a letter or a journal and forgive yourself. Writing helps to give these feelings expression in a more tangible way.

4. To help perspective and process, try to see if other unresolved emotions have arisen. These will often surface because the heart feels so much pain that the suppression of other wounds may rise to the surface, creating a sense of overwhelming raw emotion. Write in your journal or draw upon other relevant Strategies like 16 Clearing, 27 Deep Release Breathing, 53 Forgiveness, and 88 Shadow Play.

5. This is an important time to draw supportive people close to you and distance yourself from those who may lack compassion. State clearly what your needs are with friends and family, whether it's a meal, some company, a shoulder to cry on, or help with various things. Very often people want to help but don't know how best to support you. Be willing to ask for what you want. Beware to avoid any expectation you may have that others "should" know how you feel or know what you want or need at this time.

6. Remember the good times and steer your mind away from any remorse. You can't change what has happened but you can manage your mind and help yourself feel better by redirecting your focus to happy memories.

7. Beware of a protracted period of wallowing in grief. Seek professional help if you cannot seem to move beyond feelings of overwhelm grief or depression. You will help both yourself and your deceased loved one if you let them go so you can move on and they can then make an easier transition. It may help to remind yourself that we are all eternal energy beings and your loved one has simply transitioned from one form to another. A process you too will experience in time.

8. Be aware that peace and healing is possible for you.

"Everyone who lives long enough to love deeply will experience great losses. Don't let fear of loss, or the losses themselves, take away your ability to enjoy the wonderful life that is yours."
– Barbara "Cutie" Cooper

See also:

- Allow Feelings
- Clearing
- Connect with Nature
- Deep Release Breathing
- Feeling Guilt or Shame
- Forgiveness Process
- Grounding/Earthing
- Thought Power and Control

Barbara "Cutie" Cooper, *Fall in Love for Life: Inspiration from a 73 year Marriage*, Chronicle Books 2012.

Strategy 42
FEELING GUILT OR SHAME

CATEGORIES APPLIED

Addressing Addictions
Addressing Anxiety
Addressing Depression
Awareness and Mindfulness
Career and Goals
Communications and Relationships
Improving Self-Esteem

Guilt or shame are emotions that often follow regret at some kind of action or even thought. In our society there are many times when both guilt and shame can be imposed upon another person. It is used to punish, manipulate, or control someone. This says more about the perpetrator than it does about the receiver. However, even though it may be imposed there must be an agreement at some level for you to take it on board as a belief.

Some people consider it virtuous to hold on to guilt, believing that it will help them to not repeat the same behavior. Others will desperately attempt to deny it and still others will act it out unconsciously and sometimes with masochistic behaviors. It is important to be alert to any desire towards self-punishment for guilt, which may be conscious or unconscious.

Shame is reflected in humiliation or embarrassment and extreme vulnerability. It is commonly associated with childhood sexual abuse and is very destructive to emotional health and wellbeing, with massive detrimental impact on self-esteem. It can cause us to withdraw and feel very alone.

While guilt and shame are certainly different emotions, they can sometimes be confused and are similar in the seriously negative energy impact upon us. Both have a strong element of judgment.

Poor choices and learned behavior that occur through our conditioned upbringing are part of the journey of life here in Earth school that all people experience. However, retaining these feelings of guilt, fault, blame, or shame and judging yourself actually serves no positive function and can seriously impair your growth and drain your energy. It can cause you to withdraw, pull back from others and from any loving support that surrounds you.

Without resolution of these painful emotions they will accumulate and eventually affect your health because it holds the quality of this heavy negative vibration stuck in your body along with any associated beliefs like "I'm not good enough."

How Do I Address Guilt And Shame?

It's important to accept responsibility for your life and all that has happened. Any feeling of blame means that you have handed your power to the other person. This does not mean that you condone or ignore the behavior. It does mean that you see it and are willing to move on from it. You attitude is all-important here. This empowers you and gives you access to more of your available energy that you need to heal.

Recognize that behaviors that trigger guilt or shame occur when we are disconnected from our higher self. Have compassion for yourself, because rarely are we taught to acknowledge, let alone encouraged, to let that greater loving intelligence be our internal guide.

Separate you real self from your behavior. Recognize yourself as a multidimensional being. You are eternal, and while the emotions of shame or guilt can be extremely painful to the personality/ego self, they do not reflect your core essence over eternity.

Monitor your mind, which can perpetuate the thoughts and subsequent feelings that maintain these emotions and erode self-esteem. See Strategies 94 Thought: Managing the Inner Critic and 95 Thought Power and Control for more information.

On a physical level, do what you can to rectify the situation as quickly as possible. This could be a verbal apology, explanation, or any number of different things depending on the source of the emotion. Aim to restore harmony; you may need to call upon the beautiful qualities of humility and maybe courage to assist you in this. Simply sit quietly and feel into these qualities before proceeding.

In a meditative state

- Sit in a quiet space and in your mind review the scenario and make changes in a way that allows for harmony. This process of working with the mind and expressing the intention to restore harmony creates an energetic shift and also sets the intention for any future event. It is a way to retrain the mind. Remember, your thoughts and beliefs are creative and determining your reality, so ensure they are how you want things to be.

- Of utmost importance is that you forgive yourself! Feel into your heart and imagine yourself as a small child. This will help to build and connect with the compassion of your higher self. Know that whatever you did was simply a learning experience. An "unaware" part of you acted out this behavior. Then with genuine feelings of compassion, express forgiveness for yourself. See Strategy 53 Forgiveness Process for more information.
- If guilt or shame has been" imposed" upon you, through your intention, send it back to the giver. See, sense, or imagine it as streamers of energy returning to them. Be aware that you must have made some agreement to accept any imposed guilt. Then call back your own energy that you have given over to the person or situation through the acceptance of guilt or shame. See also Strategy 16 Clearing.

Ensure that you have strong boundaries if you are aware of anyone who may have an investment in you retaining your guilt or shame. See Strategies 12 Boundaries and 63 Intention/Counter-Intention for more information.

Do not hesitate to seek professional help if required.

See also:

- Accept Yourself
- Awareness: Building the Observer
- Clearing
- Feeling Worried
- Forgiveness Process
- Intention/Counter-Intention
- Review and Remake Your Day
- Thought: Managing the Inner Critic
- Thought Power and Control
- Who Am I?

Strategy 43
FEELING JEALOUSY

CATEGORIES APPLIED

Addressing Addictions
Addressing Anxiety
Addressing Depression
Awareness and Mindfulness
Career and Goals
Communications and Relationships
Improving Self-Esteem

Jealousy often arises in relationships, when one is feeling insecure and wants some kind of reassurance. It can also emerge when someone has manifested something that you desire.

When you find yourself being critical or jealous of another because of what they have manifested, it has the effect of working against your own desires. It also sends a negative energy towards the other. Learning to manage your mind is of great importance for your own success, wellbeing, and health.

> **"If someone is not receiving what they are asking for, it is not because there is a shortage of resources; it can only be that the person holding the desire is out of alignment with their own request. There is no shortage. There is no lack. There is no competition for resources. There is only allowing or the disallowing of that which you are asking for."**
> – Esther and Jerry Hicks

1. Accept the uncomfortable feelings and thoughts of jealousy and realize you do not have to reflect that in your behavior. See Strategy 6 Awareness: Building the Observer.

2. Fully bring your attention to yourself and away from the other person. Examine your own beliefs, expectations, and assumptions about the situation or the relationships and identify which ones might be holding you back.

3. Use the painful feeling of jealousy and any insights from your own self-reflection as an impetus to move you towards your own aspirations. Focus on problem solving or finding creative solutions so that you can move towards what it is that *you* desire. Incorporate this as part of your goals.

4. Jealousy rarely enhances any relationship, though clear communications may clear up any misunderstandings and resolve the issue. When you are clear in your own mind about the source and beliefs behind your jealous feelings, determine if it is wise to discuss them within your relationship.

5. Move into a feeling of gratitude for everything you have in your life at the current time. It is essential for manifesting what you want and will lift your energy frequency and help you feel better.

6. Adopt a curious attitude (not judgmental) about yourself and identify what it is that you are not doing or not allowing that has triggered this feeling of jealousy. Then take remedial action.

7. Every day, work on building your own sense of self-love and personal empowerment.

See also:

- Awareness of Awareness
- Clearing
- Communication: When You
- Competition versus Cooperation
- Feeling Disempowered
- Goal Setting
- Ideas and Inspirations
- Personal Mission Statement
- Relationships: Building Intimacy
- Thought Management: Inner Critic
- Thought Power and Control
- Values

Esther and Jerry Hicks, *The Teachings of Abraham: Ask and It Is Given*, Hay House 2004, p. 86.

Strategy 44
FEELING LONELY OR ALONE

CATEGORIES APPLIED

Addressing Addictions
Addressing Anxiety
Addressing Depression
Awareness and Mindfulness
Communications and Relationships
Improving Self-Esteem

Feeling alone can be very distressing. It can cause one to feel empty or unwanted and risk some serious health consequences: depression, low self-esteem, antisocial behavior, an increased risk of heart disease, and a reduced immune system. The desire to be with people is a natural human condition. The prison system, aware of this, uses isolation as a harsh punishment.

As multidimensional energy beings we are all interconnected, which contributes to our conscious desire to be with others. Nevertheless, there are many who suffer from loneliness who have people around them, and still others who enjoy a more secluded life and don't feel lonely at all.

Loneliness is much more a state of mind
and beliefs than it is a reality.

If you are feeling lonely it is your body guiding you that something needs to change.

At the basis of loneliness is a feeling of disconnection from your higher self or your source energy. This is fundamental to feeling connected, loved, and safe. Building self-esteem is the journey we all must take to facilitate that ultimate connection: to truly find peace with who you are and any of your perceived imperfections; to recognize that you are indeed worthy of love and that your true essence is a loving and lovable being. Then you will never feel lonely again.

"Negative emotions like loneliness, envy, and guilt
have an important role to play in a happy life;
they're big, flashing signs that something needs to change."
-Gretchen Rubin

Tips For Change

1. Attune to your higher self. Hold that intention each day along with creating a bubble of light to surround you.

2. Manage your mind so that you are only thinking positive thoughts that promote good feelings.

3. Practice focusing your mind on how you would like to be together with others so that the law of attraction can assist your co-creative desire.

4. Work on building self-love and self-esteem – *the essential cure for loneliness.*

5. Reach out and get involved with some community activity that interests you – gardening, walking, tai chi, book club, or start a new course.

6. Become a volunteer. It's a great way to connect with others and make a difference.

7. Show kindness to another. This satisfies a strong human need for supporting each other and you both get to feel good.

8. Consider getting a pet. They can be a wonderful companion and source of unconditional love.

9. Greet people more warmly than you normally would to open up to deepening friendships or possible new relationships.

10. Connect or reconnect with friends and family. The Internet and Skype can help you stay in touch if distance is an issue.

See also:

- Asking for Help
- Change: Warmer Greeting
- Communication Keys
- Connect with Nature
- Do Things You Enjoy
- Help Another
- Kindness to Self
- Music to Uplift and Nurture
- Thought Power and Control
- Who Am I?

Gretchen Rubin, *The Happiness Project*, HarperCollins, 2010.

Strategy 45
FEELING REJECTED OR HURT

CATEGORIES APPLIED

Addressing Addictions
Addressing Anxiety
Addressing Depression
Awareness and Mindfulness
Career and Goals
Communications and Relationships
Improving Self-Esteem

Rejection can result in deep hurt. There are all kinds of circumstances that can trigger a feeling of rejection. It can be related to your lover, friends, or family, something to do with your work, perhaps something you are aspiring towards, an idea, or maybe entry into a club or organization. Our natural human existence is to be part of a group – it is a very primal state that helps us feels connected.

Rejection is painful, but it need not be carried around as a burden or become a repeated story that you allow your mind to run on incessantly, since that will surely intensify the emotional pain.

A very common perception when feeling rejected is that there is something wrong with you, you don't fit in. Feeling unwanted then brings about a reduction in self-esteem.

Rejection can awaken in you previous experiences from childhood, that were not resolved. It might be feelings of abandonment by a parent or caregiver, or a whole series of perceived rejections: not being comforted when you were upset, being denied something you wanted, not being acknowledged, heard, or seen. All people experience this many times, so rejection is not a new pain but an old hurt arising once again.

How To Deal With Rejection

Understanding of the play of energy can help you to heal.

1. If you can feel some tears below the surface allow them to bubble up and cry. This will help to release the intensity of the emotion.

2. Put it in perspective: You are rejecting things all the time. So are others. It is a normal behavior. You have all kinds of likes, dislikes, and preferences. This applies to everything

in life including people. There are 7 billion people on this Earth and no two are the same. You will not be loved by all.

3. When someone rejects you it is actually saying more about who they are than it is about you. Their behavior makes sense to them. They are acting out of their own conditioning. You are not in their skin experiencing their reality. There may be all kinds of burdens, insecurities, or fears going on for them. Their life might be totally complicated and they may be trying to find a way to deal with all their stuff.

4. Don't make assumptions that there is something wrong with you.

5. The pain you feel is because you have attached to another. It is a common behavior until you come into self-love, which is the essential journey that we all must make. You have given some of your power over to them. Implicit is the message "If I am loved and accepted by another then I am okay." It is as though you are defining yourself and who you are by what someone else thinks about you, as if they are an authority. That is basically giving others responsibility for your happiness. This kind of behavior will always lead to pain; suffering, disempowerment, and happiness will surely elude you. Claim your sovereignty.

"I take rejection as someone blowing a bugle in my ear to wake me rather than retreat."
– Sylvester Stallone

6. Understand that you have a choice on how to perceive the situation. You can take rejection personally and add to the unresolved pain within, or seize it as an opportunity for greater awareness. Look for the gift.

   Perhaps this experience will lead you down a different path, which would ultimately serve you better. Even if you can't see it just yet, simply choosing to perceive it that way will certainly elevate your feeling state.

   Maybe some self-reflection of your own behaviors might reveal a negative pattern that you have exhibited and not acknowledged previously. Be grateful for the awareness that now allows you to bring about change.

   Whenever hurt or pain is present, it is also your opportunity to heal. All healing happens in the present moment. See if you can just let yourself feel the pain and allow the energy to flow through you *without any mind story to hold on to it.* See Strategy 27 Deep Release Breathing and cry if you feel you want to.

7. Practice forgiveness to help you release the energy you are holding. This must be from your heart and not just your mind. Your heart is the transformation center where healing can happen. See Strategy 53 Forgiveness Process for more information.

8. When you can accept responsibility for the rejection without blaming the other person or yourself, you will grow and become stronger and more empowered.

9. Consider carefully before you avoid or reject the person whom you perceived rejected you. Rather, see them as an angel in disguise whose gift to you is to show you how important it is to love yourself. Depending on the kind of relationship you had, strive to maintain the friendship connection if there are qualities about them that you like.

10. Don't reject yourself by running mind stories about rejection or some self-deprecating thoughts. Repeating these kind of thought-forms become a powerful energy that impacts on you and if repeated enough will become a belief system that will do nothing but create misery in your life. Manage your mind. See Strategy 95 Thought Power and Control and 3 Affirmations for more information.

11. Recognize and connect with your higher self through your heart. Ask your higher self to give you the strength to find a way through. Irrespective of what anyone else thinks about you, you are an eternal multidimensional being whose core essence is love. Allow yourself to fully embrace that truth.

See also:

- Clearing
- Communication: Conflict Resolution
- Communication: When you...
- Feeling Disempowered
- Feeling Fear
- Feeling Jealousy
- Seek to Understand
- Thought Power and Control
- Who Am I?

Strategy 46
FEELING SCATTERED: UNBALANCED

CATEGORIES APPLIED

Addressing Addictions
Addressing Anxiety
Addressing Depression
Awareness and Mindfulness
Career and Goals
Environmental Health
Improving Self-Esteem
Quick Stress Busters

Alignment in this context refers to two different states: one is the direction in which you are heading and whether or not you are responding to your own higher guidance or letting your mind rule over your heart. The other refers to your subtle bodies and whether they are feeling aligned or scattered. It can be a sense of feeling unbalanced, all over the place, often with an inability to focus the mind effectively. It is a stressful feeling that could involve procrastination, inner conflict, confusion, self-sabotage, and maybe a sense of overwhelm and a critical inner voice. It can be a situation where intent and results are not working out.

This is definitely a sign that you need to pause, align, and ground yourself. A scattered person has both wellness and safety issues at the forefront. Decision-making and reflexes are out of kilter, leaving you vulnerable to accidents and emotional triggers.

On an energetic level, when you are feeling scattered it is a reflection that your subtle bodies are distorted and that you have lost your alignment with your higher self or inner guidance.

Your natural state is in alignment with your higher self, and when that is so, you feel good, balanced, in tune with your own inspiration, and things seem to flow.

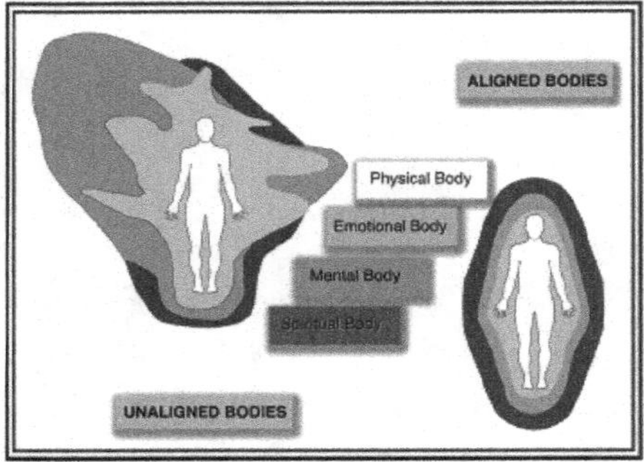

You are a multidimensional being who has three primary subtle bodies beyond your physical body, even though most people cannot see them. This is also referred to as your aura (the aura can be photographed using Kirlian photography).

When you feel balanced and centered, your four-body system is in alignment just like a nest of Russian dolls.

In order they are the physical, emotional, mental, and spiritual bodies and each impacts on the other.

The image here reflects these contrasting states.

Choose from the various options below to align, balance, and center yourself. They are different methods to bring a similar result.

Standing Alignment Process

1. Start with a few deep, long, slow breaths and place yourself in a column of light. The breathing draws your attention inwards and begins to slow the mind. The light provides a protective energy.

2. Next focus your mind on your whole four-body system. Stand with your eyes closed and your feet about a hip-width apart. Imagine you have roots of light going down your legs, out through the soles of your feet and deep into the Earth. This also helps to ground you.

3. Now gently rock your body backwards and forwards, gently swaying so that you can feel your physical body moving to and fro. After about one minute stop the gentle rocking and stand still, just feeling/noticing where you are – unmoving and connected to the Earth.

4. Then, still keeping your feet anchored to the Earth, commence a gentle rocking from side to side. After about one minute stop the rocking and find the balance point where your physical body feels in perfect alignment, weight evenly distributed over both feet.

5. Next, while maintaining the same standing posture with your eyes still closed, *in your imagination only*, repeat steps 2 and 3 with your emotional body, which is the next layer out from your physical body.

6. Then, *in your imagination only*, repeat the same steps with your mental body.

7. Finally, *in your imagination only*, repeat the same steps with the outer layer of your spiritual body until all four of your bodies feel in perfect alignment.

8. Then focus on the central point in your body, which is just below the sternum (centre of the bottom of the rib cage) and above the navel. Notice your physical, emotional, mental,

and spiritual bodies, all aligned, like a nest of Russian dolls, one encasing the other. This will give you a feeling of being aligned, centered, balanced.

Notice how different, focused, and calm you feel. This is your true foundational state, which also facilitates greater alignment with your higher self and improved intuition.

Spiral Alignment

1. Take a couple of deep, long, slow breaths to draw your attention inwards.

2. Then close your eyes and imagine roots of light coming out through the soles of your feet going deep into the Earth, just like a tree. This is to ground you.

3. Next, get a sense of where you feel the outside of your energy field is located. This includes your physical, emotional, mental, and spiritual bodies. Just trust your intuition. If, however, you find it difficult to get a sense of your energy bodies, just imagine a point about 2 meters beyond your physical body.

4. Make sure you stand with your weight evenly placed over the balls and soles of your feet. If sitting, choose an upright chair and ensure your spine is straight, feet flat on the floor and you are balanced on your chair.

5. Then starting at that outermost point of where you sense your energy bodies, imagine an anti-clockwise circle embracing the whole of you – all of your physical, emotional, mental, and spiritual bodies.

6. Commencing from the outer to the inner, begin an anti-clockwise spiral with the intention of embracing all your bodies and bringing them into balance. Maintain your focus and gently continue the spiral, winding it inwards and allowing this spiralling to take two to three minutes. Intention and focus are the keys to success here.

Figure 8 Alignment

Begin with a few long, slow, deep breaths to begin to draw your mind inwards and assist focus. It is best to close your eyes to avoid distractions.

Sit or stand in an upright posture. Then imagine a moving light in the shape of a vertical figure 8 running the perimeter of your energy field. The figure 8 is a mathematical symbol representing the lemniscate, a symbol of infinity, though it is usually depicted on its side rather vertically.

The objective and intention is to embrace your whole energy matrix, consisting of all four bodies with the center point crossing at your heart.

You have an energy center about an arm's length above your head, often referred to as the soul star and another, the earth star, a similar distance below your feet. You need to embrace both of these points as well when you run the figure 8.

Starting at your heart area, imagine a golden circle of light running in a clockwise direction up above your head and then coming down your right, crossing at your heart, and down your left side, beneath your feet into the Earth and then up your lower right side to the center point again.

At the same time of creating this figure 8 imagery in your mind's eye, hold the intention of drawing your energy field into alignment and creating a boundary to any outside energies that may otherwise be disruptive. Continue for a few minutes or until you feel aligned and balanced.

Earth Alignment

Nature has a powerful way of balancing our energies. If you are in a position to do so, find a beautiful big tree and lie on the ground underneath the branches. Trees have their own unique healing energy, as does Mother Earth. Breathe deeply for ten to thirty minutes as though the breath is coming up from the Earth, bringing her natural nurturing energy. Flesh-to-Earth contact is best to allow the negative electrons to restore balance through your skin. This will provide a balancing, grounding, and restorative feeling.

Further Option

Following any of these energetic alignment processes you may like to seek further clarification. Ask yourself, "What is, or has been behind this scattered feeling?" "What is my priority now?" – and act upon it.

When your bodies are back in alignment, what may have been obscure before becomes clearer.

If you still feel a little discombobulated go to Strategy 16 Clearing to clear your field of any interference. Strategy 23 Conscious Breathing is also beneficial and may be included to enhance your feeling state.

See also:

- Boundaries
- Clearing
- Conscious Breathing
- Feeling Agitated
- Grounding/Earthing
- Jiggling

Strategy 47
FEELING STUCK

CATEGORIES APPLIED

Addressing Addictions
Addressing Anxiety
Addressing Depression
Awareness and Mindfulness
Career and Goals
Communications and Relationships
Improving Self-Esteem

Feeling "stuck" is a term often used to indicate that nothing seems to be moving; there is a sense of being in some kind of bind, or maybe a perception of going around in circles. Sometimes it can be that you are fighting against a situation and don't feel as though you are making any progress. Because we are energy beings, energy is constantly in a state of change; we are actually not stuck but just going back and forth repeatedly between one area and another, which gives the sense or illusion of being stuck.

To address this debilitating and frustrating feeling, be aware that this is a trick of the mind. The simple acknowledgment may give you immediate relief and even a sense of direction.

If you are resisting something, as though you are pushing against a brick wall, just be aware of that and drop into a state of acceptance and allowing. That will immediately change the energy.

Further, make a list of everything that is on your mind around the subject of your "stuckness." It gets everything out there for you to see and gives you a sense of relief that it is now fully exposed so that you can be more aware of exactly what it is you are dealing with.

Next, fully focus your mind and determine to take action in one direction or another. It actually matters little which direction you choose. You really can't make a "wrong" decision. The purpose is to create a feeling of momentum again. Whatever action you take will give you greater insight. It will be a learning experience showing you either that the direction you have taken is leading you towards your objective, or it will reveal to you that there is a better way. You cannot fail, you can only learn; your direction will be clearer as a result and you will no longer feel stuck.

It is important to make a decision and then feel good about it – no regrets.

Clearing Clutter

An additional strategy for dealing with feeling stuck is to clear out your clutter. Clutter in your surroundings is a metaphor for cluttered thinking and can contribute significantly to the undesired feeling of stuckness. Removing physical clutter from your immediate environment will help. Clear out a cupboard or drawer to facilitate a shift.

See Also:

- Clearing
- Connect with Nature
- Deep Release Breathing
- Decisions: Heart Wisdom
- Decisions: Motives and Impact
- Grounding/Earthing
- Personal Mission Statement
- Thought Power and Control

Strategy 48
FEELING UNCERTAIN OR FEARFUL OF THE UNKNOWN

CATEGORIES APPLIED

Addressing Addictions
Addressing Anxiety
Addressing Depression
Awareness and Mindfulness
Career and Goals
Communications and Relationships
Improving Self-Esteem

Feeling uncertain or fearful of the unknown is a play of the mind. It is the personality/ego perspective of you wanting some kind of reassurance.

It may be habitual thinking that anything new is scary, which shows up in the tendency to stay in familiar or safe territory. This kind of thinking will result in many behaviors that will sabotage your goals. Or the trigger may remind you of a past experience that didn't go well and so your brain sends off warning signals: "Don't go there!" However, one bad experience doesn't mean they will all be like that.

Let's look at this more rationally. Anything that has not been experienced before is "new" and therefore will be unfamiliar, and it is quite normal to have some slight anxiety about it. The difficulty arises when we allow the mind to start running irrational stories that we both create and listen to. Without consciousness, the mind can create many assumptions through negative thought patterns and stories, which create drama and build much stress and fear. We can quickly slip into judgment, fear, and even hate. This kind of thinking is totally irrational and very debilitating.

Examine your thought processes and shift your attitude to quickly transform these feelings. In response to your fearful inner voice ask, "If I were to listen to you where would that lead me?"

Become comfortable with uncertainty or the unknown. Don't discard or judge something as bad or fearful just because it's new to you. Change your focus to curiosity, wonder, and excitement.

Mind Rehearsal Process

- Take a moment to connect with the privacy and safety of your own home. Feel the security it offers, close your eyes, and do some long, slow, deep breathing to center yourself.
- Then, while retaining that feeling of security, bring to mind what has been scaring you.
- Recognize that you are totally safe and begin step by step to walk yourself through the thing that has been causing you anxiety, however nebulous it is.
- Pause at every step and check with your rational mind to clarify what might play out and how you would handle the situation.
- See yourself succeeding every step of the way, facing the fear and at the same time resolving any problems or issues that arise.
- This kind of preparation will instil; a feeling of safety and familiarity.

"Nothing in life is to be feared.
It is only to be understood."
– Marie Curie

If you are still feeing some anxiety see Strategy 16 Clearing.

See also:

- Ask for Help
- Awareness of Awareness
- Beliefs Challenge
- Change Challenge
- Clearing
- Connect with Nature
- Conscious Breathing
- Deep Release Breathing
- Gratitude
- Grounding/Earthing
- Seek to Understand
- Thought Power and Control

Strategy 49
FEELING UNLOVED OR UNLOVABLE

CATEGORIES APPLIED

Addressing Addictions
Addressing Anxiety
Addressing Depression
Awareness and Mindfulness
Communications and Relationships
Improving Self-Esteem

Feeling unloved or unlovable is probably the most painful of all emotions because it is the direct opposite of our true nature as an eternal spiritual being in a human body. The essence of who we are is part of Source energy and therein lies our first clue: a magnificent co-creative being who has disconnected with our own source.

This will reflect that we have given power to the mind and have not been honoring our heart's natural expression of love and desire. It also reveals that it is an "inside" job; despite the longing to feel loved by another, it actually doesn't have anything to do with anyone outside of ourselves.

The unmanaged mind is the culprit; the fortunate part is that you and only you have the power and control to remedy this situation.

All people, are born worthy, including you.

These acutely painful feelings may have developed gradually over weeks, months, or many years as a result of your programming, or may have arisen from a perceived rejection by another. While rejection is always painful, *you do not have to reject yourself as well.*

"The biggest disease in this day and age is that of people feeling unloved."
– Princess Diana

Unfortunately this is a common reaction for an unmanaged mind. Think of it this way. Imagine a small child being rejected or even ostracized in the school playground. Your heart would naturally go out to her. You understand what it's like and your natural empathy would surface. This pain you are feeling is your inner child screaming out for *your* love and acceptance. The question then is: Will you continue to deny this spiritual being that is you, deny your recognition and your love? Or will you dig deep and connect with the innate love within your own heart and provide that comfort and reassurance to yourself? Just acknowledging, with compassion, the part that feels so unloved or unlovable can ease the pain.

The wondrous part about this transformation process is that when you start demonstrating your lovability to yourself you will organically attract others who will also love you.

The fundamental key to "undoing" feeling unloved or unlovable is to begin to manage the mind and keep your energy field clear from contamination. Become very conscious of your thinking, eliminating any negative thought patterns. When they arise, remind yourself that it is your mind and that is not the real you.

Challenge all your beliefs. Replace the negative thoughts with positive loving thoughts. Affirmations can be a great help, and so can always reaching for a better feeling thought. Find things that you are grateful for every day. It is one of the fastest and most effective ways to elevate your feeling state. Do things for yourself that show love and respect for you and don't leave that responsibility to others. Eat well, exercise, and nurture your physical body. It is your temple to house the essence of your eternal self in this lifetime.

If you are waiting on others to love you in order to feel good about yourself you will always be waiting, because that is handing over your power, and you need to reclaim it. Accept all parts of you, even the parts you consider unlovable. See your life as a series of learning experiences, not as mistakes or regrets. Realize that you have a faulty mind program running that needs fixing, and you have everything within to change it. Bit by bit and day by day you will transform this faulty mind story and awaken to the truth of your authentic loving and lovable self.

Embrace all the self-esteem processes in this program to support your awakening.

See also:

- Accept Yourself
- Affirmations
- Beliefs Challenge
- Clearing
- Feeling Lonely or Alone
- Gratitude
- Grounding/Earthing
- Kindness to Self
- Thought: Managing the Inner Critic
- Thought Power and Control
- Who Am I?

Strategy 50
FEELING UNSUPPORTED

CATEGORIES APPLIED

Addressing Addictions
Addressing Depression
Addressing Anxiety
Awareness and Mindfulness
Career and Goals
Communications and Relationships
Environmental Health
Improving Self-Esteem

There are all kinds of possible scenarios that may leave you feeling unsupported. It may be your intimate loved one that is falling short of your expectations; it may be other family members. Perhaps you are trying to complete a project and need some help with tending to children's needs or some domestic chores; maybe your feeling arises from a protracted feeling of lack of emotional support; maybe some immediate work dynamic is leaving you feeling unsupported. Here are some key points to consider before deciding your best approach for moving forward.

1. Is the primary issue a lack of effective communication? Do you expect that the other person "should" know you would like support and how this might play out? Have you asked in a friendly, kindly way for what you want? Or are you just feeling resentful because your desires are not being met?

   In loving relationships, often people express their love and care in a way that you may not recognize as supportive. Gary Chapman discusses these love communication styles as words of affirmation, quality time, receiving gifts, acts of service, and physical touch. If your primary language is expressing love through acts of service and your partner's is physical touch then you may well interpret the absence of acts of service as not feeling supported, and vice versa. It is really a misinterpretation and some good communication with a desire to understand the other can readily resolve this.

2. Do some honest self-inquiry to determine "am I supporting myself?"

   Have you lost the balance between work and living? If you are not supporting yourself then you are projecting and the other person or persons in your life are just reflecting that back to you. In this case the solution becomes: Have you taken on too much and do you need to say "no"? Do you need to join a yoga or dance class, spend time meditating, take time out to catch up with friends for lunch or a movie, maybe allow yourself a sleep-in, a walk on the beach, or a massage?

3. Another cause of feeling unsupported may be disowning a shadow aspect of yourself. We can so often see in another what we struggle to see in our own personality. So the question, which takes honesty and courage to answer, becomes, "Do I support others?" If you discover that you are lacking in this area, then you will have to address this by changing your own behavior and the energy dynamic playing out so that support can flow back to you.

4. Maybe your feelings of lack of support are long-term and stem from an earlier life experience where you have allowed your thoughts to become a belief that has created a pattern that you keep attracting through the universal Law of Attraction. Remember, a belief is just repeated thoughts and can be changed. Retrain your mind by looking for even the smallest demonstration of support and feeling gratitude. If you are still holding some resentment or hurt, seek to heal these old wounds. See Strategy 53 Forgiveness Process. Also watch your "self-talk" to ensure you are compassionate, kind, encouraging, and supportive.

5. Determine if you have given your power over to others in the belief that they will take care of you. This kind of dependent relationship will always lead to pain. It is challenge enough to accept full responsibility for your own life, let alone take on responsibility for someone else's life. Don't confuse care, love, support, and compassion with responsibility. Explore ways to empower yourself and fulfill your deepest passion, and encourage others to do the same.

See also:

- Asking for Help
- Communication Keys
- Do Things You Enjoy
- Forgiveness Process
- Gratitude
- Grounding/Earthing
- Help Another
- Kindness to Self
- Thought Power and Control

Gary Chapman, *The Five Love Languages*, Northfield Publishing, 2010.

Strategy 51
FEELING VICTIMIZED

CATEGORIES APPLIED

Addressing Addictions
Addressing Anxiety
Addressing Depression
Awareness and Mindfulness
Career and Goals
Communications and Relationships
Improving Self-Esteem

There are often experiences throughout our life where we may feel victimized. These incidents can have a dramatic impact on our life, affecting relationships, career, health, and just about every aspect of our being. On an emotional level, such examples may arise from being punished unjustly, or bullied at school, or manipulated in the workplace; maybe having a tussle with some bureaucratic system, being stalked, deprived by deceit, being conned or robbed; or, at a more physical level, when there is harm or abuse to your body through accident or intent.

All kinds of emotions can result including fear, anxiety, hate, anger, and depression, along with feelings of helplessness. Clearly this is very disempowering and the whole situation can be compounded by lack of resolution and a mind that constantly repeats the story. Even support groups can reinforce victimhood if they do not encourage ways to heal, forgive, and move on.

The primary key for healing and moving on is to accept responsibility for where you are in this moment. It is important because being responsible puts you in a position of power. That does not in any way suggest that you are to blame. Accepting responsibility allows you to determine what will happen from here; it does not give any power to the other person or situation. You do not need to rely on any one else but yourself.

If there is any kind of trauma
it is highly recommended that you seek professional help.

Rather than make any judgment about the circumstances of the individual situations, or discuss your rights from a legal point of view, the following offers an "energetic" perspective and how to help you feel better so that you can heal, grow, and move forward in your life.

First of all, understand that when you are feeling victimized you cannot move on or heal emotionally. It leaves you stuck with a sense of powerlessness. Such an undesirable feeling will be perpetuated by your perception and beliefs or the mind story that you run.

This does not remotely suggest that you are not justified in experiencing any of these feelings, which are very normal at the outset of the trigger. It is important to feel and acknowledge what you are feeling. *You cannot heal what you cannot feel*, and it is far better that these feelings be expressed rather than suppressed because they can become the unconscious driving force in your life.

However, managing your mind and understanding that "emotionalized thoughts create feelings" is of the greatest importance. It is necessary to recognize that if you keep running the same thought patterns and beliefs – repeating the same story time and again in your mind, or saying it verbally to others – you will perpetuate your current feelings of distress. It's just the way it is: cause and effect.

Understand, it is a choice.

There are a multitude of self-help strategies that can help you to heal and move on. Check through the 101 Strategies in this book to assess what feels most relevant for you at the time. This will be influenced by the nature of your experience and where you are in your processing. Among the many you can choose from, the following are considered important:

Validation. For some, it is valuable to have your story witnessed as a kind of validation. This is best done in a loving, supportive environment where your witnesses will just listen and hear your pain, not reinforce any kind of powerlessness or victimhood. This is a normal part of the healing process.

Remake the situation. In a meditative state, replay the situation in your mind and give it a positive outcome. An example might be a major conflict with a colleague over a business presentation, which left you feeling victimized. In your remake, you see the presentation going harmoniously where you are both left feeling good. The mind does not know the difference between what is real and what is just a thought, and this will change the energetics and before long lead to harmony. You may need to repeat this several times to offset the amount of times you have run the original story in your mind.

Find gratitude. Look for something to be grateful for in this situation. There is always learning that comes out of adversity and provides growth. For example, you were betrayed by someone whom you trusted with your money. You could respond by feeling gratitude that you have now established clearer boundaries. Perhaps you have also learnt to take greater responsibility for checking information rather than just trusting someone so completely. See Strategy 57. Gratitude

Release the need to be right. Be willing to let go of being right. Rather, have an attitude of "It happened – it just is." Realize that you can't change the past, and be determined to move on. Right and wrong, good and bad are forms of judgment which hold energy stuck in time and space. See Strategy 84. Release the Need to Be Right

Forgiveness. Holding on to resentment will ensure that a victim mentality is maintained and that you cannot possibly heal or resolve your pain. When you forgive another you set *yourself* free. This is extremely important for your growth and for integrated healing. Forgiveness recognizes that you can't change the events that triggered these emotions within, but you can change your *perception* of them. Healing transformation comes through the heart, not the mind, so it is important to connect with your heart and your feelings as you go through this process. See Strategy 53. Forgiveness.

Projection. Take time to reflect to see if you are projecting onto another. It is a common behavior that arises when feeling emotionally triggered. It comes from the subconscious mind and is a way of avoiding any responsibility or change that will help you move forward. See Strategy 78. Projection

Do not hesitate to seek professional help if you still feel victimized.

See also:

- Allow Feelings
- Asking for Help
- Clearing
- Conflict Resolution
- Connect with Nature
- Deep Release Breathing
- Do Things You Enjoy
- Feeling Agitated

- Feeling Anger
- Feeling Disempowered
- Feeling Fear
- Feeling Stuck
- Feeling Unsupported
- Forgiveness Process
- Gratitude
- Projection
- Release the Need to be Right
- Review and Remake Your Day
- Seek to Understand
- Thought Power and Control

Strategy 52
FEELING WORRIED

CATEGORIES APPLIED

Addressing Addictions
Addressing Anxiety
Addressing Depression
Awareness and Mindfulness
Career and Goals
Communications and Relationships
Improving Self-Esteem
Quick Stress Busters

It is common for people to mistake the emotion of "worry" for love. There is a belief that worrying about someone means that you love him or her. Worry has a low resonance and falls within a bandwidth of fear, and as such it attracts a parallel energy – a negative frequency.

An example is being concerned about the type of friendships that your child is engaged with, or the health of your loved one, or your position in the workplace, or financial burdens. The very energy you are concerned about and not wanting to happen is the same energy you are bringing towards you through the Law of Attraction. The more you worry the more evidence you see of it around you.

What's more, it leaves you feeling down and projects negativity onto the person of your concern! There is *no* upside to worry.

Instead use your mind to imagine the desired situation. Sit quietly with your eyes closed and step by step imagine your preferred outcome in detail. Embellish the examples below. Energy goes where energy flows, and this way you are contributing to a positive scenario for both you and the person or area of your concern, rather than contributing to a negative situation through worry.

1. Envisage your child having positive, loving, supportive friendships.

2. See and sense your loved one in radiant good health, full of fun and vitality.

3. Imagine you are totally fulfilled by your job and it is a wonderful means to express your passion, creativity and gifts and at the same time is financially rewarding.

4. Explore with excitement and anticipation what wonderful things would be happening with the financial abundance that is yours.

Also, look for something to be grateful for in whatever is the area of your concern. This will immediately lift you and will offer a higher vibration to anyone who may otherwise be at the center of your worry.

Where appropriate, seek help with addressing some practical issues like a financial budget. Some strong boundaries may be necessary to implement. Try to spend time in nature, which can assist your clarity and wellbeing with its more pristine environment. Ensure you clear your energy field regularly to optimize a higher vibration. If you are caring for a sick loved one, make sure you look after yourself well with diet, exercise, and rest. In summary, the more positive and healthy you can be, the more you can help others.

For a total diversion, do something creative. It is a way to exercise the brain and provide new pathways of thought, assisting you to refocus in a positive direction. It also gives you pleasure and elevates your mood.

See also:

- Asking for Help
- Boundaries
- Clearing
- Connect with Nature
- Do Things You Enjoy
- Gratitude
- Grounding/Earthing
- Projections
- Seek to Understand
- Thought Power and Control

Strategy 53
FORGIVENESS PROCESS

CATEGORIES APPLIED

Addressing Addictions
Addressing Anxiety
Addressing Depression
Awareness and Mindfulness
Communications and Relationships
Improving Self-Esteem

There are three separate Forgiveness processes below, though the one for Forgiving Self may be incorporated within either Forgiving Another or Asking Another for forgiveness. Each is done in a meditative state.

Feelings of hurt or betrayal can be all-consuming; they can hinder your clarity, seriously erode your self-esteem, inhibit your potential, and color your thoughts and everything you do in life. These feelings drain your energy and can be the trigger for the manifestation of illness or disease in your body.

This Forgiveness process recognizes that you can't change the events that triggered these emotions, but you can change your perception and release the emotional charge. Holding on to resentment or pain is effectively leaking your energy over to the other person or situation. Forgiveness means that you choose to move on and release the previously held judgment – and you don't wait for an apology.

On an energetic level, it is your judgment about the situation that is holding the hurt feelings in place. Judgment has a very inflexible, cold vibration to it, so you ultimately need to be able to release this judgment to be free.

When you forgive, you release the negative energy that you are holding stuck in your energy field and bring in light to replace it. Transformation comes through the heart, not the mind, so it is important to connect with your heart and your feelings as you do this process.

Heart forgiveness changes the victim mentality into a power mentality where you are able to bring about transformation. It is calling your power back from this person or situation that triggered your hurt response.

If you struggle to engage with the forgiveness you may find it helpful to recognize that this person was acting out of their conditioning. It is not the truth of who they are, but merely a behavior they did at the time. Remember that you too act out of your conditioning – in fact all people act out of their conditioning until they begin the awakening journey and bring consciousness to their thoughts and actions. Forgiveness is part of the process to greater consciousness.

**"When you FORGIVE
You don't change the PAST
But you do change the FUTURE."**
– Bernard C. Meltzer

While healing can be almost instantaneous once the judgment is released, that can also be the primary struggle for some. So holding the intent to forgive and working with the mind and feeling body in this way for 30 days provides insurance and sends a very strong message to the body/mind that you are committed to moving on and changing old patterns.

You will know you have been successful when can reflect on the situation without wanting to change or justify any aspect of it. You may even reach a state of gratitude for the learning that was created out of the experience. Your future will be different as a result.

30-DAY FORGIVENESS PROCESS

Forgiving Another

1. Place yourself in a golden column of pristine light. This invokes a higher vibration around your field of energy. Invoke your higher conscious to be present with you. You may want to imagine this as a pristine ball of light that descends from above your head into your heart.

2. In order to heal inner pain you must allow yourself to feel it. You can't heal what you can't feel. Breathe into your heart and allow those hurt feelings to arise. If tears arise at any stage, let them flow.

3. Then bring to mind the person with whom you hold the feelings of hurt or pain and express forgiveness towards them, repeatedly saying: "I forgive you for anything you have done intentionally or unintentionally that has caused me pain. I forgive you, I forgive you, I forgive you." Genuinely express this from your heart. Repeating this like a mantra helps the mind to stay focused as you allow the feelings to begin shifting.

Depending on the intensity of the emotion, you may find it easier in the initial stages to add the words "I choose" so that what you say is, "I choose to forgive you." This is a subtle shift but may feel easier. Later on, if it feels more appropriate, change to "I forgive you."

Note: Very often at the root of deep pain you may discover some guilt. If this occurs, at any time throughout this 30-day forgiveness process add, "I forgive myself."

So the expression becomes "I forgive you and I forgive myself." Once again you need to be able to release any judgment about self.

Asking Another for Forgiveness

This process is also done in a meditative state rather than in person. Since we are all energy beings this practice can be equally effective, though the other person may not be aware of your intent. Of course, asking for forgiveness in a face-to-face situation is a definite option, though it may be more challenging.

1. Engage step 1 as above.

2. Bring to mind the person whom you want to ask for forgiveness. Then feel into your own heart, cultivating feelings of integrity and honesty.

3. Then say to them: "Please forgive me for anything I have ever done to hurt you in any way at any time." Feel into the genuineness of your feelings and words while holding the image of the other person for a few minutes.

   While a sincere request for forgiveness changes the vibration between you, you will need to trust your intuition on the feeling response you get back from the other person to determine how often it needs to be repeated. It may be that once or a few times is enough. Your sincerity, the intensity of the issue, and the other person's willingness to let go, will influence how often you need to do this before resolution. Your intent is of utmost importance, though 30 consecutive days will certainly create a strong energetic impact.

Forgiving Self

Holding on to self-judgment for something you have done that may have hurt another has a similar negative impact on your multidimensional body as does holding on to resentment. Ultimately this can lead to health problems. Forgiving self is equally important to either of the forgiveness processes above where there are feelings of guilt.

Just as you would feel compassion for a child learning a new task, you need to direct that compassion and forgiveness to yourself. Recognize that anything you have done to hurt another has arisen because of your conditioning, whether it was forgetfulness, confusion, or a fear based reaction. Your awareness is now such that you would choose differently. The learning has happened and it is time to release the self-judgment.

Simply add the words "I forgive myself" with genuine feeling expression

----

See also:

- Clearing
- Communication: When you…
- Conflict Resolution
- Feeling Anger
- Feeling Guilt or Shame
- Projection
- Release the Need to be Right
- Seek to Understand
- Shadow Play

Strategy 54
GAG GOSSIP

CATEGORIES APPLIED

Addressing Addictions
Addressing Anxiety
Addressing Depression
Awareness and Mindfulness
Career and Goals
Communications and Relationships
Everyday Essentials
Improving Self-Esteem

The definition of gossip is: Casual or unconstrained conversation or reports about other people, typically involving details that are not confirmed as being true. It can be sharing thoughts or a story about another when there is no value to the other person knowing.

Gossip can range from some kind of small talk, news, hearsay, rumors, to intimate or malicious talk. It may be motivated by just having something to say, jealousy, to cause harm, to seek support, or detract focus away from self. Gossip may be true or untrue.

The activity of gossip can be extremely toxic and can contaminate another person through the projection of thought-forms and lead to all kinds of negative outcomes that have a domino effect. When information is spread through gossip, people often have reactions to it and start projecting their own fears onto it, adding a lot of negativity; this forms a very dysfunctional energy matrix. The impact can last for years or a lifetime.

Some Guidelines

1. Be aware that every word has its own unique vibration, which not only has a direct impact on you but adds to the collective mix of universal energies, adding to the love or fear balance.

2. When contemplating sharing some information or being part of a conversation about another, which may be considered gossip, really tune in to your own self to determine what is your intent. Identifying your motive could provide much personal awareness. Is my involvement because I want to fit in, satisfy some egoic desire to be informed, validate my own beliefs, or any other number of reasons? Bringing consciousness to your motive allows choice and may highlight the need to address some kind of jealousy, projection, or just greater self-love.

3. When you are in a conversation that looks as if it will become gossip, stand strong in your integrity and learn to directly tell people that you do not wish to discuss something that you do not think is appropriate.

4. If you experience conflict with someone and you are contemplating sharing with others, notice if your objective is to seek support. If so, be aware that is your ego at work. Tune into your higher self through your heart to determine a more appropriate approach, which may be addressing the conflict directly with them without sharing with others, or selecting someone whom you feel will provide some honest feedback and help you see a greater truth.

5. If you find yourself in a situation where you are questioned about what someone else has said to you, gently state your boundaries and desire not to participate in gossip. You may add, "You will need to ask them, not me." This may be particularly challenging if it is a friend – though a good friend is likely to be very respectful of your desires and actions.

6. Be very discerning about even listening to, or reading the news and then discussing some negative story that *you can't do a thing about.* The problem is, as you convey the story, you take on board the vibration of the words, which leaves you vulnerable, adds to your stress levels and very likely to the stress levels of others as well. It's a kind of gossip that contributes to the collective negativity within our world, which is struggling with all kinds of imbalances.

It can take courage to stand your ground and be conscious, clear, and direct in these situations, but this powerful kind of response will avoid potentially messy situations and ultimately be beneficial to all including:

- To the potential recipient/s of gossip because you are avoiding any contribution to contaminating them.
- To those wishing to engage you in gossip; when you deny this involvement you model a behavior of integrity and assist harmony in this world.
- To yourself because when you choose behaviors that are focused more on love than on fear (which is behind gossip), you add to your own sense of self-worth. This is also a reflection of self-mastery.
- Keeping your own thoughts private about your goals creates a purer, clearer, and more powerful energy matrix that avoids any contamination by others.

As human beings there are times when you feel you want to share some concern or feel the need to bounce something around with another. Be discerning and talk to a close and trusted friend whom you know you can confide in without risking it going beyond the two of you.

See also:

- Boundaries
- Do No Harm
- Honor and Respect Differences
- Intention/Counter-Intention
- Projection
- Seek to Understand
- Thought Power and Control
- Trust, Truth, and Honesty
- Truth Lover

Strategy 55
GOAL SETTING

CATEGORIES APPLIED

Addressing Addictions
Addressing Anxiety
Addressing Depression
Awareness and Mindfulness
Career and Goals
Communications and Relationships
Environmental Health
Exercise for Life
Improving Self-Esteem
Nutrition for Life

Setting goals is like planting seeds. Some seeds take longer to germinate than others and some take years before they are visible. Still others manifest very fast. Goals give you a sense of purpose and direction.

Without doubt, the most satisfying of all goals are the ones that fulfill your heart's desire. Desire is a natural human condition and as creator beings, the reality is that you are manifesting all the time whether you realize it or not. So you might as well have a focus that leads you to your preferred goals, rather than going along aimlessly or focusing on what you don't want, which is the common practice for an unaware mind.

It is important to determine your own goals without being influenced by the opinion of others. This can distract you from your own inner knowing and create confusion. Decision-making then comes through the conditioned mind, and all kinds of things can come into play to prevent you reaching your heart's desire. Adult children may find themselves living out the goals of their parents, maybe pursuing a career in IT or medicine when they really want to work in agriculture. There may be other well-meaning friends or associates who all contribute their ideas, and before long you could be burdened by ideas, logic, and practicalities that do nothing to satisfy your true purpose.

When you choose goals that come from your heart's desire you will likely find that these are also respectful of the Earth because your heart energy recognizes the connectedness of life and knows the importance of sustainability and respect for all life. Goals that come from passion evoke emotion. This is an ingredient that inspires, motivates, and helps you to feel good. It is also an extremely powerful energy for manifesting.

While material wealth may be part of your journey, be aware that if it is your primary motivator it will not fulfil the true essence of your being. Many people spend a great deal of energy striving for wealth and even achieving some success, yet remain unfulfilled. Your mind and heart must work together to understand and satisfy your fundamental purpose for being here in this earthly reality. This alignment of heart and mind provides a freedom for you to express your true gifts and have fun along the way.

Identifying Your Goals

Step 1. To identify your core goal – your reason for being here – sit quietly and breathe deeply in and out of your heart. When you feel a sense of calm, bring in a feeling of gratitude. It brings that higher vibration that allows inspiration to arise from your heart.

Then imagine you are approaching the end of your life. When you look back on it, what will make you feel completely satisfied that you achieved what you set out to achieve? It's the kind of feeling that makes you want to punch the air and say, "Yes, I did it – I really did it!"

Then, from that place of awareness, plan the steps backward that move you towards that outcome. There will likely be a multitude of steps and goals that branch out into different areas that form part of this primary one. There will also be secondary ones that enhance your life and sense of wellbeing along the way. Consider the following categories and jot down all the goals that come to mind.

- Career business: new job, self-employed, market growth
- Family: days off, trips, special events
- Financial/income: savings and investments, credit, debt reduction
- Health/appearance: weight loss, exercise, nutrition
- Making a difference: charitable giving, tithing, mentoring
- Personal growth/spiritual: education, counseling, meditating
- Other relationships: friends, mentors, business alliances, staff
- Creative: hobbies, sporting or fun activities.

Step 2. If your goals are still unclear, get clear on your values, as this will help you see what is important to you and assist your clarity. See Strategy 99 Values for more information.

Step 3. While maintaining your primary end-of-life goal, list your short, medium, and long-term goals. Your primary life goal may be included in your long-term one. It is important that you believe the fulfillment of these goals will make you feel happy.

- long-term (5 years) goal/s

- medium-term (1 year) goal/s
- short-term (1–6 months) goal/s.

So, write down your primary goal and the different goals from various categories, as in Step 1 above. A scheme like this will also reflect your values (see Strategy 99 Values). It is an overview, and now you need to plan the specific steps. You can continue with the following steps in a notebook or use a large sheet of paper so everything is visible on one page.

Step 4. Using the example with a single large poster-sized sheet of paper, draw your primary life goal in the center and all your secondary goals radiating out, giving them plenty of room so you can add further information if necessary.

For those surrounding goals that are linked to your primary goal, run a connecting line through from goal to goal to indicate this.

Other goals that are separate remain on your poster sheet, creating an overall picture of what you are striving to achieve. Every one of the goals will be like a cog in a wheel and central to a series of adjacent lines that will represent the steps you need to take. As you identify the different steps, create a small line out from your center goal circle and note the behaviour or task required.

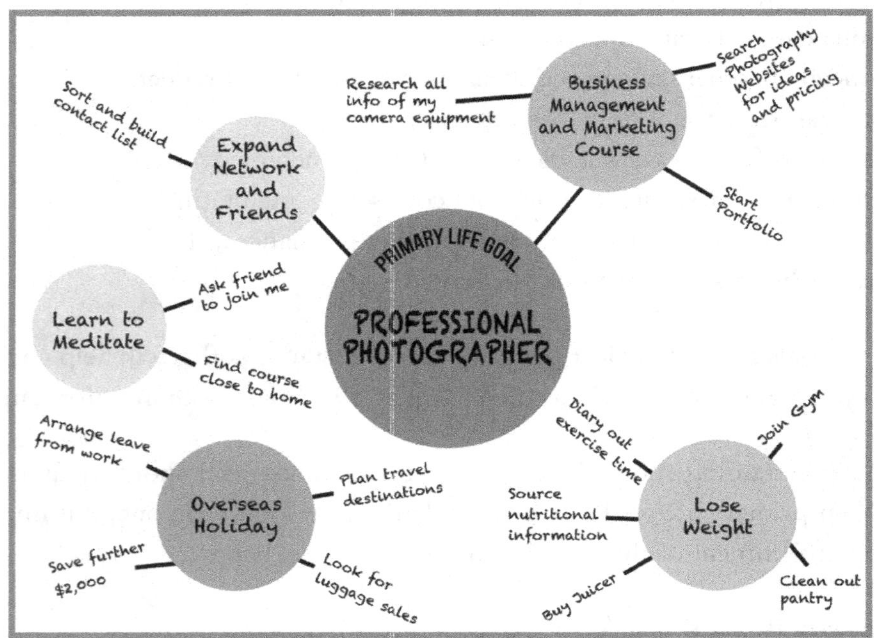

Your finished goal plan will show each of your goals, labelled in a central circle, with a series of small connecting lines labelling your specific associated behavioral tasks.

Add as much detail as you like. You may like to prioritize these behavioural tasks by numbers in a sequence of activity and assign dates to these tasks. You can add this to your daily TO DO list. Hang your goal poster on a wall somewhere where you are constantly reminded of your goals and steps you need to take.

Step 5. If you want further clarity, this optional step 5 will make things clearer by answering the questions below. You can then add your notes to your poster-sized plan:

- Why do you want this goal, or what do you aim to achieve by the fulfillment of this goal? (Your agenda).
- List the knowledge, skills, and abilities that you will need to acquire to achieve your goals.
- List the areas you are weak in and what you can do to acquire these skills, knowledge, or abilities.
- What are you willing to give up to achieve this goal? (e.g. behaviors such as alcohol abuse, blaming, avoidance, unclear boundaries, dysfunctional relationships)
- What beliefs do you hold that may be in the way of you achieving these goals?

On completion, you may find some adjustment or additions to your tasks. Be aware also that going for your goals will bring up your blocks and resistance. Continually challenge your inner voices, which will include your saboteur and inner critic. Identify all the logical excuses for not achieving your goal/s. Then identify your motive underneath your logical excuse. For example,

> Initial Motive: "It will take too long"
> Deeper motive: "I might fail and be rejected"
> Repeatedly ask yourself: "If I were to listen to you, where would that lead me?"

As you do this self-inquiry, you may realize that it is a pattern you exhibit that stops you moving forwards. With greater awareness you can choose again.

Step 6. Going for goals and achieving new things may require that you work outside of your comfort zone. This is how you expand and move towards your potential. To keep your spirits up, avoid spending a whole day in challenge; also do things you love.

Step 7. Keep returning to a feeling of gratitude to keep your vibration high and in the flow of positive energy, even when the obstacles arise. You will expand into more of your potential from overcoming each challenge.

Step 8. Create affirmations to support your goal/s and work with them habitually.

Step 9. Create a Vision Board. Collect and cut out pictures and images that reflect what it is you are wishing to manifest and paste them onto a board. Pictures are the language of the subconscious mind and create an immediate message and reminder of your desire.

Have it where you view it daily.

Step 10. Spend a few minutes each day visualizing each of your goals as though they have already happened. Connect with that deep feeling of satisfaction that you were completely successful. It is the feeling that is important as you focus on your desires. If you have difficulties experiencing the feeling, play with *WHAT IF…*, i.e. "What if this goal had manifested? What would be happening? How would I feel?"

Remember that energy goes where energy flows. This gets your creative mind working, which is more right brain and connected to your heart energy.

Step 11. Then let go and allow your goal to manifest. Do not be fixated; let the universe work with you and remain observant and act accordingly. Entertain a sense that it is coming to fruition. Be in the flow of energy and know that every choice and decision you make is building your future.

Step 12. Perform frequent goal review – as you change your goals often change.

Important reminder: To feel completely satisfied, it is not so much about acquiring things as it is about fulfilling your heart's passion or the desire of your core essence. As you follow your heart's longing you actualize your gifts. This in turn allows you to continue to realize more and more of your authentic self. See Strategy 77 Personal Mission Statement for an expanded process.

See also

- Affirmations
- Asking for Help

- Do Things You Enjoy
- Going with the Flow
- Ideas and Inspirations
- Personal Mission Statement
- Review and Remake Your Day
- Values
- Work Passion

Strategy 56
GOING WITH THE FLOW

CATEGORIES APPLIED

Addressing Addictions
Addressing Anxiety
Addressing Depression
Awareness and Mindfulness
Career and Goals
Communications and Relationships
Improving Self-Esteem

Going with the flow has a fluid and easy feeling and things just seem to unfold in your track. It's like swimming with the tide rather than against it. It's typical of the energy that reflects your alignment with your passion or your heart's guidance. And it will ultimately have positive outcomes. It's a matter of trusting that inner feeling that is always striving to guide you even if you may not be aware of the exact outcome or destination.

Going with the flow is about identifying what feels right for you as an individual and acting on that, while also respecting others' preferences.

You need also to be discerning that you have not hooked into the flow of others around you that may take you off your course. This is common when you step into the field of a group where they collectively have a similar focus. Have you ever found yourself buying a further drink or having a dessert when you really doubted that you wanted it, or buying something you didn't need when you went into a shopping center? Somehow you've got hooked into a collective field of energy that is stronger than yours, and it has a powerful affect on you. Such examples illustrate the need for keeping your own energy field clear and having strong boundaries.

Being in resistance, by contrast, is when challenges and obstacles are present. It's like trying to swim upstream. Resistance is also a reflection of being attached to a particular thing or outcome. It is often associated with a mind story that you run, believing this will ultimately serve you, but effectively you are disregarding your heart's innate intelligence and allowing the ego to drive you. It may suggest stubbornness on your part; only your honest self-reflection can determine if this is so.

Discernment is important here because if you are striving to achieve certain goals, it is common to come up against some resistance. It is often overcoming obstacles that can be part of the learning process, and this leads to your growth. Your higher self may be guiding you to do something that will empower you and your belief in yourself.

Penny Peirce has this to say:

> The Flow is the constantly evolving consciousness of all souls and all forms of life. It sources you with ideas and give your creations to others who need them, so we all evolve in the most efficient, loving way. Flow can also be an experience of alignment and unification of your body, emotion, mind and soul with an action – to the point where you can't tell if you're doing the moving or if something bigger is moving you.

Essential to going with the flow is flexibility and the willingness to change direction. It is being attuned to your feeling body so that you can interpret your own higher guidance. Learning to trust your own heart's guidance is probably the single most important thing you can do for yourself, because it will always lead you to expansion and greater love in your life. Your heart is directly associated with your feeling body, which never lies: it just feels. Unfortunately, listening to your feeling body is something we tend to unlearn as we grow up; we allow logic and practicalities, which come from the analytical mind, to be the dominating force.

Have you ever observed a 2-year-old?
They just feel and act. No thinking!

Be aware that your mind can be telling you all kinds of stories that will be influenced by your programming. If you are finding obstacles, pause and reflect inwardly to determine the possible reason for this:

- Is your higher self attempting to guide you in another direction that you are resisting?
- Are you just meeting an obstacle that you need to overcome to meet your goal and add to your learning?
- Is what you are feeling all "yours", or are you being influenced by the energies around you. If so, you will need to find some neutral space and do some clearing. See Strategy 16 Clearing and 63 Intention/Counter Intention.
- Question any thoughts before acting on them. Ask yourself "If I were to listen to you, where would that lead me?" Notice the feeling response along with the impression you get.

See also:

- Allow Feelings
- Awareness of Awareness
- Clearing
- Do Things You Enjoy
- Gratitude
- Grounding/Earthing
- Intention/Counter-Intention
- Thought: Managing the Inner Critic

Penny Peirce, *Leap of Perception: The transforming Power of Your Attention*, Beyond Words, 2013, p. 196.

Strategy 57
GRATITUDE

CATEGORIES APPLIED

Addressing Addictions
Addressing Anxiety
Addressing Depression
Awareness and Mindfulness
Career and Goals
Communications and Relationships
Everyday Essentials
Environmental Health
Improving Self-Esteem
Nutrition for Life
Quick Stress Busters

Gratitude has a very high frequency and as such attracts a high-quality energy that is basically a "feel good" vibe. Positive feelings and emotions can be measured scientifically and reflect even waves of energy on the ECG monitor by measuring the heart response – very different to negative emotions, which present on the monitor like jagged mountain peaks of varying heights.

According to research at the Institute of Heart Math,

> True feelings of gratitude, appreciation and other positive emotions can synchronize brain and heart rhythms, creating a body wide shift to a scientifically measurable state of coherence. In this optimal state, the body's systems function more efficiently, generating a greater balance of emotions and increased mental clarity and brain function.

Research by Dr. Masaru Emoto on the effect of words on water revealed that the words "Love and Gratitude" created a most beautiful light-colored crystal-like snowflake. By contrast, the words "You make me sick" created a dark distorted image.

Love and Gratitude

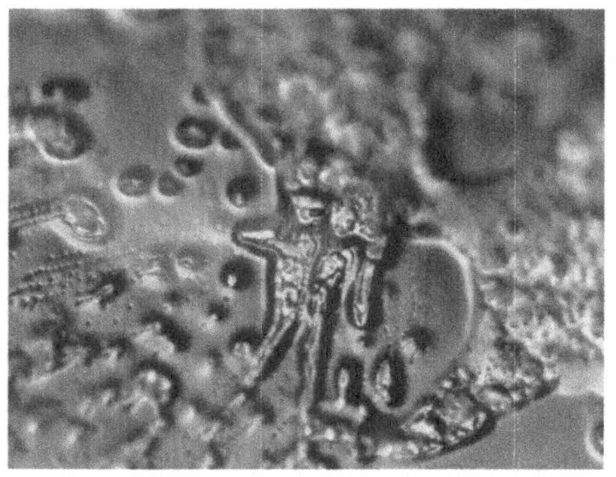
You Make Me Sick

If we were to look at all emotions on a scale from Fear at the low end to Love at the high end, like degrees on a thermometer, we would find that Gratitude is way up in the love bandwidth. This very high vibration puts you in alignment with your heart and your higher guidance. No matter what situation you are in, there is always something to be grateful for. It can be easier to evoke a sense of gratitude than it can be to evoke loving feelings, yet the high vibrations of both feeling states are similar in the beneficial qualities.

Summary findings from Robert Emmons' "Thanks! How the New Science of Gratitude Can Make You Happier" indicates that those who practice grateful thinking "reap emotional, physical and interpersonal benefits."

The science is here. When you practice Gratitude you develop more optimism, build your self-esteem, relationships improve, you have more energy and exercise more, sleep better and you become more spiritual and generally happier. Gratitude activates the heart energy, and when we are attuned to our heart we are more intuitive, have better problem-solving abilities, clearer thinking, and access to more information.

Looking for gratitude everywhere can profoundly change your life. In 2013 Thought Leaders of the World offered 21 days of gratitude in meditations through the Internet, attracting over 200,000 participants. During a meditation retreat, Stacey Robin created this gratitude symbol, and through the Internet invited the world to join in a 42-day gratitude experiment in 2009. There were 271,934 participants and reports for the key benefits are listed below:

- Feel better instantly.
- Enjoy supportive, synergistic, exciting relationships.
- Increase your prosperity and abundance.
- Experience vibrant health.
- Know peace of mind.
- Supercharge your creative juices.
- Magnetize the realization of your dreams and goals.
- Make a profound difference in the lives of many people.

While the various types of scientific research about feelings and gratitude are very affirming, we know from our own innate body's intelligence just how good we can feel when we focus on gratitude. It can be instantly transforming of all kinds of challenging emotions.

The feeling we get and the vibration it creates are amazingly powerful and freely available to us at all times. We simply need to consciously choose gratitude. Gratitude for a warm bed, an abundance of food, loving relationships, the smell of a beautiful rose – all provide that feel-good quality that enhances our wellbeing.

Each of these gratitude strategies requires that you engage the emotional body because of the high vibration that results. So first think about (the mental body) whatever is your focus of gratitude and then really feel into it (Thought + Feeling = Emotion). You will find that it can immediately bring about a positive change.

"Gratitude helps you to grow and expand;
Gratitude brings joy and laughter into your life
and into the lives of all those around you."
– Eileen Caddy.

Everyday gratitude

Look for gratitude in all kinds of things every day. Say thank you in your mind often for even the smallest things. Develop an attitude of gratitude for everything in your life and see what happens.

Gratitude lift – 1 minute

This is an "in the moment" exercise. When you are feeling a bit down, challenged, stressed or lost, *feel into* something that you are grateful for. It doesn't matter what in particular is the object of your attention; it is the frequency or resonance of gratitude that uplifts you and the energy around you. It could be simple things, like a good cuppa, a nice meal, a roof over your head, friends or loved ones in your life, a beautiful sunset, the song of a bird, a magnificent tree, opportunities for growth, an income, some kind of creative expression, good health, or anything else.

21-day gratitude list – 10 minutes

At bedtime, take a pen and paper and list at least 10 things that you are grateful for in your life. Just before you go to sleep your brainwave pattern slows down and you enter the alpha level, which is where the subconscious and so much of our unresolved issues are stored. Making this gratitude list facilitates a more peaceful sleep, uplifts your feeling state, and helps to reprogram the subconscious mind. Writing requires a deeper level of reflection than just thinking, and assists you to maintain focus. You also engage other senses such as kinaesthetic and visual as you write and read each one. The more senses you engage in learning, the more integrated the experience.

Meditation is another time when the brain slows down and enters the alpha level, so this is equally beneficial to use as part of your meditation practice and can be done at any time of day.

Repeat this process of listing at least 10 things that you are grateful for every day for 21 days. Try to extend your list so that you keep finding more things each night. Twenty-one days is the timeframe required to adopt new habits. On completion, you will notice a very tangible difference in how you feel. Repetition changes the neural pathways and boosts your immune system. Being grateful every day leads to joy.

Gratitude for people triggers

An emotional trigger is usually the result of someone who has found your wound and you are reacting to it. Without their input you may continue to live with the subconscious pain that drives you, whether you are aware of it or not. At the very least you can be grateful for the awareness that something in your body-mind has revealed itself and then for the opportunity to bring healing to the problem. Further gratitude can be for the person who actually found that button, albeit painful. It is these people (your angels in disguise), who are helping you recognize where you have inner work to do. Feeling emotionally triggered is always your opportunity for more clarity, and transformation. It is almost impossible to heal issues when the pain is not present. You can't heal what you can't feel! The pain, hurt, anxiety, distress – whatever it is – has made its presence known and this is an opportunity for healing old wounds and has the potential for a greater awareness. Greater awareness or the expansion of consciousness is an unfolding truth.

Gratitude for issues

Sounds a bit odd, you may be thinking, yet developing gratitude for problems is a way to assist their resolution and help you feel better. Problems are typically associated with negative or undesirable feelings. Consider the kind of resonance you would be creating if you chose to be grateful for the perceived problems in your life. See them rather as challenges to be overcome, opportunities for learning, expansion and growth. When you feel gratitude around a perceived problem, you not only improve your feeling state, but you leave yourself open to a new understanding rather than having a fixed kind of judgment around it. The energy surrounding that particular problem is then elevated to a more positive vibe – and as a result you may find your perception changes, a solution presents itself, or that the patterns around you alter in some way.

Because of the pattern and many rewards of these processes you will find that gratitude becomes more prevalent in your daily routine.

Experience these gratitude exercises and watch yourself change and grow, feel better, experience joy, and your world change around you.

As a final reminder, do remember to engage both the mental and emotional bodies.

See also:

- Awareness of Awareness
- Do Things You Enjoy
- Feeling Agitated
- Feeling Anger
- Feeling Challenged
- Feeling Disempowered
- Feeling Fear
- Feeling Grief
- Feeling Guilt or Shame
- Feeling Jealousy
- Feeling Lonely
- Feeling Rejected or Hurt
- Feeling Scattered: Unbalanced
- Feeling Stuck
- Feeling Uncertain or Fearful of the Unknown
- Feeling Unloved or Unlovable
- Feeling Unsupported
- Feeling Victimized
- Feeling Worried
- Thought Power and Control

http://www.heartmath.org
Masaru Emoto: http://www.masaru-emoto.net/english/water-crystal.html
Robert Emmons: http://gratitudepower.net/science.htm
www.GoGratitude.com

Strategy 58
GROUNDING/EARTHING

CATEGORIES APPLIED

Addressing Addictions
Addressing Anxiety
Addressing Depression
Awareness and Mindfulness
Career and Goals
Communications and Relationships
Environmental Health
Everyday Essentials
Exercise For Life
Improving Self-Esteem
Quick Stress Busters

Arguably the greatest healing energies ever known to humankind are right at our feet. Yes, the soles of our feet directly onto Mother Earth. Our more modern lifestyles have increasingly steered us away from the profound healing and balancing energies that are totally free. The humble shoe could be the greatest impediment to our health and wellbeing. We have gone so far away that we have been seeking a pill or some other kind of intervention to remedy all kinds of ailments that need nothing more than the free-flowing electrons that constantly emanate from the Earth's vibrational surface.

Despite our disconnect from the Earth, it's likely that at some time we've all felt the healing energies, the pleasure, the tingling or uplifting feeling that comes from a stroll with bare feet on the beach, perhaps playing on the grass in the park or your own backyard. Maybe we've attributed our improved sense of wellbeing to being on holidays, or having fun with the kids, when all along we have not been aware that our flesh-to-Earth connection is sending healing vibrations through our body.

Thanks to the research initiated by Clint Ober and others who followed, the evidence is now abundantly clear: the Earth is a living source of energy constantly providing negatively charged free electrons at its surface.

We human beings are also electrical in nature and when our bare feet meet with the Earth's surface our bodies immediately start to equalize to the same electric energy levels as the Earth.

Benefits Of Earthing/Grounding

Clinton Ober and his associates tell us that placing your bare feet on the ground does some remarkable things:

- Defuses the cause of inflammation, and improves or eliminates the symptoms of many inflammation-related disorders
- Reduces or eliminates chronic pain
- Improves sleep in most cases
- Increases energy
- Lowers stress and promotes calmness in the body by cooling down the nervous system and stress hormones
- Normalizes the body's biological rhythms
- Thins blood and improves blood pressure and flow
- Relieves muscle tension and headaches
- Lessens hormonal and menstrual symptoms
- Dramatically speeds healing and helps prevent bedsores
- Reduces or eliminates jet lag
- Protects the body against potentially health-disturbing environmental electromagnetic fields
- Accelerates recovery from intense athletic activity

If you want to feel better, then remove your shoes and socks and go sit, stand, walk, or connect your flesh with the Earth. Earth's conductors of energy include sand, soil, grass, concrete, slate, or paving. The effect, while almost immediate, varies from person to person. The key thing is to make it habitual. Even do your own little experiment. Try Earthing for 30 minutes a day for one month and notice how you feel. Then go back to your old ways just to test it out. It won't cost you anything and the potential gains are extraordinary, plus your feet will love it. Barefoot walking allows them to breathe freely, provides relaxation to tired feet, while also stretching and strengthening tendons and ligaments.

Effects Of Being Ungrounded

Many energy workers identify indications that one is not grounded: when you repeatedly bump into things; maybe trip or just can't seem to think clearly; when you are easily influenced by the opinions and beliefs of others, or feel detached from your feelings. Some of life's more harsh experiences can on some level leave you with a sense of not really wanting to be here, although it may or may not be articulated. This often arises as a result of unresolved trauma or emotional wounding, which can lead to addictive behaviors.

Even some meditative practices without the process of energetically connecting to the Earth can tend to take one out of the body. This can significantly affect your energy field by retracting it up from the Earth. As a result, you also become more vulnerable to accidents because you are not fully occupying your body.

Not being grounded inhibits your ability to manifest your goals. If you wish to transform anything you must totally inhabit all your multidimensional bodies and be present and grounded on the Earth. It is also essential to bring about healing in your physical body. You must be fully present in your physical body in order to truly heal and transform any imbalance.

Being grounded helps you to really feel and allows you to respond appropriately in your body by being more connected to the Earth's forces of which you are a part, more attuned to your subtle nervous system, your energy bodies, your instincts and your higher conscious levels – in fact to everything in your life.

Earthing For Survival

Most of the Earth's creatures live with a natural connection to the Earth Mother, and yet humankind has cut itself off from her, and become insensitive to her constant giving of life. As human beings living in this world, our connection with the Earth energy is vitally important for all our survival needs.

Despite the plethora of technological devices that seem to be steering humanity to clearly unsustainable thinking and actions, with the relatively recent revelations about Earthing, perhaps it could be the way ahead for our very survival as a species on this beautiful planet. When we ground with the very being that provides all our resources for living in this existence, we begin to realize that we are all connected and that many of our actions and inactions are inherently damaging. Grounding allows us to rediscover the natural order of things and it may be that with that awareness we can move forward with the essential respect and compassion necessary for our mutual evolution.

When we build a loving connection with the Earth she also provides us with a level of protection from many of the unseen negative energies in our universe. She is after all our Earth Mother.

Grounding/Earthing Exercise

Remove your shoes and sit or walk for 20–30 minutes with flesh to earth contact.

When this is not possible do this energy-grounding exercise. It works on the premise that energy follows thought.

Hold the intent to connect with Mother Earth and visualize, sense, or imagine that you have roots of light (just like tree roots) coming out through the soles of your feet that go deep into the heart of the Earth.

If sitting cross-legged in meditation, do this exercise by imagining roots of light coming out from the base of your spine. This will have the added benefit of ensuring that you fully inhabit your body following your practice.

Aim to feel or sense your energy going down into the core of the Earth. You can enhance this process further by cultivating a sense of gratitude for all that she gives. Then strive to feel the Earth's energy being returned to you and coming up through your whole body.

Just a few minutes each day will strengthen your connection.

See also:

- Awareness of Awareness
- Boundaries
- Connect with Nature
- Feeling Agitated
- Feeling Scattered: Unbalanced
- Jiggling

Clinton Ober, Stephen Sinatra, and Martin Zuker, *Earthing: The Most Important Health Discovery Ever?* Basic Health Publications Inc. 2010, p. 11.
Dr. Stephen Sinatra, https://www.youtube.com/watch?v=XumPQLTzPWI

Strategy 59
HELP ANOTHER

CATEGORIES APPLIED
Addressing Addictions
Addressing Anxiety
Addressing Depression
Awareness and Mindfulness
Career and Goals
Communications and Relationships
Improving Self-Esteem

When someone is feeling down, they have lost their connection with their higher self. They may be anxious about something, running a negative story, grieving for some kind of loss or inability to control some of life's circumstances, feeling powerless or unloved. Low self-worth could well be a prevailing condition. A friendly smile, a willingness to be present and listen can be the very best medicine.

Our actual presence with them is one of the greatest gifts humans can give each other. Most often the root of all our problems arises from a feeling of disconnect – not feeling heard, seen, valued, or respected. Just acknowledging another and what they are feeling is very precious and helps us feel connected. It is not about agreeing or disagreeing, just validating them for where they are.

Expressing their concerns to an empathic listener can help them become clearer, and this is often enough for them to be able to move on. If it feels relevant you might like to draw from Strategy 18 Communication Keys.

Be alert to a common misbehavior of sympathizing with someone, or worrying about them, particularly if they are in your closer connections. When this occurs, you join with them in perpetuating the lower vibration, which helps neither of you. You are much more likely to be of benefit if you can be light-hearted and keep your focus in the positive. When you are positive, your energy can entrain another to uplift them, though you need to take care with your own boundaries.

Be aware of any tendency within yourself to want to "fix" or rescue another. This can often be projection of your own unresolved emotions or your own need for recognition. True unconditional support is when you can leave the other person empowered, perhaps helping them to see how they can take responsibility to elevate their emotional state.

If they are repeating a negative story you could remind them that this is perpetuating their current feeling state and suggest a number of other Strategies in this program relevant to their situation: Strategies like 10 Beliefs Challenge, 27 Deep Release Breathing, 29 Do Things You Enjoy, 87 Seek to Understand (play some of their favorite music), or any of the techniques in 98 Thought Power and Control, or 57 Gratitude will create an instant lift, though acknowledging your compassion for them might be enough on its own to help elevate them.

There may be occasions that even your best efforts may fail to uplift them. This is the great balancing act: to be present and compassionate and know when you need to stand back and just allow them to be in their current emotional state and know that all things will pass.

"It is one of the beautiful compensations of this life that no man can sincerely try to help another without helping himself."
– Ralph Waldo Emerson

Help Another Physically

Helping another person not only offers assistance to them, but it also leaves you with a good feeling. It is part of our innate nature to be loving and caring and there are numerous studies to validate the positive impact of such caring on our own health, happiness, and even longevity. Helping another to achieve their goals is a sure way to help yourself achieve your own goals.

Providing support need not be a major effort. It can be very simple things requiring little effort, time, or cost, like giving up your place in a queue at the bank, post office, or theatre; carrying someone's shopping to the car; assisting a neighbor to take their bins out for collection.

Consider volunteering in your community. Join Rotary or the local Lions club. There are plenty of opportunities that can enrich your life, such as reading at the local school or hospital, caring for animals, assisting someone with gardening, or transporting elderly people to appointments.

If your commitments create limited time consider helping with small business loans in developing countries from as little as $25.00 (see http://www.kiva.org). You may like to ponder the practice of "Gif-tiv-ism". It is radical acts of generosity that can change the world. Great people like Gandhi, Mother Teresa, Cesar Chavez, and Nelson Mandela all share a remarkable trait of generosity. Simple small acts of giving feed the soul of the giver and the receiver.

"Our human compassion binds us the one to the other – not in pity or patronizingly, but as human beings who have learnt how to turn our common suffering into hope for the future."
– Nelson Mandela

The Contrast: Intentionally "Not Helping"

Be aware of any tendency towards a behavior that could inhibit, obstruct, or undermine another that may arise from feelings of inadequacy, jealousy, or fear of their success over you. Withholding information that may be useful to them is a certain way to inhibit your own success. It is behavior of the egoic mind, which feels threatened in some way, and it does not understand that support and cooperation for another is really at the core of the human heart and recognizes that we are all connected. Helping another is a direct way to maintain flow and facilitate your own ease of manifestation. At the same time you get to feel good about yourself.

See also:

- Boundaries
- Beliefs Challenge
- Competition versus Cooperation
- Deep Release Breathing
- Do Things You Enjoy
- Gratitude
- Honor and Respect Differences
- Seek to Understand
- Thought Power and Control

Strategy 60
HONOR AND RESPECT DIFFERENCES

CATEGORIES APPLIED

Addressing Anxiety
Addressing Depression
Awareness and Mindfulness
Career and Goals
Communications and Relationships
Everyday Essentials
Improving Self-Esteem

All people have their own unique skills and qualities and yet we are all made of the same stuff. Each one of us is programmed according to our early life experiences including our genetics, parenting, education, culture, and religion. This is not a better or worse situation. It is just the way it is.

The challenge is to recognize that all people are conditioned and most will identify themselves with the illusory mind unless they have been educated otherwise. The human mind forms opinions and wants to make judgments, create labels, and make some kind of conceptual identity about another. This assigns them to a form of limiting box and it inhibits your own ability to view both them and life from a more expansive view.

Mark Waldman, a researcher in communication, spirituality, and the brain, states:

> The moment we repeat a certain thought, the more "real" that thought becomes. Because everything we believe in also has a corresponding non-belief, the brain does something odd. It rejects any information or anyone, that interferes with that belief. It's a natural neurological process and it explains why human beings are so prone to prejudice. The moment we identify ourselves with one group (political, religious, social or even a sports team) the less respect we show toward people who are members of different groups.
>
> We need to remind ourselves that our labels – our beliefs, our memories, even our perceptions of the world – are not real. Instead they are arbitrary categories that our brain uses to organize the sensations coming in from an unknown world.

That is why raising awareness is so important and help us to see these often unconscious patterns of behaviors that seek to separate rather than unite. True self-empowerment comes from unraveling all our conditioning and seeing the play of the mind and how our thoughts and beliefs dictate our behavior – all of which is within our power to change. Irrespective of different people's beliefs, values, and experiences, we are all connected. It is important to be open to new ways of thinking and be willing to learn from another.

Do not judge another for their differences, but rather look for the sameness.

Judgment carries a very harsh and negative energy that detracts from your vibration and has a negative impact on the other person.

Acceptance of another for who and what they are allows energy to keep flowing freely as it is meant to do. It does not mean you have to agree with another or even condone their behavior. It's just a matter of accepting them as a person, and understanding they have been conditioned just like you, and then be discerning and setting clearly defined boundaries that respect your own values as well as the other person.

The more we seek to understand about others, the more our knowledge and awareness expands of both them and ourselves. We become open to new perspectives and this facilitates connecting to that instinctive compassion that resides within, allowing benefit to another, but also helping to feel good about ourselves.

"If you want others to be happy, practice compassion.
If you want to be happy, practice compassion."
– The Dalai Lama

See also:

- Awareness of Awareness
- Boundaries
- Beliefs Challenge
- Judgment Effect
- Projection
- Release the Need to be Right
- Seek to Understand

Mark Waldham, Neurowisdom-ebook.pdf 10 Mind Blowing Discoveries About the Human Brain No. 7.

Strategy 61
IDEAS AND INSPIRATIONS

CATEGORIES APPLIED

Addressing Addictions
Addressing Anxiety
Addressing Depression
Awareness and Mindfulness
Career and Goals
Improving Self-Esteem

There is no shortage of positive ideas, but unfortunately many of them never come to birth and remain in the thought realms. Human beings are naturally creative and always desiring. Remember, everything we experience in this universe is as a result of the collection of humanity's thought processes.

"Good" ideas are associated with "good" feelings that add to the harmony on this planet, and yet many will not take the required action to bring them into manifestation. This is like denying your inspiration – the light within you or your higher guidance – all of which is leading you towards your greatest potential and purpose.

The common reason for this is a lack of self-worth arising from stories people have told themselves, fears about change, and overcoming challenges that are an inevitable part of growth and bringing a new idea into manifestation. These ideas and inspirations are keys to your growth, how you feel about yourself and success in life.

Every single person has their own unique energy signature and their own gifts, talents, and abilities that are meant to contribute to this earthly life. When you respond to your heart's desire you feel good about yourself. Every time you call on some inner courage and will to overcome a challenge and step out of your comfort zone, the result is a feeling of increased self-esteem and self-worth and of course, a closer step towards the manifestation of your ideas.

Set goals and take action steps to bring your positive ideas to fruition. When you act upon inspiration, the universe will keep guiding you if you stay grounded and attuned to your heart. It may be better not to share your inspirations initially in case you do not have a supportive audience. If the idea feels good, just do it.

See also:

- Change Challenge
- Decisions: Heart Wisdom
- Decisions: Motives and Impact
- Do Things You Enjoy
- Goal Setting
- Go with the Flow
- Grounding/Earthing
- Intention/Counter-Intention
- Personal Mission Statement

Strategy 62
IF SERIOUSLY ILL: UNDERSTANDING INTEGRATED HEALING

CATEGORIES APPLIED

Addressing Addictions
Addressing Anxiety
Addressing Depression
Awareness and Mindfulness
Career and Goals
Communications and Relationships
Environmental Health
Everyday Essentials
Exercise for Living
Improving Self-Esteem
Nutrition for Life

Resolving serious illness requires courage and a compassionate, curious, and willing attitude towards change that embraces what needs to be done at a physical level as well as what has to be addressed at an energy level. This is because your physical body is a reflection of your subtle bodies: your emotional, mental, and spiritual selves. What impacts on one of these bodies will also impact on the others.

The body has a supreme intelligence and naturally knows how to heal itself if you allow it and provide the right environment. To understand true healing we must acknowledge the spiritual aspect of self: the eternalness of your energy. Energy can never be eliminated, only change in form much as a tiny seed grows into a magnificent tree and eventually dies and goes back to the Earth. Life and wellbeing is not just about the body and mind, but rather about eternal growth and integration as each person does the consciousness journey to awaken to their true authentic self that recognizes the connection with all life.

If you are seriously ill, first of all attempt to get an accurate diagnosis of the cause of the health condition. Obviously treating the cause is going to be far more efficient than treating symptoms. While it may not always be a simple process to identify the cause, the seven areas below can be a helpful guide and may allow some kind of elimination, though the imbalance may comprise more than one element. See also Strategy 13 Causes of Health Imbalance.

1. Genetic disorders
2. Inadequate exercise
3. Karma
4. Harmful oral consumption, lack of nutrition
5. Insufficient sleep

6. Environment
7. Unresolved emotional issues.

"When the diagnosis is correct, the healing begins."
– Carl Jung

Wellness Checklist

Do what you can to purify the temple of your physical body. This may mean exploring and eliminating some of your bathroom products or checking for household or environmental toxins. The average home is very toxic, with a multitude of chemicals and hazardous materials. Notice if deterioration in your health followed the purchase of new furniture or furnishings and check for possible toxins. See also Strategies 30–34 Environmental Health for more detail.

Where possible, ensure the food you eat is organic, nourishing, full of life force energy and free of preservatives, antibiotics, artificial flavors and colorings. Basically eat fresh organic food – no processed foods. You may need to detoxify the body and seek some professional help to ensure your digestion and other organs are working in harmony and able to process your food effectively. There have been many advances in gut health and this can be a significant contributor to all kinds of different maladies. See also the Nutrition Strategies 72 and 73.

Exercise if your health condition allows. Check with your doctor if in doubt. While this is of great benefit to you physically it is also helpful on an energetic level as it brings light into the body. The more light, the more wellness ensues.

Make certain that rest and restful sleep are part of your daily regime, and as much as possible, get outdoors among the healing energies of nature, and soak up some sunshine. Perhaps one of the most beneficial and easiest things we can do for our health is grounding – a simple, no-effort process that is totally free and available to all. Grounding, or Earthing, has an abundance of health-promoting benefits only recently understood by science. See Strategy 58 Grounding/ Earthing for more information.

Ensure you support your body with appropriate supplements of minerals and vitamins. Supplementation is important today due to the increasing toxicity in our environment and our foods.

Repeatedly use your mind to run light through your body, and particularly to affected areas. Do it while meditating, while walking, showering, before sleep, upon waking, any time and as many times as you can think of it. Illness, disease, or pain will have darker, lower vibrational energies. Disease cannot exist where there is light within the physical body; the more light you bring into your body, the more harmony, balance, vitality, and physical wellbeing you will experience.

Check with your doctor for side effects of any medication you may be taking. Understand that anything artificial in the body has to work through the body organs and can create disharmony. Consider a second or third medical opinion. A doctor who is supportive of complementary therapies can be a great asset to support your inner healing journey.

Consider consulting with complementary practitioners who understand energy. Different ones may give you various pieces to the cause of your condition. Explore the growing field of metaphysics.

Review any immunisations you may have had and research possible effects.

Commonly Overlooked Areas

Investigate some of the less commonly explored areas related to health and wellbeing:

There are many environmental toxins, some unseen, which can have a slow and insidious impact on health. Having the head of your bed against the same wall as your outside meter box is providing a very toxic input of electromagnetic radiation while you sleep, for instance. You may live in an area where you get the drift of pesticides and herbicides from crop spraying. Our world and our homes have become very toxic and it is wise to explore these areas thoroughly. See also Strategies 30–34 Environmental Health for further details.

Check with your dentist for oral health. Every tooth is on an energy meridian, which has a direct relationship to different organs and glands in the body. Some liver or bladder problems may be triggered with an unhealthy incisor, or problems with your heart by the back molars. Ask your dentist to advise you of any specific tooth which has a root canal filling and explore the association to your presenting symptoms. Any amalgam fillings, which contain mercury, may also be problematic. See also Strategy 74 Oral Health for more information.

The temporomandibular joint or TMJ is where the lower jaw and the upper jaw connect. It is the most complex joint in the body and can be the cause of several health problems. It might be as a result of injury to the jaw or neck area, teeth grinding, poor dentistry, stress, or some kind of arthritic condition in the TMJ. Symptoms may include fibromyalgia, chronic fatigue, dizziness, sleep disturbance, face, neck, shoulder, back and headache pain. Seek a TMJ specialist or Bowen therapist or consider other gentle modalities, which may provide correction.

Geopathic stress is essentially the study of Earth energies and their effect on human wellbeing. The Earth is a living, pulsating being with natural flows of energy. The installation of cables, excavations, fracking, or any various man-made alterations can intensify the Earth's stress. There are fault lines, water veins, Hartman and Curry lines. If, for example your bed is above a crossing point of these lines your health's vulnerability is increased as it reduces your immune system.

Dr. Carstens MD (wife of former German Federal President Karl Carstens) wrote a study in 1985 stating that there were 700 cases documented worldwide where terminal cancer patients had regained their health without any conventional treatment after their sleeping area had been moved from a geopathic stress zone. Other research is available. See http://www.royriggs.co.uk/www.royriggs.co.uk/GEOPATHIC_STRESS_RESEARCH.html

Other conditions that may be signs of regular exposure to geopathic stress are chronic body pain, restless sleep, irritability, behavioral problems, and neurological disabilities. If you feel better away from home it can be a good indication that you are living in geopathic stress. A professional dowser or geomancer can help to identify any geopathic stress.

The more pristine our environment, the healthier our bodies.

"A wise man should consider that health is the greatest of human blessings, and learn how by his own thought to derive benefit from his illnesses."
– Hippocrates (460–377 BC)

Generally speaking, any physical health imbalance has been a long time coming. Any abuse to the body's temple through addictive oral substances like cigarettes, alcohol, or sugar foods will have a time lapse before organ imbalance occurs. If we expose our bodies to any of the environmental toxins so prevalent in our world today then our physical bodies will suffer, but so will our subtle bodies. Every physical imbalance has an emotional component and is the trigger for stress.

Any stored emotional hurt will manifest first out in the subtle bodies and eventually will reflect as disease, illness, or pain in the physical body. This delay is because the physical body is the densest of all the subtle bodies and so any manifestation takes longer.

Emotional (Energetic) Causes

Emotional causes of health imbalances are a huge and often neglected area, though increasing recognition is occurring of this nebulous energy.

In 1975, psychoneuroimmunology was the term that emerged to describe interactions between behavior, brain, and the immune system. Increasingly our scientists are moving into the world of vibration in order to understand the impact and interconnection of mind, body, feelings, and our environment. Quantum physics and epigenetics form the new science, which recognizes that we as energy beings are interacting within a world of seen and unseen energies in our environment.

The emotional, mental, and spiritual bodies are generally not seen with normal eyesight but can be photographed using Kirlian photography. These bodies are referred to as the aura beyond the physical body. Our energy bodies are constantly changing depending on our feeling and thinking state of being and our environment. In essence, the more negativity we think and feel, the less vitality, wellness, and light is within our field of energy.

Any emotional issues that remain unresolved will reflect in your energy bodies as dark or stagnant energy. That is because energy is meant to be in a constant state of movement or flow, as are all things in this universe. The function of your mind is to create coherence between beliefs and reality. As you change your beliefs you change your biology and your cells can grow healthy.

Unresolved emotional issues are most often associated with judgment of some kind. A belief that it should not be that way or should not have happened. Human beings are constantly making judgments. Making something right or wrong or good or bad or superior or inferior. It is a human construct – entertainment for the egoic mind, which makes comparisons. In the world of spirituality there is just cause and effect, actions, and consequences. Being in judgment prevents you from seeing your own denied personality aspects, instead projecting out onto others in a superior way. While this is quite a normal human condition for the unenlightened, it is also the energy that contributes to massive physical and emotional disharmony in our own bodies and in the greater world which can lead to major conflict and war. There is no loving vibration associated with judgment, just a cold, dark, heavy, fixed kind of energy.

Being discerning by contrast, allows you to acknowledge another's reality, while you may not choose it for yourself. Unlike judgment, there is no emotional charge associated with discernment, which has a freer, lighter, more flexible kind of energy.

Judgment is a heavy load to carry, which not only drains your energy, but also has a negative impact on others. While it is unlikely that the human race will desist from this behavior any time soon, being aware of its effect can be a great help to understanding the play of energy and help you with your own healing. Notice any time you are in judgment and simply let it go. Realize that everyone has been conditioned just like you and it does not help you or anyone else to stand in judgment of another's behavior.

> **"The doctor of the future will give no medicine, but will interest his patient in the care of the human frame, in diet and in the cause and prevention of disease."**
> – Thomas Edison (1847–1931)

Tips For Emotional Healing

1. Make a list of all people with whom you still have unfinished business and practice **forgiveness** with every one of them. See Strategy 53 Forgiveness Process.

2. Release any resentment or blame from past traumas, people, or experiences. **Accept responsibility** for yourself and call back your power so you can heal.

3. Healing requires that you must **release your emotional story**. Immediately stop any repetitive story about past hurts or unresolved emotional issues. Going over these repeatedly is feeding the negative energy and keeping you trapped. See also Strategy 95 Thought Power and Control.

4. Live with **gratitude** every day – it is fundamental to healing because of the higher vibration it evokes. It builds your immune system, lowers blood pressure and just makes everything better. Search until you can find something to be grateful for in any wounding and allow that to be your focus. It might be for a greater strength that you developed as a result or a new direction that fulfilled a deep desire.

5. **Being really honest** with yourself is essential for your own healing. Acknowledge any aspects of yourself that you would prefer to deny like guilt or shame and find deep compassion for yourself by connecting with your inner child. View all your life experiences that you judge harshly as learning experiences. Denying shadow aspects or continual projecting onto another will hold the energy stuck. Be open to new understandings and ensure you are willing to make changes and foster a real passion for truth. It is the unfolding of a greater truth that will expand your awareness. Refer to Strategies 83 Release Resistance, 84 Release the Need to be Right, 14 Change Challenge, and 98 Truth Lover for greater detail. Meditation and mindfulness practices will greatly assist you to become the observer of your mind.

6. **Attune to your feeling body** in a curious way to see what is there. Notice also if you are attached to your body's dysfunction: Is there some kind of pleasure or satisfaction about your physical or emotional disharmony, like getting the attention you wanted? Notice if the fear of change has resulted in you justifying your behavior and defending any dysfunctional perceptions of energy. Once these obstructions to healing become conscious you can change them. Adopting a regular meditation practice will assist awareness. See also Strategies 4 Allow Feelings, 7 Awareness of Awareness, 14 Change Challenge.

7. **Explore and challenge all your beliefs** and most particularly anything that is not positive. These repeated thought-forms create an attracting energy affecting the way your body functions. Identify the five people you associate with the most, as these will have the strongest influence on your development and your beliefs. See Strategies 10 Beliefs Challenge and 68 Major Life Influencers for further information.

8. Understand that *you can't heal what you can't feel.* So any kind of continued suppression or denial of emotions will leave the energy stuck within your multidimensional self. The more you **open to feelings**, the more awareness can arise. All healing happens in the present moment. When what has been previously suppressed or denied can be felt *without any judgment* or story, the energy can return to its place in the space-time continuum and the emotional charge is transmuted. It is not necessary to delve into any details of the situation even though the mind will likely want to know. It's just to feel what was previously judged or rejected and held so that the energy can be released. The body's innate intelligence knows how to process it and where it needs to go to restore balance. Allowing feelings without judgment produces the greatest strides in your evolutionary process. Meditation and observing the mind assists this process. Also, use strategies 27 Deep Release Breathing,

96 Toning, or any of the relevant Feeling Strategies, or whatever else you feel drawn to in the 101 Strategies to help you transmute your pain.

9. Be vigilant about managing and **directing your mind to wellness,** not focusing on your illness. Ensure your attention and your intention towards healing is your focus. Energy follows thought. The Mindfulness and Breathing Strategies can assist you to do this, and the practice of meditation. See also 95 Thought Power and Control.

10. **Clear your energy field** regularly. Thought-forms and environmental energies all impact on you. Any kind of illness, pain, or disharmony will have a lot of lower vibrational or dark energy associated with it. Though well intentioned, even the *worrying* thoughts of your loved ones can add to the negativity in your field. Clear your field several times a day and constantly draw light into your body. Darkness cannot exist where there is light. See Strategy 16 Clearing for more details.

11. Find ways to help yourself feel good, such as lots of **laughter** – jokes, movies, watching some of the u-tube antics of pet cats or dogs, helping others, beautiful music, or being in nature. Feeling good is in the higher love vibrations, which create positive impact on the cells in the body.

12. If you have given **your personal power** to anyone else to make you happy you will always be wanting, and in doing so you will be attracting lower vibrational energy. The same applies if someone has given their power to you for their happiness; it is a heavy burden to carry and not your responsibility. When you don't claim your sovereignty, you deprive yourself of your own sense of authority and it creates much emotional pain through co-dependent relationships. Own your personal power, and encourage others to own theirs and share your love from that foundation.

13. It is essential to be fully present and grounded in your physical body here on Earth to bring about any healing. Be alert to any tendency to avoid this reality, which can happen when there is physical or emotional pain and the desire to avoid it rather than address it. Walking on the Earth barefoot, and imagining roots of light coming out of the soles of your feet, assist the grounding process and bring with it a huge range of proven health benefits. This is reflected in Strategy 58 Grounding/Earthing.

14. Constantly work at building **self-love**. This is absolutely fundamental to provide the healing vibrations. Self-love increases each time you overcome a fear, or open to a new truth. It

is like gathering all the parts of your authentic self back together to become whole once again – your heart opens to allow the natural flows.

The bulk of the healing Strategies in this program address this vital issue of building self-esteem and self-love. Adopting a meditation practice is highly recommended. It will assist the undoing of your conditioning and bring you into present time, which is where healing can happen.

"Love heals all that it touches and
Love opens doors that have been closed."
– Tom Kenyon and Virginia Essene

In summary, it is essential that you accept responsibility for "what is" before any healing can take place. With that foundation, be prepared for action. True integrated healing requires an active internal process that addresses the energetic cause of the imbalance. The conscious mind is unlikely to have the answers. It is about going beyond the limitations of the egoic mind and opening up to all the channels of energy to flow within yourself. It is about restoring the misplaced energy that occurs as a result of faulty belief systems and unresolved issues. It is about the alignment of your multidimensional bodies and restoring balance and harmony.

Real healing expresses the intention to investigate and release any negative patterns that impact on the physical, mental, emotional, and spiritual self. When the energetics have been resolved, healing happens. There is a new understanding, and the nervous system and behavior are restored to balance and harmony; the heart is open – loving feelings are present and energy flows as it is meant to.

See also: most of the 101 Strategies.

Tom Kenyon and Virginia Essene, *The Hathor Material*, 1997, p. 62.
Bought Movie/Documentary - http://www.boughtmovie.net

Strategy 63
INTENTION/COUNTER-INTENTION

CATEGORIES APPLIED

Addressing Addictions
Addressing Anxiety
Addressing Depression
Awareness and Mindfulness
Career and Goals
Communications and Relationships
Environmental Health
Exercise for Living
Improving Self-Esteem
Nutrition for Life

Intentions travel ahead of your conscious awareness, so setting your intention ahead of time is planting the seeds to your preferred outcome, and this facilitates its manifestation.

Intention is a function of both *awareness* and *attention*. It is not just setting an intention and forgetting about it, perhaps believing, or at least hoping, that because you have set an intention it will automatically play out, though this is a common illusion.

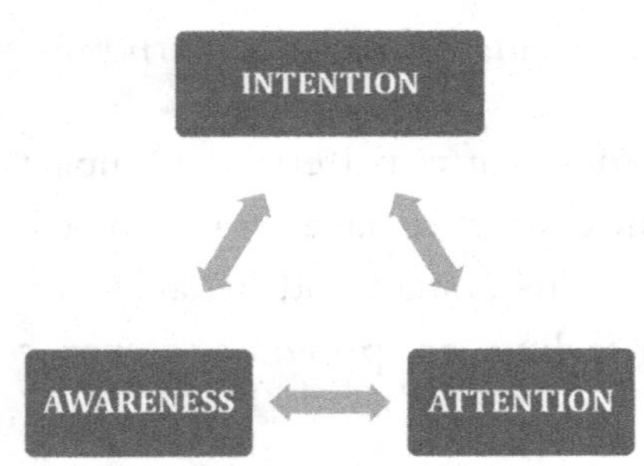

It is about paying *a*ttention to your *i*ntention. The seed is planted and now you have to nurture it to facilitate its growth.

Without holding your focus in this way your intention can quickly become overridden or lost in your unconscious patterns and behaviors.

Intentions are most successful when you are both aligned and attuned to what it is that you desire to achieve.

It is being alert to your mind and any distractions so that you can return quickly to your intention. Intention is the energy of thought and we live amid a sea of different thought-forms, from ourselves and others, that constantly affect us. Setting your intention at the start of each day creates a smoother pathway to your desires through focus and a greater feeling of clarity – it is planning ahead. Practice this each day and observe and enjoy the difference it makes.

Daily exercise: Start each day by deciding your intention. Include both your attitude and what you want to achieve through your behaviors. Such an example might be choosing to be kindly, open and flexible while communicating with others. You may want to complete a project you have been working on, or resolve some challenges with a planned meeting or numerous other tasks.

A **counter-intention** is the opposite of your intention. This can arise as a result of your own conflicting thoughts and beliefs and leads to sabotaging your desired intention. These are often subconscious or unconscious and can occur anytime there is inner conflict. Common examples of this often arise with New Year resolutions where you express your intentions of some new practices you plan to adopt and may even start out – then somehow, often unconsciously, you abort.

Intention:	I'm going to increase my exercise regime
Counter-intention:	*I don't really have time*
Intention:	I'm going to lose weight
Counter-intention:	*If I lost weight a whole lot of things would change and maybe that would challenge my relationship*
Intention:	I'm going to give up sugar
Counter-intention:	*I so love chocolate and I would feel so deprived not to have it.*

If you are not clear or mindful you will constantly compromise your best intentions. A good strategy to remedy this kind of pattern is to regularly ask yourself, "If I were to listen to you where would that lead me?" Of course it is essential to be totally honest with yourself. Regular self-inquiry will also develop clarity and mindfulness.

Counter-intention from others

Counter-intention can certainly come from others, and more likely those you know who have an investment in you not changing, or in your lack of success. Your intention may be to save money for a holiday; as you come closer to your goal a family member keeps arguing why you should stay home to be with an unwell father, or perhaps you have adopted a daily meditation practice and your flatmate is feeling threatened by your growth and so keeps making a lot of noise despite your request for quiet at that time.

The counter-intention from another can contribute a lot of negative energy and result in you aborting your goals, sometimes leaving you puzzled how that happened.

The way to offset this is to:

- do some reflective self-inquiry to check that you are not opposing yourself though your own inner conflict.

- keep your energy field clean of others' thought-forms.
- ensure clear boundaries. (If there is a pattern of this kind of sabotage behavior coming from another, it may sometimes be appropriate not to share your goals, and/or find another way to communicate your concerns towards resolution.)

Counter-intention arises from the energy within your own field or energy matrix, whether it is your own thought-forms or those of others.

See also:

- Awareness: Building the Observer
- Boundaries
- Being: Mindfulness
- Beliefs Challenge
- Clearing
- Goal Setting
- Personal Mission Statement
- Protection
- Thought Power and Control
- Values

Strategy 64
JIGGLING

CATEGORIES APPLIED

Addressing Addictions
Addressing Depression
Addressing Anxiety
Awareness and Mindfulness
Exercise for Living
Quick Stress Busters

Jiggling is a rhythmic pulsation of the body, affecting both the inside and outside of your body. Julie Henderson is a psychologist specializing in somatics and author of *Embodying Well-Being*. She says: "Whatever supports the right rhythms of pulsation, supports life, liveliness and well-being. Jiggling certainly does that."

Jiggling helps to reduce muscle tension by shaking all the muscles. It's great for the organs and assists your kidneys and adrenals to flush their toxins. It gets the blood flowing freely in your body, improving circulation, and can be energizing and grounding.

Jiggling can help bring body awareness by stimulating whole body movement. It helps you to connect with and "feel" your body. It assists you to become "present" with your body often releasing stored or stagnant energy. It's great for those who are very mind-focused, and it's fun!

In case you need instructions:

> Stand with your knees softly bent, arms by your side, teeth slightly apart to ensure a relaxed jaw, and just start to jiggle your whole body. Allow every body part to hang loose and limp as you jiggle. Let your breathing adapt as it wishes. Continue for a minimum of 5 minutes.
>
> You may find allowing your voice some expression enhances your enjoyment – feeling the vibration that the jiggling makes through the sound of your voice.
>
> When you finish your jiggling just stand quietly with your eyes closed for a few minutes to feel the continuing effects.
>
> Enjoy! And entice your family to join in.

See also:

- Body Breath Awareness
- Feeling Agitated
- Feeling Scattered: Unbalanced

Strategy 65
JUDGMENT EFFECT

CATEGORIES APPLIED

Addressing Addictions
Addressing Anxiety
Addressing Depression
Awareness and Mindfulness
Career and Goals
Communications and Relationships
Everyday Essentials
Improving Self-Esteem

Judgment must be used with great caution to avoid negativity and suffering. Judgment is something human beings have created and do repeatedly. It imposes a kind of identity label on another person. When we pass judgment, we are making something right or wrong, better or worse, good or bad, superior or inferior. It carries a kind of "power over" attitude, which also creates a mirror effect, meaning whatever it is that you are judging also has a power over you. When there is no judgment there is no loss of power and therefore no suffering. It is an activity of the egoic mind and extremely destructive to others because of the projected negativity, and to ourselves because it holds our own perceptions in a fixed view, often closed to a greater truth.

Judgment Versus Observation

Judgment is not the same as observation. We naturally observe, and constantly make decisions upon what we see, feel and think. Observing a situation for what it is, is not making judgments. It is perceiving, witnessing, seeing, and being discerning, but not making anything right or wrong.

Like everything in this world, words too have a particular vibration – their own unique energy signature. Some of the words of lower resonance include jealousy, criticism, anxiety, and anger, which all come within the bandwidth of fear. The higher vibration words are love, compassion, appreciation, peace, gratitude, openness, and so on, which all come under the bandwidth of love. To help you sense the effect of judgment, take a moment and just *feel into* the vibration of the word *judgment*. You will find it has a very fixed kind of energy: harsh, inflexible and heavy, even cold. It is a word that falls into the fear bandwidth. Now take a moment to feel into the word *compassion* and notice the difference in the frequency. Compassion has a soft, warm, flowing, gentle, yet strong kind of feel to it.

You Make Me Sick

Research by Dr. Masaru Emoto discovered that water reacts to different words, prayers or music and changes its crystalline structure. Water exposed to positive words formed beautiful aesthetically pleasing and symmetrical shapes and negative words formed distorted kinds of shapes. From this perspective alone, can begin to appreciate how words impact upon our bodies, particularly when we consider that our bodies are primarily made up of 60–80% water

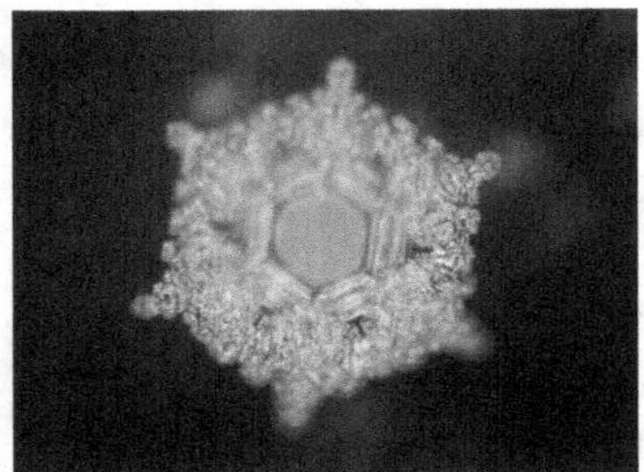

Love and Gratitude

The impact of judgment on another has the effect of sending streamers of energy across to whoever is the focus of your judgment. This connects you to their energy system and then you become vulnerable to picking up whatever it is that they are feeling. So if they are feeling agitated or angry then you, too, can take that on board. More likely it will be without any awareness that this has occurred as a result of you hooking into their energy field through your own judgment.

The reverse also applies, that the other person is affected by what is going on for you; if you are judging them it certainly won't be a positive impact. We are all responsible for our own thought-forms. Basically the way you think is either adding to positive, neutral or negative vibrations in your environment. We are each totally responsible for our own energy field. To awaken to the greater truth of your real self, and add more harmony to this planet, we need to use great discretion before judging another. It is better to observe, and seek a higher understanding.

When we judge something it is like holding the energy related to our judgment stuck within our energy matrix, which is constantly interacting and resonating with the physical body. When it has a strong emotional charge to it, the energy can't move – it becomes fixed. This is the activity of the egoic mind. It is in contrast to our true nature of an evolving loving human energy being in the flow of life.

Holding on to resentment, criticism, or anger (all forms of judgment) will over time work its way through the outer mental and emotional energy bodies into the physical body and present as some kind of malady. This is because the held energy becomes stagnant as the activity of judgment holds back the natural flow. Such an example would be judging another for betraying you and holding on to the resentment. While you are holding that belief of another person's wrongdoing, be aware that the energy associated with it is adversely affecting *your* energy system.

It is important to understand that all our thoughts about others arise from our own conditioned mind – our own programming through our childhood upbringing within the culture and society in which we live. Every time we make some kind of judgment about another, those thought-forms have to work through the filters of our own subconscious mind where all the programming is stored. It is an extremely limited kind of perception that may have nothing whatsoever to do with a greater truth. We could say it is like having the mouse's view rather than the eagle's view. Everyone else has also experienced conditioning that dictates the way they think and behave.

To put it into perspective, it is maybe helpful to recognize that all laws and rules are man-made laws laid down by different religions, cultures, governments, and individuals. These rules do not arise from nature, where there is simply cause and effect. It is the human who has declared something to be right or wrong, good or bad.

You can perhaps see how misguided, futile, and potentially harmful judgment can be. The activity of judgment causes a massive negative impact in this world – at its worst creating wars.

A Preferred Way

Instead of judgment use *discernment.* Discernment allows you to see the situation for what it is without making it right or wrong. There is no attachment to it. It respects that others have different opinions and values and you do not have to agree with them. Recognize that everyone has been conditioned just like you and don't allow your mind to make polar opposites like good or bad, superior or inferior. Discernment is a way of seeing any differences and acknowledging another's reality and choices without making them wrong. Then make choices and create boundaries for yourself according to that perspective.

Rather than being fixated on something, which is what judgment does, *create preferences* without attachment to outcomes. Preferences allow expression of your desires. Attachments will always lead to pain.

Imagine going to a social function of a friend where there is a lot of swearing and perhaps some drug use, which is not the kind of environment that appeals to you. Rather than judging those doing that behavior, or your friend, simply acknowledge to yourself and your friend that this is not consistent with your preferences and leave. You have created boundaries that support you without making the others wrong or you superior in any way.

Observe also in yourself any tendency to always be right. This too is an activity of the egoic mind, which seriously limits close relationships and will inhibit your ability to know a deeper truth. Instead, express your opinion and understanding and leave yourself open to a greater truth. Acknowledge the limitations of your knowledge and the lenses through which you view things.

Strive to understand the other person's beliefs and behaviors. Remember that they are totally influenced by their conditioning in the same way as you. Their behavior makes sense to them. If the circumstances seem appropriate, ask, "Help me to understand …" And be curious and open.

Fellow employees in the workplace might judge a colleague who has some kind of ritual behavior before eating his lunch as weird and unsociable, without understanding that it is part of a blessing associated with his religious culture.

Always strive to create harmony and build trust with another. *Look for the commonalities and the sameness* rather than focusing on differences. Be open to new understandings.

"Real magic in relationships means an absence of judgment in others."
– Wayne Dyer

Judgment of self is also an extremely unhelpful activity of the egoic mind. This kind of self-criticism does little more than erode your self-esteem while adding to the negativity in your field of energy. Instead, simply notice your behavior as a neutral observer in a curious kind of way – not making anything right or wrong, good or bad; just noticing the mind and what is going on. Observing without judging keeps energy in flow and allows you to be conscious and make other choices.

Beware also of any tendency to judge yourself that you are judging yourself!

Ultimately, judging another is like saying to the universe, "I don't understand this and so I need to experience what this is like for my soul's evolution." This is a common spiritual pathway for growth, building consciousness, and developing compassion for all beings. And so it is often said, that you become what you judge.

Unfortunately, in our world there are some situations where judgment results in harm to another. Our true core essence finds such behaviors totally abhorrent: harm to a child, forced child marriage, mutilation, the abuse or suppression of women, torture, animal cruelty. Hearing or witnessing any thing like this awakens in us a kind of knowing that this is not the way it's meant to be. It is against our true nature. When this occurs, it is not about being a silent witness or condoning such behaviors, but rather using your discernment and doing what you can to remedy the situation.

The people doing these kinds of acts are totally disconnected from their Source energy. They are acting from their programming. We know too, that often arising out of these traumatic events will come great learning for the perpetrator and even the victim. We are inspired by people like Nelson Mandela, Aung San Suu Kyi, and Mahatma Gandhi, and many other unsung heroes, who each experienced great adversity yet through their courage, ability to forgive, and inner strength have made a significant contribution to bring about change to the world.

Additionally there are many unseen negative energies that attach to our energy field, most often without our awareness or consent. They reflect an accumulation of negative thoughts and fears by humanity and other low vibrational forces, all of which can leave us feeling out of balance or unwell. Such circumstances require us to take full responsibility for keeping our multidimensional body clear, cleaning up our own negativity, and claiming our sovereignty. The more we do this the more we strengthen our energy field and diminish the negative effects by bringing awareness to these abuses. It is perhaps obvious that the more love and light we bring into our world the less darkness and greater harmony will exist. See Strategy 16 Clearing for more information.

Ultimately we are all responsible for our own thoughts, decisions, and actions. When these challenging situations occur, it is far better to connect with our higher self and determine our response with heart-connected consciousness. This is the way we can bring awareness and change in the most harmonious way possible.

Anything that is not of LOVE just needs LOVE.

See also:

- Boundaries
- Control versus Preferences
- Do No Harm
- Honor and Respect Differences
- Projection
- Release the Need to be Right
- Seek to Understand

http://www.masaru-emoto.net/english/water-crystal.html

Strategy 66
KINDNESS TO SELF

CATEGORIES APPLIED

Addressing Addictions
Addressing Anxiety
Addressing Depression
Awareness and Mindfulness
Communications and Relationships
Improving Self-Esteem

Be kind to yourself and do things that nurture you. Don't wait for others to nurture you.

It is all too common to project onto another, desiring their input to help you feel better about yourself without taking responsibility for your own wellbeing; perhaps wanting compliments, recognition, or some kind or praise. This is clearly very disempowering. It leaves you just *wanting*, as though you can't be happy unless someone else is acknowledging you.

When you treat yourself well, others will treat you well – not the other way around. That is because of the energy that you vibrate. As you demonstrate your own level of love and respect, it carries a certain positive frequency that people pick up on either consciously or unconsciously.

Buy yourself flowers, play beautiful music, have a bath surrounded by candles, go for a walk on the beach, say loving supportive things to yourself, get a massage, take some time out with your favorite book.

"Simple kindness to one's self and all that lives is the most powerful transformational force of all. It produces no backlash, has no downside, and never leads to loss or despair. It increases one's own true power without exacting any toll."
– Dr. David Hawkins

See also:

- Accept Yourself
- Affirmations
- Connect with Nature
- Grounding/Earthing
- Exercise for Living

- Laughter Medicine
- Music to Uplift and Nurture
- Nutrition: Best Food Options

David Hawkins, *Power Versus Force*, Hay House, 2007, p. 128.

Strategy 67
LAUGHTER MEDICINE

CATEGORIES APPLIED

Addressing Addictions
Addressing Anxiety
Addressing Depression
Awareness and Mindfulness
Communications and Relationships
Improving Self-Esteem
Quick Stress Busters

Laughter releases those feel-good hormones that we all enjoy. Doctors describe "mirthful" laughter as "internal jogging" because of the health benefits. It can lower blood pressure, improve alertness, memory and creativity, reduce stress, give your internal organs a bit of a work-out, and boost the immune system, much like moderate exercise. It can regulate the body's vital functions and even reduce pain because the pituitary gland releases its own pain-suppressing opiates. Above all, it just makes us feel good.

Laughter in relationships has a way of connecting people and creating a positive ambience. Children laugh on average 200 times a day, while adults average only 20 times per day. Laughter supports social relationships, and as we know, can be incredibly contagious.

Here are some fun activities to choose from or create your own:

- Watch comedy movies or standup comedy routines.
- Play with a child. Even 2 adults willing to connect with their inner child can bring about the same effect.
- Walk around like a monkey with bent knees and feet a hip width apart, then begin stomp around like a Sumo wrestler facing his opponent.
- Try kissing without touching noses.
- Try kissing only touching noses.
- Make up funny stories that one person starts and then continue, each taking turns as the story evolves.
- Play tag with a soft squashy ball.
- Do this fun exercise with one or more people. Make a big *"Ha"* sound from your belly, then do a few together, then do a few with the one breath. *"Ha Ha Ha."* Try and copy the other person's style.
- Talk with a funny voice while sticking your chin out.

- Stand in one spot with knees slightly bent and arms hanging loose and start jiggling. Let your voice echo the vibration that your body is making. Great to do with another person.
- Start laughing (about nothing) in the company of others. After the initial peculiar looks, before long others will join you and there will be a lot of joy around.
- Join a Laughter club and share in the fun created by the deep laughter, the healing and company offered.

From an energetic perspective laughter raises your frequency, bringing light into your field; it puts you in the love bandwidth where all healing takes place.

Whenever you bring more light or love into your field, you also impact on others in your surrounding. We know how contagious laughter can be.

See also:

- Do Things You Enjoy
- Grounding/Earthing
- Mantras
- Music to Uplift and Nurture

Strategy 68
MAJOR LIFE INFLUENCERS

CATEGORIES APPLIED

Addressing Addictions
Addressing Anxiety
Addressing Depression
Awareness and Mindfulness
Career and Goals
Communications and Relationships
Improving Self-Esteem

All humans are heavily influenced by other people's thoughts, attitudes, and behaviors, and we are vulnerable to the plethora of seen and unseen energies in our environment. We are constantly filtering, accepting, or rejecting all kinds of people, information, and ideas based on our conditioning as a child and our experiences and perceptions. Growing up, we adopt many erroneous beliefs, which can seriously limit our sense of worthiness and completely color our life. Unaware, this constant flow of influences can lead us totally away from our true desires.

Complete this exercise to identify your primary influencers.

Using a blank sheet of paper, draw a circle in the middle of your page, which represents you.

Then, surrounding you, draw a circle for each of the primary people in your life – around ten. This could be family members, business associates, friends, work colleagues, etc. Indicate the strength of their influence upon you, (irrespective if it is positive or negative) by the **size** of the circle and the proximity to you.

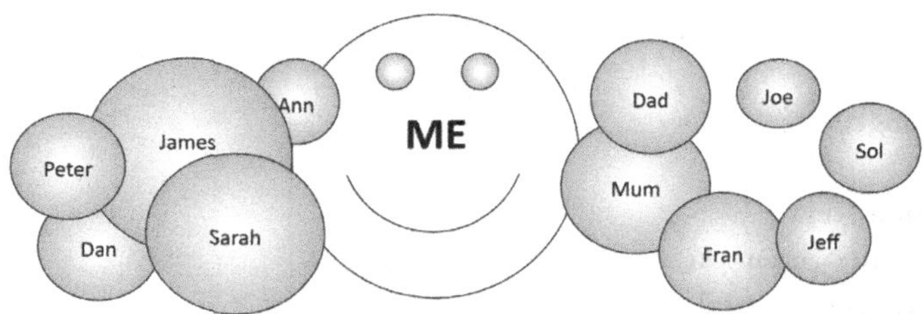

Now really reflect and determine how positive these influences are by shading in each person's circle with a colored pen. What is not colored in reflects any negative impact.

To go even deeper with this awareness process, you may like to consider the following questions:

- Is the way I have drawn these circles telling me something more – consider overlapping circles, any circles bigger than your own, connection of one circle to other/s?
- Am I holding on to some kind of resentment? Do I need to do some forgiveness work?
- Am I projecting my own judgment onto another and denying an aspect of myself?
- Is another projecting their negativity onto me?
- If I have been aware of the negative influence, why have I allowed it to continue?
- What specific boundaries could I put in place to remedy this situation?
- Do I need to share my deeper feelings with another?

Through a kind of osmosis, we will become most like the five or six people we associate with the most or listen to the most. If these primary influencers in your life are not reflecting the kind of person you aspire to be, you will find it more than challenging to grow and fulfill your goals.

Once you have identified who these primary influencers are in your life, then determine if they mirror the kind of energy you want to attract. If their impact is not favorable, what will you do about it?

Seek out people who are loving, positive, and successful. Spend time with those who inspire you and listen to the ones you admire and respect whose behavior and language are congruent.

Being truly consciousness of these influencers empowers you with choice.

See also:

- Awareness: Building the Observer
- Boundaries
- Beliefs Challenge
- Clearing
- Communication Keys
- Intention/Counter-Intention
- Thought Power and Control
- Values
- Who Am I?

Strategy 69
MANAGE KEY TENSION AREAS

CATEGORIES APPLIED

Addressing Addictions
Addressing Anxiety
Addressing Depression
Awareness and Mindfulness
Career and Goals
Improving Self-Esteem
Quick Stress Busters

Stress and tension can creep into the body resulting in muscular restriction, pain, and headaches. We are often unaware of tension until we become conscious of pain or restricted movement. The body tends to store tension in key areas such as the brow, jaw, neck, and shoulders, the abdomen, and the hands. This is typically as a result of the thinking mind.

Just taking a few minutes to focus on these areas one by one can release tension from the body before it becomes unmanageable. Listed below are two different ways to proceed. Each will take just a few minutes.

1. Relaxation Through Contrast

In this process you are going to achieve relaxation through the opposite sensation of tension. This is a good way to recognize the feelings of tension that may creep into your body. It assists body awareness and your ability to reduce tension before it reaches an unmanageable level.

Sit or lie down as you prefer. Starting at the top of your body in the forehead, you go though each muscle area and focus there with your mind for a few seconds, then tense it. Hold it for a few seconds, then relax.

Be careful to isolate each muscle group first so that you don't reengage other body areas. It's important to release quickly after holding each part for just a few seconds. This will avoid any tendency towards cramps or pain. Proceed in the following order:

> **Forehead**: Focus for a few moments on your forehead, then to tense these muscles, raise your eyebrows as high as possible … Hold for just a few seconds, fully feeling the tension, then let them return to their normal position. Breathe deeply, then just fully feel the contrast of heaviness and relaxation.

Jaw: Focus on your jaw for a few seconds, then to tense these muscles clench your teeth tightly together and pull back the corners of your mouth as hard as you can. Hold for a few seconds, then totally relax. Take a deep breath and ensure that your teeth are slightly apart with your tongue resting on the bottom of your mouth. Notice the difference between tension and relaxation in your jaw.

Neck: Focus on the muscles in your neck and try to isolate them from the rest of the body, then try to push your head down and hold it back at the same time. Hold the tension, feel it, and let go, taking a deep relaxing breath.

Shoulders: Focus your attention in your chest, shoulders, and upper back. To tense these muscles take a deep breath, hold it, push your shoulder blades back towards each other. Feel the tension, and then let go. Breathe easily and feel your shoulders heavy and relaxed.

Abdomen: To tense the abdomen, simply try to make your stomach as hard as you can. Imagine you are about to be hit in the stomach by a medicine ball. Hold the tension for a few seconds, and then relax, allowing the muscles to give up their hold completely. Allow the breath to carry the tension out of your abdomen; you may experience warmth spreading through your torso.

Hands: Focus on your hands and make a fist… Hold it for a few seconds, and then let go. Allow any tension to ooze out through the tips of your fingers. Do this two or three times until both hands feel totally relaxed, comfortable, and easy.

The advantage of the relaxation through contrast helps you to recognize how much tension is in your body through the opposite effect of tension and relaxation. An alternative is just to direct your attention to different body parts, and use the breath to assist your focus by breathing into each key tension area.

2. Relax Key Tension Areas

Sit or lie down as you prefer. Close your eyes and draw your attention inward. Hold the intention that you are going to focus on key body parts and as you do so release tension with an outward breath. Ensure you maintain deep breathing throughout this relaxation process to assist the movement of energy within your body.

Brow: Starting at the brow, fully focus your attention here and notice if you are holding any tension. Take a few deep breaths along with holding your focus in this area and release the tension with every out breath.

Jaw: Move down to the jaw. When the jaw is relaxed your teeth will be slightly apart with your tongue resting on the bottom of your mouth. Give your full attention to your jaw, then release any hold you have with the out breath. Take 2 or 3 long breaths in this manner.

Neck: Now focus on the neck. Tension in the neck will often result in limited mobility or rotation. Keep your awareness here with the intention of releasing all stress and tension with every out breath. Breathe deeply for 2 or 3 breaths, letting go with every out breath while staying fully focused on your neck.

Shoulders: Tension in the shoulders will often result in your shoulders being up closer to your ears and affecting both the upper chest and back. Gently lift your shoulders back and down and feel them soften down further as you exhale, releasing all tension and stress. Continue for 2 or 3 releasing breaths until they feel relaxed and heavy.

Abdomen: The abdomen is also called the seat of emotion. It is where we store a lot of unresolved emotion. The media encourages us to hold the belly in without awareness of the emotional impact this can have. Give your full attention to this area and then allow your belly to go really soft as you breathe out. Continue breathing in and breathing out all tension until your belly feels really soft, spongy, and relaxed.

Hands: The final key tension area is the hands. Rest your hands comfortably on your lap, a chair, or the floor; direct your full attention there and allow every out-breath to carry away any tension out of your hands with it. Repeat for 2 or 3 breaths.

See also:

- Awareness of Awareness
- Clearing
- Conscious Breathing
- Deep Release Breathing
- Feeling Agitated
- Feeling Anger

- Feeling Challenged
- Feeling Disempowered
- Feeling Fear
- Feeling Guilt or Shame
- Feeling Jealousy
- Feeling Rejected
- Feeling Scattered: Unbalanced
- Feeling Stuck
- Feeling Uncertain or Fearful of the Unknown
- Feeling Victimized
- Feeling Worried
- Jiggling
- Music to Uplift and Nurture
- Shadow Play
- Thought: Managing the Inner Critic
- Thought Power and Control

Strategy 70
MANTRAS

CATEGORIES APPLIED

Addressing Addictions
Addressing Anxiety
Addressing Depression
Awareness and Mindfulness
Communications and Relationship
Improving Self-Esteem
Quick Stress Busters

Mantras are intrinsically related to sound, and sound is reverberating in everything in this universe. Mantra means sacred utterance – a word, formula or prayer, which is chanted or sung, though it can also be chanted silently. Mantras emerged around 5000 years ago from the mother Indo-European language Sanskrit, which is a universal cellular sound language that vibrates deeply within, connecting us all.

Mantras seem to feed the soul. They are often used as a spiritual process. They can still the mind and open your heart to the divine flow of energy gaining greater awareness and self-transcendence. Chanting mantras can be mystical and magical as the body vibrates through the singing meditation. They can be quite emotive and tend to evoke color and mood, simply because of their musical qualities. They can also be childlike. As you relax, the mind often generates imagery spontaneously.

It is said that they were initially the property of holy people who had the highest spiritual knowledge and knew the power of sound. They knew that by refining sound they could create deep healing responses in the body. The scientific effect of these sound vibrations, physically and emotionally, was suppressed for many years though these healing benefits are more commonly known today.

Mantras speak equally to all people, irrespective of religions or beliefs.

While mantras are usually associated with the practice of meditation, we can also chant them at any time of day: doing the dishes, walking around, shopping, or in the shower. However, chanting mantras while sitting in a meditative state and maintaining a deeper focus will have a stronger impact on your multidimensional body.

If using a mantra as a meditation it is not necessary to relax before going into meditation. The mantra maintains the mind focus helping to avoid distracting thoughts and the body will begin to relax.

TYPES OF MANTRAS

- "**Om**" is without doubt the most popular mantra and in fact is often used at the beginning and end of mantras and prayers. The various definition of "Om" is wholeness, the cosmic "yes." Om is said to contain all the wisdom in the universe, the sound of infinity and immortality, the unification of masculine and feminine, a sacred formula. According to Wikipedia, other spiritual interpretations include a human longing for truth, reality, light, immortality, peace, love, knowledge and action.
- **Om Shanti Om** is an invocation for inner peace.
- **Om Shree Dhanvantre Namaha** is an invocation for healing energy.
- **Om Mani Padme Hum**. There is no simple translation, but it is often said to be praise to the jewel in the center of the lotus. It is the most widely used of all Buddhist meditation mantras and evokes the golden light of the Bodhisattva of Compassion.
- **The Gayatri Mantra** is the most universal of all Hindu mantras, invoking the universal Brahman. It is considered to be not different from the divine entity that forms the content of the mantra.
- Mantras can also be just the simple names of deities or invocations to deities: **Ram, Buddha, Jesus, Christos, Kali, Hare Krishna, Om Namah Shivaya**
- All words in all languages carry a specific energy vibration, which reflects the quality of the word. A Westernised mantra can be: **I AM** with a translation of immortal spirit; **I AM THAT I AM; I AM ALL THAT I AM.**

Play with the mantra and feel into the different sensations that they evoke in you. You may find the longer mantra give you something to get your teeth into. They can keep you more alert when you relax deeply. They are often chanted 108 times to really allow full immersion into the quality and vibration of the sound.

Mala, or prayer beads, consist of a string of 108 beads and are often used in conjunction with chanting mantras 108 times. There are numerous and varied explanations for the reason for 108 repetitions. Two are that the number is said to represent the amount of major *nadis* or energy lines in the human body, and chanting the mantra balances the body; and that 108 signifies the wholeness of the divinity, perfect totality.

Guidelines

Prepare a quite space where you won't be interrupted and set the intent to sing the mantra with love and devotion. Focus on your heart and then observe your breath for a few minutes. Select a mantra and start repeating it silently.

It helps to synchronize your mantra in some way with your natural breathing or heartbeat, so that it becomes more of a circular kind of process. As you chant aloud, it will intensify the feeling response as you activate your voice and the vibration it carries through your whole body. It is important to be open to feeling the sound vibrations within your body. Let yourself fully surrender into the texture and rhythm of the mantra. Envelop yourself in the flow of sound, conscious of the capacity of frequency for healing. Let the mantra carry you along.

Stay with the mantra. Notice when your mind is spacing out and bring yourself back into presence with the whole of the mantra experience. If you are losing your focus, say the syllables more precisely or accentuate the rhythm. Enjoy yourself.

At the end of the mantra journey, just sit quietly for a few moments and allow yourself to feel the lively effects of your mantra chant and the energy of the vibration pulsing through your whole body.

For a most delightful musical accompaniment, recordings of mantras by Deva Premal and Miten * are available. These can provide wonderful array of healing vibrations to the listener.

See also:

- Music to Uplift and Nurture
- Toning

* www.devapremalmiten.com

Strategy 71
MUSIC TO UPLIFT AND NURTURE

CATEGORIES APPLIED

Addressing Addictions
Addressing Anxiety
Addressing Depression
Awareness and Mindfulness
Environmental Health
Improving Self-Esteem
Quick Stress Busters

All things are made of energy and as such have a frequency or vibration. Sound from every source emanates frequencies that are beneficial or detrimental to your psyche and body. Some sounds, like the dentist's drill, seem to grate to the very core of our being; a mosquito sharing your bedroom when you are trying to sleep can have the effect of elevating your stress levels. Other sounds, like waves crashing on the shore or the song of a bird, can be calming, uplifting, and nurturing to our very core.

Music can entertain or tap into our creativity and facilitate expression through making some kind of sound. It could be using a musical instrument or anything else – like drumming on a plastic bucket, playing with spoons, or tapping a stick on a hard surface. Music can sometimes express what we struggle to say in words; it can inspire or tell a story, as it has done in early cultures from time immemorial, and in our era as an accompaniment with movies.

Throughout time, music has been used in shamanic rituals and sacred ceremonies. It can be used to effect change in brainwave patterns and restore harmony to the physical body by helping to release blockages. Classical music is well known for the particular resonance it creates, which has a soothing and uplifting effect: calming for the sick and agitated, flourishing for the plants, gentle receptivity for animals, and we know of the beautiful crystal patterns sound can make in water. Some music (without words), which has a rhythmic 60 beats per minute can assist your brain's ability to focus and be a useful aid in study, artwork, or other activities that require concentration.

Music is very personal and does not work for everyone in the same way. When selecting music to nurture yourself, avoid heavy metal music or anything that has negative words.

The words in some songs can trigger different emotions and either add or detract from your state of wellbeing. If choosing music with song, make sure they speak to your heart and uplift your soul.

Use beautiful music to replace some television or computer time – great when you come home from a busy day at work or when you want to motivate yourself with study, house cleaning, or some creative pursuit.

There is an ever-expanding world of beautiful music from classical to modern spiritual music and mantras.

Just a few of the modern spiritual music sources are:

- Christine Morrison. http://www.christinemorrison.com/
- Tom Kenyon. http://www.tomkenyon.com/home.php
- Deva Premal and Miten. http://www.devapremalmiten.com/
- Kip Mazuy. http://www.bliss-music.com
- Geoffrey Gurrumul Yunupingu.

See also:

- Connect with Nature
- Grounding
- Mantras
- Toning

Strategy 72
NUTRITION: BEST FOOD OPTIONS

CATEGORIES APPLIED

Addressing Addictions
Addressing Anxiety
Addressing Depression
Awareness and Mindfulness
Environmental Health
Improving Self-Esteem
Nutrition for Life

Eating whole foods is essential for good health and wellbeing. This includes fruits, vegetables, nuts, seeds, and grains, tubers, legumes, and fungi. Whole plant foods still look like the original form of the plant. It means foods that are unprocessed and unrefined as little as possible and free from additives or other artificial substances. Pesticides, chemicals, antibiotics, and artificial hormones are common in today's plant and animal farming practices; the intent is to boost production at the expense of reduced nutritional value or cruel factory farming practices which deprive animals of their natural habitat. One of the major problems with contaminated and unhealthy foods is how it plays havoc with your gut health which in turn can trigger all kinds of chronic diseases, diarrhoea, IBS, obesity, arthritis, allergies as well as be the cause of anxiety and depression.

You may like to consider reducing the amount of meat you eat or consider a vegetarian diet, which significantly reduces many of the common health risks such as strokes, obesity, diabetes, heart disease, and cancer, leading to a longer and healthier life – in addition massively reducing the greenhouse gas emission produced by livestock, which according to a Worldwatch Institute report in 2009 was 51%.

Organic

Eating organic food is clearly best for your health and wellbeing, though it is not always available and at times the cost may be prohibitive. Growing your own or buying from farmers' markets are viable options.

Where possible choose organic produce, which is grown and handled without the use of synthetic chemicals, artificial fertilizers, food irradiation, or genetically modified organisms (GMOs). Organic farming methods produce foods that are naturally higher in nutrients and much lower in pesticides, chemicals, and additives than food from conventional farming methods. Pesticides, chemicals, and additives in food have been linked to some diseases and birth defects. By eating organic food you can dramatically reduce your exposure to these harmful chemicals.

The biggest study ever into organic food – a four-year E.U.-funded project – found that organic food is far more nutritious than ordinary produce, and can help improve your health and longevity. http://www.twnside.org.sg/title2/susagri/susagri018.htm

Locally Grown

Typically locally grown food is freshest and so offers more flavor and a better texture. Food naturally has maximum nutrition when freshly harvested. Often local farms use organic farming methods also. There are many other benefits to buying foods that are locally grown: supporting families in your community, avoidance of GMO produce (typically licensed to large factory farms), and the protection of genetic diversity. It builds stronger communities and minimizes the concern of the environmental impact of transport.

Home Grown

Growing your own produce without all the harmful chemicals can be a most rewarding and enjoyable experience while satisfying your nutritional needs. You also get the health bonus of being out in nature. Even growing a few vegies in pots can boost your nutritional input if you don't have the space or time for a full vegie garden.

These options make sense for a sustainable future while optimizing our health.

According to Friends of the Earth Australia (http://www.foe.org.au/articles/2012-02-21/new-pesticides-and-food-report) the top twenty Australian foods with Most Pesticide Detections 2000-2011 are:

Apples	15.2%	Tea (imported)	1.6%
Wheat	13.2%	Barley	1.4
Strawberries	10%	Tomatoes	1.3
Pears	9.5%	Apricots	1.2%
Grapes	6.4%	Canola	1.1%
Lettuce	4.1%	Flour	1.1%
Nectarine	3.7%	Carrots	0.8%
Peaches	2.3%	Plums	0.8%
Bread	2.1%	Green Beans	0.8%
Biscuits	1.6%	Others	20%

A non-profit organization, the Environmental Working Group (www.ewg.org) in the USA, have provided a Shoppers' Guide to Pesticides in Produce. Here are their findings:

1. Of the forty three different fruit and vegetable categories tested, the following had the highest pesticide load, making them the most important to buy organic versions, or to grow organically yourself

   15 Foods to Buy Organic

   Apples
   Sweet bell peppers/capsicums
   Nectarines
   Cherries
   Grapes (imported)
   Potatoes
   Kale/collard greens
   Peaches
   Celery
   Strawberries
   Lettuce
   Pears
   Spinach
   Blueberries

2. The following had the lowest pesticide load, and consequently are the safest conventionally grown crops to consume from the standpoint of pesticide contamination:

   12 Foods You Don't Have to Buy Organic

   Broccoli
   Cabbage
   Kiwi
   Sweet peas (frozen)
   Pineapple
   Avocado
   Cantaloupe
   Sweet Potatoes
   Mushrooms
   Eggplant
   Banana
   Asparagus
   Mango
   Sweetcorn (frozen)
   Onion
   Watermelon
   Grapefruit

Some people are more sensitive to pesticides and chemicals than others, but these insidious toxins for human health seem to becoming so pervasive that a study by the Environmental Working Group (www.ewg.org) found 287 toxic chemicals in the umbilical cord of pregnant mothers including pesticides, mercury, fire retardants, and Teflon chemicals. Do you really want to disregard these findings?

See also:

- Environmental Health: Consumables
- Environmental Health: Water
- Nutrition Keys

World Watch Institute http://www.worldwatch.org/node/6294Published in *World Watch Magazine*, 22(6) 2009.
Friends of the Earth Australia (http://www.foe.org.au/articles/2012-02-21/new-pesticides-and-food-report)
E.U. Funded Press Release 10/29/2007
Documentary film "Bought" http://www.boughtmovie.net.

Strategy 73
NUTRITION KEYS

CATEGORIES APPLIED

Addressing Addictions
Addressing Anxiety
Addressing Depression
Awareness and Mindfulness
Career and Goals
Environmental Health
Everyday Essentials
Exercise for Living
Improving Self-Esteem
Nutrition for Life

"People are eating more and more artificial food, and getting fatter and sicker. In fact, more people are chronically ill today than at any time in the history of the world."
– John and Ocean Robbins, Food Revolution Summit 2013

The information contained below is general information and does not constitute individual health or nutritional advice. Any person with a medical condition should consult his or her medical practitioner.

Poor eating habits can contribute to many chronic lifestyle and health imbalances, affecting your mood and the brain resulting in fatigue, anxiety, brain fog, depression and your ability to sleep soundly. An unhealthy diet can not only cause ill health, but could also lead to death. As an energetic living organism, our four-body system responds best to foods that are natural and full of life force. Different foods contain different combinations of nutrients, vitamins, and minerals. Variety is essential to satisfy all of your body's nutritional requirements. Remember that your body's natural state is wellness.

Recognize your body as a vehicle, which requires the right fuel and maintenance to keep it in good working order. This naturally includes exercise and plenty of fresh water. Neglecting your body's needs can cause irreparable damage with illness and disease.

Be aware: Everything you put in your mouth, on your skin, including the air you breathe and the environment you live in, has an impact – not only on your physical body, but your emotional, mental, and spiritual wellbeing also. University research on 80,000 people in both the UK and US found the more fresh produce people ate the happier they felt (see reference below).

There is a plethora of different diets around which often do more to confuse than to clarify what is best for you to do. The greatest insight will come from understanding your body's nutritional needs in conjunction with really listening feeling and observing your own body.

Good Nutrition

Eat in moderation and choose whole foods. Whole foods are the most nutrient-dense (in contrast to calories). They look like they did when they were picked or came out of the ground.

Eat plenty of **fresh fruit, vegetables, nuts, seeds, and legumes** to provide fibre to your diet. Enhance flavors with herbs and spices. These help to stabilize your blood sugar and assists in the management of cholesterol. Grains are also a good source of fibre; see also Wheat below.

Eat a **low fat** diet to keep you lean and boost your immunity; the general recommendation is around 15% of all daily calories. Beware, however, that when manufacturers reduce or eliminate the fat, they typically replace it with something that simply tastes good; too often this is simple carbohydrates such as sugar, more sodium, and thickeners. So without the filling effect of fat in foods, you are left hungry and tend to eat more.

Eat a **low sugar** diet.

Research shows that beyond weight gain, sugar can take a serious toll on your health, worsening conditions ranging from heart disease to cancer. Some physicians go so far as to call sugar a toxin (CBS NEWS April 1, 2012). Sugar also seriously affects tooth decay.

Beware of sugar substitute found in many foods, which can be highly toxic, for example Aspartame and Saccharin. See also Strategy 30 Environmental Health: Consumables.

A good sugar substitute is Xylitol (extracted from various fruits and vegetables) or Stevia (a herbal leaf sweetener). Other alternatives are: honey, coconut sugar, date sugar, maple syrup, fruit juice, honey, agave extract.

Avoid soft drinks high in sugar. Apart from the toxic affects it can lead to anxiety.

Beware also of high sugar content in processed foods like breakfast cereal, mayonnaise, peanut butter, sauces, and many microwave meals. It comes in the form of sucrose: table sugar, dextrose (corn sugar), and high-fructose corn syrup. Fructose interferes with our hormones, our brains, and our ability to regulate appetite, and so perpetuates eating.

Avoid **table salt.** It is chemically stripped of its companion elements, and manufactured salt contains aluminium, which has been implicated as a major cause of Alzheimer's disease. Sodium is found in nearly all processed food; it increases blood pressure and adds to your risk of stroke or heart disease. It mingles with other elements and stimulates appetite so can really be a contributing factor to stacking on the weight. Refined table salt can create craving for salt because it is not meeting the body's needs. It is just sodium and chloride and added iodine.

By contrast, **natural salt** like Himalayan salt, sea salt, and rock salt contain around 70–80 valuable mineral elements and does not contain any chemical additives. Natural salt has numerous health benefits, which are vital to our body's functions. Natural salt helps to:

- regulate blood sugar (VIP for diabetics)
- prevent varicose veins and spider veins on the legs and thighs
- clear congestion and mucus in the lungs and nasal passages
- remove excess acidity from the cells of the body
- regulate sleep
- prevent the gout type of arthritis
- maintain healthy bones
- extract excess acidity from body cells and brain cells to assist proper brain functioning.

When the body is short of salt it means the body is really short of water.

Avoid **fast foods, which** have little nutrition and are usually high in fat, calories, cholesterol, and sodium. Fast foods are usually cheap and convenient because they are made using cheaper ingredients such as GMO products, high-fat meats, refined grains, added sugars and fats instead of nutritious foods such as lean meats, fresh vegetables, and fruit. They can result in serious health problems such as high blood pressure, heart disease, and obesity.

Avoid **processed foods**, which have little nutrition. Processed food has been altered from its natural state and is either bagged, canned, jarred, or boxed and has a list of ingredients on the label. What you eat has far-reaching effects, not only on your physical body but on also your general wellbeing. Fresh fruit and vegetables, preferably organic without the use of herbicides, pesticides, antibiotics, and hormones are obviously best.

Take care with **wheat.** Wheat is one of the most common food allergies and one of the most widely used products in processed foods. It is found in breakfast cereals, breads, pasta, and myriad other processed foods. Other names include bulghar, durum, durum flour, and durum wheat, Einkorn, Emmer. The bulk of the wheat grown today has toxins and is not as it used to be. Gluten is a protein found in wheat and is causing growing health problems.

Increasingly, wheat is being found to be at the basis of numerous health conditions: obesity, heart disease, arthritis, neurological impairment, diabetes, and various digestive problems. You may find eliminating wheat from your diet brings you much more vitality and feeling of wellness.

Avoid **Monosodium Glutamate** (MSG). It is also known as sodium glutamate and is the sodium salt of glutamic acid. It is added in vast amounts to processed foods to mask flavors and improve the taste of cheap or bland foods that can lead to cravings. Glutamic acid from food sources can get into the brain, injuring and sometimes killing neurons.

Reactions can include:

- rashes, itching, burning, numbness
- migraines, headaches
- asthma
- irritable bowel syndrome
- chest tightness, heart palpitations, heart arrhythmia, anxiety
- irritability, restlessness, sleep disturbance.

Eating Tips

1. Preferably, eat when you are hungry rather than by the clock. This increases body awareness and is more harmonious to your body's needs for sustenance.

2. Before you eat, look at your food and think about where it has come from including each of the different ingredients and their original environment. This helps to bring awareness to the food you are eating, its source, quality, and nutritional value. It also brings consciousness to the fact that the Earth provides everything to sustain you. Give thanks for the food you are about to eat. Gratitude increases the frequency of the food and your frequency. One idea is "I give thanks for this food and all life that has contributed to this abundance before me."

3. Your body's system priorities change in different circumstances and so it is best not to eat when the digestion of food could be compromised. This occurs when you are stressed, angry or upset, you are feverish, or just before going to bed. When emotions

are high, there is a tendency to eat quickly and your body doesn't break down the food properly or get the signal that it is full.

4. Eat mindfully. Don't eat at your desk or while watching television or any other kind of media. It's hard to be conscious of the food you are consuming and how it feels if your mind is elsewhere. This can easily result in overeating or addictive eating. Give attention to your food while eating. Really taste what is going into your mouth, and maintain awareness through the whole chewing and swallowing process.

5. Chew your food thoroughly before swallowing to facilitate good digestion. It signals your stomach that food in on the way.

6. Don't overeat. Feel satisfied but not bloated when you've finished a meal. If you are still hungry after eating, a wait of 20 minutes will often dispel the desire to eat.

7. Avoid water at least 30 minutes before eating or 1 hour after eating to maximise digestion.

8. Healthy food that is cooked and presented in an attractive manner can improve your sense of wellbeing by increasing the level of pleasure you feel about it. Sensory benefits are derived from the taste, smell, and texture of different foods and its colorful appeal. It can also encourage mindful eating.

9. To assess your reaction to different foods, develop a habit of tuning into your body after eating and ask yourself – "How does my body feel?" Notice if you feel bloated, if you feel a heaviness or discomfort in any way. Notice any cravings, change in body temperature or allergic reactions. Notice any peaks or troughs in your energy levels.

While you may struggle to have so much consciousness around your everyday eating habits, even doing it occasionally but regularly will certainly heighten your body's response to what you are consuming.

Supplements

Current research confirms that we can no longer get the essential nutrients from our food alone. Contributing to this is the depleted soils, pesticides, antibiotics, and other toxic effects that permeate so many foods. It is recommended to supplement even the best diet with nutrition to promote resistance to disease. This includes high-daily nutritional supplements such as essential multivitamins, antioxidants, and minerals.

Be aware, many of the "cheaper" supplements are passed through the body without absorption.

"If you can only afford one or two supplements, then make them Magnesium and a good multi vitamin."
– Dr. Carolyn Dean M.D., N.D.

Cravings

It is common that *food cravings* can indicate a negative reaction in your body. See the chart below to identify what you body really needs. Reproduced with permission from Dr. Colleen Huber: http://natureworksbest.com/naturopathy-works/food-cravings

If you crave this...	*What you really need is...*	*And here are healthy foods that have it:*
Chocolate	Magnesium	Raw nuts and seeds, legumes, fruits
Sweets	Chromium	Broccoli, grapes, cheese dried beans, calves liver, chicken
	Carbon	Fresh fruits
	Phosphorus	Chicken, beef, liver, poultry, fish, eggs, dairy, nuts, legumes, grains
	Sulfur	Cranberries, horseradish, cruciferous vegetables, kale cabbage
	Tryptophan	Cheese, Liver, lamb, raisins, sweet potato, spinach
Bread, toast	Nitrogen	High protein foods: fish, meat, nuts, beans
Oily snacks, fatty foods	Calcium	Mustard and turnip greens, broccoli, kale, legumes, cheese, sesame
Coffee or tea	Phosphorous	Chicken, beef, liver, poultry, fish, eggs, dairy, nuts, legumes
	Sulfur	Egg yolks, red peppers, muscle protein, garlic, onion, cruciferous vegetables
	NaCl salt	Sea salt, apple cider vinegar (on salad)
	Iron	Meat, fish, poultry, seaweed, greens, black cherries
Alcohol, recreational drugs	Protein	Meat, poultry, seafood, dairy nuts
	Avenin	Granola, oatmeal
	Calcium	Mustard and turnip greens, broccoli, kale, legumes, cheese, sesame
	Glutamine	Supplement glutamine powder for withdrawal, raw cabbage juice
	Potassium	Sun-dried black olives, potato peel broth, seaweed, bitter greens
Chewing ice	Iron	Meat, fish, poultry, seaweed, greens, black cherries
Burned food	Carbon	Fresh fruit
Soda and other carbonated drinks	Calcium	Mustard and turnip greens, broccoli, kale, legumes, cheese, sesame
Salty foods	Chloride	Raw goat milk, fish, unrefined sea salt
Acid foods	Magnesium	Raw nuts and seeds, legumes, fruits
Preference for liquids rather than solids	Water	Flavour water with lemon or lime. You need 8 to 10 glasses per day
Preference for solids rather than liquids	Water	You have been so dehydrated for so long that you have lost your thirst. Flavour water with lemon or lime. You need 8 to 10 glasses per day
Cool drinks	Manganese	Walnuts, almonds, pecans, pineapple, blueberries
Pre-menstrual cravings	Zinc	Red meats (especially organ meats), seafood, leafy vegetables, root vegetables
General overeating	Silicon	Nuts, seeds, avoid refined starches
	Tryptophan	Cheese, liver, lamb, raisins, sweet potato, spinach
	Tyrosine	Vitamin C supplements or orange, green, red fruits and vegetables
Lack of appetite	Vitamin B1	Nuts, seeds, beans, liver and other organ meats
	Vitamin B3	Tuna, halibut, beef, chicken, turkey, pork, seeds and legumes
	Manganese	Walnuts, almonds, pecans, pineapple, blueberries
	Chloride	Raw goat milk, unrefined sea salt
Tobacco	Silicon	Nuts, seeds; avoid refined starches
	Tyrosine	Vitamin C supplements or orange, green and red fruits and vegetables

Reproduced with permission from Dr. Colleen Huber
http://www.naturopathyworks.com/pages/cravings.php

An **alkaline body** is a healthy body. High fat and high sugar diets create acidity, increasing the need for the millions of antacid tablets purchased every year. This can result in serious digestive problems

For overall health and wellbeing *exercise* is essential. Generally speaking, to maintain a healthy weight, ensure calories consumed equal calories burned.

Website Links For More Detailed Information About Nutrition
Nutrition Australia – Frequently Asked Questions about nutrition. http://www.nutritionaustralia.org
Independent scientific health researchers who have reviewed the data, facts and findings; applied the knowledge at their own personal level; and stand with their evidence that the Facts are Indisputable. http://www.advancedhealthplan.com/

Nutritional Fact Sheets
World's healthiest foods. http://www.whfoods.org/cookhealthy.php
The George Mateljan Foundation is a non-profit organization with no commercial interest or advertising. It is a new force for change to help make a healthier you and a healthier world.

Dr. Mercola is the number one website for Natural Health. You can subscribe to a free Natural Health Newsletters loaded with Health Articles and Information you can really use! www.mercola.com. You can also search for advice about an extensive range of health issue and have access to research with proven practical solutions.

Dr. Carolyn Dean MD ND, promotes natural health remedies. http://drcarolyndean.com/

Research on MSG. http://www.advancedhealthplan.com/msgstudy.html

Jeff Hays made a documentary film Bought about the truth behind vaccines, GMO'S and Big Pharma http://www.boughtmovie.net.

A naturopathic website which indicates what your body needs when you have food cravings. http://www.naturopathyworks.com/pages/cravings.php

Australia's No. 1 Natural Health website Comprehensive descriptions and articles of interest about many of the natural therapies available in Australia including practitioners. http://www.naturaltherapypages.com.au/

See also:

- Nutrition: Best Food Options
- Oral Health

- Environmental Health: Consumables
- Environmental Health: Water

D.G. Blanchflower, A.J. Oswald, & S. Stewart-Brown, "Is psychological well-being linked to the consumption of fruit and vegetables?" *Social Indicators Research,* October 2012.

Strategy 74
ORAL HEALTH

CATEGORIES APPLIED

Awareness & Mindfulness
Improving Self Esteem
Nutrition for Life

"Oral health is fundamental to overall health, wellbeing and quality of life. A healthy mouth enables people to eat, speak and socialize without pain, discomfort or embarrassment. The impact of oral disease on people's everyday lives is subtle and pervasive, influencing eating, sleep work and social roles. The prevalence and recurrences of these impacts constitutes a silent epidemic. Dental caries is the second most costly diet-related disease in Australia."

– National Advisory Committee on Oral Health

Poor oral hygiene can be the cause of major health issues. Factors such as an unhealthy diet, excessive use of sugar, tobacco use, and harmful alcohol use all significantly contribute to toxicity. The vast majority of gum and teeth problems occur first *between* the teeth where bacteria build up.

Brushing alone is not enough to maintain healthy gums and teeth. Daily use of dental floss and regularly stimulating the gums are also considered important. Gum stimulation not only removes waste from the tissue but also increases the blood flow, which brings both oxygen and nutrition to that area.

Oral health is often a neglected area in diagnosing a multitude of other health problems. Numerous health imbalances can be associated with the mouth, teeth and jaw. Clenching or grinding teeth can lead to headaches and muscular damage around the jaw. This often occurs during sleep. The temporomandibular joint is the hinge that connects your jaw and your skull. It can be the source of much discomfort resulting in difficulty with chewing, swelling in the face, dizziness, neck and shoulder pain, and ringing in the ears.

About Fluoride

Fluoride compounds are salts that form when the element fluorine combines with minerals in soil or rocks. There is much debate about the use of fluoride, which is added to our water supplies by councils despite the objection of many individuals. While it has been found that topical application of fluoride on teeth results in fewer tooth cavities, this does not justify the inclusion of fluoride in our water supplies in the same way that a sunscreen used to protect skin would not be orally ingested.

It is also argued that fluoride is an "endocrine disruptor." It has a detrimental affect on many tissues in the human body including bones, the brain, the thyroid gland, and the pineal gland.

Dental fluorosis is a condition that presents as cloudy spots and streaks on the teeth, causing a defect in tooth enamel commonly found in the developing teeth of teenagers. Despite the poison warnings on fluoridated toothpastes, many children swallow this harmful substance.

According to the British Fluoridation Society *One in a Million: The facts about water fluoridation* (2012), Australia is among the world's highest percentage of a population (80%) drinking artificially fluoridated water.* www.bfsweb.org/onemillion/onemillion2012.html (updated November 2012)

The reader is encouraged to research to their own level of satisfaction. Some useful links are below.

Root canal or **Endodontics** is a treatment that replaces the root of the tooth or infected pulp with a filling. While it appears that most work well, there can be insidious problems. If you have health issues that are not resolving, check against the energy meridians related to the tooth of any root canal filling you have to see if there is a relationship. This could open the door to problem solving.

Energy Meridians (Teeth)

Each tooth is located on an energy meridian, which is related to the different bodily organs. Some organic health imbalances may be as a result of an unhealthy tooth. Root canal fillings, and amalgam fillings can be the unexplored cause of many health anomalies. Regular dental check-ups help to identify possible issues. Further insights may be available through a complementary practitioner who can do some muscle testing.

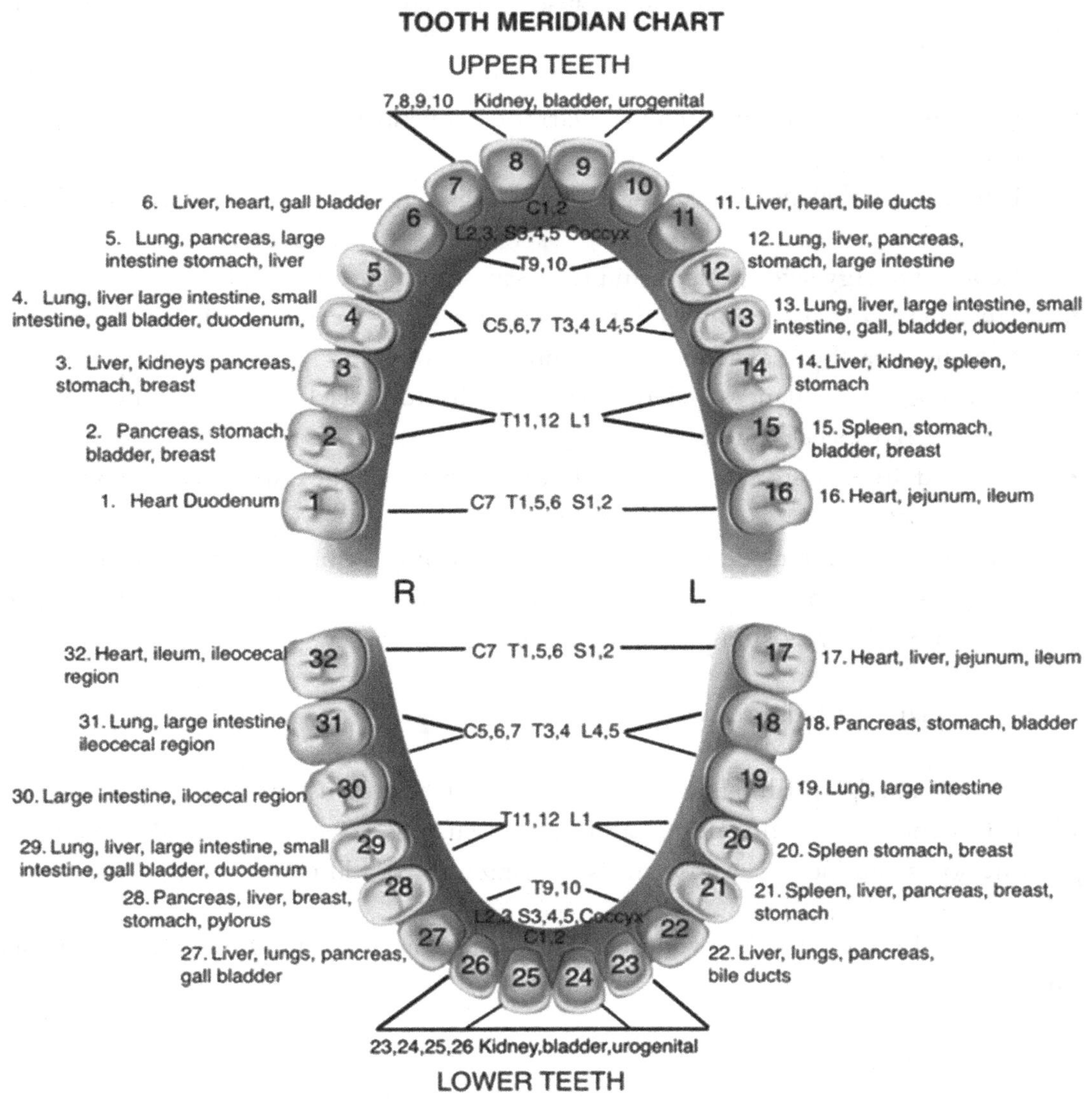

Dental Amalgam (Mercury)

It is now widely known that the dental amalgam (mercury) used for fillings is the most poisonous, non-radioactive, naturally occurring substance on our planet. The World Health Organization has stated that there is no safe level of mercury. Toxic mercury vapor continually releases from the amalgam fillings, with around 80% of it entering and accumulating in your body. It can be the cause of many health symptoms, the severity of which are influenced by the number of fillings, how long you have had them, how they are stimulated and how often.

Symptoms of mercury poisoning are vast because it has such a destructive effect on the immune and detoxification systems.

- Digestive upsets including colitis, diarrhoea/constipation, weight loss,
- nausea/vomiting
- Emotional imbalances including mood swings, aggressiveness, anxiety, fits of anger, depression
- Reduced energy levels, apathy and restlessness and chronic tiredness
- Muscular/skeletal – cramps, joint or muscular aches, weakness, stiffness, numbness
- Irregular heartbeat, anaemia, chest pain
- Neurological imbalances including, learning disorders, lack of concentration, memory loss, slurred speech, numbness
- Oral and throat: chronic coughing, bleeding gums, metallic taste, mouth inflammation, sore throats
- Other symptoms include allergies, excessive blushing, genital discharge, gland swelling, hair loss, insomnia, loss of sense of smell, excessive perspiration, renal failure, cold and clammy skin, vision problems, and water retention.

There are also many related diseases.

Removing these amalgam fillings can also result in a tremendous amount of mercury being absorbed into the body if not done carefully, because as soon as the drilling starts the temperature soars and mercury vapor starts pouring into your lungs.

Safety measures for mercury removal used by dentists who understand these matters include precautions such as:

- Safety glasses

- Breathing pure bottled oxygen through a nasal tube and the dental mask across the nose, and rubber dam
- Copious amounts of cold water to keep the temperature low while the filling is being drilled
- Clean-up suction device around the tooth
- Powdered charcoal and chlorella placed in your mouth under the rubber dam (this has the ability to absorb mercury particles before they get absorbed into your system).

For a balanced discussion on root canals see http://www.mgoldmandds.com/rctchoices.htm
http://fluoridealert.org/
http://www.mercuryfreenow.com/layperson/symptoms.html
http://www.healthcarealternatives.net/toothbody.html

See also:

- Nutrition: Best food Options
- Nutrition: Keys
- Environmental Health: Electromagnetic Fields
- Environmental Health: General
- Environmental Health: Personal Products
- Environmental Health: Consumables
- Environmental Health: Water
- If Seriously Ill: Understanding Integrated Healing

Strategy 75
PAIN DIALOG

CATEGORIES APPLIED

Addressing Addictions
Addressing Anxiety
Addressing Depression
Awareness and Mindfulness
Communications and Relationships
Improving Self-Esteem

It is often said that pain is an inevitable part of life but suffering is optional. Pain is the sensation and suffering is the mind story associated with the sensation. There are many and varied mind stories – things like:

- I don't deserve this pain.
- This shouldn't be happening.
- I can't be happy with so much pain.
- There is too much pain in my life.
- I hate pain.
- Nobody deserves to feel this kind of pain.

Suffering will ensure you keep the pain. Your body has a supreme intelligence and knows how to heal itself. Pain is the body's way of trying to communicate with you. It wants your attention and has likely been striving to get it for some time, and you may have been missing or ignoring the earlier cues. Pain, either physical or emotional, is often associated with resistance. It can be resistance to feeling some challenging emotions that you didn't know how to process and are stuck in your multidimensional body, or an attachment to a belief and resistance to a greater truth. All of which can be compounded by a contaminated energy field.

Dialoging with pain is a way to access your intuition and try to get to the source of the pain. It is a means to increase your awareness and understanding about yourself. When you dialog with pain it can provide you with greater insight into the condition you are experiencing. Insight and introspection = awareness, and awareness gives choices. It will take honesty and courage and you really must be willing to trust and surrender to this inner communication. There is most definitely a part of you that knows exactly what is going on.

You will need a writing pad and pen for this exercise.

To help establish the appropriate attitude for the dialog process. Imagine the pain represents a child part of you that has desperately wanted your attention for a long time and you have continued to ignore it. Now this inner child feels ignored, abused, resentful, and not trusting that you will ever take care of it. So as you attempt to connect with the pain you will need to be patient, compassionate, and present.

When you feel you have the appropriate attitude, take yourself into a quiet meditative state by doing some deep breathing as though the breath is coming in and out of your heart center. Keep your attention on your heart breathing for a few minutes to bring you into present time and facilitate a connection to your inner knowing.

To discern between you as the "Questioner" (or you may prefer to call it "Conscious Mind") and the part of you which is the "Pain," just create a new line for each and preface with a Q or CM for Questioner and P for Pain - then just let it flow. There are no fixed rules. It may start like this:

> Q – Feel into the pain you are experiencing and say hello to it. Ask "Would you please dialogue with me, I want to understand you better?"
>
> P – There may be a sense of "Oh yeah? Maybe."
>
> Q – "I can recognize that you may not believe me or trust me but I am sincere and really want to understand you better."
>
> P – "Mm mm maybe, let's explore a little then?"
>
> Q – "Thank you, Pain. I really appreciate your willingness to dialog with me. I wondered what it is that you are trying to convey to me. What is the behaviour or thoughts that I have been doing that is behind your communication?"
>
> P -....... (continue on)

Continue writing what comes into your mind. Do not challenge the response; just be grateful for the communication and continue to record the conversation.

You may also find that you have a flowing dialog from the pain without the need for questions. If this is not the case you could ask questions like:

> "Pain, if you were to have a name, what would you be called?"

You may find it is the same as the name of someone you have an issue with or it might be an emotion like frustration or something else entirely.

While in this meditative state of mind, another option is to ask these questions with your eyes closed. Often the mind will give you images that provide insight into your question. You may also discover that as you go about your day when you are not thinking about it, a deeper understanding just drops into your awareness.

Other possible questions could be:

- What is it that I am avoiding or denying?
- If I were to drop any preconceived ideas what would be revealed to me?
- If I were to experience instant healing, what beliefs would I need to release and what behavioral change would I need to implement?
- If I truly surrendered, how would my life be different?
- Is there some kind of toxin in my body that is causing this pain?
- Is there some kind of geopathic stress affecting my home?

It is recommended that you focus and dialog regularly with your pain until the desired shift occurs. Patience is so important. Remember, your body has an innate wisdom. Your job is to fully attune to it with love and compassion.

See also:

- Affirmations
- Allow Feelings
- Ask for Help
- Awareness of Awareness
- Being: Mindfulness
- Clearing
- Deep Release Breathing
- Environmental Health: Electromagnetic Fields
- Environmental Health: General

- Environmental Health: Personal Products
- Environmental Health: Consumables
- Feeling Anger
- Feeling Challenged
- Feeling Fear
- Feeling Guilt or Shame
- Feeling Jealousy
- Feeling Stuck
- Feeling Uncertain or Fearful of the Unknown
- Feeling Victimized
- Feeling Worried
- Forgiveness Process
- Going with the Flow
- Gratitude
- Grounding/Earthing
- Manage Key Tension Areas
- Pain Focus
- Seek to Understand
- Shadow Play
- Thought Power and Control
- Toning
- Trust Truth and Honesty
- Truth Lover

Strategy 76
PAIN FOCUS

CATEGORIES APPLIED

Addressing Addictions
Addressing Anxiety
Addressing Depression
Awareness and Mindfulness
Communications and Relationships
Improving Self-Esteem

(Note: This Strategy to address pain does not constitute medical advice. Please consult your practitioner.)

Pain is something that we all experience at some stage in our life, and understanding the play of energy involved may prove very helpful.

There are different degrees of pain and different causes, classified most commonly as either acute or chronic. Acute pain may be as a result of surgery, some kind of accident that has resulted in broken bones, skin abrasions, burns, or childbirth. It could be mild or severe but does not typically last longer than 3–6 months. Chronic pain is ongoing, often despite the apparent healing of any wound. It can present physically as muscular and/or nerve pain, limited mobility, or a disease like cancer or arthritis.

Pain is an indication that something hurts. The pain may present as soreness, cramping, discomfort, aching, burning, stabbing, prickling, or tingling. These sensations arise from the thousands of receptor cells under our skin that sense light, heat, cold, pressure, touch, and pain; these nerve receptors send a message up the spinal cord to your brain and other body parts. Pain can be mild or severe and variable with different people.

Pain is always the body's way of saying *"PAY ATTENTION!"*

Pain is typically not something we embrace or welcome, despite the supreme intelligence and integrity of our body. Our human body, and more specifically our "feeling" body, is our internal guidance system, telling us what feels good and what feels bad. It is arguably one of the greatest gifts we have as human beings and is commonly the most abused or disregarded. We will often go to great lengths to manipulate, avoid, or deny our feelings, or at least the ones we don't want or don't want to acknowledge, on either a physical or emotional level.

People respond differently to their individual pain. One way is to initially acknowledge the pain but consciously choose to ignore it and just press on with life's activities, or the exact opposite and allow the pain to stop all activity, consuming their mind with constant negative thoughts without any suggestion of exploring the message the pain is striving to communicate. Another is to immediately use distractions by adopting different kinds of behaviors: things like eating for comfort, watching television, being consumed by the variety of computer-type technologies, being busy being busy, or using drugs, alcohol, or shopping – anything to desensitize or suppress the pain. Some also blame the different body part for causing so much pain, e.g. "I hate that my back causes me so much pain."

For some, the actual fear of pain causes the body to go into resistance. This will also inhibit the movement or flow of energy and can significantly contribute to the degree of tension and pain.

From a *vibrational* perspective, pain reflects energy that is stuck in the body and unable to move. As with all life forms, we are in a constant state of change and through it our energy is meant to be always flowing.

The human body has seven primary energy centers called chakras, which basically means spiralling fields of energy. This is where the exchange of energy takes place with the universe and our bodies. These are invisible to the naked eye and are affected by how we think, feel, and behave, and therefore reflect in our physical, emotional, mental, and spiritual bodies, all of which are interrelated.

A healthy body reflects a constant flow of energy coming into and out of our bodies uninhibited through the primary energy centres. Energy practitioners refer to this as *chi*, *prana*, or life force energy. The expression "going with the flow" is when you are in alignment with your higher self and your energy is flowing unencumbered.

Pain arises from conflict

What causes energy to become stuck is judgment, making something right or wrong, good or bad. It often has fear at its foundation. It is an attachment to a belief or story that we have created in our mind. We are holding it fixed and don't want to let it go on some level of our being. Notice within you any kind of satisfaction or pleasure you derive from your pain and how much it becomes part of your language. These are all clues to your possible resistance.

Strive to have a positive attitude and appreciation that your body is doing its very best to try to communicate with you. Be willing to really tune in and listen.

Eckhart Tolle speaks of pain in this way:

> **The greater part of human pain is unnecessary. It is self-created as long as the unobserved mind runs your life.**
>
> **The pain that you create now is always some form of non-acceptance, some form of unconscious resistance to what is. On the level of thought, the resistance is some form of judgment. On the emotional level, it is some form of negativity. The intensity of pain depends on the degree of resistance to the present moment, and this in turn depends on how strongly you are identified with your mind.**

Without denying the immense gifts medical science provides for us, it is useful also to recognize that we often celebrate medical science each time it finds a way to distance us from our pain, but this potentially prevents us from *understanding the cause* of the disharmony we have created in our bodies.

Consider just the simple over-the-counter painkillers available to us as a quick fix to a headache or some other discomforts that our feeling body is trying to communicate – "Hey listen to me - I want your attention!"

Before reaching for pain medication in the first instance, use the signal as an opportunity to tune into your body and the message it is trying to convey to you. Strive to find a natural approach first. It could be that by taking medication you actually add to the problem, as all drugs have side effects and adverse reactions.

Pain is not static. You are not static

This pain relief process uses the mind to do the exact opposite of the common tendency of resistance. The objective is to give your undivided attention to the pain and to describe what it is that you are feeling. It is really *surrendering into* the pain.

The purpose of sharing this process, adapted from a technique by Dr. Elan Z. Neev, is more to look at the dynamics playing out on an energetic and causal level and move out of all resistance.

Pain Relief Process

Ensure that you will not be distracted by anything going on around you. Close your eyes and take your attention inwards. Connect yourself to the Earth by imagining roots of light going down into the Earth just like tree roots. This is important because when we experience pain there can be a strong desire to be out of your body, but you must be fully in your body to facilitate healing. Breathe a few long, slow, deep breaths while focusing all your awareness on your breath. At the same time, make sure you don't run any mind story, or think about the process or anything else, as this too will inhibit your focus; just let the breath consume your full attention for a few minutes. When you feel your mind has become quieter, adopt an attitude of curiosity about your body and the pain, as though you really want to get to know every single thing about it. There is no resistance: you are giving it your full attention by being present with it. Leave yourself open to new experiences of pain rather than being fixed by any past episodes or expectations of any future outcomes.

Your role is to stay totally present with it while describing it in great detail. You can verbalize this quietly to yourself, though speaking aloud may assist your ability to concentrate better. Proceed by responding to the following questions. Finish each question before you immediately move on to the next. You may find it will assist your focus to use your hands to gesticulate as you describe it.

1. Where specifically in your body is the pain located?
2. How deep is it? Is it on the surface or deep within?
3. What size is it? Use measurements like 6 inches or comparisons like the size of a basketball.
4. What color is it? Use your imagination and guess if you don't seem to see a thing.
5. What shape is it? A blob, like a star, round, square, oblong, spiky, etc.
6. Does it have any sound, a pulse, or vibration? Or some other movement, like groaning, tapping, throbbing, whistling, grinding, pounding, swishing, clicking, or tapping?
7. What is its texture? Bristly, rough, spiky, smooth, rough like sandpaper?

Once you have answered all these questions go back to the beginning and repeat the process in the same order. Without resistance your body's energy can shift.

Maintaining your focus in this way allows you to keep your *attention* on your *intention* of fully being present with the pain. As you do this you will notice your responses to the questions vary and your pain diminish.

1. Where specifically in your body is the pain located?
   In the left side of my head and down into my left shoulder

2. How deep is it?
   Feels like about 3 inches under my skin

3. What size is it?
   Like the size of a tennis ball

4. What color is it?
   Red with black swirls

5. What shape is it?
   Kind of round with a bumpy surface

6. Does it have a sound, pulse, vibration or some other movement?
   It's like an erratic throb that kind of moves around

7. What is its texture?
   A bit lumpy

Now start at the beginning again and repeat each of the questions, maintaining a curious attitude responding with your considered answers. Realize this is not the same moment as it was before, so don't anticipate based on previous responses. This is a different now moment.

1. Where in your body is the pain located?
   In the left side of my head near my ear

2. How deep is it?
   Feels like it's just below the surface of my skin

3. What size is it?
   It feels like the size of a lemon

4. What color is it?
   Just red now

5. What shape is it?
   More of a blob kind of shape

6. Does it have a sound, pulse, vibration, or some other movement?
   An even kind of pulsing sensation

7. What is its texture?
   Kind of smooth and glassy

   Keep repeating this cycle of questions with your responses while maintaining full focus on the pain until you are feeling comfortable.

Don't be limited by the questions. If you feel so inclined, ask other questions. Focus on each question one at a time, maintaining your curiosity and respond fully before moving on to the next one.

Repeat the process of this curious, industrious kind of description until you find no more to describe. This teaches you to know your pain intimately without resistance. The effect of this total acceptance allows all tension to go and the pain often goes with it.

Helping Another In Pain

This is lovely to do with a partner who simply asks each question, waits patiently for your response, and then pauses with a breath, creating just the right amount of space before asking the next question. Working with a partner allows you to stay in a quiet reflective state with your eyes closed, retaining total presence with your pain. Nevertheless, once you've done this a few times you will likely remember the questions without having to read them. It is a cyclical process.

Always remember that pain is your plea or your signal from your feeling body or internal guidance system to pay attention. Pain is not static, and you are not static. Feeling pain fully, without any story or judgment attached, facilitates its movement through the body – and often out of it.

Helping a Child in Pain

A common reaction to seeing a child in pain is to distract him from genuine pain in the belief that it helps him somehow. While this can be beneficial for the superficial and frequent knocks and bumps of an energetic child, it is unhelpful for the more painful experiences. It is no wonder the majority of people grow up wanting to resist any sign of pain.

When a child has a fall or a bump of some kind and it's obvious to you that he doesn't need any medical intervention, then you might respond with "You're okay"as a loving reassurance.

If, however, there is genuine pain, consider using this Strategy as it teaches body awareness and how to connect with the child's feelings without going into resistance.

> Example: Comfort the child with contact or cuddles and express genuine empathy and compassion for him and his pain. If it seems that he needs more support, say something like, "I know a way that we might be able to make the pain go away. Do you want to try it?" Then proceed with the series of pain relief questions above. You may want to adjust your language to suit the child's age.

When there is an emotional hurt, there can be a tendency for a child to think there is something wrong with him, as though he is deficient or not good enough. Reassure him by reminding him how lovable he is. Then ask him where he can feel that emotional hurt/pain in his body and guide him with the same series of questions. This teaches the child a great coping mechanism of allowing his feelings to be without resistance and without being judged; it allows his energy to flow and may well result in complete resolution of the pain.

When we bring our mind into presence, as with this Pain Focus Strategy, the body's stuck energy can move. You may also want to explore Strategy 23 Conscious Breathing where the breath is used as the focus to bring you into presence.

Do not hesitate to seek medical assistance if pain persists.

See also:

- Allow Feelings
- Ask for Help
- Awareness: Building the Observer
- Being: Mindfulness
- Clearing
- Deep Release Breathing
- Environmental Health: Electromagnetic Fields
- Environmental Health: General

- Environmental Health: Personal Products
- Environmental Health: Consumables
- Feeling Agitated
- Feeling Anger
- Feeling Challenged
- Feeling Disempowered
- Feeling Fear
- Feeling Guilt or Shame
- Feeling Jealousy
- Feeling Lonely or Alone
- Feeling Rejected or Hurt
- Feeling Scattered: Unbalanced
- Feeling Stuck
- Feeling Uncertain or Fearful of the Unknown
- Feeling Unloved or Unlovable
- Feeling Unsupported
- Feeling Victimized
- Feeling Worried
- Forgiveness Process
- Going with the Flow
- Grounding/Earthing
- Manage Key Tension Areas
- Pain Dialog
- Projection
- Thought Power and Control
- Toning

Eckhart Tolle, *The Power of Now*, Hodder, 1999, p.27.

Dr. Elan Z. Neev, *Wholistic Healing: How to Harmonize Your Body, Mind and Spirit with Life, for Freedom, Joy, Health, Beauty, Love, Money and Psychic Powers*, 1977.

Strategy 77
PERSONAL MISSION STATEMENT

CATEGORIES APPLIED

Addressing Addictions
Addressing Anxiety
Addressing Depression
Awareness and Mindfulness
Career and Goals
Communications and Relationships
Improving Self-Esteem

A personal mission statement is a truly valuable process to help you define and attract the energy you want, what you want to accomplish, and who you want to become in every area of your life. It is a lovely adjunct to goal setting.

Writing a personal mission statement forces you to think deeply about your life, clarifies your purpose and the reason you are here on the Earth. It identifies what is really important to you and will reflect your gifts, talents, and passion. It also helps you to remember your true authentic self.

Lauren Gorgo distinguishes desire from want: "Wanting is at the ego level and comes from a place of separation, lack, of not having… whereas desire is at the soul level and is the basis, or the motivation for every level of creation."

Too often people adopt a path they have been told to follow by well-meaning parents, teachers, or significant others. This can have a disastrous negative impact and take you totally off the path of expressing your own unique calling. It can lead to depression and a reduced immune system because there is a lack of passion and drive – there is no heart involved.

Creating a mission statement is standard practice for high achievers. It is a means to focus your energy through your actions, behaviors, and decisions towards the things that are most important to you. Having clearly defined values sets your priorities and helps to keep you on track. They tell you how you want to spend your time and your life. All your goals will be based on your mission statement and part of your daily action plan.

Your personal mission statement will often reflect some aspect of your life wounding. As you work through the pain and weaknesses, you are able to transform them into your strengths and clear out the misconceptions that would otherwise limit you. You may also find you become a teacher for others who may experience something similar.

Some Guidelines

1. Sit quietly with eyes closed in a meditative kind of state and breathe into your heart. It can help to put your hand on your heart to assist you to focus there. Then bring in a feeling of gratitude. This is a way of connecting you to the higher vibration of your heart and identifying what it is that your soul wants. Imagine that you are approaching the end of your life and looking back. What are the things that would give you that deep sense of satisfaction that you lived the life you wanted and completed your personal mission? Who is the person you want to become? What qualities, strengths, and attitudes will you have? What is really important to you? What does your core essence long for? See if you can get a clear sense of how it will feel to be this person. Jot it down.

2. These further steps about identifying your values and what is really important to you will enhance the process. A simple way to do this is to jot down the following:

    a. List five characteristics of the one or two persons you admire most. What is it that attracts you about them? What qualities, strengths, skills, and attitudes appeal to you?
    b. List five things you enjoy doing.
    c. List five things that interest you.
    d. List your current strengths, talents and abilities.
    e. List the strengths, talents, and abilities that you would like to develop.

    Ensure that your list creates good feelings when you contemplate your values. Beware of identifying these values just from the mind, which may involve "should," or your parent's values, or some significant other person in your life. See Strategy 99 Values for a more comprehensive process.

3. Next, maintaining that heart connection, define your life roles. These may be roles in relation to your profession, family, community, or other areas in your life. Define how you would like to be described by others in each of these roles.

4. Then write a draft of your personal mission statement, making it as succinct as possible, perhaps just a few lines. Your mission statement must evoke good feelings from you. Then you know you have your heart involved and have connected with your higher guidance. There will be a sense of deep satisfaction and happiness.

5. When you are happy with it, post it on your desk or somewhere you will see it every day. Use stick figures, colors, or symbols to embellish and enhance your mission statement.

6. Refer to it frequently and use it as a standard to assess all your activities. It is most helpful to keep you on track.

7. Review your personal mission statement periodically to keep you connected with your deepest aspirations and assist you to stay in harmony with yourself. You will know, because if you are not living according to your values and fulfilling your deepest desires you will likely feel depressed and disconnected from your higher self.

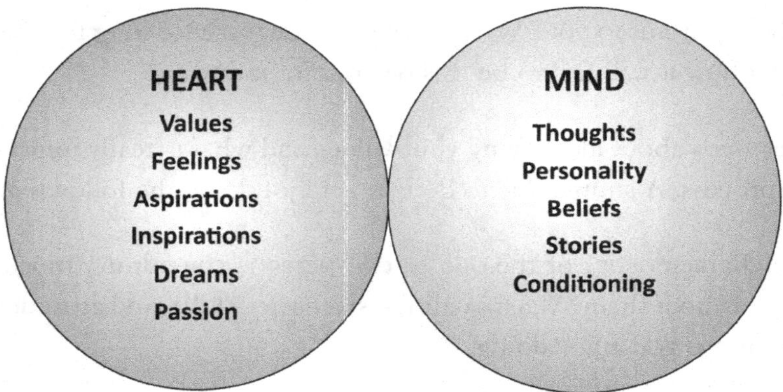

Your heart is associated with your feeling body and your feelings will never lie to you – they just feel. Be careful, however, not to run negative mind stories, which also create feelings. The mind is associated with the egoic/personality self and it has been subjected to programming and conditioning. Without awareness, your mind can and will deceive you.

Always *feel* into what your heart desires and follow its supreme intelligence.

See also:

- Awareness of Awareness
- Decisions: Heart Wisdom
- Decisions: Motives and Impact
- Do Things You Enjoy
- Goal Setting

- Ideas and Inspiration
- Major Life Influencers
- Values
- Who Am I?
- Work Passion

Lauren Gorgo March 2013, http://thinkwithyourheart.com

Strategy 78
PROJECTION

CATEGORIES APPLIED

Addressing Addictions
Addressing Anxiety
Addressing Depression
Awareness and Mindfulness
Career and Goals
Communications and Relationships
Everyday Essentials
Improving Self-Esteem

Projection is behavior of the egoic or personality mind. It involves seeing and judging in another what is part of your own psyche, but unconscious or denied. It is the ego's way of protecting its preferred identity. These denied aspects of self are sometimes referred to as "the shadow." The shadow is a defence mechanism whereby a person subconsciously denies their own dysfunctional thoughts, motives, desires, and feelings, and, in order to reduce their own anxiety, projects them onto someone else without realizing what they are doing.

Projection is commonly reflected by the other person mirroring your own denied behaviour. Or something you judge harshly, which might include criticism of another who is showing you what you don't have the courage to do yourself. Judgment, anger, attack, criticism, defence, and justification are typical of the reactions so often directed towards another, enabling us to keep a comfortable distance from our own dysfunctional behavior.

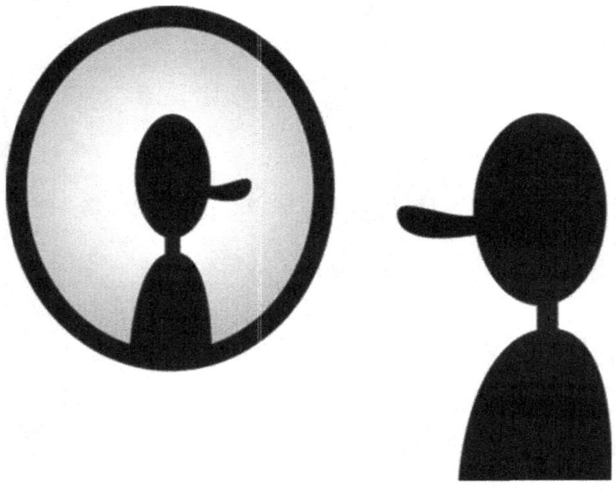

Perhaps one of the most common projections is that someone doesn't like you and so you avoid them, enabling you to remain unconscious of the mirrored behavior that *you actually don't like them.* It can also reflect a lack of self-love or the more intense form of self-loathing.

This emotional reaction is the ego/personality's way of continuing the avoidance, denial, or suppression of a shadow aspect of self. It may be associated with an unresolved painful experience within your own life.

Projection allows you to feel better about yourself by protecting the conscious mind from something you judge harshly, and thereby keeps you from the truth.

It takes courage, humility, a desire for truth, and honest reflection to help you recognize what issues, beliefs, and judgments you hold… *what you can see in another, but not in yourself.* Beware not to judge yourself as you discover these projections; rather, celebrate your awareness and the opportunity for growth and integration – we all have a shadow. It's the integration of the shadow that gives us peace and freedom and brings more light into our multidimensional self.

Some forms of projections are:

Judgment is an activity of the mind; a belief that something is right or wrong, good or bad. It has the energy of "power over" and a desire to control, whether it's a person, place, or thing.

"The way that man spoke to his child was appalling.

Justifying is the inner self-talk you use to give consent to the mind or the negative ego in order to continue with a certain belief or behavior that you know at a deeper level is not supporting you or giving you the results you want. Justifying inhibits growth or a greater truth that you know at a deeper level awaits you:

"There was no point in sharing that information with my colleague because they would have used it to manipulate the situation."

Defending your behavior is an attempt to create protection from any hurt – keeping you safe. The real effect of defensive behavior is preventing the truth from being revealed and leaving you in illusion where the key trigger/s remains intact:

"Of course I haven't completed that job. Haven't you noticed what's been happening and how busy I've been?"

Denial is the behavior of pretending something doesn't exist or is not happening. It could be denial of feelings, thoughts, or behaviors. It is a means to keep the truth from yourself so that you can remain in illusion. Denial or suppression of your own painful feelings will still be driving you through the subconscious:

"I was not angry, I simply stated the facts as I saw them."

Criticism is another form of judgment: a kind of prejudice or disapproval. It is making an analysis about something with either a superior or inferior declaration:

"That presentation was really pathetic. She didn't provide enough detail and she seemed all over the pace. A five-year-old could do better."

Attacking is a behavior you exhibit when you feel seriously threatened. It can be exhibited by sharp criticism or lashing out to those who dare to reflect a truth that you deny. It is not possible to be open to truth when you are in attack mode. Attacking has venom behind it:

"You are an absolute idiot. I hate you and I want nothing to do with you or your family ever again. If I see you around here again I'm going to punch your lights out."

These examples are typical of a situation where projection perpetuates the disharmony. It prevents you from being able to access truthful memories, intentions, and experiences, keeping you from a higher truth. It keeps your shadow self locked away in the unconscious, unaware of its existence.

Understand that any and all projections will ensure you keep the pain and possible pattern and remain unconscious. It requires a lot of energy to keep the truth suppressed and it also means you inhibit the real depth or potential of the good feelings that are part of your natural state.

Whatever is causing you a degree of anxiety is your *reaction*, and resolution or healing requires that you accept responsibility for your feelings and *you* make changes, not the other person.

Key Points

- You can't see in another what is not within you.
- You can't change another, you can only change yourself.
- Remember that your perception is your perception; it doesn't mean it is the truth.
- Your thinking is filtered through the subconscious mind and all your programming.
- When you are triggered, your feeling body has awakened to some painful belief, unresolved event or issue. It is having a *re*-action.
- When you project onto another, you send energy streamers over to that person.
- Everyone has a shadow side that must be integrated before enlightenment.
- Holding on to resentment is a constant drain on your energy system.
- There is an energy match: the spiritual Law of Attraction is at play here.
- All people are conditioned, just like you.
- Blame ensures you get to keep the problem.
- Your opportunities for greater consciousness come through people pushing your buttons. They are like angels in disguise.

The process below involves some questions of self-inquiry and an open attitude towards a greater truth. It can totally liberate you, expand your awareness and facilitate more love and harmony in your life. Be kindly and compassionate to yourself as your begin to own your projections, just as you would a child learning something new. The awareness may not always happen in the first instance, but the intent to know a greater truth will set the energy into play along with your potential for greater consciousness.

1. *"I am feeling triggered!"*
You are aware that you are having an emotional reaction. You may even recall other times when you have felt the same way.

2. *"Okay, I recognize I'm defending my thoughts or behavior about…" (e.g. not being available)*
This attitude shows acceptance and responsibility for your own feelings, which are the first step towards any kind of transformation to heal past hurts, change negative beliefs and undesirable patterns of behaviors.

3. *"There is something in my energy field that is attracting this – what is it? Or "What is this person or situation is trying to show me?"*

This reflects that you are willing to look at things from another perspective and is a gift in waiting. It is an opportunity to integrate a shadow or disowned aspect of yourself and heal old wounds.

4. *"Thank you for providing this healing opportunity."*
When you are triggered, you are in the "feeling" and all healing happens in the present moment. Feeling gratitude immediately elevates your feeling state and connects you with your heart.

5. *"Show me truth!"*
A willingness to know a greater truth leaves you open to change your perspective and embrace the learning.

6. *"Okay, I choose to accept full responsibility for what I am feeling. What behavior change do I need to make to stop attracting this energy?"*

The key here is to change your own behavior and not expect another to change theirs. When you do that, you vibrate differently and therefore attract a different energy. This is how you integrate the learning and grow.

These steps help raise consciousness and keep the energy flowing. Depending on the situation you may need to do some forgiveness work. See Strategy 53 Forgiveness Process. You will know you have been successful when either the person seems to behave differently or your buttons are no longer being pushed.

Feeling Projection.
Just as you have projected onto other people, others will also have projected onto you. It's what we keep doing until we understand the effect of our thoughts and behaviors and begin to manage them. Often we attribute these uncomfortable feelings to any number of others things like feeling agitated, disgruntled, or angry without a known trigger. When a person projects a lot and those affected by this negativity begin to clean up their energy field and return any projections back to the sender, it can feel like psychic attack to the initial sender – they can feel like the victim when it is just their own negativity returning to its source. You will appreciate the benefits in learning to manage projection and in clearing your own energy field as well. See Strategy 16 Clearing for more information.

Seeking Support.

When lost in projection, it is common to seek support from others around you to validate and justify your feelings. This is a way the ego/personality reinforces its denial of truth. *Observe yourself* for any time you share your story about something with view to seeking support.

When we are able to successfully process our past hurts and pain, these triggers no longer remain active in our energy field so we are less likely to attract that kind of negativity. The effect is that the shadow aspect of self is owned and integrated and so there is no reaction, just observation or awareness. Our vibration is higher and so we are now attracting more loving exchanges.

Real self.

Projection is a common behavior until we understand and accept responsibility for all our feelings and the direction of our life. It is very common where there is a lack of self-esteem, and so working on self-love is an integral part to eliminate projection. It is important to realize that any negative projection is not coming from the "real" you. Our natural state is deeply loving and compassionate. It is part of our core essence and what all human beings deeply desire beneath the periphery of anything outside of self. The negativity is coming from the subconscious programming that we all experience and must undo to awaken to real self.

We can see this evidenced by the loving projections we make about others. Reflect how you notice kindness demonstrated by another, generosity, or how compassionate a particular person is, or how charming, honest, or patient another might be. All of these positive attributes or qualities are part of your core essence or you wouldn't be able to recognize them as such.

See also

- Awareness: Building the Observer
- Beliefs Challenge
- Clearing
- Do No Harm
- Gag Gossip
- Honor and Respect Differences
- Judgment Effect

- Release Resistance
- Release the Need to be Right
- Seek to Understand
- Shadow Play
- Truth Lover

Strategy 79
PROTECTION

CATEGORIES APPLIED

Addressing Addictions
Addressing Anxiety
Addressing Depression
Awareness and Mindfulness
Career and Goals
Communications and Relationships
Environmental Health
Everyday Essentials
Improving Self-Esteem
Quick Stress Busters

We all live in a sea of different energies, which are constantly affecting our thoughts, feelings, and behaviors. To be as clear as possible and optimize our wellness, it is essential to regularly cleanse your energy field of the different forms of negativity that permeate our world. See Strategy 16 Clearing for details.

In addition, we need to build and strengthen our energy field. The more we do this the stronger, happier, and healthier we will be and the more light becomes part of our energy matrix.

Light is the vibration of loving energies. Where light abounds, darkness is not. Working with the light certainly enhances your energy matrix and does provide a level of protection. It is nevertheless compromised if you have fearful thoughts or engage in some kind of negative behavior or you are in an environment where there is a lot of negativity. If this occurs, first do some cleansing and then the following protective strategy.

Light Ball

1. First, anchor yourself to the Earth by imagining roots of light coming out of the soles of your feet just like tree roots. Imagine them penetrating deep into the Earth creating a light-anchor. (As we are living on the Earth we need to exercise our connection to be fully here to manifest our goals and heal our bodies of any imbalance.)

2. Then envisage before you a brilliant ball of pristine white light larger than you. Imagine that you are stepping into that ball of loving light and feel, sense, or visualize that your field of energy is expanding out from your heart.

3. Affirm that you are grounded, safe, and protected.

It is the combination of intention and *attention on your intention* that strengthens the effectiveness of this protective energetic shield. Practice putting yourself in the light often: As you wake each morning, when in the shower, before you eat, as you get in your car or the bus, as you enter a building, as you walk, when you meet another, as you reenter your home, when you go to bed.

The more you do it the more you build your protective energy. Try it every time you change from one activity to another.

Mirror Ball

An optional variation is to proceed with steps 1– 3 above then envisage the ball of light to have a mirror facing the outside, so that anything that is projected to you within your sphere is reflected back to the source.

Sleep

It is common to pick up lower vibrational energies during the sleep state if we venture out into the astral realms. Often we can wake tired, depleted or out of sorts. To avoid this occurrence, it is a good idea to instruct your subconscious not to go into the astral realms but stay within to rejuvenate, restore and heal your body. It affords a level of protection as well.

Other practices that strengthen your light body are meditation, prayer, gratitude, loving thoughts, and affirmations. Chanting the ancient mantras is also beneficial. It is the vibratory effects of the sound rather than the meaning of the word that produces the power. If using prayer, make sure you connect with the highest possible vibration of love and light within your belief system such as God, Source energy, or sovereign self.

When you can recognize that you are a sovereign being – incredibly powerful, creative, and loving at your central core, you are giving yourself strong protection in the same way as you develop self love you attract higher vibrational people and experiences into your life.

There are various external things that may also be supportive such as crystals, gemstones, essences, or symbols.

See also:

- Awareness: Building the Observer

- Boundaries
- Clearing
- Connect with Nature
- Environmental Health: Electromagnetic Fields
- Mantras

Strategy 80
QUICK BREATH AFFIRMATION

CATEGORIES APPLIED

Addressing Addictions
Addressing Anxiety
Addressing Depression
Awareness and Mindfulness
Career and Goals
Communications and Relationships
Improving Self-Esteem
Quick Stress Busters

This Quick Breath Affirmation is helpful if you are feeling emotionally triggered and it is not opportune to go into processing – perhaps because you are in a social situation, tending to children, or in the midst of some work task.

Take a moment to connect to the Earth by imagining you have roots of light coming out through the soles of your feet. This is important to ground you (fear can have the opposite effect), then while breathing deeply, chant to yourself "I choose truth and I choose love." Or you may prefer "I choose to know the truth and be peaceful." Keep repeating it over and over until you feel the energy shifting.

Incorporating the words 'I choose' in these affirmations alerts your mind to the fact that you do have choice in this moment and you are able to redirect your mind to elevate your feeling state.

The simple act of connecting to the Earth not only grounds you but can help to ease the fear, recognizing the constant support of your human existence as well as her natural healing energies that are always available. The deeper breathing keeps the energy moving (fear causes energy to become stuck in your energy body) and the words express the intention that you are willing to explore a deeper truth. The combination of grounding, breath, and language will help you dissipate the charge, without going into resistance, which will leave you open to learning more.

Remember, the ultimate truth will always lead to love!

Depending on the intensity of the emotional trigger, you may find that just redirecting your mind is enough to give relief. Affirm "I choose to feel peaceful," "I choose truth and calm," or whatever else feels appropriate, or "I choose love." When you direct your focus to these positive choosing statements, it elevates your frequency and increases your feel-good hormones.

Remember, energy follows thought and you attract what you focus on – so focusing the mind in this way facilitates a more peaceful feeling state.

See also:

- Affirmations
- Deep Release Breathing
- Conscious Breathing
- Gratitude
- Thought Power and Control

Strategy 81
RELATIONSHIPS: BUILDING INTIMACY

CATEGORIES APPLIED

Awareness and Mindfulness
Communications and Relationships
Improving Self-Esteem

Intimacy in this context is a close personal loving relationship with a partner; it is so much more than just physical closeness. It is being present, honest, vulnerable, and emotionally close. It can be reflected without touch and without words, though these can most certainly be incorporated as a significant part of intimate expression.

There are a multitude of different fantasies about intimate relationships. Many of them based on the some kind of romantic myth that somehow becomes part of our social conditioning and can end up creating immense pain and resentment. Before we can have a truly intimate relationship it is important to be able to identify and let go of conditioned beliefs. Beliefs like "romantic love always lasts" or "once in love always in love," or "there is a knight in shining armour just for me."

Very often the desire for an intimate, deep, loving relationship comes from a desire to be loved and needed. This kind of longing for love and attention from another can create a destructive and unhappy cycle.

Needing to be needed arises from a lack of self-love – a feeling that I am only worthy if someone needs me. It can lead to attempts to please the other along with some kind of expectation that the other will behave reciprocally. If this does not happen (and it often doesn't), it leads to resentment and emotional pain. The unsatisfied desire then leads to a further longing to be loved and needed, and so the cycle continues. The person who needs to be needed to feel good about themselves will often attract people who will just take advantage of them without any real appreciation. Without awareness of this pattern, it will continue.

Intimacy in relationship (and it doesn't necessarily mean sexual) is someone who is present with you – someone whose heart is open to your heart, who can be with you in a way that allows his or her vulnerability to show through. This is so much more than just a sexual relationship, and yet many will look for intimacy through the physicality of many sexual relationships. They go from one to another in search of a deep, loving relationship that remains unsatisfied. Intimacy involves the whole of you: your physical, emotional, mental, and spiritual self.

An intimate relationship recognizes that you must be in contact with your own feelings. It is a closeness that is expressed through your body and through your eyes, sometimes with and sometimes without words or touching.

Understand that you can't possibly express intimacy if you are disconnected from your own feeling body. This can happen when the thinking mind is allowed to rule rather than trusting your heart or feelings to guide you in the moment; thinking about ways to connect with your partner, rather than just being present and trusting your feelings to lead you.

Being aware of your own feelings is the very essence of intimacy – feeling open and vulnerable.

It takes time to build intimacy in a relationship and it requires awareness of your own motives, a willingness to keep building your own self-worth outside of any relationship, courage, honesty, and trust.

Tips for Building Intimacy

1. Get clear on your motivation for intimacy and recognize if it is coming from a needy space; if so, find ways to build your own inner resources, which will increase your self-love and allow more love to come to you. Keep checking within to build your own body awareness and skills at being present. *"What am I feeling and where in my body am I feeling that?"*

2. Use "I statements" and express your feelings in your interactions. This facilitates clear communications and assists your own awareness.

3. Be willing to work through any conflicts. This will ensure that you accept full responsibility for your own feelings, at the same time expressing your felt experience as accurately and succinctly as possible. Remain open to new perspectives.

4. Express your love and gratitude every day to your partner: for their qualities, words, or behaviors that nurture you. Don't assume they know how you feel. Communicating in this way helps to build trust with your partner as well as giving a gift that invites the feelings of the enjoyment of being acknowledged, valued, and loved by another.

5. Practice being totally "present" with your loved one. That means allowing your whole self to be there, allowing whatever you feel to arise, at the same time really listening attentively.

6. Be open and honest about what gives you the most pleasure in your sexual encounters. This allows your partner to respond to your deepest desires. The more you can relax into the experience the more you can feel.

7. Lie closely with your partner just a few inches apart but not touching. Have eye contact and tune into your own body, at the same time maintain awareness of your partner's body. As you become aware of your own feelings and sensations, begin to describe them to your partner – how you feel and specifically where any sensations are located. Invite your partner to do the same. Keep the exchange of sharing in this intimate way about what feelings you are experiencing without any attempt to analyze them.

   Analyzing will engage the mental body and detract from maintaining presence with your feeling body – just stay with the expression of feelings and their location. Be specific and honest. Your sensations will keep changing and become more dynamic with more aliveness and sexual arousal.

See also:

- Allow Feelings
- Awareness: I Statements
- Awareness of Awareness
- Communication: Keys
- Communication: When you….
- Honor and Respect Differences
- Relationship: Key Question
- Trust, Truth and Honesty

Strategy 82
RELATIONSHIPS: KEY QUESTION

CATEGORIES APPLIED

Addressing Addictions
Addressing Anxiety
Addressing Depression
Awareness and Mindfulness
Career and Goals
Communications and Relationships
Improving Self-Esteem

Relationships come in all shapes, sizes, and ages. It is through relationships that we can learn a great deal about ourselves. Most people recognize that relationships do require some effort to keep them strong and positive; without that, misunderstandings, conflict, and disharmony can reign.

You can ask this simple rating question: its main purpose is so that you really hear and understand the other person while seeking ways to enhance your relationship.

> "On a scale of 1 to 10, how would you rate the quality of our relationship during the last week?"

Of course, the same can be asked as an overall question:

> "On a scale of 1 to 10, how would you rate the quality of our relationship?"

The question, and the response you get, can reveal wonderful insights into how to improve the harmony between you, how to build trust and deepen understanding. It is important to always ask with sincerity.

This same question can be applied to numerous other topics, both personal and business, to give valuable insights also.

"On a scale of 1 to 10, how would you rate……?

- My parenting
- My listening ability
- My communication style
- My management style

- This food
- This meeting
- These facilities
- My service
- Our date/vacation
- My teaching style
- This product/s
- My performance
- Our website
- This book/recording/movie?

This level of sharing is useful for understanding the other person better and gives you the opportunity to choose to respond to the information or not. It is not a requirement for change – just a potential learning experience.

For any answer that scores less than 10, ask, "What would it take to make it a 10?"

The response will provide further clarity that could inspire ideas for solutions, negotiations, and more harmonious relationships. In addition, it will allow for greater personal awareness. (This rating question was inspired by author Jack Canfield)

See also:

- Communication: Conflict Resolution
- Communication: Family Agreements
- Communication Keys
- Communication: When You…
- Projection
- Relationships: Building Intimacy

Strategy 83
RELEASE RESISTANCE

CATEGORIES APPLIED

Addressing Addictions
Addressing Anxiety
Addressing Depression
Awareness and Mindfulness
Career and Goals
Communications and Relationships
Exercise for Living
Improving Self-Esteem
Nutrition for Life

Resistance, avoidance, denial, suppression, repression, are all behaviors associated with the egoic or personality mind. They reflect that aspect of mind that has experienced hurts and wounding and doesn't want you to experience them again. It is always attempting to keep you safe, but it doesn't realize that it also blocks your ability to heal and grow and holds you in a pattern of fear and resistance.

We experience resistance when fear or anxiety arises. Without awareness, rather than be present with the emotion and allow it to move through, we attempt to suppress it. It's an old survival pattern that the child learns to do when she lacks guidance to process these difficult feelings. The problem is that all that is suppressed still drives us through the subconscious mind and leads to greater levels of unconscious behaviors.

When we are in resistance, we are disconnected from our own internal higher guidance system, and are blocking the natural flows of energy. The stronger the resistance, the more disharmony, suffering, and struggle you will experience. Without addressing the source of the discomfort, the intensity will build, requiring more effort to resist; the results are even greater disharmony and more unconscious outcomes. This is typical of addictive behaviors.

Resistance is like boosting the importance of the egoic mind as though it has a superior intelligence that knows how to guide you. When you do this you find that everything in your world becomes a struggle. It is giving power to the part of the mind that has all the unresolved pain and wounding, somehow expecting that it knows how to move forward to greater wellbeing. This is an impossible task when we consider that all our behaviors and thinking must run through the filters of the subconscious mind where all the old wounding exists; this is the reason patterns develop unconsciously.

What you resist will persist.

Surrender and allowing, on the other hand, lead to acceptance. These are the qualities that counter resistance and eliminate struggle. These higher vibrational states are associated with the intelligence of your heart and connect you to universal consciousness and the immense wisdom and power of it.

In a surrendered state you connect to your true nature, to source energy, and can tap into who you really are.

Resistance can manifest in all kinds of different ways but ultimately it is about resisting feeling: resisting those painful emotions that are tucked away in the subconscious mind; resisting a truth that may feel too uncomfortable; resisting a behavior that would bring too much challenge to your feeling state.

Some Forms Of Resistance

- Being busy being busy with any kind of behavior reflects the avoidance of just *being* when feelings can arise.
- Holding tension in your body requires effort, though often it creeps up without awareness as we avoid feeling.
- Doing any addictive behavior – smoking, drugs, food, IT work, social media, TV, sex, exercise, etc.
- Projecting judgment onto others is most often our own behavior that we disown.
- Worrying about anything is using the mind in a negative way, and demonstrates a lack of faith or understanding of the bigger picture.
- Constant thinking keeps you in the mind, darting from one thing to another; it can totally inhibit feeling.
- Self-judgment or criticism is a denial of real self.
- Being attached to a particular point of view, a person or thing; you cannot be open to a greater truth when fixated.
- Attempting to control… a situation or person.
- Repeating an old story is a behavior that reinforces a victim mentality and inhibits growth
- Being single-minded and pushing against…
- Ultimately resisting acknowledgment of your true self – the real you.

One fresh thought,
one act of surrender,
one change of heart,
one leap of faith,
can change your life forever.
– Robert Holden

Process To Release Resistance

Being aware of your resistance behaviors is the first step to resolving these destructive patterns and having the intention to let go and move on. Take time to reflect and identify where you are in resistance. This is a way of accepting responsibility and directing your focus.

Use your breath to breathe into the resistance and where you feel it in your body.

Then commit to the inner journey to build self-love. This is such an essential ingredient to all kinds of healing. It means learning how to say "no" and creating strong boundaries, nurturing yourself with compassionate and loving behaviors and self-talk, learning to manage the monkey mind and observing its tendencies and patterns.

Scan the strategies in this program for further inspiration and tools to move you forward.

See also:

- Allow Feelings
- Awareness of Awareness
- Awareness: Building the Observer
- Beliefs Challenge
- Being: Mindfulness
- Deep Release Breathing
- Going with the Flow
- Gratitude
- Key Tension Areas
- Projection
- Thought: Managing the Inner Critic
- Thought Power and Control
- Trust, Truth and Honesty
- Truth Lover

Strategy 84
RELEASE THE NEED TO BE RIGHT

CATEGORIES APPLIED

Addressing Addictions
Addressing Anxiety
Addressing Depression
Awareness and Mindfulness
Career and Goals
Communications and Relationships
Improving Self-Esteem

In the world of spirituality there is no right or wrong, just actions and consequences. Needing to prove yourself "right" implies the opposite, that something or someone is wrong and judgment is thus created which creates disharmony, much of which can be avoided.

Behind the need to be right is often low self-esteem. It is typically accompanied by some arrogance, sometimes stubbornness and a "power over" kind of attitude. It reveals an attachment to a belief. It is so often people who push our buttons that help us see our beliefs and our attachments to them.

Needing to be "right" also reflects a need to control, or a deep desire for recognition. It takes courage and a degree of humility to look at this aspect of self and the emotion or agenda underneath it. This requires a genuine willingness to be open to a higher truth and may lead you to an awareness of some shadow aspect of self previously denied. There is always a gift in awareness because it provides choice and the opportunity for change.

The important thing to understand is that when you have a strong desire to be "right," when whatever you do or say evokes a certain kind of response because of this judgmental attitude, you set up the energy for conflict and disharmony. So to facilitate a more harmonious outcome, you must be willing to own your own feelings and beliefs and respect others' beliefs and feelings even though they differ from yours. Remember, beliefs are just repeated thought-forms that may contain no elements of truth. You can agree to disagree and still retain harmony.

Even in your rightness about a subject,
when you try to push your
rightness toward another who disagrees,
no matter how right you are,
it causes more pushing against. In other
words, it isn't until you stop pushing

that any real allowing of what you want can take place.
– Abraham Workshop 2003/05/17 Boston M.A.

Letting go of the need to be right can be particularly challenging for people in leadership positions who have little awareness or ownership about their own feelings, preferring a more dictatorial approach. However, you can certainly lead and give direction without making someone else wrong, and often avoid conflict by so doing.

Being open to the beliefs, ideas, and creativity of others shows great respect and may provide a new perspective that can lead to better outcomes for you and others who may be involved. It's helpful to understand and accept that all people are programmed according to their upbringing and they – just like you – are on the human awareness journey, consciously or otherwise. Respect others' choices and beliefs and be willing to just let it go and enjoy a more harmonious outcome as a result. It will ultimately work in your favor by avoiding the conflicting energy.

See also:

- Beliefs Challenge
- Competition versus Cooperation
- Go with the Flow
- Honor and Respect Difference
- Seek to Understand
- Should versus Could

Strategy 85
REVERSE COUNT BREATH

CATEGORIES APPLIED

Addressing Addictions
Addressing Anxiety
Addressing Depression
Awareness and Mindfulness
Career and Goals
Communications and Relationships
Improving Self-Esteem
Quick Stress Busters

Breathing continues every hour of the day, with or without your awareness. It is both voluntary and involuntary. Becoming more aware of this vital breathing process is essential to maximize the many benefits on both a physical and emotional level.

Bringing attention to the breath brings you into present time (where all healing takes place), raises consciousness, reduces your stress levels, increases the flow of oxygen to your body and mind, and helps to release tension from your body.

An anxious mind cannot exist in a relaxed body.

A relative short but effective process to improve your wellbeing is by counting the breaths backwards; it tends to create a stronger focus than counting forwards.

Sit upright on a chair so that your lungs can expand and contract with ease or lie down flat on your back. Start from fifty and with every exhalation count backwards. Continue counting without losing awareness. If you lose track, simply start again from fifty. The whole time ensure a kindly attitude towards yourself. When you reach zero, end the practice and sit in the stillness. Repeat this often to maximize benefits.

See also:

- Awareness of Awareness
- Awareness: Building the Observer
- Body Breath Awareness
- Conscious Breathing
- Deep Release Breathing
- Quick Breath Affirmation

Strategy 86
REVIEW AND REMAKE YOUR DAY

CATEGORIES APPLIED

Addressing Addictions
Addressing Anxiety
Addressing Depression
Awareness and Mindfulness
Career and Goals
Communications and Relationships
Improving Self-Esteem

All our thoughts, beliefs, and experiences add to the mix of who we are and whether what we experience enhances or detracts from our life. All of it also affects those whose lives we touch.

We are all in Earth school and through our life experience we start to understand how our thoughts and actions evoke a certain response. We begin to see that if we are positive and loving that we will attract positive and loving thoughts, experiences, and people into our lives. The more aware we become, the more we can see that we are at all times being affected by the Universal Law of Attraction.

"Anyone who has never made a mistake has never tried anything new."
– Albert Einstein

Self-compassion is important to avoid the harshness of judgment for our learning experiences. By using the mind in a creative way, we can begin to change some of the unhelpful patterns we may have developed unconsciously. This process need only take a few minutes.

At the end of each day before you go to sleep, review your day. Notice anything that did not leave you or another (that you are aware of) with a positive impact. Then, just like in a movie, do a cut, remake and replay those situations in your mind with the preferred outcome. The mind does not know what is real and what it not real; it just responds to your thinking and feeling state.

Doing this nightly review is a way to reprogram the mind. It is an opportunity to get creative without distraction or feeling under pressure, as may be the case in the moment during your day. It allows you to re-create your preferred outcome using the power of your mind. Doing so just before sleep is when your mind moves into the "alpha" level of consciousness where all the subconscious programming is stored, so maximizing the positive impact.

There are many benefits of this simple and effective process:

- Promotes awareness
- Helps you to feel better by bringing in more positive energy rather then brooding over a past event.
- Facilitates change and prepares you for the next time, by planting a new seed from any undesirable pattern.
- Leaves the last thought/action associated with the particular incident in a positive "manifesting" energetic state.

See also:

- Awareness: Building the Observer
- Do No Harm
- Intention/Counter-Intention

Strategy 87
SEEK TO UNDERSTAND

CATEGORIES APPLIED

Addressing Addictions
Addressing Anxiety
Addressing Depression
Awareness and Mindfulness
Career and Goals
Communications and Relationships
Environmental Health
Improving Self-Esteem
Nutrition for Life

The definition of "understanding" includes the power to comprehend and a friendly or harmonious relationship. We can have understandings about our problems, about a subject, a process, or a situation. Understanding can also refer to agreements made: "If I cook, he does the dishes."

In a world with so many differences and opposing beliefs, there is often conflict with its negative consequences. We are social creatures, and relationships and getting on with others are essential parts of our survival. It is also through relationships that we learn about ourselves, including our beliefs and any unfinished business we might have.

It is our individual responsibility to maintain existing relationships and establish new ones. If we seek to understand those connections better, everyone is enriched by the experience.

The simple act of pausing and reflecting momentarily to seek understanding can facilitate harmony, eliminate the harshness of judgment, and have a huge impact – not only on you, but on others and on your environment.

Understanding also facilitates change. We, or others, are more likely to make adjustments if we have a better understanding. Understanding facilitates a greater awareness of cause and effect, which is the driving force in our world. Travel and living in different cultures can open us up to many different beliefs, attitudes, and behaviors as we notice what is normal for others.

- **Seek to understand yourself:** *What is my body trying to tell me with this pain? I wonder what was in that food that made me feel nauseas? Why am I procrastinating when I really want to do that course? Why am I so judgmental of them?*

- **Seek to understand another person:** Separate their behavior from their true spiritual self. Be aware that just like you, the other person's behaviour is sensible to them at the time. – *I wonder what is going on for them that they are so critical? I wonder why she took offence at my suggestion?*

  When it seems like an appropriate opportunity, you may like to ask "Help me to understand from your perspective." It enhances your communication by sincerely listening and showing respect by your desire to comprehend the situation better.

  It's not about being nosy or prying into another's business but rather about opening yourself up to a different perspective and learning more about your own beliefs and behaviors.

- **Seek to understand the environment:** *I wonder what will be the outcome of continued earth fracking? I wonder about all the steps that have happened to get this food to my plate? What will happen with genetically modified food and who is really behind it?*

"Everything that irritates us about others can lead us to an understanding of ourselves."
– Carl Jung

We can comprehend the value of this when we consider that all people experience conditioning and think, talk, and act from their conditioned existence. Often we project judgment onto another what is part of our own "denied" behavior. So seeking understanding is a way to build consciousness and greater harmony, not only for self and others but for our communities and the environment in which we live.

Why seek to understand?

- Ever felt misjudged by another and reflected that they don't understand?
- Ever judged someone for their behavior without knowing any background?
- Ever had conflict with another where it's someone you know or barely know without making any attempt to understand their perspective?
- Ever made consumer decisions without reflecting on the environmental impact of your purchase?
- Ever felt unwell after eating?
- Ever noticed how much better you feel after having skin-to-Earth contact?

What are the benefits of seeking to understand?

- It expands our knowledge base.
- It improves self-awareness, enabling us to be more conscious and responsible for our thoughts and actions.
- It helps us to be more respectful of differences and less judgmental.
- It minimizes conflict and enhances harmony.
- It assists us to make change.
- It builds relationships and connections.
- It helps to open our hearts, to be more considerate and to build compassion.
- It builds self-esteem: when we understand and accept others we also become more "free" to be our true self rather than playing roles.
- It leaves us open to a greater truth.

It becomes obvious then, in the bigger picture that the more we direct our energies to seek to understand, the more harmony we create in our own life and the greater world.

See also:

- Awareness: Building the Observer
- Being: Mindfulness
- Challenge Your Beliefs
- Honor and Respect Differences
- Projection
- Judgment Effect

Strategy 88
SHADOW PLAY

CATEGORIES APPLIED

Addressing Addictions
Addressing Anxiety
Addressing Depression
Awareness and Mindfulness
Improving Self-Esteem
Quick Stress Busters

This is a process that helps connect with your shadow side. It is also a powerful way to release the intense energy of stored anger. Everyone has shadow aspects. Denial of them will most assuredly inhibit your potential because it takes effort to keep these shadow parts suppressed. Such avoidance will build anxiety and often results in unconscious outbursts of unwanted behavior. By contrast, owning and accepting that they are part of you stops the denial and gives you choice in the moment. You may even find that what you initially perceive as a negative aspect of yourself may be useful for you at different times of your life. An example might be a fighter shadow aspect that may be useful one day to protect your family if they are threatened.

Privately acting out the behavior in the shadow play brings it into full consciousness and releases much of the uncomfortable energy, reducing anxiety and tension. It leaves you feeling freer and happier and in a position to make choices that serve your positively. The important thing is to recognize that all people have a shadow side and not to judge yourself when you connect with it.

Just remain in the observer position as you play out your shadow consciously. That is observing, noticing, and allowing but *not judging*. Judging creates non-acceptance and will hold some of the energy within.

Shadow play is a totally private process. It is about you and your feelings. You will appreciate some kind of isolation, and perhaps even darkness. It can be done at night while out walking alone, which allows for running, kicking, swearing, or whatever vigorous movement your body wants to release. Swimming can also be effective where you can thrash about without causing any harm to yourself or others. You can also do shadow play when you are alone or in the privacy of your bedroom with doors and windows shut. A few soft pillows may prove handy for any punching or thrashing that you feel inclined towards. This is a time for releasing the pent-up energy that the shadow creates.

The Process

1. Choose a safe and private environment where you will not disturb another or hurt yourself.

2. Surround yourself in a large blue bubble. This is to ensure that you do not energetically project out onto another. Then beyond that, place a large golden bubble of light. This provides protection for you and your energy field.

3. Invite your shadow self into full consciousness with the intention of giving it expression. A few deep breaths holding that intention will bring it to the surface, but be aware that any self-judgment will inhibit it. Keep your focus inward with an attitude of tolerance until you have connected with this shadow or angry aspect.

   Close your eyes and begin to breathe deeply, feeling more and more into the part of you that is feeling agitated and wants expression. Keep your focus inward until you have connected with this shadow or angry aspect.

   Then just let it flow. At the same time, remain the observer of your own behavior without any judgment. This part within, may want a lot of verbal expression, swearing, kicking, finger-pointing, thrashing legs and fists, sexual gestures, pacing, making faces, or other behaviors less common for you. Don't try to suppress any of it. Don't judge any of it. Just let yourself act it out, fully realizing that it's all a play and it's not about allowing these aspects of self to rule your life. You are simply providing the opportunity for expression in a controlled and conscious way.

4. Be aware of your inner critic or any other part of you that wants to criticize or moralize about what you are doing; let them have expression also while remaining clear about your intent. Just keep going until all that suppressed energy has been vented.

5. When finished, imagine a cone shaped galactic vacuum of light to clean up any negative energy surrounding you. This is a way to transmute any negative energy left around you and your environment. Then envisage the brightest, most pristine white light everywhere in the vicinity and totally embracing you, penetrating through all layers of your multi-dimensional self.

The release of stored anger or intense energy by acting it out is typically quite quick; it can bring a much greater sense of calm, and, depending on the circumstances, could also bring a feeling of empowerment. On conclusion, you might find this whole play quite amusing, or you may find yourself being quite moralistic. If so, do a little forgiveness prayer for yourself. Remember, in this private experience, the only person judging you is your own mind.

Do not hesitate to seek professional help if you have any concerns.

See also:

- Accept Yourself
- Allow Feelings
- Awareness: Building the Observer
- Clearing
- Conflict Resolution
- Feeling Fear
- Forgiveness Process
- Honor and Respect Differences
- Projection
- Thought Power and Control
- Thought: Managing the Inner Critic
- Toning

Strategy 89
SHOULD VERSUS COULD

CATEGORIES APPLIED

Addressing Addictions
Addressing Anxiety
Addressing Depression
Awareness and Mindfulness
Career and Goals
Communications and Relationships
Exercise for Living
Improving Self-Esteem
Nutrition for Life

The use of the word "should" reflects a contradiction between your thinking and your behavior, an incongruity that will result in a negative feeling. It also implies "duty" – some kind of moralizing. Allowing the mind to be the superior guiding force will always lead to pain because it disconnects you from your own inner guidance, which comes from your heart. Sometimes the beliefs around your thinking are those you have taken on from others; your heart is trying to tell you something else and so there will be an inner conflict.

"Should" is used very commonly in everyday language and does little more than erode one's sense of self-esteem by implying guilt. It also carries the negative energy of judgment. Be alert also to the self-talk of the inner critic, which is always striving to put you down. It is extremely important for your self-esteem to be both aware of the inner voice and manage it. Eliminating "should" from your vocabulary will contribute to your wellbeing.

Instead try these alternatives… Where you would normally say "should" replace it with "could":

I should visit my mother more	versus	I could visit my mother more
I should meditate daily	versus	I could meditate daily
I should clean the car more regularly	versus	I could clean the car more regularly
I should get out in the garden more	versus	I could get out in the garden more
I should spend less on eating out	versus	I could spend less on eating out

You will notice a much softer feeling to the alternatives. There is no self-criticism; rather, it invites conscious choice with a kind of curiosity to explore the situation further.

Another option is to bring even more awareness to the situation by including:

If I were to… (Then ponder the likely consequences).

Often we just judge ourselves by using words like "should" and feel the discomfort of the inner conflict without taking time to explore in greater depth, which may provide insight and a harmonious solution. Consider these same examples:

1. *If I were to visit my mother more,* I'm sure she would be appreciative and I know that would leave me feeling good. I can leave work a little earlier on Tuesdays.

2. *If I were to meditate daily* I've no doubt I will be less stressed and all I have to do is give up 20 minutes in bed in the morning. I would certainly feel better about myself too and be less of a grump around my family.

3. *If I were to clean the car more regularly* I know my wife would love it, but it's just not up there on my priorities. Perhaps I could suggest she might like to take responsibility for getting it cleaned at the car wash.

4. *If I were to get out in the garden more* I just know that would be good for me and would give me a chance to be outside in nature, which is a much healthier contrast to my normal workday. I guess it's time to reevaluate and maybe give up watching some sport on TV.

5. *If I were to spend less on eating out,* I would have to prepare more meals at home and that would take more time, but then we would certainly be eating more healthy meals and maybe we could all chip in and make cooking more of a family responsibility rather than just mine. That would also help develop the children's cooking skills.

If "should" is a common part of your language it shows you that you are not in full alignment with your heart energy. When you are in alignment, your feelings, values, and behaviors are congruent and you feel good. Be conscious of your speech and inner self talk and strive to eliminate "should" from your language. When you honor and respect yourself you build integrity and it helps others to know you better. You can still be kind, helpful, and compassionate without feelings of guilt, obligation, and duty.

See also

- Awareness: I Statements
- Awareness of Awareness
- Awareness: Building the Observer
- Being: Mindfulness
- Challenge Your Beliefs
- Help Another
- Seek to Understand
- Thought: Managing the Inner Critic
- Thought Power and Control
- Values

Strategy 90
SIMPLIFY YOUR LIFE

CATEGORIES APPLIED
Addressing Addictions
Addressing Anxiety
Addressing Depression
Awareness and Mindfulness
Career and Goals
Everyday Essentials
Improving Self-Esteem

Simplifying your life can be quite transformative and remove a lot of anxiety and perceived pressures. It can be easy to get on a treadmill, making lots of acquisitions and getting involved in many different things because of implicit expectations, or being ego-driven and so lose sight of what is really important to you.

Identify your values

Identifying what is really important to you in your life will bring clarity and allow you to discard what is not. First evaluate how you spend your time: work, leisure, family time, and all your commitments. It's easy for things to become habitual without ever thinking about the value of these activities. List the 5 most important things and ensure you have time for these things. Eliminate the activities that are not enhancing your life or wellbeing. The movement, sorting, and discarding will free up quite a lot of energy. Once done you will be much better organized, with a clearer sense of space.

Clear out your stuff

Go through your household items including clothing and discard what is not used, together with all those gifts that you have been given but you don't like. Go through your kitchen drawers and cupboards and discard all those things you have accumulated over time but don't use. Do the same in the outside shed. Simply removing clutter can help you feel so much better – whether it's big furniture items or a cluster of things. Op Shops, Men's Sheds, Community Groups could be happy recipients. Once done you will be much better organized.

Ground yourself regularly

Grounding requires no effort – just intention and visualizing your own energy going deep down into the Earth through the soles of your feet. Better still is flesh-to-Earth contact and it provides immense health benefits. So many of the behaviors that we do and purchases we make are because we believe it will make us feel good, and grounding, or earthing as it is also called, enhances our wellbeing without expenditure or accumulation of stuff. It also reminds us of our connectedness and our life support system.

Limit your exposure to TV

Watching television consumes time, and many of the shows can have a negative impact on your mental and emotional energy system. It can be a major impediment to family communications, and significantly distract you from other activities that enhance wellbeing. Instead get out some board games or cards, play with your family, go for a walk, call a friend, write in a journal, play some music, sit and watch nature, or read a good book.

Limit your exposure to the electronic media – phone, computer, and games

The media technology so prevalent in our society today has distinct advantages and disadvantages. Mobile phones have become almost like an appendage; computers can be all-consuming, keeping you tied to work and on alert 24 hours a day, 7 days a week. Review all your computer connections and lists that you are on including forums like Facebook, Skype, and Twitter. Really evaluate if these connections enhance your life. Press the delete button, get off lists, and cease circulating emails. Your body will also enjoy the health benefits from the reduced electromagnetic frequencies that mess with your own circuitry.

Minimize travel

If you find you spend a lot of your time traveling to either extended family or work, consider moving closer. This will not only save time and money, but could also extend and enhance family time and be better for the environment.

Limit your spending

Consumerism has created an unsustainable practice and caused suffering to the planet and stress to consumers. Habitual spending is often the cause of a lot of financial stress, particularly through the availability of credit cards, which can create an illusion of your real financial situation. Also, purchases create more stuff that you have to store, clean, learn how to use or maintain – all of which can add to your stress levels and unnecessarily complicate your life.

In the Western world we have about 3 times more space than we did fifty years ago and yet we collectively spend millions of dollars on storage. The result – too much stuff. Despite the popular belief that material possessions will make us happy, it is most commonly a short-term experience. Do yourself and the Earth a favor when contemplating any purchase. Pause, and consider:

- Do I really need this?

- Do I have something that will already perform this function?
- Where has this come from?
- What has been involved in the making of this?
- Who has been involved in the making of this?
- What effect will it have on the planet?
- Where will it go when I'm done with it?
- Will it contribute to my life?

Check out this website about the Story of Stuff: www.storyofstuff.com, which is suitable for the whole family. It shows the process of making, using, and throwing away stuff, with a twenty minute cartoon about trash. It is one of the most watched environmental-themed movies of all time.

Plan days off

Plan days off ahead of time to spend time with family, fulfill recreational desires, or whatever you need to bring balance into your life.

Downsize your home

If you no longer need such a large house, finding something that accommodates your current needs will result in less expense, and give you more time because of less cleaning and less stuff that surrounds you. Maybe you have a large garden that demands more of your time and energy than you want to give at this stage of your life. The process of moving house can be time-consuming but it also provides a wonderful opportunity to do some serious culling while considering what is really important to you.

Give up multi-tasking

Multi-tasking increases stress levels and stops you being in the present moment with each chore. Better to give your full attention to each task and do them one at a time.

See also

- Grounding
- Values
- Work Passion

Strategy 91
SLEEP TIPS

CATEGORIES APPLIED

Addressing Addictions
Addressing Anxiety
Addressing Depression
Awareness and Mindfulness
Career and Goals
Communications and Relationships
Environmental Health
Improving Self-Esteem

Restful sleep is fundamental to wellness. It is the time the body uses to recharge and repair itself and the mind processes the events of the day and gives you the energy you need to start your new day, enhancing performance and memory. Irrespective of how healthy your habits are, if you are not getting enough sleep your health will be compromised. The average person needs around seven to nine hours of sleep each night.

Effects Of Sleeplessness

Sleeplessness will upset your mental and emotional balance, adding to stress levels. Common effects are:

- Irritability
- Anxiety
- Depression
- Poor concentration
- Memory challenges
- Impaired motor coordination
- Reduced patience
- Mood swings
- Reduction in your coping skills
- Heightened pain sensitivity

Understandably, insomnia will lead to safety risks at home, in the workplace, or driving a motor vehicle. Sleep deprivation can lead to serious health problems, including anxiety, depression, a weakened immune system, increased risk for heart disease, heart attack, heart failure, irregular heart beat, high blood pressure, stroke, and diabetes.

Cause Of Sleeplessness

The cause of sleeplessness is often symptomatic of another problem, so identifying the cause is most helpful with a view to determining the optimal remedy or treatment. Exercise, diet, nutrition and eating patterns all have a large effect on the quality of your sleep. For example though it may not be obvious to you, addressing digestive problems could ultimately resolve any sleep disorders. Digestive problems can lead to anxiety, fatigue, depression, leaky gut, parasites, mal absorption of vitamins and minerals, and disrupt the serotonin and melatonin levels in the brain which help control your mood and sleep cycle.

There are indeed many factors that influence both the quality and quantity of your sleep. You may have difficulty getting off to sleep; you may wake through the night or wake feeling unrested. Sleep disturbance can be triggered by physiological, psychological, and environmental influences. There are times when planetary influences such as solar flares or full moon affect your energy and leave you feeling more agitated, anxious, or emotional. These influences are more challenging to address, but sometimes just understanding this and knowing it will pass allows more acceptance, which can be beneficial to how you perceive things.

Do what you can to treat the cause of any symptoms appropriately:

- Itchy or irritated skin
- Restless legs
- Disruptive bed partner
- Asthma, or breathing problems
- Allergies
- Coughing
- General recovery from illness
- Sleep apnea
- Reflux or digestive problems
- Physical pain
- Jet lag
- Hot flushes due to menopause
- Pregnancy discomfort
- Frequent urination
- Withdrawal from drugs or medication
- Mineral deficiency

- Depression
- Emotional pain or distress such as anxiety, grief, or worry.

Your Bedroom Environment

There are a lot of factors which influence your bedroom environment. The following are worthy of consideration.

- The best room temperature recommendation is 17–20 degrees. Remember, your body is always regulating itself according to its environment, so when it is at its optimal temperature the less hard it has to work.
- Stale air in your bedroom can leave you feeling foggy in the head and hinder your intake of fresh oxygen. Try a little fresh air with a slightly opened window.
- Make sure your bedroom is just used for sleeping and sex.
- Ensure that you can make your bedroom dark, or use a sleep mask.
- Be aware also of an accumulation of dust mites that live off human skin cells. Poor ventilation, high humidity, indoor air pollution such as cigarette smoke and high temperatures about 20 C or 70 F all create the ideal breeding ground for these creatures. They can be the cause of allergies and many uncomfortable nights.
- Is it time for a new bed? You spend about a third of your life in bed so it's a good investment to have a supportive base to enhance your sleep.
- Maybe your bedding needs to change, but first do your research. A lot of pillows, sheets, and doonas are made of or include synthetics, which can cause allergies and other health problems. Generally speaking, wool that is free of harmful chemicals is best because it allows you to breathe, regulates your body temperature, and is hypoallergenic. Make sure the weight of your covering appeals to your comfort. Some prefer a blanket to the lighter weight of a doona. Consider sleeping on earthing sheets (products available on the Web).
- Find the perfect pillow that supports your head and neck and is free of any harsh chemicals that could impair your health or your quality of sleep. A drop of lavender essential oil on your pillow may assist. If you like to sleep on your side a pillow between your knees can enhance your comfort.
- Make your bedroom feel welcoming. Ensure it is clean, tidy and uncluttered.
- Avoid red, burgundy, or dark somber-colored linen such as black and brown. All colors carry a frequency that influences how you feel. The red tones can be stimulating and energizing and the darker tones oppressive. White is the best followed by pastel colors

- Generally speaking loose, soft nightwear is ideal to enhance your personal comfort, though this may be contra-indicated for pregnant or lactating mothers who prefer breast support or aids for other physiological conditions. Sleeping naked may be your preference, though it is best to wear something like a T-shirt around your shoulders if you are prone to stiff necks, which may otherwise disturb your sleep
- Minimize noise – use ear plugs if necessary.
- Avoid any electrical equipment that emits invisible energy, particularly close to your head. Common things like clock radios, phones, chargers, computers, and televisions are not only an impairment to restful sleep but strong caution is recommended because of the potential for more serious health problems because of the electromagnetic fields.
- Check for any geopathic stress that could be interrupting restful sleep. Ley lines, watercourses, or other kinds of Earth energies can have a significant impact both on your health and sleep pattern. You may need to engage a professional geomancer.
- Clear the unseen energy in your room. We have all walked into places that don't feel welcoming even though we can't see anything. Open the windows wide before bedtime to get a free flow of fresh air through. See Strategy 16 Clearing for more information.

Behaviors To Facilitate Restful Sleep

1. Make sure you try grounding. As easy and effortless as it sounds, many of the above symptoms may reduce or disappear with regular earthing/grounding. Our modern lifestyles have disconnected us more and more from the profound healing and balancing energies of Mother Earth, with her constant flow of negatively charged free electrons. We, too, are electrical in nature and when we are barefoot and connect flesh to Earth our bodies immediately start to equalize to the Earth's electrical energy levels. Approximately 30 minutes each day flesh to Earth is a good start – also excellent to do as soon as possible after flying to remedy jet lag which can be very disruptive to sleep as your body tries to adjust to its new time zone. See Strategy 58 Grounding/Earthing for more information.

2. Avoid daytime napping.

3. Where possible, it is best to retire around the same time every night to assist your body clock to establish routine.

4. Clear your own energy field by imagining yourself bathed in pristine white light. See Strategy 16 Clearing for more information.

5. Avoid fluids that result in the need to get up to go to the toilet.

6. Avoid stimulants 4–6 hours before sleep: alcohol, caffeine, and nicotine.

7. Avoid any spicy, fatty, heavy or large-quantity meals before bed and allow your digestive system to rest and recharge.

8. Around 30–40 minutes of exercise is great to do several times a week. It can improve metabolism, decrease inflammation, and help move stuck energy, all of which can assist you to make you feel physically tired and enhance sleep quality. This is best done no later than two hours before bed.

9. Read your favorite spiritual book before your close your eyes (nothing stimulating).

10. Avoid any stimulating TV or computer viewing just before bed. The light from the screens stimulates the brain preventing deep sleep and the electromagnetic fields impact negatively.

11. Check if any medication you may be taking could impair restful sleep.

12. Beware of adopting behaviors to help you sleep that could ultimately disrupt your sleep pattern, such as drinking alcohol, taking sleeping tablets.

13. Sometimes it helps to have a small snack before sleep. Banana, cheese and crackers, a small piece of chicken or turkey, or a glass or warm milk all contain Tryptophan, which is an amino acid that causes sleepiness. If you have woken after being asleep any of these small snacks may help you get back to sleep.

14. Play peaceful, relaxing music before bed to get you into wind-down mode.

15. Release body tension by focusing and relaxing body parts. Start at the top of your body and work down, focusing on each body part and breathing light into it and exhaling any tension. The imagery of light purifies the energy body and is a great accompaniment to focusing and relaxing the physical body.

16. Review your day from the moment you woke, taking about 3 minutes to complete the whole process to where you are now. Avoid engaging in one particular thing, though you may be tempted. It is a way to help release the mind from the busyness of your day. Also see Strategy 86. Review and Remake Your Day.

17. Make a Gratitude List before you go off to sleep. Write down as many things as you can think of that you are grateful for: a warm bed, food to sustain you, the smell of a beautiful flower, a loving friend or family, etc. These positive last thoughts before sleep are more likely to seep into the subconscious and induce peaceful sleep. See Strategy 57 Gratitude for more information.

18. Avoid in-depth discussions that stimulate mental activity before bed.

19. Avoid checking the time during the night.

20. Don't take your problems to bed. Try to sort them out before your bedtime. Write down possible solutions before going to bed.

21. Manage your thought processes. Fearful or negative thoughts create anxiety and impair your ability to relax and sleep. By contrast, positive loving and relaxing thoughts all help the both body and mind to relax. Even if you are not sleeping, being content with not sleeping will help create the mood to facilitate sleep.

22. To help you quiet down a busy mind, patiently count backwards on every out-breath from 100. Reverse counting requires a stronger focus then forward counting. See also Reverse Count Breath Strategy 85.

23. Try to keep your eyes open until you are so sleepy that you must close them.

24. Repeat affirmations – (positive affirming thoughts) somewhat like a mantra:

    - I choose to feel relaxed and peaceful.
    - I love my bed and rest my body and mind.
    - I choose to release the thoughts of today and focus on resting my body now.
    - I breathe light into my body with every breath – cleansing, releasing, relaxing.

Oral Supplements

Melatonin is sometimes referred to as the sleep hormone. It is a natural hormone made by the pineal gland whose primary function is to regulate our body clock. As we age it becomes less efficient and can be the cause of increased insomnia in the older population. Your doctor can prescribe it.

Vitamin B 12 plays a role in melatonin production and has several other health benefits. It is readily available from supermarkets, chemists, and health food stores. Take during the day to reap the sleep benefits at night,

Ziziphus Jujube is a fruit used in traditional Chinese medicine for the treatment of insomnia and anxiety. Herbs such as Valerian, Hops, Lavender, and Skullcap are beneficial to assist relaxation. These are found in some herbal teas, called Sleepy Time Tea, Chamomile, and others, or check with your herbalist, health food store, or homeopath.

There are numerous other supplements that may address symptoms of sleeplessness. Magnesium is a mineral that has many benefits for all kinds of health imbalances, including easing restless legs, reducing anxiety, and relaxing muscle tension. Calcium and iron can also be important.

See also:

- Affirmations
- Being: Mindfulness
- Body: Breath Awareness
- Clearing
- Conscious Breathing
- Connect with Nature
- Deep Release Breathing
- Grounding/Earthing
- Review and Remake Your Day
- Simplify Your Life
- Thought Power and Control

Strategy 92
SOLITUDE

CATEGORIES APPLIED

Addressing Addiction
Addressing Anxiety
Awareness and Mindfulness
Career and Goals
Communications and Relationships
Improving Self-Esteem

Life can be so busy and full that sometimes solitude is what we need to regenerate ourselves or process some feelings. It's like having a retreat from the world. With all kinds of media that connect us with those outside of ourselves, it can seem impossible to be free of the various kinds of communication media. While these certainly have many benefits and facilitate connections with others, they can also be demanding and distracting from what we really need at a particular time. Emails, texts, phones, social media forums, blogs, and newsletters all place a demand on our attention, let alone newspapers, radio, television and work. The unfortunate truth is that it can develop into an addiction.

Solitude allows us the time and space to dig deep into self, tap into our creativity and find a deeper truth, peace, and beauty. It can improve our mood and memory and lower stress away from the stimulants and busyness of life to find a deeper truth, peace, and beauty. The aloneness or isolation from others can help us to observe our own thinking, question all those beliefs that we have inherited, find our own inner voice and inner strength. Quiet and minimal distractions allow us to be more in the moment and appreciative of the smallest things in life – to be in the flow without distractions.

Find some quiet space for yourself by severing your outside connections for a while. You might choose just an hour, or more of a retreat type of experience amounting to days or even weeks of isolation. Consider a day a week away from all forms of media including your phone.

Depending on your preferences, the options are many, from a quiet walk in a beautiful garden or beside the sea, to a more protracted time tucked away perhaps in a country area.

It is possible to just have spontaneous periods of solitude within your family home. If living with others, some prior clear communications and negotiation would be necessary to make this happen harmoniously. If family members feel threatened by this, alleviate their anxiety by stating clearly that it's just your need and not about them. You are more likely to be supported in your solitude if you take the time to gently and kindly explain your objectives to others.

Some helpful tips if sharing space with another:

a. Put a sign on your door saying "QUIET TIME."
b. Wear a cap or hat with the prior understanding that while you wear your hat you are having quiet time and are not around.
c. Hang a sign around your neck, rather like a billboard that has a sign on either side of your front and your back (QUIET TIME, INNER TIME, TIME OUT or SOLITUDE).

Use any creative process that works for you and enjoy the many benefits that can come from a period of solitude such as greater clarity and creativity, peace, rest, release, and recharge.

See also:

- Do Things You Enjoy
- Honor and Respect Differences
- Kindness to Self
- Major Life Influencers
- Simplify Your Life
- Truth Lover

Strategy 93
SWITCHING PROCESS

CATEGORIES APPLIED

Addressing Addictions
Addressing Anxiety
Addressing Depression
Awareness and Mindfulness
Career and Goals
Communications and Relationships
Improving Self-Esteem
Quick Stress Busters

An immense amount of stress and anxiety arises from an unmanaged mind and attempts to multi-task. Multi-tasking is often revered, but its true impact is seldom understood. Though we may often say "I've got a lot on my mind", the mind is actually not thinking of two things at once but rather switching from one to the other. Research revels that every time you switch between tasks from one thing to another it saps your mental energy, as well as costing you time as you refocus. The more complex the task, the greater is the time lost.

By contrast, being totally focused with the task at hand allows you to be more productive, present and in flow (that's a feel-good state). A busy mind darting from one thing to another creates stress, affects your physiology, and impairs your ability to be conscious. This applies not just to work tasks, but to any and every thing you do.

For example, let's say you've dropped the children at school and you arrive at work. Rather than continue thinking about an earlier discussion with a family member and all the things that need to happen and after-school activities, shopping and what needs to get finished at work today, just sit for a moment. *Reflect* on family and what you have just done. Then consciously choose to *Release* all the associated thoughts. A moment more, and now *Rest* your body and mind by focusing on a couple of deep breaths to recharge and bring you into presence. Feel or sense the Earth beneath you to tap into that vital source of energy and then switch into work mode and prepare for the next project.

Continued thinking about all the things that have happened in the past or will happen in the future is both distracting and stressful. Just bring your mind to the task at hand.

Find times in your day where you use this switching process. You could incorporate it through the changing tasks in your work day such as before and after meetings, phone calls, work tasks, refreshment breaks, and before you return home. The same could apply then – after leaving the supermarket, before dinner, tending to children's needs and, most importantly, switching off before sleep.

Switching Process – 3 R's
You have been focusing on your task at hand. Then when you are about to change to something else.

> **Reflect** on what you have just done. It is a way to satisfy the mind's desire to continue processing.
>
> **Release.** Now hold the intention that it's time to release from the previous activity. It is a way of giving the mind an instruction showing your intent rather than allowing it to dart from one thing to another.
>
> **Rest.** In these few moments your body/mind can make the transition from one task to the next and allow you to be mindful in your next task. Connect with the Earth and few deep breaths will give an instant recharge.

And so the pattern continues: you are focusing on your task and about to make a switch. Remember the 3 Rs: Reflect, Release, Rest. The switching process may take less than a minute but it will reward you with more energy, more time because of your relaxed state, and increased productivity. It does take practice but the rewards are well worth it.

When and where possible, though it may not always be convenient, if your day includes learning something new, have a little nap just afterwards. It is a way to help your body/mind integrate what you have just done. It can be like a small reward and can add pleasure to any task. Start yawning to facilitate the mood. Just open your mouth wide and jiggle it about a bit and before long you will be yawning and slowing down. After a brief nap, you will feel revived and be ready for the next task.

See also

- Awareness: Building the Observer
- Being: Mindfulness
- Feeling Challenged
- Feeling Scattered: Unbalanced
- Intention/Counter-Intention
- Thought Power and Control

Strategy 94
THOUGHT: MANAGING THE INNER CRITIC

CATEGORIES APPLIED

Addressing Addictions
Addressing Anxiety
Addressing Depression
Awareness and Mindfulness
Career and Goals
Communications and Relationships
Everyday Essentials
Improving Self-Esteem
Quick Stress Busters

The inner critic is a self-created inner voice that everyone has. It is a very judgmental kind of voice that is often disparaging, unkind, insensitive, super-critical, and even relentless in its personal attacks on us. It always seems intent to sabotage any goals or aspirations, irrespective of how strong our desire or yearning might be for change. It could even seem that we are providing a residence in our head for the voice of our parents, teachers, or significant others who may have played a role in our upbringing. Yet this inner voice is something that we have unconsciously created and adopted as our own.

It is as though the mentality of the inner critic is to criticize us more than anyone outside us so that it won't hurt as much when others criticize us! The result is a seriously detrimental impact on our self-esteem. A strong inner critic will always be present with people who suffer from addictive behaviors.

The inner critic is part of the negative ego that has been conditioned. It is associated with the mental body. It is an unmanaged part of the mind that simply has to be trained so that our conscious mind becomes the driver.

The self-talk generated by the inner critic creates negative feelings and emotions which directly influences our behavior. Every time we allow the inner critic to drive us, we empower it. To turn that around, we have to disempower it, and this can be done by the way we choose to respond to this critical voice within our mind.

Experiment with these four different strategies to find which one works best for you. Then keep practicing until you master it.

How To Disempower The Inner Critic

When you are aware of it,

1. Say to yourself, "Oh, thanks for popping in and showing me my thoughts!"

   This response acknowledges the inner critic in an accepting way, and so avoids any kind of resistance. Without the judgment of the appearance of your inner critic (which would otherwise bring negativity), you increase the harmony.

2. Sing "Happy Birthday" to it. Or even sing your favorite nursery rhyme. It's a way of belittling the inner critic and disempowering it.

3. Befriend it. Try to understand your inner critic like a friend or parent who is worried or fearful. Any kind of resistance is another way of activating that particular energy. The objective is to transform rather than resist or deny its existence. The common expression "What you resists persists" is a perfect example.

   We all know how worry can bring out our fears, often resulting in negative expressions that don't help the situation or our communications. Let us suppose the inner critic is really concerned about something and so is totally focused on the negative possibility of what may transpire. It's not that it wants the negative to happen, just that it is worried that it will occur… and so that becomes the projection in the voice of the inner critic.

   A strategy is to engage with it in a curious, kindly way, as you would a friend, and you will reduce its negative intensity. An example in response to your desire to commence a course could be:

   > **Inner critic:** Don't be ridiculous, who are you kidding – you're not up for study.
   >
   > **Self:** Okay, I hear you and wonder if you are feeling really worried about my ideas to start that new course. What is the real core of your concern, because I'm really keen to keep moving forward in my life?
   >
   > **Inner critic:** What if you're the only one who fails and get really hurt? Then how are you going to feel?

> **Self:** Well, I suppose that is a possibility, but I won't really know unless I try and every time I try, at least I will learn something and feel as though I am moving forward. I can't possibly reach my potential if I keep playing it safe, plus I really want to learn more about that subject.

Note that there is *no resistance* to hearing the Inner Critic. The responses from it tend to be softer and your understanding of its agenda greater. This puts *you* back in the power position.

Key to all healing is to love the unlovable.

4. In this process we talk ourself up the *emotional scale.* Just as the gauge on a thermometer measures the temperature from low to high, so too can we use an emotional scale from fear at the low end to love at the high end to make ourselves feel better. The inner critic always operates at the fear end of the scale and this is obviously what makes us feel pretty shabby. So the task is to talk up our emotions towards the love end of the scale. * This process of talking yourself up the emotional scale is one often recommended by Abraham/Hicks in their books, CD's and workshops.

Here is another conversation you might have:

> **Inner critic:** You idiot, don't you ever learn! How many times do you have to experience this humiliation before you get it? You may as well give up now and just keep doing your job. At least that would avoid the embarrassment of further failure.
>
> **Self:** Okay, I didn't pass the test again. But at least I did a lot better this time and I can really identify my weak areas that I need to work on. I can see that I didn't allow enough time for the longer essay and I had so much I wanted to put in the paper. I know next time will be better. Anyway, it took a lot of courage for me to try again and I can feel good about myself for that, much better than if I didn't try at all. I also know that every time I put myself out there I'm really giving myself every chance to succeed. I choose to see it as a learning experience; it's just a matter of time and I will persevere because I know I can do it.

When you engage in this kind of inner dialog, talking yourself up the emotional scale, you effectively raise your vibration, feel better, and disempower the inner critic.

PRACTICE, PRACTICE, PRACTICE until you master the inner critic. It Is one of the most powerful things you can do to increase your self-esteem and move towards your potential.

See also:

- Beliefs Challenge
- Clearing
- Feeling Anger
- Feeling Challenged
- Feeling Disempowered
- Feeling Fear
- Feeling Guilt or Shame
- Feeling Jealousy
- Feeling Lonely or Alone
- Feeling Rejected or Hurt
- Feeling Scattered: Unbalanced
- Feeling Stuck
- Feeling Uncertain or Fearful of the Unknown
- Feeling Unloved or Unlovable
- Feeling Unsupported
- Feeling Victimised
- Feeling Worried
- Thought Power and Control

* Abraham/Hicks http://www.abraham-hicks.com

Strategy 95
THOUGHT POWER AND CONTROL

CATEGORIES APPLIED

Addressing Addictions
Addressing Anxiety
Addressing Depression
Awareness and Mindfulness
Career and Goals
Communications and Relationships
Everyday Essentials
Improving Self-Esteem
Quick Stress Busters

All thought carries a resonance, frequency, or vibration, and so what you think is what you vibrate. Positive loving thoughts enhance your wellbeing; negative fearful thoughts not only detract from your energy system, but will eventually make you unwell. That is because thoughts impact on your physiology and biology. The Universal Law of Attraction says, "That which is like unto itself is drawn," which means our frequency is always attracting a match – responding to what you vibrate.

On an energy level it means that somewhere in this sea of energy that surrounds us all are the imprints of all prior thoughts and feelings – ours and others. Our multidimensional bodies are connected with others and the frequency or quality of that thought remains in the psychic atmosphere impacting on both our own energy field and others. The more you focus on a particular thought-form, the more you tap into that collective field of energy.

We are indeed incredibly powerful creator beings.

You will notice that when you focus on a particular thought, it becomes increasingly easy to continue in that vein of thinking, because the Law of Attraction is making more of the same kind of thoughts available to you. It doesn't matter whether it is something you are observing, remembering, or, contrary to the popular misconception that we cannot control our mind, we are in fact the only one responsible for doing so. What goes on in our mind is our own activity, though the myriad energies in our environment can and do affect us, and that is why it is so important to regularly clear our energy field (see Strategy 16 Clearing).

As a co-creative being, we are constantly creating our reality by every thought we think. And so it is often said, "You get what you think about whether you like it or not." Thinking is like planning a future event. Worry is planning what you don't want to happen.

George Bernard Shaw once said, "Those who cannot change their minds cannot change anything."

Feeling gratitude and appreciation is a way to attract more of your desires and just feel good. It is very important to learn to mange your mind because as you do, and consciously choose positive thoughts, you not only affect yourself but those closest to you, and your frequency adds to the energy mix in the atmosphere which impacts on all others.

'Manage' is the operative word for mind because even practiced meditators who regularly experience stillness of mind will tell you that you can never know when the next thought will come. The key is to notice the quality of your thoughts.

The more positive the thoughts, the better you feel;
the more negative the thoughts, the worse you feel.

All people will experience pain in their life but the majority of spiritual teachers all over the world recognize that it is the unmanaged mind that creates the suffering and holds us in a world of illusion – sometimes not even understanding our own actions.

There are two primary ways to learn to manage the mind. They are, in essence, observing the mind and training the mind. These strategies simply require consciousness and a focus on the objective.

Thought + feeling = emotion
Emotions are the children of thoughts.

Observing The Mind

Observing the mind is also commonly referred to as mindfulness. It is when you simply observe the mind as though you are the watcher of your thoughts. There is a space between you as the thinker of your thoughts and you as the observer of your thoughts. To use an analogy, imagine that you are on the platform of a train station as an observer. While on the platform you are watching the train go by. The train represents your thoughts. So you are the observer (on the platform) of your thoughts (the train). You are observing your train of thoughts and while you are doing that, consciousness is present. You are aware of the thoughts, you are not lost in the thinking process. You are conscious that you are thinking, and that space created in the witness position allows you choice in terms of how you will respond to the thought.

Your awareness or mindfulness is lost when you become absorbed in your thoughts. It is as though you have jumped from the platform onto the train along with your thoughts and you are off on an "unconscious" creative journey in your mind. You have again become the thinker and not the witness of yourself as the thinker. That is, until once again you realize that you are thinking, and then you can return to become the observer on the platform watching the train of thoughts go by. This is a constant cycle. When you are lost in thought your body-mind can carry you on an emotional journey as your feeling body responds to the unmanaged thoughts of the mind.

Mindfulness allows us to feel and not react, to observe and choose how to respond. Becoming mindful is a wonderful skill to develop. You will begin to see and understand how illusory the mind is. While the personality (egoic) mind so frequently considers its thoughts important, as you become increasingly observant of the mind it's interesting to notice that an enormous amount of your thoughts aren't even useful or even complete – often just a few words before darting off onto another thought, and another thought, all the time sending out energy vibrations, some that enhance or detract from our wellbeing.

**It is the repetition of becoming the
observer of your thoughts that
will reduce the emotional impact of your
thoughts, heighten consciousness,
and thereby increase choice and greater wellbeing.**

Be aware that your subconscious programming will be influencing all your thinking. When you are not conscious, the mind will automatically default to the subconscious. So all those subconscious beliefs that you picked up as a child and haven't yet challenged, will be your filter system. In the first seven years of life the brain is designed to download a massive amount of information about how to be in this world. The young child takes on board many beliefs without the ability to discern their quality and what to choose and what not to choose. Understandably, there will be many beliefs that do not serve you, including those that are self-deprecating in some way.

**"Watch your thoughts, for they become words
Watch your words, for they become actions.
Watch your actions, for they become habits.
Watch your habits, for they become character.
Watch your character, for it becomes your destiny."**
– Author unknown

Training The Mind

Training the mind is slightly different to observing the mind in that it is more pro-active. In fact you will need at least a 5 to 1 positivity ratio. It is not, however, meant to replace mindfulness. It is an additional practice and requires that you constantly choose positive and affirming thoughts, chanting affirmations perhaps 50 to 500 times a day (see Strategy 3 Affirmations), looking for the positive in every situation and expressing gratitude many times each day. In these activities you are not so much observing what has arisen in the mind, as consciously choosing and directing the mind to positive thought-forms.

The brain has a preference to embed negative memories because the organism needs to respond to future threats faster than our conscious minds can respond.
- Mark Waldman

From a physiological perspective anything you do think or feel connects to your brain cells. When you learn anything new like walking or riding a bike, new neuron connections are formed and they become stronger and stronger the more you practice.

It's somewhat like changing the flow of water running down a hill. The water will always flow in the same trail until some rocks or vegetation are moved to establish a different pathway. In a similar way the unmanaged mind will continue using the same habitual thinking processes until you change them.

This perhaps has more meaning when you consider that some researchers say we have between 60,000 and 80,000 thoughts per day and around 90% of those are the same as yesterday.

Negative thinking is seriously debilitating and a habit that doesn't serve you. You developed it and you can change it. It simply requires your awareness to do so and it will transform your life. Be alert too, to any negative mind story that you habitually run. These can be based on past experiences or events that allow your mind to hold you stuck in perpetual negative thinking about a particular issue or story.

Remember, we *always have choice* to think what we want, though be aware that if your energy field is contaminated you will find it more difficult to maintain a positive focus (see Strategy 16 Clearing for more information). With intention and awareness we can change old habits, including the way we perceive things and the emotions we choose in each moment. These negative thought control techniques all require the awareness that you are thinking negatively and as such not enhancing your state of wellbeing.

In addition to the mindfulness practice of observing the mind, experiment with these other process for training the mind. You may like to try these different processes one at a time or, if you prefer, a combination of them. An example might be 2 & 6 or 1 & 3 or other variations, as you feel so inclined.

NEGATIVE THOUGHT CONTROL TECHNIQUES

1. Observe/notice that you are experiencing a negative thought and let it go. Don't respond. And most important, don't judge yourself. This is a very important process to build the all-important role of the observer within you.

2. Call out "Stop!" or "Cancel!" either out loud or in your mind.

3. Say "I flood my mind with light" and imagine white or golden light running through and purifying your mind.

4. Immediately replace the negative thought with a positive thought (something unrelated), for example, "I dread talking to him after that conflict" versus "I'm looking forward to going to the movies on Saturday."

5. Immediately replace the negative thought with the opposite, for example, "I'll never be able to face that person after our argument" versus

   "I know I can find a positive, creative way to reconnect with him."

6. Replace any negative thought with thought/s and feelings of gratitude. Gratitude has a very high resonance and facilitates a good feeling. The gratitude could be for any number of different things: loving relationships, your home, a beautiful rainbow, a warm bed, the song of a bird, your favourite color or piece of music, or even your growing awareness with your increasing mind power.

   Gratitude is great to use when you are experiencing concern and worry that can leave you feeling depleted and powerless to help to another who may be at the center of your concern. Use this gratitude process to fully focus your self-talk in all that you appreciate. The important thing is to get into the feeling state or vibration of gratitude, not just the mental aspect of the words uttered.

> Example: "My husband is ill and I don't know what else I can do!"
>
> "I am so grateful we have this time together. We are closer than we have ever been before. We have so many supportive friends and family around us. I've enjoyed experimenting with new recipes to help his diet. I know it is helping him and he is enjoying them. We are so lucky to have lived so many years together. I love him dearly. I know the power of love and nothing can take that away"
>
> More information on gratitude is available in Strategy 57.

Both observing the mind and training the mind are very empowering processes and each will take practice.

To start your day

As you wake each day your mind moves through the alpha (subconscious) level to the beta (outer conscious) level. Make sure your first thoughts of the day are totally positive and/or filled with gratitude. This will help to reprogram the mind and set the tone for your day.

Throughout your day

Twenty to a hundred or more times a day, pause for a moment; check within and ask: "Where is my awareness? What am I thinking and how am I feeling?" It is perhaps obvious that the more you do it the more awareness you can develop.

You may find it helpful to use reminder triggers like this: after you have used your phone, each time you walk through a doorway, or sit down or stand up, before or after any bathroom activity or exercise, or putting something in your mouth. This is even more powerful if you say your response out loud or write down your thoughts and feelings. It really helps you focus and heighten awareness. Further it brings in other senses (kinesthetic, visual, audio) which all facilitate easier integration.

Before sleep

Your mind will transition from the beta level of the outer conscious to the alpha level of the subconscious as you drift off into sleep. This is a great opportunity to reprogram the mind and set you up for restful sleep. Make sure you thoughts are focused positively. Gratitude is always a great enhancement.

See also:

- Being: Mindfulness
- Beliefs Challenge
- Clearing
- Gag Gossip
- Judgment Effect
- Projection
- Feeling Agitated
- Feeling Anger
- Feeling Challenged
- Feeling Disempowered
- Feeling Fear
- Feeling Grief
- Feeling Guilt or Shame
- Feeling Jealousy
- Feeling Lonely or Alone
- Feeling Rejected or Hurt
- Feeling Scattered: Unbalanced
- Feeling Stuck
- Feeling Uncertain or Fearful of the Unknown
- Feeling Unloved or Unlovable
- Feeling Unsupported
- Feeling Victimized
- Feeling Worried
- Forgiveness Process
- Gratitude
- Seek to Understand
- Thought: Managing the Inner Critic

Mark Walkman, *10 Mind Blowing Discoveries About the Human Brain Ebook*.pdf p9

Strategy 96
TONING

CATEGORIES APPLIED

Addressing Addictions
Addressing Anxiety
Addressing Depression
Awareness and Mindfulness
Career and Goals
Communications and Relationship
Improving Self-Esteem
Quick Stress Busters

Toning is a form of sound healing, and while there are many practitioners who work in this way, it is also possible to be your own therapist. Everything in this universe has a particular vibration unique to itself. We as individuals have our own individual frequency that we vibrate through our physical and subtle bodies. It is made up of all of our thoughts, beliefs, life experiences, genetics, and behaviors.

We all know the power of sound and how some sounds are very abrasive, like a jackhammer going for hours at a time, a dog barking incessantly, or the sound of some alarm or persistent mechanical sound; even a mosquito sharing your bedroom at night can be irritating. Sound vibrations also affect our nature friends. Dogs and other animals can become very distressed at the sound of fireworks or lightning and thunder; our beautiful ocean giants, the whales, suffer dreadfully from the deafening sounds of sonar blasts, which can cause them to starve to death.

Cymatics is the study of visible sound, which may be water or sand on the surface of a plate, diaphragm or membrane which then mirrors the symmetries found throughout the natural world. The origin of cymatics goes back around 1000 years to the early African tribes who would divine future events by noting the patterns of sand on a drum*

As humans, we also know how music can enliven us and get our foot tapping, or how a beautiful classical piece can be very calming to the senses. There is also some music that can be offensive or at least unappealing to our senses depending on your musical taste.

Toning is in the same family as singing. In ancient times singing was said to cleanse the spirit by cleaning our inner world of darkness. Toning is rather different. There is no melody, words, rhythm, or harmony, and the sound is produced in a different manner from singing. It. is a way of using vocal sounds that creates a particular vibration in the body that can restore balance and harmony – somewhat like having an internal massage. It enhances your ability to breathe more effectively through the intake of oxygen and allows your body's energy to restore its natural flows, improving your energy levels and your ability to focus.

Toning is great to use when you are feeling agitated, upset, stuck, or just out of balance in some way. It can create a vibration that actually frees the irritation you are feeling and restore harmony. Toning can release anxiety, anger, jealousy, trauma, or stuck or stagnant energy. It can impact on your physical, emotional, mental, and spiritual bodies, resulting in a sense of calm and balance.

Regular practice with toning assists you to become more attuned to your feeling body and facilitates expression of your uniqueness. It can awaken you more to yourself as a spiritual energy being having a human experience. Toning can be done in the privacy of your own home, in the car, or out in nature somewhere.

How To Tone

1. Close your eyes, and breathe deeply in and out for a few breaths to quiet and prepare your body/mind. This allows you to come into presence.

2. Feel into your body where the disharmony exists and maintain your focus there. You may sense tightness or a stabbing feeling somewhere in your torso or something more vague. Just attune to whatever part of your body calls your attention with the intention that you want to express the appropriate resonance through your voice to release any imbalance.

   Your body has a supreme intelligence and it will oblige if you can relax into it and allow yourself to give expression to the stored energy.

3. Then take a long slow in breath and on the out breath allow a sound to manifest as though it is coming from the area of discomfort. Let your full voice carry that sound vibration for as long as your breath will allow. Allow your focus to shift from the bodily discomfort to the actual sound or the feeling of the sound because it will create a resonance in your body.

4. Repeat several times, tuning into the body, deep in breath, toning as you exhale and altering your toning as you feel is appropriate, always allowing your voice freedom of expression.

To release the stored energy and bring about transformation, you may need just a few tonings in conjunction with your breath, or you may find you need to repeat for fifteen minutes or so. It depends on the degree of blockage and your ability to be free with your voice.

You will know when it is complete because you will feel better.

See also:

- Deep Release Breathing
- Feeling Agitated
- Feeling Anger
- Feeling Challenged
- Feeling Disempowered
- Feeling Fear
- Feeling Grief
- Feeling Guilt or Shame
- Feeling Jealousy
- Feeling Lonely or Alone
- Feeling Rejected or Hurt
- Feeling Scattered: Unbalanced
- Feeling Stuck
- Feeling Uncertain or Fearful of the Unknown
- Feeling Unloved or Unlovable
- Feeling Unsupported
- Feeling Victimized
- Feeling Worried
- Mantras
- Music to Uplift and Nurture

* Cymatics http://www.cymatics.org

Strategy 97
TRUST, TRUTH, AND HONESTY

CATEGORIES APPLIED

Addressing Addictions
Addressing Anxiety
Addressing Depression
Awareness and Mindfulness
Communications and Relationships
Improving Self-Esteem

Trust, truth, and honesty go hand in hand.

As very young children we are naturally innocent, playful, spontaneous, truthful, and trusting. All these energies relate to the essence of our heart. Then some of our perceptions and life experiences result in hurt and pain and so we begin to shut down those more vulnerable aspects of self as a means of self-preservation.

We learn to distort the truth or lie to avoid getting hurt or into trouble and sometimes just to get our own way. This is typical of a conditioned upbringing that we all experience as children.

The energetic effect of this is actually closing down or creating a protective field of energy around our heart so we are less vulnerable. This reduces our sensitivity and inhibits our ability to feel and consequently impairs our ability to experience the joy of love and connect to our higher guidance.

Without an understanding of the longer-term effect, and lack of guidance to heal past wounds, this closing down has a high cost of self-sabotage, affecting every part of our life. It limits our ability to see through the self-imposed limitations and illusions we have created and will seriously erode self-esteem; it will inhibit intimacy in relationships and limit our potential for success in every area of our life.

Everyone experiences trust issues as part of life's journey. Building consciousness is the process of undoing all that conditioning, challenging our beliefs, and being open to a higher truth.

Trust comes from understanding and recognizing that there is a greater wholeness, a greater Truth that your heart actually knows.

In spiritual terms, your heart is known as the great transformer. This is where true healing happens; where forgiveness takes place, where truth, compassion, and love are felt and where true intimacy can be experienced. When you notice and respond to the truth of your heart, your whole life can change. The deeper you go into your heart and trust your feelings the faster your life will be transformed, attracting more of the loving resonance or vibration associated with the heart's wisdom. Wanting to know truth or aspiring to truth will always lead to more love in your life, even though there may be some pain or obstacles to work through.

For both personal and professional relationships to be successful and harmonious there must be a strong foundation of integrity or truthfulness. Without honesty, you basically have a relationship built on lies or deceit, whether it is with another or even yourself. While the truth can sometimes be painful, it provides the essential foundation for healthy, happy, and successful relationships, bringing greater consciousness and an expanded sense of love and wholeness into your life.

We all like to relate to people who walk their talk. We respect people where there is honesty, clarity, and clear boundaries. It helps to build our trust towards them. We know where we stand with people like this.

When we demonstrate honesty with ourselves, we not only learn to trust our own intuitive processes and feel connected with our source guidance, but we also feel good about ourselves and this increases our feelings of worthiness.

Trust, truth, and honesty must be chosen from among the alternatives if you are to experience self-love, create the life you want, and fulfill your heart's desires.

Understanding Motives

Much of our ability to be honest and open to a greater truth requires that we understand our motives. This is part of building awareness. Often motives are veiled in subconscious or unconscious beliefs and programming. Questioning and challenging all your thought processes, beliefs, and behaviors will help you to get clear about your motives.

You will need to dig deep and be really honest with yourself because your ego or personality mind has an investment in keeping you safe from the pain of past hurts; without consciousness, old patterns will continue. Constant self-inquiry will build your awareness and assist you to cut through the illusions you have created, resulting in greater self-love and a more truthful perception of your multidimensional self.

If you can't be honest with yourself, it will be impossible to be truthful to another.

> Example: Let's say you have made a commitment to yourself to improve your fitness level and lose some weight. If you justify to yourself that you avoided going to the gym today or going for walk because you didn't have time, without examining if there is a deeper truth or motive behind that activity, you miss the opportunity for expanded awareness and you will likely continue with subconscious sabotage patterns.
>
> If, however, you responded that you preferred to spend that time watching television, then that awareness immediately takes ownership for your behavior and you are authentic. You have revealed to yourself one of likely many opposing beliefs that you hold. One part of your personality is inspiring you towards things you want to manifest and the other part does not want change.

It is vitally important that you have compassion for yourself as you uncover these less truthful aspects and understand that many were born out of a need for self-preservation. Behind the resistance, there may be some fear associated with getting fit and healthy because it means giving up a victim mentality or believing that your relationship may change if you become more attractive. Dig deep into your motives to find out the real reasons for your behavior. With every initial response to self-inquiry ask yourself "What is the motive beneath my motive?" There will often be a deeper truth as you answer that question.

This kind of self-honesty actually helps to purify the mind of inner conflict. It will make you more alert to any sabotage behaviors and allow you to choose which inner voice you will regard. Your heart is always aspiring you to greater truth and expansion, so feeling into your heart as you make these self-inquiries will be most beneficial.

Be alert also to doing a behavior that you actually believe is wrong. It is extremely damaging to your own sense of worthiness because it compromises the truth that your heart knows.

"Whenever you have truth it must be given with love, or the message and the messenger will be rejected."
– Mahatma Gandhi

Common Motives for Dishonesty

- Wanting to be liked, or seek approval
- Avoiding confronting a painful situation so that you continue to live a lie

- Being attached to a particular belief that you are not prepared to challenge
- Wanting to avoid your own shadow aspect (devious, manipulative, guilty, jealous, ashamed, greedy, etc.)
- Fearing criticism
- Cheating because of lack of skills and wanting to get ahead
- Identifying with a skeptical part of you that just wants to be right
- Avoiding something you don't want to do
- Not wanting to hurt the feelings of another – this is where your *intention* is all-important. Share the truth with love and compassion and never with intention to wound another.

Process to Feel Your Truth

Go and stand in front of a mirror, feet slightly apart, arms relaxed. Feel or sense yourself grounded with mother Earth and beautifully aligned with your higher guidance. Imagine yourself in a protective column of golden light; this creates a more purified field of energy around you. Close your eyes and breathe long, slow, deep breaths into your heart.

As your mind begins to become quieter with your deepened breathing, feel how your body feels. This attunement to your body provides a benchmark of what you are feeling so that you notice any change.

When feeling relaxed, aligned, and centered, feel into the silence and space and just be in a state of allowing. Then bring into your mind the situation that you are seeking truth about. Take another deep breath and hold it, to help your mind to become still and notice the resonance of your body as you silently, look deeply and softly into the mirror observing your heart's knowing through your own eyes.

As it is so often said, "You can see the truth in someone's eyes." This is a moment of deep intimacy where you can allow the truth to arise, notice what feeling sensations are communicating with you. Again, take a deep breath and hold it while feeling the truth.

See also:

- Awareness: Building the Observer
- Awareness: I Statements
- Awareness of Awareness
- Beliefs Challenge

- Communication: When you …
- Feeling Challenged
- Feeling Guilt or Shame
- Major Life Influencers
- Release the Need to Be Right
- Truth Lover

Strategy 98
TRUTH LOVER

CATEGORIES APPLIED

Addressing Addictions
Addressing Anxiety
Addressing Depression
Awareness and Mindfulness
Career and Goals
Communications and Relationships
Improving Self-Esteem

If truth is important to you then you need to look within and without. It is a twofold process of personal and environmental exploration because each is impacting on you. Becoming a "truth lover" and aspiring to truth will always lead to more of what every human desires, which is more love in your life. While it may reveal some lumpy bits along the way that need to be addressed, the insights and revelations bring greater consciousness, wholeness, and truth.

If you "feel into" the quality of the word "truth" you will notice it has a very calm, peaceful energy about it. It just is. What is true doesn't need anyone's support – it will survive no matter what. Truth is not owned by anyone.

Surrender, acceptance, openness, and tolerance are all qualities that will assist in this awakening process, and it is just that: an awakening process, a constant unfolding and revelation of a greater and greater truth. It is as though the blinkers come off and you can see from a broader perspective, or, to use another analogy, instead of having the limited mouse's view from the ground, you are able to see from the expansive eagle's view from the sky.

All of life's experiences, whether you interpret them as "good, neutral, or bad," create the opportunity for growth, and yet this is not automatic. Often our reactions and experiences are patterns of behavior that we don't entertain as possibilities for greater awareness and empowerment. Two people may have the exact same experience, but their individual perception of it and how they then choose to respond determines whether there will be greater consciousness – a greater truth as an outcome or not. One may stay stuck in anger or resentment and another will choose to embrace the learning, accept responsibility, and move on. Growth requires a willingness to let go of previously held perceptions – the release of a fixed view. It is a desire and a willingness to embrace truth that allows the doors to open to facilitate personal and spiritual growth.

We are living in a world where much of the truth about what really goes on in our world has been obscured by lies, corruption, and manipulative information to distract the discerning truth seeker. The Internet has certainly assisted in the exposure of corrupt actions by governments, churches, banks, newspapers, and numerous companies and corporations. For some it has become a known and acceptable reality that many people in positions of power will lie and deceive for personal or monetary gain. Our complacency as individuals contributes to the disharmony and corruption we observe.

As the great Mahatma Gandhi once said, "Be the change you want to see."

It can be a harsh reality to recognize that we can see in others what we deny in ourselves. The imbalances all around us are our constant reminder of what we need to address within ourselves and what we need to stand up for to create a more harmonious world. The truth remains even when it is ignored.

Having a love or a passion for truth will always keep you striving for the eternal and unchanging universal truth where All Is One and One Is All. As many great spiritual teachers have said,

The truth will set you free.

On a personal level, if you are feeling triggered emotionally, see it as a signpost that there is a greater truth awaiting you. It is your signal through your feeling body that there is disharmony and some energy is stuck and often a new perspective to embrace. There can sometimes be resistance or even emotional pain, because it means you have to let go of your previous view or attachment. It may require owning some aspects of self that you do not like, perhaps judgment about another that is really part of your own behavior that you have previously denied. It may require releasing attachments to certain beliefs, forgiving or apologizing to someone for a misinterpretation.

On an environmental level, as an individual we are not able to address the myriad things in our world where we would like to see change and truth reside. Let your heart be your guide to wherever there is a passion within you for change. That is your calling to make a difference.

One must be very discerning when wanting to create change outside of self because judgment of another can contribute to the existing negativity. Your intent must be honorable and heart-focused with a view to bringing greater harmony into this world; it must not be driven by the egoic mind to score points or be right. Let your higher self guide you to do what you can to contribute to the restoration of harmony and truth. Donate money, write to your politicians or people in power, contact companies, become an active voice through the Internet, stop purchasing products from stores that do not respect your values for truth. There is no doubt that when we join together in a loving force for truth we can and will create change in our world. That real truth that you feel deeply and honestly is powerful because it is real.

To be conscious and free requires that you tell the truth to yourself and be willing to tell the truth to others. It is your wake-up call and a means to accelerate your growth because resistance is minimized. Becoming a truth lover allows you to be open to a different perspective, a new understanding, and a greater truth that will continually unfold. Becoming a truth lover encourages others around you to do the same. Such is the path to freedom, love, and greater awareness.

This process is sometimes called moving through the veils of illusion made with the mind and awakening to the heart's truth. The effect is one of transforming fear into love, raising your vibration and just feeling better, more empowered, and attracting more and more love into every aspect of your life. It is also the process *of remembering the truth of who you really are.*

No matter what path you choose, always have a passion for truth. It will liberate you and our world.

See also:

- Awareness: Building the Observer
- Beliefs Challenge
- Major Life Influencers
- Release the Need to Be Right
- Seek to Understand
- Truth, Trust, and Honesty
- Who Am I?

Strategy 99
VALUES

CATEGORIES APPLIED
Addressing Addictions
Addressing Anxiety
Addressing Depression
Awareness and Mindfulness
Career and Goals
Communications and Relationships
Improving Self-Esteem

Without consciousness, so much of our life is living out the values of others through belief systems that we have inherited. Beliefs come from parents, teachers, religion, culture, society, or the many forms of media that are bombarding us with the latest product assured to make us feel better. Very often our parents or teachers want us to comply with their values; if we honor their preferences, we can find ourselves disconnected from our own essence and not living in the integrity of what really feels right for us. This results in unconscious behaviors, feelings of dissatisfaction, boredom, depression, and a lack of direction without goals to inspire us towards our highest potential.

Dr. Sidney Simon, educator and author*, says that without values, we tend to be apathetic, indecisive, inconsistent, and conforming. There is a tendency to follow a path of least resistance that responds to the programming of the unaware mind.

By contrast, having clear values by its very nature invokes clear boundaries shaping our attitudes, and behaviors that are decisive, consistent, self-empowering and success-oriented. Values exist whether we are aware of them or not. Having clear values clarifies our desires and makes our goals meaningful. They are our guiding principles. It enables us to get clear on how to spend our time and live our life with purpose and a deep sense of satisfaction and fulfillment.

If you value family life and you are engaged in very long working hours that inhibit that fulfillment you will feel stressed and experience inner conflict. If you value sustainable practices that support the Earth and future generations and you are working in a company that does not respect these principals, then you will not be able to give your best and feel job satisfaction. It just doesn't go well together, and it will have a constant undercurrent of conflict detracting from your wellbeing.

Desire is part of the human condition, but without clear values those desires can just be focused around what you don't want. This usually arises from some challenges that people have previously experienced, such as an unreliable car, conflict in relationships, or financial burdens. This is so much more limiting in the world of possibilities because of the negative association of "I don't want ..." and the magnetic effect of the Law of Attraction.

Desire in a positive association could be for a new car, the perfect loving partner or soulmate, or financial abundance; it could be for the ideal career that provides just the right amount of challenge, stimulus, and satisfaction, perhaps free creative expression, deep family bonds; or it could be for spiritual growth or a deep sense of integrity.

Identifying your own values is a way to honor yourself. You are unique. There is no one else in the world just like you and yet you have the same core structure of all beings irrespective of race or religion. Underneath all aspirations remains an innate desire to love and be loved and to have a sense of purpose and belonging.

When you identify your values and you live by them, your behavior is congruent with your values, and that has a direct impact on building your self-esteem and sense of self-love – the very foundation to living a happy and successful life.

Some core human values are kindness, compassion, and connectedness. They are life-affirming values and we see these become more prominent in times of great distress that may be caused by personal trauma or by natural disasters such as floods, fires, tsunamis, and earthquakes. It awakens us to the true nature of our humanness.

Values

Abundance
Accomplishment
Accountability
Accuracy
Adaptability
Allowance
Assertiveness
Attunement
Awareness
Balance: Life
Belonging
Beauty
Being the Best
Calm Assurance
Cheerfulness
Clear-Mindedness
Compassion
Commitment
Competency
Connectedness
Contentment
Cooperation
Courage
Curiosity
Creativity
Credibility
Decency
Dedication
Dependability
Dignity
Discernment
Efficiency
Empathy
Empowerment
Endeavor
Enjoyment/fun
Equality
Ethics
Excellence

Fairness
Faith
Family
Fidelity
Flexibility
Flow
Freedom
Friendliness
Future generations
Generosity
Gentleness
Grace
Gratitude
Growth, personal
Growth, professional
Harmony
Health
Honesty
Hope
Honor
Humility
Humor
Independence
Influence
Innovativeness
Inspiration
Integrity
Intimacy
Intuition
Innocence
Intelligence
Spiritual intelligence
Kindness
Learning
Legacy
Love
Loyalty
Making a difference
Mastery
Merit
Non-judgment
Open Communication
Openness
Optimism
Passion
Patience
Peace
Positivity
Practicality
Preparedness
Purity
Quality
Receptivity
Reliability
Resourcefulness
Respect
Respect for nature/earth
Responsibility
Security
Self-actualization
Selflessness
Self-reliance
Self-respect
Sensitivity
Serenity
Service
Simplicity
Spiritual Intelligence
Spontaneity
Stability
Strength
Support
Surrender
Temperance
Thankfulness
Timeliness
Thoughtfulness
Tolerance
Trustworthiness
Truth-seeking
Understanding
Unity
Usefulness
Unconditional love
Vitality
Worthiness
Wisdom

Five Steps to Identifying Your Own Values

1. Note down your responses to the following:
    - Brainstorm or choose your values from the list above.
    - Then answer the following questions to help clarify further.
    - Reflect upon people you admire most. What is it about them that appeals to you? What values do they exhibit?
    - What is worth living for, what is it that evokes a feeling of passion with you?
    - What is really important in your life?
    - Reflect upon times in your life when you have felt most fulfilled and identify the desire that was met.

- Why do you believe this value is important to you?
    - What behaviors do you exhibit that support this value?

    These values will evoke good feelings and reflect the energy of your heart's desires.

2. While there could be a very long list, hone it down to your priorities of about fifteen values. Avoid the word "happiness" as it is assumed that this is a consequence of living your values and it tends to be too abstract when used in this way. Instead identify specifically what it is that you feel or believe will make you happy.

   For example, these might be an intimate relationship with your partner, quality time with family, continued learning and growth, job satisfaction that respects the Earth, a feeling of connectedness in your community, feeling that you are making a difference, speaking your truth and living your life with integrity, being positive and grateful, practicing compassion and respect, honoring your body with good health practices, demonstrating patience.

   Prioritize your list by starting with your top value. Try to minimize your values to keywords like the list below :

    1. Family
    2. Health
    3. Making a difference
    4. Learning
    5. Growth
    6. Connectedness
    7. Respect for Earth
    8. Intimacy
    9. Integrity
    10. Compassion
    11. Respect
    12. Positivity
    13. Gratitude
    14. Social justice
    15. Patience

3. Then review your list to see where you are out of alignment with your values. As an example, if you have loving relationships as your top value but you are often attacking them

with negative emotions and bad moods, you will experience a lack of personal fulfillment. Or if you selected health and you regularly eat fast food, or skip meals and forgo exercise, you will be dissatisfied.

Use the following criteria to identify a true value:

- It is a heartfelt passion, something that is really important to you.
- It is something you choose quite freely from among others.
- It is considered and reflected upon even if you feel you have grown up with it ingrained in your belief systems.
- It is something that you freely affirm publicly and act upon repeatedly.

Values that do not yet meet the above criteria are in a state of "becoming." They are something that you are aspiring towards.

4. With these values now clarified, including the ones that are in a state of becoming, list them somewhere so that you can see it often. Ensure you use the words as part of your everyday language to remind you and assist the integration of the chosen value.

5. For the values that are in a state of becoming, decide what you can do about it to bring it more into your conscious way of being and *take action* to make it happen.

Review

Be aware that even though values tend to be fairly stable, they can change as you change and grow. Someone at the beginning of their career may have a lot of emphasis on values that reflect success and satisfaction through abundance, learning, creative expression, security, independence, but as time goes on and you begin a family your higher values could change towards family, health, life balance, etc.

Someone who experiences a life trauma can have a dramatic change in values – developing more sustenance from values of spiritual intelligence, compassion, health, peace, kindness, harmony, connectedness.

Refer to this list whenever you are making any important decisions. The prioritization of your values will point you towards the optimal answer to the question.

Having clear values is fundamental to the success of your goals and sense of wellbeing. It helps you to be in integrity – to walk your talk. Without them, you will be heavily influenced by those around you.

See also:

- Beliefs Challenge
- Goal Setting
- Decisions: Heart Wisdom
- Decisions: Motives and Impact
- Personal Mission Statement
- Major Life Influencers
- Intention/Counter-Intention

*Humble thanks for the inspiration of this strategy on values clarification by Dr. Sidney Simon – American Professor of Humanistic Education. http://www.dcbsites.com

Strategy 100
WHO AM I?

CATEGORIES APPLIED

Addressing Addictions
Addressing Anxiety
Addressing Depression
Awareness and Mindfulness
Career and Goals
Communications and Relationships
Improving Self-Esteem

Who am I? is a very deep and powerful question that is good to ponder.

Often people might respond to this question with the roles they play: a mother, father, teacher, businessman, electrician, IT consultant, gardener, etc. Or they may lose their identity through a painful life experience and believe they are that way because *that* happened to them. Some may think of themselves as the body/mind. All of these titles, roles, and perceptions are very limiting and do not embrace the totality of your true essence as a spiritual being.

Recognize yourself as an eternal energy being. Like everything else in this universe, energy can never be exterminated, only change in vibration. Shift your perspective from a human being with a spiritual body to a spiritual being having a human experience. As you embrace this understanding you will be able to use your energy in more creative and productive ways, and claim your sovereignty.

As multidimensional beings, we live amid a sea of different energies. You are a human being with vibrating fields of energy interacting with other vibrating fields of energy in this vast universe. All things in this universe are vibrational in nature. Energy is never static; it is always moving and changing.

Your physical, emotional, mental, and spiritual bodies are all interacting together and with other energies in your environment. You are connected with all life forms.

Some Key Points

Science tells us that our physical bodies are made up of around 99% space, creating the illusion that we are solid.

Quantum physics tells us that our experience of reality is determined by our thoughts and beliefs.

The human heart's magnetic field of energy can be measured several feet away from the body and is the largest electromagnetic field in the body (sixty times greater than the brain).

To assist you in this expanded state of awareness experiment with the three different exercises below.

Exercise 1. Who Am I?
Sit quietly and hold the intention to connect to your higher self. Ground yourself to the Earth by imagining roots of light coming out through the souls of your feet, then take several deep breaths, focusing on your heart energy and then see what arises as you ask the following questions:

- Who am I?
- Where have I come from?
- Why am I here?

These questions open the door to spiritual self-discovery. Repeat periodically.

Exercise 2. Dis/Identification-Identification Exercise *
It is recommended to read this exercise aloud every day for a minimum of twenty one days until it sinks in to become part of your reality. This will deepen your understanding of the "real you" and facilitate growth and change.

> **Dis-identification**
> I have a body but I am not my body. My body may find itself in different conditions of health or sickness. This has nothing to do with my real self or the real "I."
>
> I have behavior, but I am not my behavior. All my behavior comes from my thoughts and beliefs. If I am not fully conscious of these, I may sometimes behave inappropriately. Even though I behave well or poorly, I am not my behavior. This has nothing to do with my real self, my real "I."
>
> I have emotions, but I am not my emotions. If I am not fully conscious, my emotions are sometimes negative and sometimes positive. As I become more conscious, this will

change. Though a wave of emotions may overtake me, I know I am not my emotions. My true nature will not change. "I" remain the same.

I have a mind, but I am not my mind. My mind is my tool for creating my emotions, behavior, and body, as well as what I attract into my life. If I am not fully conscious, my mind sometimes runs me, instead of me controlling my mind. My mind is a most valuable tool, but it is not who "I" am.

Identification
I am a sovereign being. I am eternal. I am a center of pure consciousness. I am a center of will and personal power, capable of being the cause and creator of every aspect of my life. I am capable of directing, choosing, and creating all my thoughts and emotions, my behavior, the health of my body, and the kinds of things I magnetize into my life. My core essence is pure love.

This is **Who I Am!**

Exercise 3. Mantras *
These mantras can be used separately or together and will help you to awaken to your expanded self. Energy follows thought. Learn them off by heart and chant them often. Great to do anytime, though in meditation, upon waking, or before sleep all connect with the alpha level and allow the message to sink in to the subconscious mind. Chant them while exercising, doing household chores, feeling a bit down, or feeling great to affirm your real self.

I AM
I AM all that I AM
I AM one with the universal mind
I AM love
I AM light
I AM peace
I AM truth
I AM

And/or

I AM sovereign
I AM free
I choose love through eternity

See also:

- Affirmations
- Awareness of Awareness
- Awareness: Building the Observer
- Being: Mindfulness
- Truth Lover

*** Inspired by Michael King http://michaelking.id.au/**

Strategy 101
WORK PASSION

CATEGORIES APPLIED

Addressing Addictions
Addressing Anxiety
Addressing Depression
Awareness and Mindfulness
Career and Goals
Communications and Relationships
Environmental Health
Improving Self-Esteem

It is important to really love the work you do, given the huge chunk of time it consumes in your life. The kind of work that you engage in is a way for you to express yourself: your creativity, your consciousness, your core essence. The manner in which you participate in work provides a reflection of basically how you perceive yourself in the world.

When you are engaged with work you love, there is passion, energy, a sense of freedom, love; you are in flow and extremely productive. This benefits not only you but all those around you. When you are in joy with your work you are fulfilling your life's purpose – your potential, and your puzzle piece in terms of your greater purpose and your spiritual connection is strong. When you work among others who also love their work there is real synergy and productivity.

Implicit in loving your work is that you will have balance with family life and friends and look after your health. Without time to nurture these important relationships, (fundamental to your coexistence in this world), feelings of disconnection will arise and stress levels will increase. The potential for added stress increases without clear boundaries that support all aspects of your life.

Some people spend around half their life attending to, going to, or leaving from work. Even if you have a 40-hour week the traveling to and fro can quickly extend your work-related hours by a further ten or more hours depending on where you live. Many who work for themselves may spend even longer hours in work engagement. For numerous others, the digital age has dramatically expanded their ability to work from just about anywhere, with higher expectations making them accessible around the clock to their workplace.

Ultimately you must create appropriate boundaries and make choices that support your health, the work you love, and the people you love.

If you realise that your work is not satisfying or fulfilling you, look both at the work itself, and to the places within yourself where your intentions may be obscure, where you are unclear, or in resistance or denial.

Maybe you are at a turning point in your life and your heart is calling you in a different direction. Or perhaps your spirit has moved on and your egoic mind is holding you stuck.

If your work is leaving you feeling unfulfilled, what is it in your life that you are not doing for yourself? Are you living the life your parents wanted? Notice if there is some conflict in work relationships: what is that showing you about your attitudes, beliefs, and expectations? Are you judging another, wanting them to change and not looking at yourself and your own behavior?

Your work provides an immense amount of information on how you feel about yourself, which then reflects in your behavior. We will always behave according to our beliefs, whether they support us or not. That is why self-inquiry is so very important to bring about greater consciousness.

Mind and logic are useful tools in our human existence, but allowing the mind to dominate and dictate the work you do in such a significant part of your life will seriously inhibit your ability to feel good and connect with your deepest longing. It is doubtful that you will be able to find love and joy within your work and you will likely feel depressed and disconnected from your spiritual essence because you are not fulfilling or expressing your innate creative gifts.

Feeling good, experiencing love and joy, connected to your longing and spiritual essence are all qualities of the heart. Remember, it is the superior intelligence of your heart or feeling body that really knows your deepest desires and is always striving to move you towards that.

Consider the wise words of the great Sufi mystic Jalal ad-Din Rumi (13th century):

"Everyone has been made for some particular work,
And the desire for that work has been put in every heart."

These words remind us of the true value and importance of the kind of work we do. How are you living your life? How are you expressing your creativity, your gifts, your true purpose? Are you in fact fulfilling your heart's desire? If you do not love the work you do, inner work is required.

Tips To Help You Identify Your Heart's Passion
Sit quietly and ponder this thought: if you were approaching the end of your life, what is it that would give you that resounding feeling of deep satisfaction – "Yes" I did it!" Then work backwards from there, setting yourself goals towards that completion. (See Strategy 55 Goal Setting for more information)

Ask yourself:

- What is important to you?
- What is it that you most enjoy doing?
- What would you do if you could only do one thing for the rest of your life?
- What makes you smile from the inside?
- Is there something you've always wanted to do but abandoned at some time?
- What do you wonder or dream about?
- What do you avidly read about?
- What are your favorite movies and the message they bring up for you?
- What do you enjoy talking about that leaves you feeling good?
- What activities make you feel good about yourself?
- What would you do if you knew you couldn't fail?
- What are your values and goals?

It can indeed be a challenge to keep your heart's passion at the forefront when surrounded by a consumer-driven culture that neglects the core of your spiritual essence. It is this kind of distortion that leads to stress and unhappiness. It is obvious we are more productive, more creative, and happier when we feel good in our job. Accepting a job promotion, based on remuneration or title, can be a step away from what is really important to you.

Watch the mind and the obstacles it will strive to create for you. Be alert to the inner critic and those sabotage voices that reveal old belief systems that you may have subconsciously or unconsciously inherited. It could be beliefs like: "Seize any opportunity for promotion," or "You don't have enough of what it takes to move into that area."

Reflect deeply and ask yourself "Do I really believe that?" Dig deep into your beliefs because you will always behave according to them, even if they are totally untrue or detrimental to your wellbeing. Such is the importance of making the unconscious drivers conscious.

Ask these inner voices, "If I were to listen to you, where would that lead me?"

Remember your higher self, your I AM presence, your spiritual self – whatever it is that you call that precious part within, will always be leading you towards your potential, towards greater love, joy, and expansion. When you follow your heart's guidance and pursue your passion, you have a deeper connection with yourself and others; you naturally express greater love, compassion, and appreciation. You are connected with your core authentic self where higher awareness, wisdom, and intuition flow.

See also

- Awareness of Awareness
- Awareness: Building the Observer
- Boundaries
- Comfort Zone Expansion
- Decisions: Heart Wisdom
- Decisions: Motives and Impact
- Do Things You Enjoy
- Goal Setting
- Ideas and Inspirations
- Major Life Influencers
- Personal Mission Statement
- Values
- Who Am I?

CONSCIOUSNESS TIPS FOR CHILDREN

The most profound form of learning is to be a model for your children.

Demonstrate consciousness through your own behavior. Refer to the multiple strategies within this program for your own development and realize you cannot teach your child what you do not know how to do for yourself, though continued practice will effect change.

The first four years of a child's life involves a massive amount of learning that really comes like downloads of information. This is when the bulk of the subconscious programming takes effect, nevertheless it begins in utero. As all pain and suffering arises from the mind it is obvious that one of the greatest gifts you can give children is to help them manage the mind and find a way to process their emotional pain so that it is not stored in their energy matrix. This means helping the child to connect to their heart and *feel* what is there. It is the most empowering thing you can do to help your child.

If you encourage your children to stay connected to Source Energy, they will remain clear minded; they will remain optimistic; they will remain enthusiastic. They will remain balanced; they will remain flexible. They will remain in a state of grace. They will remain in a state of Well Being. And they will make wonderful choices.

- Abraham/Hicks

KEY TIPS

1. Teach your children that they are loved, powerful, creative, important, valuable, and worthy.
2. Avoid any negative name-calling. Separate any undesired behavior from them as a person, e.g. "That was a silly thing to do" rather than "You are a silly person."
3. Your children are sensitive little beings and pick up on your energy as well as what you do and say. Attempting to hide any disharmony teaches children to suppress their negative emotions and creates a toxic atmosphere. Explore ways to be truthful and reassuring at the same time. Truthfulness builds trust and demonstrates integrity, qualities that will serve them well through life.

4. Teach your child to honor their feelings as the special part within them that helps them to steer their way through life. It's good to know what feels good and what feels bad or what you like and what you don't like.
5. Teach your children to manage their mind – happy thoughts make you feel good, negative thoughts make you feel bad. And help them realize it is always their choice what to think.
6. Teach your children the source of everything that supports them and guide them to express gratitude and appreciation for everything that comes from Mother Earth: This encourages a beautiful connection that will sustain them throughout their life. Help them to understand about the Earth kingdoms of mineral, plant, animal, and human. Teach them how they provide everything we need for this earthly existence – their food, the different sources and how things grow, their clothing (fabrics made of cotton which comes from plants or wool from sheep), their toys (plastics come from oil, wood from trees etc.), their home, bed, transport, books, entertainment sources and how we all need to contribute and share with other people in our world.
7. Teach your children about equality and that all people are spiritual, irrespective of different skin colors, cultures, religions or behaviors. We are all connected.
8. When things don't work out in a way the child wants – teach them to look for
    a. What they could have done to make the situation work out better
    b. The positive aspects, irrespective of any outcome.
9. Connect with your child before you strive to correct any behavior. When you are connected (heart to heart), it builds feelings of safety and trust.
10. Help your children to feel connected within their families, schools and communities.
11. Arrange short family meetings where children are encouraged to help find solutions to problems. This empowers children to build skills of creative thinking and problem solving and builds feelings of connection and openness. Avoid using these times to lecture your child.
12. Encourage your children to flush their bodies with brilliant sunlight and place themselves in a big bubble of light as a means to cleanse their higher light body and afford some energetic protection

Helping Your Child Process Challenging Feelings

- If your child is really upset just hold them with total presence. Being truly present and hearing your child validates and acknowledges them and their feelings. It is in the feeling and acceptance that the emotional pain can dissolve. Avoid pacifying with something oral; avoid patting or rocking, or any attempts to justify, minimize, or devalue the intensity of their feeling – just look at them and hold them. This kind of presence assists the child to process through their painful feelings at the same time feel safe.

- While being totally present with your child, ask what is it that is upsetting them. Adopt a really curious attitude about their emotional pain as though you want to know everything about it. This encourages them to explore and build their own self-awareness.
- Ask: "Where in your body do you feel it?" – e.g. tummy, chest, throat?
- Ask: "What does it feel like …?" – e.g. like a football is in my belly, all wishy-washy, like there is sword fight going on in my tummy, all tangled up in my throat, like my legs are made of jelly, or hot and burny.
- If they are struggling to identify their feelings attempt to label it in a questioning way, ask "Is there something in you that is feeling angry, sad, left out etc.?"
- You may even inquire if this feeling has a name or could they draw it?
- If the child is being overly dramatic about some situation, take care to avoid getting sucked into the drama as this would only serve to perpetuate the situation. Attempt to direct the child to the feeling awareness in their body, but if there is too much chaos at the time return to it after the event when things have settled down – see 4, 5, and 10 above. Avoid any submission to a child's dramatization if they didn't get their own way. You do not want to teach the child manipulative behavior.

Parent Alert – Electronics

An unfortunate truth is that today's children are exposed to much more media technology than ever before with the harmful effects of electromagnetic radiation compounding the issues. According to the Heart Math Institute, "Overstimulation from today's media technology is causing millions of children to experience an array of problems, including attention deficit at school and home, overtiredness and emotional developmental delays."

There is growing evidence about these health concerns available through multiple resources on the Internet. Do your utmost to determine what is right for you and your family.

It is recommended that you create strong boundaries with technology for your children and help them to understand why this is beneficial. Demonstrate through your own behavior.

ABRAHAM/HICKS: http://www.thesecret-lawofattraction.net/abraham-hicks-quotes.html
Heart Math Institute – http://www.heartmath.org/free-services/articles-of-the-heart/children-and-media-technology.html

AFTERWORD

Understanding the cause of any health imbalance allows you to focus your attention in the relevant area to address the condition more specifically. Many of these external causes can be tackled with relative ease once you are aware of them. For example, certain environmental energies can be minimized or eliminated once you become aware that particular bathroom products are behind your skin irritation, or realize that your bed is above some geopathic stress lines causing your sleep disturbance. Noticing that a root canal filling you have is on the same energy meridian as some bowel problems can prompt a trip to the dentist to explore possible solutions; adopting a regular exercise program can provide many health benefits that your body needs and to trim down some excess weight and reduce anxiety; changing your diet, improving your intestinal health and having more whole foods may remedy your lack of energy and improve the appearance of your skin and your general mood.

Then there are the unresolved emotional issues that block the body's natural energy flows and cause health imbalances. These can be more challenging to link to the specific cause if the world of metaphysics is new to you. You may, however, recognize that you need to adopt Strategy 53 Forgiveness Process because your feelings of hurt and betrayal remain after some years and this is playing out in your physical body as constipation, diarrhea or some lower back problems. Perhaps you realize that one of the reasons people seem to take advantage of you is because you don't have strong boundaries and you have just been diagnosed with cancer because of the suppressed anger and resentment you have not yet managed to resolve; a persistent cough may reflect the loss and grief following a relationship breakup.

Learning to manage your mind could ward off acute anxiety, panic attacks or reduce your blood pressure which may otherwise lead to a heart attack or stroke. The mind is the cause of your emotional pain and needs to release the belief systems, fear, or judgment that is at the causal level and the body just needs to feel what has been suppressed, avoided, or denied to free the stagnant energy so that it can move back to its place in the space-time continuum. Your subtle energy bodies also need to be cleared of any interference from the astral realms.

Going directly to the specific cause can be a faster way to facilitate your body's healing and instigate a more pro-active approach. Nevertheless, as you adopt these strategies and integrate them into your way of being, there must be behavior change if the body is to continue the healing process.

Some clues to the emotional link of your physical imbalance may be found in various sources on metaphysics that cross-reference the physical condition with the perceived psycho-emotional issue. The following list is just a small sample. Naturally you must use your discernment at all times. At some level of your multidimensional self, you know the cause, so being truly open to a new perspective and a greater truth is an essential ingredient in the process of healing.

- Annette Noontil, *The Body is the Barometer of the Soul*, Gemcraft, 1998.
- Louise L. Hay, *Heal Your Body*, Specialist Publications, 1988.
- Inna Segal, *The Secret Language of your Body*, Blue Angel Publishing, 2009.
- Christiane Beerlandt, *The Key to Self-Liberation*, Beerlandt Publications, Ostend, 2001.
- Dr. Caroline Mace *Anatomy of the Spirit*, Bantam 1996, *Why People Don't Heal and How They Can* Harmony Books 1997, *Sacred Contracts*. Harmony Books 2002 and others.

Printed in the United States
By Bookmasters